Rise of Saffron Power

This volume looks at the impact of the landmark 2014 elections and the subsequent Assembly elections which have transformed the ideological discourse of India. It discusses a variety of topical issues in contemporary Indian politics, including the Modi wave, Aam Aadmi Party and the challenges it is confronting today, Hindutva and minorities, the decline of the Congress party, changes in foreign policy, as well as phenomena like 'love *jihad*' and *ghar wapsi*. It also draws together political trends from across the country, especially key states like Uttar Pradesh, Punjab, Kerala, Tamil Nadu, Telangana and Seemandhra, West Bengal, Jammu and Kashmir, and Meghalaya.

The volume will be of great importance to scholars and researchers of Indian politics, public policy, sociology, and social policy.

Mujibur Rehman teaches at Jamia Millia Central University, New Delhi, India. He has received graduate research training at the University of Texas, USA, the University of Heidelberg, Germany, and the Indian Institute of Technology (IIT), New Delhi. He wrote his doctoral dissertation on the Politics of India's Economic Reform (1991/92–2004). He has edited *Communalism in Post-colonial India: Changing Contours* (Routledge 2016). The paperback edition of this volume will be released in 2018 with a Foreword by Romila Thapar. Presently he is working simultaneously on a book manuscript on Indian Muslims and on the politics of anti-Christian violence in India.

'This collection has very useful, very thoughtful essays that cover a wide range of issues surrounding the emergence of Hindutva, both at the level of governance and of culture and the growing relation between the two. It will add measurably to our understanding of an undeniably powerful and alarming development in India since the 1980s, which has now taken on the proportions of an emergency.'
— **Akeel Bilgrami**, *Sidney Morgenbesser Professor of Philosophy and Professor, Committee on Global Thought, Columbia University, USA*

'Mujibur Rehman has assembled a fine group of scholars to contribute excellent pieces on the rise of saffron power in the aftermath of the 2014 parliamentary elections in India. This book will leave you better informed and more concerned about the far-reaching implications of the growth of Hindu nationalism.'
— **Amrita Basu**, *Paino Professor of Political Science and Sexuality, Women's and Gender Studies, Amherst College, USA*

'Essential reading for anyone working on contemporary Indian politics, Mujibur Rehman and his contributors expertly assess the changes in the Indian electoral landscape reflecting the rise of (and challenges to) "saffron power".'
— **Katharine Adeney**, *Professor and Director of The Institute of Asia and Pacific Studies, Faculty of Social Sciences, University of Nottingham, UK*

Rise of Saffron Power
Reflections on Indian Politics

Edited by Mujibur Rehman

LONDON AND NEW YORK

First published 2018
by Routledge
2 Park Square, Milton Park, Abingdon, Oxon OX14 4RN

and by Routledge
711 Third Avenue, New York, NY 10017

Routledge is an imprint of the Taylor & Francis Group, an informa business

© 2018 selection and editorial matter, Mujibur Rehman; individual chapters, the contributors

The right of Mujibur Rehman to be identified as the author of the editorial material, and of the authors for their individual chapters, has been asserted in accordance with sections 77 and 78 of the Copyright, Designs and Patents Act 1988.

All rights reserved. No part of this book may be reprinted or reproduced or utilised in any form or by any electronic, mechanical, or other means, now known or hereafter invented, including photocopying and recording, or in any information storage or retrieval system, without permission in writing from the publishers.

Trademark notice: Product or corporate names may be trademarks or registered trademarks, and are used only for identification and explanation without intent to infringe.

British Library Cataloguing-in-Publication Data
A catalogue record for this book is available from the British Library

Library of Congress Cataloging-in-Publication Data
A catalog record for this book has been requested

ISBN: 978-1-138-89727-4 (hbk)
ISBN: 978-0-429-50632-1 (ebk)

Typeset in Sabon
by Apex CoVantage, LLC

To

Barbara-Harris White, for her affection and path-breaking empirical work on India;

Eleanor Zelliot, for introducing me to Ambedkar's work. Without her work, I would have perhaps, like hundreds of others, looked at Ambedkar merely as the Chairman of Drafting Committee of Indian Constitution, not as a thinker or philosopher;

And last but not least, to Bashiruddin Ahmed, one of India's early psephologists, who was a great source of inspiration for me. I hope I will live up to some of his expectations through my publications on politics.

Contents

List of figures   x
List of tables   xii
Notes on contributors   xiii
Acknowledgements   xvii

Introduction   1
MUJIBUR REHMAN

1 'Yes, but not in the South': the BJP, Congress, and regional parties in South India   44
JAMES CHIRIYANKANDATH

2 India's foreign policy and Hindutva: the new impact of culture and identity on the formulation and practice of Indian foreign policy 2014–2017   62
ARNDT MICHAEL

3 Allegories of 'love *jihad*' and *ghar wapsi*: interlocking the socio-religious with the political   84
CHARU GUPTA

4 Understanding the BJP's victory in Uttar Pradesh   111
SUDHA PAI AND AVINASH KUMAR

5 Election 2014 and the battle for India's soul   130
HARSH MANDER

Contents

6 Collapse of the Congress party 154
ZOYA HASAN

7 Explaining the inconvenient truths of Indian political behaviour: Hindutva, Modi, and Muslim voters in 2014 168
MUJIBUR REHMAN

8 The dance of democracy: election 2014 and the marginalised and minorities 191
RUDOLF C. HEREDIA

9 Aam Aadmi Party's electoral performance in Punjab: implications for an all India political scenario 215
PRITAM SINGH

10 The 'people' and the 'political': Aam Aadmi and the changing contours of the anti-corruption movement 237
NISSIM MANNATHUKKAREN

11 The 2014 national elections from the margins of modern India 263
UDAY CHANDRA

12 Big national parties in West Bengal: an exceptional outcast? 279
MAIDUL ISLAM

13 National elections in a tribal state: the 2014 Lok Sabha elections in Meghalaya 297
CORNELIA GUENAUER

14 Electoral politics in Jammu and Kashmir (J&K) and the problem of communal polarisation 317
AIJAZ ASHRAF WANI

15 Lok Sabha elections in (un)divided Andhra Pradesh: issues and implications in Telangana and Seemandhra 347
RITU KHOSLA

16 An inquiry into the causes and consequences of the saffron whirlwind that swept Uttar Pradesh in the 2017 Assembly election 368
MUJIBUR REHMAN

Index 389

Figures

1.1	National vs. regional parties all India: 1957–2014	45
1.2	National vs. regional parties in the south: 1957–2014	46
1.3	All India share of seats for national and regional parties – 2014	59
1.4	National and regional parties' share of seats in the south – 2014	60
3.1	Covers of *Panchjanya* and *Organiser*, 7 September 2014	87
3.2	An appeal to Hindu brothers	89
3.3	'Hindus Beware: Love Jihad'	92
3.4	Front and back covers of Ram Muttalik's book *Love Jihad: Red Alert for Hindu girls*	95
3.5	Poster stating that 'Garba Venues' should only allow Hindus	97
3.6	Cover of the magazine: *Himalaya Dhvani*	99
4.1	Second position gained by parties out of total seats lost by them in the LSE 2014 in UP	114
4.2	Position of BJP and its ally (Apna Dal) in the Assembly segments during the LSE 2014 in UP	115
4.3	Average loss margin	115
4.4	Position of non-NDA parties in the Assembly segments in UP in LE 2014	117
4.5	Change in BSP's and SP's votes share in LSE 2014 over LSE 2009	120
4.6	Change in absolute vote share of BSP and SP in constituencies with more than 30 per cent of the SC population	121
4.7	Phase-wise total vote percentage and victory margin of BJP in UP	124

Figures xi

4.8	Average victory margin of BJP vis-à-vis other parties in constituencies with more than 20 per cent Muslim population in UP	125
14.1	Overall voter turnout in J&K in 2004, 2009, and 2014	325
14.2	Vote share of National Conference in Parliamentary elections from 1977–2014	330

Tables

1.1	INC, BJP, and CPI/CPM share of seats from the south in Lok Sabha elections: 1989–2014	56
4.1	Position of parties in the Lok Sabha elections in UP since 1989	113
4.2	Support to various political parties across castes/communities in 2014	116
7.1	Muslim voting pattern in national elections, 1999–2014	169
7.2	Survey-based estimates on Muslim voting preference, 2014 and 2009 (in %)	170
9.A.1	Vote share and results of General Elections 2014 for Punjab state	232
9.B.1	Religious composition of India's population 2001 and 2011 (%)	234
9.B.2	Religious composition of Punjab's population 2001 and 2011 (%)	234
9.B.3	Punjab's religious communities as a share of their all India population 2001 and 2011	235
9.B.4	Sikhs as a share of different Indian states' population 2011 (%)	235
14.1	Constituency-wise voter turnout in 2009 and 2014	326
14.2	Jammu and Kashmir Lok Sabha result 2014: change in seat and voter share of parties	326
14.3	Jammu and Kashmir Parliamentary constituency-wise Lok Sabha result in 2014	329
15.1	National Election Study 2014: Telangana	351
15.2	National Election Study 2014: Residual Andhra Pradesh	352
16.1	Muslim MLAs in Uttar Pradesh	378

Contributors

Uday Chandra received his PhD in political science from Yale University, USA, in 2013. His research lies at the intersection between critical agrarian studies, political anthropology, postcolonial theory, and South Asian history. He has published in the *Law & Society Review*, *Critical Sociology*, *Interventions*, *The Journal of Contemporary Asia*, *Contemporary South Asia*, and the *Indian Economic & Social History Review*. He has co-edited volumes and journal special issues on the ethics of self-making in modern South Asia, subaltern politics and the state in contemporary India, caste relations in colonial and postcolonial eastern India, and social movements in rural India.

James Chiriyankandath is Senior Research Fellow in Indian politics and history at the Institute of Commonwealth Studies, University of London, UK, and editor of *Commonwealth and Comparative Politics*. His interests include the politics and contemporary history of South Asia and the Middle East, especially the comparative study of religion, nationalism, and conflict; and electoral and party politics in South Asia. His edited books include *Electoral Politics in India. A Changing Landscape* (1992) and *Parties and Political Change in South Asia* (2014). He has also published widely on Indian politics and history and contributes in *The Annual Register*.

Cornelia Guenauer is a PhD candidate at the Department of Social Anthropology/Johannes Gutenberg University of Mainz, Germany, and a scholar of the Heinrich Boell Foundation. Her PhD thesis is titled 'How to make a difference: electioneering and politics of identity in India'. She has studied Politics of South Asia, Social Anthropology, and Musicology in Heidelberg and Mainz and has been working as lecturer at the Department of Social Anthropology in Mainz. Her research interests include identity politics, diversity studies, political communication, democracy, and ethnomusicology.

Charu Gupta is Associate Professor in the Department of History, University of Delhi, India, since 2009. She has been a Fellow at the Social Science Research Council, New York, and the University of Oxford, and many other places, and visiting faculty at Yale University, among others. Her major publications include, *Sexuality, Obscenity, Community: Women, Muslims and the Hindu Public in Colonial India* (2002), *Contested Coastlines: Fisherfolk, Nations and Borders in South Asia* (2008). She is currently working on life narratives of five writers in Hindi, who wrote on diverse topics in early twentieth-century India.

Zoya Hasan is Professor Emerita, Centre for Political Studies, Jawaharlal Nehru University and former Dean of the School of Social Sciences, JNU. She is currently a member of the Hindu Centre for Politics and Public Policy, and a member of the Editorial Board of the *International Political Science Review, Secular Studies* and the *Journal of Human Development in India*. Her recent books include *Congress After Indira: Policy, Power, Political Change (1984-2009)* and *Politics of Inclusion: Caste, Minority*. A collection of her essays titled *Democracy and the Crisis of Inequality* was published in 2014. Her book titled *Agitation to Legislation: Negotiating Equity and Justice in India* will be published in 2018.

Rudolf C. Heredia received his PhD from the University of Chicago, USA, in 1979, and taught sociology at St. Xavier's College, Mumbai, India, where he was the founder director of the Social Science Centre. At the Indian Social Institute, Delhi, he was director of research, editor of *Social Action*, and more recently a research consultant. Among his more recent publications are *Changing Gods: Rethinking Conversion in India* (2007) and *Taking Sides, Reservations Quotas and Minority Rights in India* (2012). He has published in journals like the *Economic and Political Weekly* and other journals and newspapers. He is currently working on collective violence in India.

Maidul Islam is Assistant Professor of Political Science at the Centre for Studies in Social Sciences, Calcutta, India. His first book, *Limits of Islamism: Jamaat-e-Islami in Contemporary India and Bangladesh* (2015), based on his DPhil thesis at Oxford University, was nominated by the Cambridge University Press in 2016 for Association of Asian Studies Bernard S. Cohn Book Prize, meant to honour innovative scholarship across discipline and country of specialisation for a first single-authored monograph on South Asia. He has contributed in academic journals, edited volumes, and newspapers. His research interests are in political theory, identity politics, cinema, and contemporary South Asian politics.

Ritu Khosla is an Assistant Professor in the Department of Political Science, MCM DAV College for Women, Chandigarh, Punjab, India. Her research focuses on electoral politics, territorial politics, and political economy in a comparative manner. Her doctoral research is on the demand for new states in India with a comparative analysis of Telangana and Gorkhaland movements. Currently, she is working on the electoral politics in the state of Punjab with a focus on the impact of 'AAP effect' in the state elections.

Avinash Kumar is Assistant Professor at the Centre for Informal Sector and Labour Studies, School of Social Sciences, Jawaharlal Nehru University, New Delhi, India.

Harsh Mander is a social worker and writer based in India. He is associated with social causes and movements, such for communal harmony and justice, tribal, dalit, child and disability rights, homeless people, and bonded labour. His books include *Unheard Voices: Stories of Forgotten Lives* (2001), *Fear and Forgiveness: The Aftermath of Massacre* (2009), and his newest, *Ash in the Belly: India's Unfinished Battle against Hunger* (2012), among others. He regularly writes columns for *The Hindu* and *The Hindustan Times*. He teaches courses on poverty and governance in the Indian Institute of Management, Ahmedabad, and St Stephen's College, Delhi.

Nissim Mannathukkaren is Associate Professor in the International Development Studies Department at Dalhousie University, Canada. His main research interests are focused on left/communist movements, development and democracy, modernity, the politics of popular culture and Marxist and postcolonial theories with a geographical focus on India. He is the author of *The Rupture with Memory: Derrida and the Specters that Haunt Marxism* (2011). He has published in journals such as the *Journal of Peasant Studies, Third World Quarterly, Journal of Critical Realism, Economic and Political Weekly,* and *Dialectical Anthropology*. He is a regular contributor to the major national and global media.

Arndt Michael holds a PhD in International Relations from the University of Freiburg, Germany, where he has lectured at the Department of Political Science, since 2004. His main areas of expertise include India's Foreign Policy and European Foreign Policy. His publications have appeared, inter alia, in *Harvard Asia Quarterly, India Quarterly,* and *India Review*. His book *India's Foreign Policy and Regional Multilateralism* (2013) received the Arnold-Bergstraesser Award 2012 for Political Science (University of Freiburg, Germany), the Cecil B. Currey Book Award 2013 from the Association of Third World Studies (ATWS, USA), and the Gisela Bonn Award 2013 from the German-Indo-Society.

Sudha Pai is Professor at the Centre for Political Studies (CPS) and Rector (Pro-Vice Chancellor) Jawaharlal Nehru University, New Delhi, India. Her research interests include Dalit politics, agrarian politics, and globalisation. Some of her major publications include *Dalit Assertion* (2013), *Democratic Governance in India: Challenges of Poverty, Development and Identity* (2001, with Niraja Jayal Gopal), *Political Process in Uttar Pradesh: Identity; Economic Reforms and Governance* (edited, 2007), and many others.

Pritam Singh teaches economics at Oxford Brookes University, UK. His books include *Economy, Culture and Human Rights: Turbulence in Punjab, India and Beyond* (2010) and *Federalism, Nationalism, and Development: India and the Punjab Economy* (2008). He is on the editorial board of several journals including *World Review of Political Economy, South Asian History, and Culture* and *Journal of Punjab Studies*. He has been a visiting professor at Jawaharlal Nehru University, Delhi, and Moscow State University, Russia.

Aijaz Ashraf Wani is senior Assistant Professor at the Department of Political Science, University of Kashmir, Srinagar, India. His research interests include governance, South Asian politics, Indian politics, Jammu and Kashmir politics, and peace and conflict. His research work has been published in number of national and international journals. He is presently working on his book pertaining to governance in Kashmir.

Acknowledgements

This book is partly an outcome of a major international conference that I put together after the 2014 Parliamentary election at the Jamia Central University, New Delhi, India. Funded by a grant from the Indian Council of Social Science Research (ICSSR), New Delhi, the conference was a great success and was attended by enthusiastic students and scholars from Jamia and outside. Some participants have contributed chapters to this volume. There were few who made presentations at the conference but could not contribute for a variety of reasons and the select list includes the following: BBC journalist and author Mark Tully, former minister Mani Shankar Aiyer, former editor of *the Hindu* Siddharth Vardarajan, noted journalist from *The Telegraph*, Sankarshan Thakur, Janata Dal(U) spokesperson Pavan Verma, Sandeep Shashtri, Malvika Kasturi, Prasenjit Bose, noted Dalit scholar Chander Bhan Prasad, late Praful Bidwai, Prof Ramu Manivannan, Head of Department of Politics and Public Administration, Madras University, noted documentary maker, Anwar Saheb, Hilal Ahmed, Rizwan Quiser, and a few others.

I would like to record my gratitude to my present Vice Chancellor, Prof. Talat Ahmed for facilitating the grant within the University at a very short notice.

Special words of gratitude to the following scholars who accepted my invitation to contribute and have demonstrated enormous patience during the preparation of this volume: James Chiriyankandath, Sudha Pai, Pritam Singh, Zoya Hasan, Nissim Mannathukkaren, Uday Chandra, Arndt Michael, Cornelia Guenauer, Avinash Kumar, Ritu Khosla, and Aijaz Ashraf Wani. The volume's content could not have acquired the depth and richness that it possesses now without their contributions.

The subject of election has fascinated me since my childhood. It has been a privilege to grow up amid heated political discussions on

xviii *Acknowledgements*

Indian elections at home and also at various institutions. I went on to study in Delhi, Europe, and America. I would like to acknowledge that Prof Walter Dean Burnham, one of the pioneers of American elections studies, is mainly responsible for generating serious scholarly interest in me for the subject. The two years he served as my faculty advisor and multiple conference courses I took with him during this period at Burdine Hall at the University of Texas, Austin, USA, played a major role in encouraging me for developing scientific understanding of elections. I would also like to acknowledge Prof Rob Moser, now the Chair, Department of Government, the University of Texas, Austin, and Prof Daron Shaw, a specialist on American elections: these are two other scholars who made significant contributions to my aspirations to study electoral politics. My future works on the subject would bear more footprints of what I learnt from these scholars.

Over the years, I am indebted to many scholars and friends in helping me to grasp the complexity of Indian politics either through discussions or their writings. And in many instances both. They include the following: Amrita Basu, Upendra Baxi, Romila Thapar, Geeta Patel, Nandini Deo, Ayesha Jalal, Neeti Nair, Sana Aiyer, Martha Nussbaum, Craig Calhoun, Robin Lewis, Sugato Bose, Neil Devota, Pradeep Chibber, Milan Vaishnav, Akeel Bilgrami, Narayan Lakshman, Riaz Ali, John Echeverri-Gent, Robert Hardgrave, Sumit Ganguly, Robert Owen, Mohammed Ayoob, Jyotsna Singh, Dipesh Chakravarty, Yasmeen Saikia, Aseema Sinha, Barbara Harris-White, Nandini Gooptu, Indranil Roy, Bhabani Nayak, James Chiriyankandath, Katherine Adeney, Yunas Samad, Wali Aslam, Gregory Burns, Ravinder Barn, Stephen White, Eleanor Newbigin, Rochana Bajpai, Gurharpal Singh, Ramin Jehanbegloo, R. Sudarsan, Sachin Dewan, Mohsin Khan, Dwaipayan Bhattacharya, Maidual Islam, Swagato Sarkar, Prasenjit Bose, Rob Moser, Sunila Kale, E. Shreedharan, Rudra Chaudhuri, Swagato Ganguly, Theoder Ratgeber, Martin Gaenszle, Fabian Falter, Ines G. Zupanov, Renaud Colson, Palermo Francesco, Alber Elizabeth, Karl Kossler, Amitabh Kundu, Abu Saleh Sharif, Rowena Robinson, Noor Baba, Vijaya Rao, Radu Cariumaru, Philip Oldenberg, V. S. Sambadan, Rahul Mukherjee, Tanvir Aijaz, Aftab Alam, Anindita Sahoo, Sunita Reddy, and several others.

Special thanks to Tom and Linda for their assistance. Specially to Tom, who had to stay up the whole night to give comments on some occasions.

My good friends Daman Singh, Andrew Buncombe, Keith Topping, Steven and Lori Young, Nishant and Sherry, David Peace, Mark Klassen, and Edward Oakley for their encouragement and support in the pursuit of my intellectual life. It is always a matter of great joy to have arguments with Edward and often disagreeing with him on politics.

Special thanks to Maddy Crowell for finding time to give feedback on the manuscript despite her hectic professional commitment, and for her encouragement.

I also would like to thank Ekta Niranjan, Dipin Kaur, Simin Akhter, and Dipyaman for their assistance in copy editing parts of the material.

I also wish to acknowledge the permission given by Sage and Paul Wallace for the publication of Sudha Pai and Avinash Kumar's paper; HarperCollins for publishing Zoya Hasan's paper, and Archiv Orientalini for the permissions for Charu Gupta's paper.

Last but not the least, Aakash Chakrabarty and Brinda Sen for their support in the preparation of this volume. And my colleagues at Jamia, particularly at the Centre for their support, particularly during the organisation of the conference.

Mujibur Rehman

Introduction
Mujibur Rehman

The results of the 2014 Parliamentary election and several other state elections – particularly that of Maharashtra and Haryana in October 2014; Jammu and Kashmir (J&K) in November–December 2014; Assam in April 2016; Uttarakhand and Uttar Pradesh in February 2017;[1] Gujarat and Himachal Pradesh in December 2017, Tripura and Nagaland in 2018 – reflect unprecedented electoral growth of the Bhartiya Janata Party (BJP), indicating a fundamental ideological shift in Indian politics.[2] During this period, despite Modi's efforts to run a high voltage campaign akin to his 2014 run, the BJP lost quite a few Assembly elections such as New Delhi in February 2015, Bihar in 2015, West Bengal in April 2016, Tamil Nadu in May 2016, and Goa in February 2017. Its victory in Gujarat Assembly election in December 2017 possessed more features of its shortcomings as a ruling party than its strength. It showed not how invincible but how vulnerable it could be as an incumbent in the face of mounting resistance.

Overall, the BJP won more than it lost; its victory in Himachal Pradesh, Maharashtra, and Delhi civic elections in 2017 (that too in the post-demonetisation period) are evidences of the BJP's continual rise. In February 2015, during the Delhi Assembly election, the BJP lost to the Aam Admi Party (AAP) which won sixty-seven seats with 54 per cent vote share. On the other hand, the BJP's vote share did not change much. It obtained 33.07 per cent vote share in 2015, a slight increase from the 32.1 per cent in Delhi Assembly election held in December in 2013.

The series of the BJP's victories represents a dramatic expansion of its electoral base, whose impetus could be traced to the 2014 electoral victory. Therefore, the regime change resulting from the 2014 Parliamentary elections is qualitatively different from the political transitions resulting from the other Parliamentary elections such as that of 2009 or 2004 (as well as 1996 or 1984 or a few more). Like that of 1977, the 2014 election is a watershed moment in India's postcolonial democracy. Table 1.1 presents the details regarding seats and vote share in various national and state parties.

If the 1977 election is etched in political imagination for restoring faith in India's electoral democracy by stigmatising *Emergency*[3] as the most dreadful word in political vocabulary; then 2014 deserves to be recognised for planting firmly the crude template of majoritarian politics in India's political landscape. The 2014 electoral transition therefore represents more than a routine regime change, and it has greater significance for scholarship on Indian democracy.

At this point, the National Democratic Alliance (NDA) coalition runs twenty-one state governments (in addition to the centre) that spread over all regions of India; while in 2014, when Modi came to power, the NDA was running only six state governments from India's north and western regions. The Congress party today runs only in three states (if Meghalaya works out it would be four, at the time of writing it was not clear), out of which Karnataka and Punjab are relatively larger ones. The BJP is also the single largest party in both the houses of Indian Parliament, *Lok Sabha* and *Rajya Sabha*. For the first time in modern Indian history, both the Constitutional positions of the President and the Vice President are represented by the BJP's nominees. According to scholars, the BJP should be able garner majority in both houses by 2018 which would give the Modi government a free hand to pursue its policies, inter alia, and its ideological agenda (Vaishnav 2017a).[4]

The Modi-led BJP and its government's ideological agenda is dictated by Rashtriya Swayamsevak Sangh (RSS) with which it shares a symbiotic relationship. For years, the RSS masqueraded as a cultural organisation and refused to acknowledge its political face. But these days, the RSS asserts its political identity with aggressive audacity and pride.[5] In the most self-evident fashion the RSS–BJP relationship is announced on the BJP's official website as follows: 'The Bhartiya Janata Party (BJP) is today the most prominent member of the family of organisations known as the "Sangh parivar" and nurtured by the Rashtriya Swayamsevak Sangh (RSS)'.[6] The RSS's exclusionary and violent ideology has even encouraged historian Irfan Habib to compare it with IS.[7] Deen Dayal Upadhyaya (1916–1968), a prominent RSS thinker and former President of the Bhartiya Jana Sangh (BJS) is the main philosopher of the Modi-Shah-led BJP, according to the BJP's website. '*Integral humanism*' is regarded as the party's core philosophy, which is based on the four lectures delivered by Upadhyaya between 22 and 25 April 1965 in Mumbai. Prime Minister Modi in his maiden speech in the Lok Sabha (Lower House of Parliament) on 11 June 2014 declared proudly that he is a follower of Deen Dayal Upadhyaya.[8]

Propelled by the Modi wave, and its consequent domino-effect in various regions, the BJP's electoral rise is far more dramatic than what the party experienced in the wake of Ayodhya movement in the 1980s.[9] Amid widespread anger against the United Progressive Association (Two) (UPA-II) government, and overwhelming disenchantment with non-Congress, non-BJP political parties, the Modi-Shah leadership has brought new fervour, commitment, and energy to its cadres and supporters, contributing to what I describe as rise of the *saffron power*.

Currently the two prominent aspects of the 2014 election at the core of scholarly discussions are as follows: one is the unprecedented nature of the election campaign that Narendra Modi unleashed, lasting several months between 2013 and 2014, and the other is its outcome that ended the 'coalition jinx'[10] after almost three decades, leading to a stable majority national government. According to one of America's prominent South Asianist, Amrita Basu:

> The BJP's dramatic electoral victory in 2014, enabling it to form a government without the need for coalition partners, represents a remarkable new conjuncture in Indian politics. The scale of its victory is explained by a variety of factors- anti-incumbency sentiment, the popularity of Modi's neoliberal agenda, the BJP's expensive, media-savvy campaign, the impact of youth vote, and Modi's personal popularity.
>
> (Basu 2015: 30)

Making of the saffron system

Various electoral and political strategies of the Modi-Shah leadership have been driven by ambition to expand the BJP's domination in all regions of India, almost the way the Congress party did in 1950s and 1960s. Rajni Kothari once famously described the domination of the Congress party in India's party politics to be a **Congress system**.[11] Today, the question is this: are we witnessing the emergence of the **saffron system**?

The BJP's rise, or what I describe as the rise of '*saffron power*', has no comparable example in the history of modern India's party politics. Its domination, nonetheless, is unlikely to become the Congress party's mirror image. In other words, the BJP would not be able to replicate the electoral map of the Congress party in terms of precise constituencies or regions all over India, owing to the variation of historical and political conditions.[12] Moreover, the political consequences of the BJP's electoral domination will be substantively different from that of the Congress in terms of ideology, institutions, and political culture: some of which are already evident since 2014.

The most worrying aspect of this domination could be its potential in restructuring of the state–citizen relationship by causing disequilibrium in the society–community relationship across various castes, regions, and religions. This would be fuelled by a majoritarian aggression that would rejuvenate the Brahminical social order. Consequently, this could cause massive sectarian violence and the subversion of human rights in multiple social domains. Mob lynchings by *gau rakshaks*[13] in various parts of India,[14] and the 2017 Sharanpur violence against the Dalits by the Thakur castes are some of the accompanying consequences of the saffron system.[15]

For the BJP, this electoral domination in and of itself is an extraordinary accomplishment. Why has the BJP been able to achieve this domination, while other parties have failed? Is it owing to its Hindutva ideology? Are there other factors? What could be its implications for India's democracy?

To analyse the implications raises a plethora of other questions: (a) Why and how has this ideological shift occurred in the context of issues raised and strategies formulated by rival political parties during the 2014 election and afterwards? (b) What are the possibilities of its consolidation? (c) What is the consequence of the terminal decline of the Congress(I)? (d) What is the future of the Left parties? (e) What might be the impact of the regional parties? And (f) What consequences would this have for dynastic politics?

The contributions made in this volume have attempted to shed light on these questions, though they by no means provide concrete answers. Nevertheless, rich insights could be gleaned from some of these narratives about the new ideological terrain unfolding in India's political landscape.

That any political leader/political party needs to have an electoral majority in Uttar Pradesh (UP) to govern India has been one of the prominent rules of thumb in India's electoral politics. Apparently, former Jana Sangh leader Syama Prasad Mukherjee[16] had once said, 'India, that is Union of States, that is, Uttar Pradesh', just to indicate how decisive Uttar Pradesh is to India's power politics. The BJP's victory in Uttar Pradesh in 2014 Parliamentary election (it won seventy-one out of eighty-one Parliamentary seats) and its more stunning victory in the 2017 Uttar Pradesh Assembly election (it received

312 out of the 384 seats it contested in Assembly) has encouraged many to forecast the return of Modi to power in the 2019 Parliamentary election.

Omar Abdullah's tweet, 'At this rate, we might as well forget 2019 & start for planning/hoping for 2024' represents such a defeatist mindset of India's rival opposition parties.[17] The collapse of Bihar's *Mahagathbandhan*[18] (2015–2017), causing the Janata Dal (JD) (U) leader, Nitish Kumar, to return to the National Democratic Alliance (NDA) by forging an alliance with the BJP to reinstall the Bihar government under his Chief Ministership, crushed any remote possibility of building a credible anti-BJP, anti-Modi coalition pre- or post-2019 Parliamentary election. Nitish Kumar's remark that 'No one can beat Modi in 2019 Lok Sabha polls'[19] sums up the future of the anti-Modi coalition and the futility of the experiment. The fragile opposition parties in present India continue to be the greatest advantage for Narendra Modi, who now stands as an undisputed populist leader of an underperforming regime in New Delhi. Adam Roberts summarised it most persuasively in an op-ed in the *New York Times* on 9 July 2017:

> Much else is no nearer to happening under Mr. Modi than under Mr. Singh. Few formal jobs have been created, as labor laws remain painfully restrictive. Nobody dares talk about creating freer markets in agriculture, lest that upset villagers. It is still hard, without political help, to buy land to build a factory. And in too many sectors – such as makers of steel, fighter jets and even sex toys – state-owned firms crowd out private ones. Mr. Modi has not done much to fix such problems, beyond telling state governments to try.[20]

If there will be an alternative to Narendra Modi in 2019, the most crucial challenge remains to be in the unity of various opposition parties. Efforts such as the gathering of opposition leaders in Chennai on 3 June 2017, on Karunanidhi's birthday; in New Delhi on 17 August 2017 in a meeting hosted by Sharad Yadav to save India's '*sanjhi virashat bachhao*' (save the composite culture); in Patna, Bihar, on 27 August 2017; Lalu Yadav's "*BJP hatao and Desh Bajao*" rally in which fifteen parties took part;[21] and a few others by Sonia Gandhi appear more ceremonial/ritualistic and half-hearted.[22]

It is worth recalling a comment made by Biju Patnaik[23] during the 1996 election campaign in Bhubaneswar (that I attended) in the presence of V.P. Singh, India's former Prime Minister: 'I was in Uttar Pradesh recently. People said to me: "Get united, there is no need to come; If you guys (opposition leaders) are not united, there is no need to come as well".[24] Thus, the challenge to Narendra Modi's future after 2019 depends on the unity of opposition parties, whose fragile nature presents the BJP with an overwhelming advantage. Consequently, the saffron system seems irreversible, and its growth is likely to flourish at various levels of India's political structure, though some setbacks are expected in its evolution owing to various internal and extraneous factors.

Narendra Modi, Amit Shah, and the Modi wave

The key difference between the BJP that lost the 2009 Parliamentary election to Sonia Gandhi and Manmohan Singh–led United Progressive Alliance (UPA) and the BJP that became victorious in 2014 and afterwards is the role played by the duo Narendra Modi and Amit Shah.[25] By giving an innovative spin to their campaign strategy derived from their rich experiences of past Gujarat elections, the Modi-Shah leadership was able to choreograph the BJP's dramatic electoral expansion by exploiting existing political conditions characterised by fragmented, directionless opposition, and massive disenchantment of voters towards the UPA.[26] In my view, the plausibility of setback to the BJP's juggernaut or the weakening the saffron power is higher in the destabilisation the Modi-Shah leadership through internal implosion rather than from any challenge or offensive that India's opposition parties could orchestrate either in the 2019 elections or later.[27]

Narendra Modi has proved to be an exceptionally savvy politician in matters of political campaigning, strategy formulations, and running an election machine.[28] Having successfully decimated his rival parties, mainly the Congress(I),[29] in three consecutive Gujarat Assembly elections (in 2002, 2007, and 2012) and having defeated the Gandhis[30] on these three occasions, he embarked on the 2014 national campaign with great confidence. India's national electoral battlefield was no doubt far greater in size as well as depth compared to Gujarat, but the key players (such as the Gandhis) were the same, and the background of seething discontent against the United Progressive Alliance-two (UPA-II) (2009–2014) regime made things easier for Modi.

Born on 17 September 1950 in Vadnagar, a small town in North Gujarat's Mehshana district, Narendra Modi grew up in a modest family of the Ghanchi caste, a caste of oil pressers.[31] Early in his life, he showed great interest in political activities. As a member of the Rastriya Swayam Sevak Sangh (RSS) and later Akhil Bharatiya Vidyarthi Parishad (ABVP), he played active roles in various socio-political movements in Gujarat.[32] Modi was General Secretary of the Gujarat BJP in 1988 and later he was national General Secretary in 1995 and in 1998. He played key roles in organising Nyaya Yatra in 1987 and Lok Shakti Yatra in 1989, showcasing his organisational skills. Modi became Gujarat Chief Minister in 2001, where he served till he got elected as India's Prime Minister in 2014. He was a key campaign manager in many elections – particularly for L.K. Advani. During Narendra Modi's journey from an ordinary worker (*karya karta*) in the BJP to its prime ministerial candidature on 13 September 2013, he has honed his oratory skills to enthuse voters, connect with masses, and disarm critics, thus making him the political leader that he has become today. He earned a good part of his skillsets during his tenure as Gujarat Chief Minister.[33] According to Aakar Patel,[34] a long-time observer of Modi, he could be compared with Lalu Yadav or even with Bal Thackeray for his rhetorical power.[35]

Narendra Modi was made Chairman of the BJP's 2014 Election Campaign Committee (BNCC) at its Goa conclave on 9 June 2013.[36] On 13 September of the same year, he was declared as the party's prime ministerial candidate.[37] He emerged as its star campaigner, dominated the public discussions, and unleashed a campaign that was unprecedented in modern Indian history.

Surprisingly, Modi's rise to this position was opposed fiercely by the BJP's patriarch L.K. Advani. We have little knowledge about the reasons for Advani's public resistance even now.[38] After the unprecedented victory, L.K. Advani, together with Murli Manohar Joshi (another dissident), was dropped from the BJP's powerful Parliamentary body. They were included in *new margdarshak mandal*, an ornamental position, and stand politically marginalised.[39] The complete grip of Modi-Shah over the party was evident by the absence of Advani in the foundation laying ceremony for the new BJP headquarters that Prime Minister Modi and Amit Shah recently took part in: a seventy-room building on Deen Dayal Marg in New Delhi. It is going to be hi-tech, eco-friendly, and cover a plot of 8,000 square metres.[40] Also, the decision to not consider neither L.K. Advani nor Murli Manohar Joshi, two former Party presidents, for the post of either President or Vice President is another unmistakable signal of Modi-Shah's grip over the party and the government.

Major opposition parties, particularly of the UPA coalition, rather naively believed that Narendra Modi's candidature had given them a walkover in 2014. They believed the blot of the Gujarat 2002 riot was compelling enough to deny Modi the Prime Ministership, and by its logical extension, deny the BJP from any opportunity to form an NDA government in the event of an inevitable necessity to form a coalition. This perception of opposition leaders was driven by the understanding of the Indian electorate, which understood the details of the 2002 Gujarat genocide; opposition leaders assumed that its alleged key architect, Modi, would face resistance from voters, which would contribute to the BJP's electoral debacle. In the final analysis, this was a flawed assumption.

A large bulk of voters, it is plausible, had little idea about the genocidal dimensions of the 2002 riot except that it was riot like any other riot.[41] For many Muslims, it was a *danga(riot)* like any other danga(riot). But Modi had other plans, and he executed them with great efficacy – much to the surprise of his opponents and even his supporters. Being aware of the 2002 riot's adverse implication for Muslim votes, Modi began a Muslim outreach through Zafar Sureshwala, who organised meetings with Muslims of several groups to refashion Modi's anti-Muslim image.[42] Muslims in some parts of India, particularly in Uttar Pradesh, Gujarat, and Karnataka did vote for the BJP and Narendra Modi (Rehman 2018).[43]

Assuming the public resentment towards the UPA-II government, Modi unleashed a multipronged strategy to seek out a full majority in the 2014 election. Opposition parties led by the Congress party were resigned to the preordained destiny of coalition government. On the one hand, the BJP's Modi-led campaign appeared well organised, and smoothly executed, as it spread all over the country; on the other hand, the opposition campaign appeared remarkably less coordinated, far less in number, fewer in turnout, and often failed to enthuse crowds. According to Pradeep Chibber and S.L. Ostermann, the BJP and Modi were able to attract more vote mobilisers in 2014 election[44] (Chibber and Ostermann 2014).

To many, the Modi wave was evident in the enthusiasm of massive crowds who showed up in the sea of audience, signalling the rise of a national mass leader with a substantial acceptance. Although many opposition leaders indulged individual attacks on Modi, there was barely enough of a coordinated strategy to take on the Modi campaign. At the individual level, leaders like Rahul Gandhi, Omar Abdullah, Lalu Yadav, Mamata Banerjee, Mulayam Yadav, Digvijay Singh, Salman Khurshid, and others, unleashed assaults on Modi. Some of those attacks were outright uncivilised, and Modi was not far behind in giving them back. For instance, Derek O Brien of the Trinamool Congress called Modi, 'Butcher of Gujarat'; Salman Khurshid called him 'impotent'; and Omar Abdullah criticised him as a leader who lacks courage.[45]

The Modi campaign not only attacked the United Progressive government (Two)'s very corrupt, inefficient regime with quips like *Maa-Beta ki Sarkar* (government run by mother–son duo); Modi also presented his Gujarat model as an alternative to address the issues of poverty, unemployment, and security of India. Opposition parties, especially the Congress party, were barely able to defend against the misrule of the dynasty; they even failed to highlight the shortcomings of the Gujarat model that became apparent with state-wide protests that were organised by Hardik Patel.[46]

During the 2014 campaign, Modi unleashed slogans like *Maa-Beta Ki Sarkar*,[47] *Acche Din*,[48] *Gujarat model*,[49] *Chaiwala*,[50] and *Chapan Inch Ka Chati*:[51] each becoming a buzzword across the country. Curiously, some of these slogans have even been used by adversaries to remind Modi of his positions and postures on various issues in recent months. Some of these slogans might return during the 2019 election and even later.[52]

Amit Shah, who runs the BJP's election machine has worked with Modi for many years as a member of his Cabinet in Gujarat and was one of Modi's influential ministers in Gujarat.[53] In an interview with Patrick French, Shah categorically stated that he would not disclose when and how his friendship was forged with Narendrabhai (Modi).[54] Shah first met Modi when he was fourteen years old according to a report in *The Week*.[55] Shah had joined the BJP in 1986, a year before Modi. He was accused of being a key conspirator to the Sohrabuddin[56] encounter case in Gujarat, for which he was arrested on 25 July 2010[57] and was incarcerated for three months. He finally managed to get bail and resumed his political life at a national stage by leading the BJP's election campaign in 2014.

It is instructive to read former Solicitor General Gopal Subramanium's comments on Amit Shah in his nine-page letter to Chief Justice of India, R.M. Lodha, explaining why he was withdrawing his consent for appointment as a Supreme Court Judge against what he said was 'a very carefully orchestrated drama to scuttle his elevation'.[58]

In the letter he wrote:

> *I may add, that I have never met Amit Shah and I have only seen his photographs in the newspapers recently. I may also add that, in the course of the hearing of the bail application of Amit Shah, I had said that his liberty should not be infringed and he may be allowed to be enlarged on bail but remain outside the State of Gujarat. This is only to indicate that I had no personal vengeance or any kind of grudge against the said Mr Amit Shah.*

Consider this: had Amit Shah been denied bail and remained imprisoned, what would have happened to the 2014 campaign? It is plausible at least that the BJP's campaign for the 2014 election and its outcome could have been different in Uttar Pradesh, which would have impacted directly the formation of the BJP government at the Centre after 2014. In the event of an inevitable coalition government in New Delhi like 1998 or 1999, even Modi's ambition to become Prime Minister could have collapsed given his polarising personality.

On 9 August 2014, Amit Shah, became the President of the Bhartiya Janata Party(BJP), India's new largest party. In 2017, he entered Rajya Sabha from Gujarat, and his income rose by three times between 2012 to 2017.[59] Gopal Subramanium, who ironically is considered one of India's brightest attorneys (and who could have become the longest serving Chief Justice of India [CJI]) had to withdraw his consent for a Supreme Court Judge's position owing to Modi government's concern for his appointment. Mr Subramanium's nomination was finalised by the UPA government, but not confirmed.

These decisions have implications for the central argument laid out in this narrative regarding India's ideological shift towards the Hindu right. For India to take an ideological turn, there is a need for judicial consent in the form of verdicts and other forms of judicial interventions which would further imply 'court packing'[60] as an important strategy for various BJP governments. Clearly, the United Progressive Alliance (UPA-II) government could not foresee this ideological aspect of the 2014 election.

The Congress party viewed the 2014 election as a routine affair and conducted it as if the party destined to rule again – even if it fails to win the majority, directly or indirectly (say even by offering outside support as it did to Chandrasekhar government in 1990). Curiously, the UPA-II government went out of the way to approve extension of Dr Mahesh Rangarajan as the Director of Nehru Memorial Museum Library (NMML), New Delhi, for another ten years only few hours prior to the end of its reign.[61] These two decisions only indicate how complacent and short sighted the UPA-II government and its coalition parties appeared, and how indifferent these parties were towards the massive ideological shift that the Hindu right has propelled.

The election slogan that the BJP framed for the 2014 election, '*Sabka Vikas Sabka Sath*' (Development for All, Support for all), had masked its Hindutva ideology and its extremist and exclusionary agenda. Narendra Modi is the first prominent Hindu right political leader who understood clearly that the Hindu right agenda could not be introduced upfront to the Indian people. Pragmatism demands that it has to be a back door agenda. Perhaps he recognised the most effective way of forming an electoral majority is not by pursuing the Hindu right's political agenda as an electoral programme, but by formulating and campaigning on the basis of a wider agenda that could have a *catch all* appeal among voters of different regions. Hence, the '*sabka sath sabka vikas*' campaign slogan in 2014.

Another distinguishing characteristic of Modi is his direct access to India's big capital that no other Prime Minister in India's history had ever had. Considering that India's elections are an extremely expensive exercise – almost everyone deals with big capital through intermediaries[62] – it is this which makes Modi a far more enduring player both in the BJP and in national politics. This is another advantage Modi had against Advani besides age.[63]

More than four years later, a considerable reassessment of the 2014 election has already been done. The Gujarat model stands exposed to the massive agitation of Patels and Dalit protests owing to assault on Dalits by cow vigilante groups in Una, which led to the resignation of Gujarat Chief Minister, Anandiben Patel.[64] The impact has been such that *India Today*, an English weekly, published a story titled, 'GUJAROT: Can Modi Save His Home State? The BJP's Crisis Intensifies After Anandiben Patel's Exit' as its 15 August 2016 (Special Issue) cover page. During the Uttar Pradesh Assembly election campaign in 2017, Narendra Modi barely uttered the phrase, '*Gujarat model*', from his lips and yet the BJP had a resounding victory. The story was similar in case of Gujarat Assembly election in 2017, though the election was competitive, yet the BJP won it (the victory was more of a face-saving type) and formed the government. I doubt the phrase '*Gujarat model*' would ever return to Modi's vocabulary or his campaign speeches in 2019 or in any election before or after.

In fact, the phrase '*Gujarat model*' did not return during the campaign for the 2017 Gujarat Assembly elections in which Mr Narendra Modi addressed thirty-four rallies in a span of fifteen days across the state. At the end, the BJP managed to win ninety-nine seats with a vote share of 49.1 per cent as opposed to the Congress party led by Rahul Gandhi, which won seventy-seven seats with a vote share of 41.4 per cent. The loss of sixteen seats that the BJP has in Gujarat Assembly elections (from 115 seats it had in 2012 to the present 99 seats in 2017) is generally explained by commentators owing to anti-incumbency against the BJP government. The fact is that the vote polled by the BJP has marginally increased from 47.85 per cent in 2012 to 49.1 per cent in 2017. In the case of anti-incumbency, there should be a decline in both seats and vote share, but in Gujarat case, there is a loss of seats but no decline of vote share. How could then anti-incumbency explain the Gujarat results? The reason, I would argue, lay on the conversion factor in the First Past Post System (FPPS) in which vote share fails to be translated into seats. There are similar instances in many elections, say for example, Bharitya Janata Party (BJP) won only three seats even if it had polled 32.78 per cent and Congress party won no seats despite polling 9.7 per cent votes in Delhi Assembly Election in 2015. How would, however, we explain the success of the Congress party in Gujarat? Clearly, the opposition presented a well-organised, issue-driven campaign compared to what it had done in past Gujarat elections in 2012 or 2007 or 2002. Despite the BJP's rather less-than-glorious win, its saffron social base has remained intact. It has been widely acknowledged by the commentators that neither the Gujarat model nor development (or vikas) was part of the campaign rhetoric of Modi or the BJP, which suggests that there is some kind of an enduring character to the saffron base in Gujarat today.

Writing on the 2017 Assembly election, noted journalist and biographer of Narendra Modi, Nilanjan Mukhopadhya made following observations:

> Muslims of Gujarat are completely missing from the ongoing electoral discourse, despite being almost the every tenth person in the state and featuring prominently, albeit as the villanised 'other', in most recent polls. This 'absence' or exclusion is not just in terms of a minuscule number of candidates from the community. No issue specifically concerning Muslims is being raised in any elections speech or publicity material.[65]

Muslims constitute 5.9 per cent of rural populations and 14.75 per cent of the urban population. Ahmed Patel happens to be the last Muslim to be elected from Lok Sabha, and ever since he was nominated to Rajya Sabha, no other Muslim has been nominated to the lower house. By all means, the BJP's victory in Gujarat or Himachal Pradesh contributed to the deepening of the Hindutva project.

RSS's role in the 2014 election and after

The unprecedented electoral success in the 2014 Parliamentary election and a few other state elections such as Maharashtra, Haryana, Assam, Chattisgarh, and Jammu and Kashmir (J&K) has been attributed to rather dedicated roles of the Rashtriya Swayamsevak Sangh (RSS) members. The RSS was deeply committed to Modi's victory, it is often argued. This claim is made with such force that it appears as if the RSS now has the secret formula to win any election in India if it so desires.

As early as July 2013, various RSS outfits huddled in Amaravati as part of a *Manthan Shivir* and contributed to the preparation of a blueprint for the 2014 polls.[66] After the election victory, seen as a result of the Modi wave and the strategic role of Amit Shah (for which Modi had complimented Shah as the 'Man of the Match' of the 2014 elections), the RSS chief Mohan Bhagwat reacted by saying the BJP's 2014 win was not a one-man show.[67] However, analysis of various state election results[68] following the 2014 election suggests that neither Modi's nor the BJP's electoral success is entirely uninterruptible.[69] No doubt, however, the RSS is clearly given exaggerated credit for its role in the 2014 election.

The fact remains that the RSS enjoys substantial influence in the preparation of the Modi government's agenda. At the oath-taking ceremony, several BJP MPs were heard mentioning the name of *Sangha* as part of their oath. A preponderant majority of key figures of the BJP's national and state politics are nurtured in the RSS as part of its cadre. Modi government ministers attended an RSS meeting between 2 and 5 September 2015, as part of the RSS's government appraisal programme. It was also attended by representatives of fifteen RSS affiliate organisations such as Vishwa Hindu Parishad, Bhartiya Mazdoor Sangathan, Swadeshi Jagaran Manch, etc.[70] Many currently serving BJP Chief Ministers – Devendra Padnavis of Maharashtra, Manohar Lal Khattar of Haryana, Shiv Shankar Chauhan of Madhya Pradesh – are directly drawn from the RSS cadre. Ram Madhav, also from the RSS background, plays a prominent role in various political affairs currently, and was a key player in the BJP's government formation in Kashmir.

However, the RSS's desire to influence the government goes back as early as that of the 1977 Moraraji Desai government, in which Advani and Vajpayee were a part. During the long years of Vajpayee government (1998–2004), there were occasional reports of troubled relationship between the RSS and the Vajpayee's government. In an interview with me, Jaswant Sinha, India's former finance minister and now a major Modi critic, had attributed the loss of his finance portfolio in the Vajpayee Cabinet owing to the RSS's pressure.[71]

In the coming years, the RSS's role and influence would grow in India's governance, contributing to the ideological shift both within and outside the government. According to Walter Anderson, 'the RSS will increasingly take on the ever more difficult task of mediating differences within the sangh parivar. This will be increasingly difficult as the interests of its various constituents will grow wider'.[72]

At the same time, there is resistance to the RSS, and it is most violent in Kerala. According to a report published in NDTV, New Delhi, during the past seventeen years between 2000 and 2017, sixty-five RSS/BJP members were killed; whereas eighty-five CPM and eleven Congress and IUML workers were killed as part of political violence.[73] Yet, there is a clarion call often heard among some secular leaders of India's opposition parties for a '*Sangh mukta Bharat*' (Sangha-free India) as a counter-objective to what Modi has declared '*Congress mukta Bharat*' (Congress-free India). Unfortunately, the evidence of their commitment to achieve this objective in terms of strategy or campaign appears patchy and disappointing.

The RSS today is a global organisation. Its proverbial defensive attempt at veiling itself as a cultural organisation is barely heard in any platform. In a recent meeting in Nagpur, Mohan Bhagwat addressed sixty-five members of Hindu Swayamsevak Sangh (HSS) (RSS's international wing) declaring that only India could save the world from the clutches of capitalism.[74] The Indian diaspora, however, has been a huge patron of the RSS in the West (particularly in the USA) consciously or subconsciously for many years (Nussbaum 2007).

Implications for non-BJP parties

The future growth and influence of saffron power is contingent upon the state of non-BJP parties and the nature of the challenge they could present to the BJP at various levels of local, state, and national elections. Ever since the Modi's rise, there has been a great deal of talk over the future of the Congress party – particularly its revival and ability to put together a viable coalition to challenge the BJP. While there is clearly an ideological space in Indian politics, the evidence for the Congress party to be able to stand up for the historic role necessary to arrest the ideological slide towards the Hindu right seems negligible. The fact remains that all of the 31 per cent of the Indian voters who voted for the Modi leadership in 2014 and in various state elections are neither hard-core believers nor fellow travellers of the Hindutva project. A good bulk of them are voters who were disenchanted with a non-performing, complacent UPA regime at the Centre and in other states. A majority of them would abandon their support for Modi and the BJP in the face of credible challenges to the BJP or the Modi government, as evident in the New Delhi Assembly election in 2015 and a few other elections.

The decline of the Congress party is inevitable. According to Jairam Ramesh, a prominent Congress leader, the Congress party is facing an existential crisis, different from what it faced in 1977 or later between 1996 and 2004, which he describes as an electoral crisis.[75] It is plausible that the party could gather a few more seats in the next election, but there is little evidence that it can go back to its heydays and become a pivotal institution or election machine. In part, the dynastic nature of its politics is mainly responsible for this decline.

Will the decline of the Congress party mark the end of dynastic politics in India? While the Nehru-Gandhi family represents the most prominent example of India's dynastic politics, this trend is far more deep, widespread, and transparent across ideological lines. There is also considerable presence of dynastic politics in the BJP itself despite the claim that the RSS largely controls its politics.

While Narendra Modi strategised his attack on the Nehru-Gandhi family, no evidence has been found in his commitment to take on dynastic trends in his own party till date. To name a few, leaders like Vijaya Raje Scindia, Jayant Sinha, and Avinash Thakur remain key players in the BJP and its governments. Dynastic parties no doubt present a major threat to Indian democracy and undermine its democratic potential. De-dynastification is clearly an important requisite for Indian democracy if it is serious about building a modern India based on merits and ability. Also, it is true that dynastic parties have their shelf life, though no one knows how many generations it would take to set into a decline mode. On average, dynastic parties appear not to last more than four to five generations at best, demonstrating most of their vigour in the first two or three generations. In large part, the survival of a dynastic party also hinges on what sort of electoral competition it is facing. The decline of these dynastic parties is inevitable because they invariably put higher premium on *loyalty* than on *ability*. In the case of the Congress party, Ghulam Nabi Azad would always be more sought after and appreciated than Mamata Banerjee or Sharad Pawar. In the context of Assam, Gogois are more wanted than Hemant Sharma.[76] Kanchan Chandra's book titled *Democratic Politics: State, Party and Family in Contemporary Indian Politics* (Cambridge 2016) presents an incisive analysis of dynastic parties of modern India.[77] Scholars such as Christophe Jaffrelot and others have often argued that what India has seen is a regionalisation of politics.[78] In fact, what we also witness in this unfolding drama of regionalisation is indeed a multiplication of dynasties, which they have not been able to notice for some reason.

The 2014 election has also showed a significant decline of the Left party's presence in Parliament. With the further consolidation of Trinamul Congress (TMC) led by Mamata Banerjee, solid signs of the electoral decline of Communist Party of India (Marxist) party in West Bengal are now evident. The more specific question is whether the CPI(M) and its allies would be able to retain their stronghold in the three states West Bengal, Kerala, and Tripura? At this point, it would be preposterous to ponder over their expansion to other regions. The West Bengal Assembly election results in 2016 clearly have not shown any evidence of CPI(M)'s revival in the state, though the story is rather positive in Kerala.[79]

Scholars would continue to debate whether there is indeed stagnation or decline setting in the Indian Left at least in the electoral arena. In a recent article entitled, 'The Decline of the Left: A Causality of Ideological Contradictions' V Krishna Ananth argues at the end that, 'Only a miracle can help it revive, and restore its relevance' (Ananth 2016: 166). Beyond this, however, if one takes into account Naxalite/Maoist politics, a very different portrait of the future of Left politics in India emerges. India's Ministry of Home Affairs, since 19 October 2006, has been running a separate department to look into what it describes as 'Left Wing Extremism (LWE)' in which it clearly records that the states like West Bengal, Odisha, Bihar, Telangana, Maharashtra, Madhya Pradesh, Uttar Pradesh, Chattisgarh, and Jharkhand are affected by LWE. Electoral results are not the most reliable indicator to show the strengths of Left radicalism that has, according to Ministry of Home Affairs reports, been spreading in different regions of India.

Scholarship on India's election studies

While elections as a theme/sub-theme is well established as part of research on Indian politics, studies on electoral studies as a discipline/sub-discipline is yet to mature in India. Without doubt, a substantial amount of writing has been seen in recent years, but the bulk of scholarship lacks rigour and depth by a global standard. Furthermore, persuasive answers to some key questions of India's electoral politics or Indian voting behaviour continue to elude us.

For instance: Why did southern voters vote for Indira's Congress in 1977, unlike the Northern voters who voted against her party? In order words, why didn't the *Emergency* excesses count in the south as much as it did in the north ? How do we explain the Indira wave in 1984? Why could not the 2002 genocide prevent Modi and his

Gujarat BJP from winning Gujarat repeatedly? Why did not the 1984 pogrom prevent the Congress(I) from winning the Delhi state at least? What sort of roles do crime or corruption play in voting decisions? Why do prominent activists like Medha Patkar fail to win elections? While Indian voters generally look smart in their voting decisions, why do they embrace dynastic parties? A list of similar questions could run endlessly, calling for serious research to advance the sub-discipline of India's election studies.

Since the mid-1990s, when the National Election Survey (NES) study was launched by the Centre for the Study of Developing Societies (CSDS), New Delhi, there has been a steady flow of books, monographs, essays, and articles on Indian elections. This enterprise has built up a decent data set, though it remains narrowly focused; and its ability to address the multilayered complexity of India's socio-economic and cultural issues remains rather limited. Compared to other data sets – such as for America (some examples are *American National Election Studies, Gallup, Pew Research Center, Electoral Integrity Project, National Annenberg Election Survey*, etc.) and for Europe (some examples are *Comparative Study of Electoral Systems, European Election Database*, etc.) – the NES database is rather limited. However, it has been useful for qualitative and quantitative research to some measure, which deserves appreciation. In a very well-researched chapter titled *Data and the Study of Indian Politics*, Steven Wilkinson, political scientist based at Yale University raises a very valid concern regarding Indian data, which is about its reliability, and not just about elections, but also on other issues (Wilkinson 2010: 587–599).

Prior to the launch of the CSDS's NES in 1996, there were few studies done at the CSDS, New Delhi, mainly under the academic leadership of Bashiruddin Ahmed with the active patronage of Rajni Kothari. Bashiruddin Ahmed along with Rajni Kothari spent the academic year 1968–1969 in the Stanford University campus at the Centre for Advanced Studies in the Behavioural Sciences. They were sponsored and mentored by Gabriel Almond. In a chapter titled 'An Intellectual History Of the Study of Indian Politics', Sussane Rudolph and Lyod Rudolph present a fascinating story on how Rajni Kothari was able to build up research on Indian politics at the CSDS (Rudolph and Rudolph 2010: 555–586). Unlike the Ahmed-led study that was discontinued, the NES has been continuous since the mid-1990s. Moreover, Professor Ahmed, also as the chairperson of Indian Council of Social Science Research (ICSSR), one of the major funding agencies for the NES in 1996, played a key role in the revival led by Yogendra Yadav.

Bashiruddin Ahmed and Samuel Eldersveld's book, *Citizens and Politics: Mass Political Behaviour in India* (1978), remains a major contribution in the field. A small community of scholars of varied abilities have been regularly writing on various dimensions of Indian elections ever since the NES began. Their numbers have not grown to the extent to cover all regions or elections (Parliamentary, state, or panchayat level). Some satisfaction, nonetheless, can be drawn as the state of scholarship is not as dismal or inadequate as it used to be prior to the mid-1990s.

A very accomplished French scholar, Stephanie Tawa Lama-Rewal, neatly summarises the broad contours of research in India's election studies by presenting a typology of election studies published since the late 1980s. She argues that this research is characterised by (a) the importance of regional parties and regional politics; (b) the formation of ruling coalitions at the national and regional levels; and (c) the polarisation of national politics around the Congress, the BJP, and the 'third space' (Lama-Rewal 2009).

Moreover, a few major Indian journals and magazines such as *Economic and Political Weekly* (EPW), *Frontline*, and *Seminar* have become credible platforms for election analysis. The explosion of private media, print and broadcast, has also created new platforms for public discussions on various election related issues. Considering Bashirruddin Ahmed's contribution to this field, I dedicate this book to him along with distinguished Oxford economist, Barbara Hariss-White and noted American scholar Eleanor Zelliot, as the writings of these scholars have helped me to deepen my understanding of Indian politics from various perspectives.

A few words on the *Sage Publications* series on India's Election Studies edited by Paul Wallace and Ramashray Roy is necessary at this juncture to grasp the richness of emerging scholarship on Indian elections. Unlike the first four volumes, which were jointly edited, the current volume on the 2014 election, titled *India's 2014 Elections: A Modi-led BJP Sweep* (Sage 2015) is edited by Paul Wallace alone. It is dedicated to Ramashray Roy, who is no more. Contributors to these volumes, a good mix of extremely accomplished scholars and relatively young ones, were invited from different parts of the world. I have drawn inspiration from this series. My endeavour is to supplement this by furthering the discussion. A new database called *Trivedi Centre of Political Data*, now established at Ashoka University, Sonepat, Haryana, will become a prominent source of scholarship on India's electoral studies, I hope.

I would like to make some comments on select publications on Indian elections and related themes to lay out the broader intellectual context. For instance, Steven Wilkinson's *Votes and Violence: Electoral Competition and Communal Riots in India* (Cambridge 2004) is a major research at the interface between ethnic violence and India's electoral politics. Democratic states protect minorities, according to Wilkinson, when it is in their government's electoral interest to do so. According to Wilkinson, when two particular conditions are met, first, when minorities are crucial part of their current support base, and second, if one of their coalition partners in a coalition government depends on minority support, then the politicians in government take extra interest in protecting minorities. In other words, invariably the protection of minorities is driven more by power calculus than by any normative considerations such as minority rights or pursuing equality among citizens of varied ethnic or religious backgrounds.

Milan Vaishnav's *When Crime Pays* (Harper 2017b) presents crucial insights to the role of money and muscle in India's electoral politics. Based on extensive fieldwork between 2008 and 2014, Vaishnav raises five specific questions to pursue his inquiry. Some questions are these: What incentives do individuals with serious criminal reputations have to take part in the electoral sphere? Why do political parties choose candidates with a serious criminal past? What are the implications of the presence of criminal politicians for democracy and accountability? Briefly, the book presents a framework for understanding the nexus of crime and democracy in modern India. Politicians tied to criminality not only survive but thrive in India's competitive politics because of the money they are able to marshal and the vacuum of governance they are able to exploit. I further suggest that Muslim politics would remain with in the framework of nationalist secular politics despite the offensive from the Hindutva forces.

Another important contribution is the research by Tariq Thachil's *Elite Parties, Poor Voters: How Social Services Win Votes in India* (Cambridge 2014). Why do poor people often support political parties that do not champion their material interests? According to Thachil, politically motivated, private provisions of local public goods by the BJP's movements affiliates persuade poor voters to vote for the BJP.

Some recent books that have received attention include an edited volume by Sandeep Shastri, K.C. Suri, and Yogendra Yadav, *Electoral Politics in Indian States: Lok Sabha Elections in 2004 and Beyond* (Oxford 2009). With chapters on Mizoram, Sikkim, Manipur, Goa together with other major states of India such as Uttar Pradesh, West Bengal, Bihar, Karnataka, Maharashtra, Jammu and Kashmir,

Gujarat, Haryana, Rajasthan, Delhi, Punjab, Jharkhand, Arunachal Pradesh, etc., the collection presents a broad coverage of elections in various states with an insightful overview of India's electoral development in 2004 and beyond. Another volume, *Party Competition in Indian States: Electoral Politics in a Post-Congress Polity* is edited by Suhas Palshikar, K.C. Suri, and Yogendra Yadav (Oxford 2014). Also, there is Mukulika Banerjee's *Why India Votes? Exploring the Political In South Asia* (Routledge 2014) that presents a detailed ethnographic account of voting behaviour and the competing interests of India's political elites based on extensive fieldwork in various Indian states.

Also, there are indeed many valuable works at the interface of party politics and public policy issues reflecting on electoral issues. That tradition continues even today. For instance, Katharine Adeney and Lawrence Saez's edited volume, *Coalition Politics and Hindu Nationalism* (Routledge 2006) and Sanjay Ruparelia's *Divided We Govern: Coalition Politics in Modern India* (Oxford 2015) are examples of this genre.

Additionally, there are academic journals taking an interest in publishing special issues on Indian elections. On the 2014 election, three academic journals, among others, deserve special mention. The first one is *Journal Of Democracy* (October 2014) an issue that published contributions by three political scientists, Sumit Ganguly, Ashutosh Varshney, Eswarn Shridharan, and one economist Rajiv Kumar.[80] The second prominent journal is *Contemporary South Asia* (Vol 23, May 2015) that published a special issue edited by Louis Tillin. Contributors for this volume included scholars like James Manor, Christophe Jaffrelot, Adam Michael Auerbach, Andrew Wyatt, Oliver Heath, Smitana Saikia, and Louis Tillin herself. Another crucial intervention is made by a Sage Journal, *Television and New Media* (May 2015). It devoted a special issue on the role of media in 2014 election; it was jointly edited by Paula Chakravarty of New York University and Srirupa Roy, a political scientist based in Gottingon, Germany. Contributors to this issue include scholars such as Ravinder Kaur, Sanjay Srivastava, Sriram Mohan, Vipul Mudgal, Somnath Batabyal, Christophe Jaffrelot, Brita Ohm, Joyajeet Paul, Lawrence Liang, and Aswin Punathanbaker. Likewise, in a major European journal, SAMAJ,[81] scholars Balveer Arora, Stephanie Tawa-Rewal, Christophe Jaffrelot, Gill Veniers, and Rekha Chaudhury wrote on a series issues concerning the 2009 election.

Another crucial dimension neglected in Indian election research is writings on campaign and campaign-related issues. India's election campaign is a festival of its own kind at any level – and they are as diverse as India is. And yet the scholarship is almost non-existent. Prashant Jha's *How BJP Wins* (Harper 2017) is a welcome contribution. One does draw interesting insights from, say memoirs or biographies of political leaders of various parties. Some politicians such as Krishna Bose, Maharani Gayatri Devi, Sharad Pawar, M.L. Fotedar, Margaret Alva, K. Natwar Singh, Somnath Chatterjee, Jyoti Basu, Atal Vihari Vajpayee, L.K. Advani, Jaya Jaitley, and many others have either written memoirs or their biographies are published, giving interesting insights to their campaign experiences. It is high time that major South Asian studies departments in various parts of the world should begin to encourage scholars (particularly at the doctoral level) to work on campaign literature for serious scientific analysis. This would help deepen our understanding of Indian voting behaviour.

Despite the national and global media's abiding interest in reporting on Indian elections, research interest on it remains rather limited. Hardly any major conference/workshop was held on the 2014 election in universities and research institutions in neighbouring South Asian countries. Political scientist Mohammed Waseem hosted a conference in Lahore University of Management Sciences (LUMS), Lahore, Pakistan, which unfortunately I could not attend despite being invited. It is one of the few conferences held in the region on Indian elections that I am aware of. If Indian democracy is expected to be role model for the region, a greater number of academic activities should be held for scholarly discussions and writings on Indian elections and its polity in South Asian region. For some reason, the idea to have discussions and scholarship on the domestic politics of South Asia region escapes our policy makers and scholars who shape minds in state power. A curious case is South Asian University, New Delhi, which does not have a Department of Politics with a focus on domestic politics, though it has a Department of International Affairs. One wonders what kind of understanding of regional friendship or development can emerge in the absence of a healthy understanding of domestic politics of various countries in South Asia!

Notes on chapters

The contributions in this volume cover a diverse set of themes pertaining to the 2014 election and the ensuing political and electoral developments. Much of these are focused on particular states, such as southern states, Uttar Pradesh, Jammu and Kashmir (J&K), West Bengal, Meghalaya (in the context of northeastern states), Punjab, Telangana, Gujarat, Chattisgarh, and Jharkhand and a few others.

Additionally, some of the contributions address themes germane to the rise of the BJP and its politics, for instance, a chapter on 'love jihad' and *ghar wapsi*, the decline of the Congress party, the voting behaviour of Muslims, the impact on Christians, and foreign policy and Hindutva.

While scholars have already attempted considerable analysis of the Modi wave – not much analysis has been on the non-Modi wave in 2014 and later. The chapter by James Chiriyankandath, ' "Yes, but not in the South": the BJP, Congress, and regional parties in South India' addresses the most fascinating puzzle of contemporary Indian politics: why and how have the southern states (Andhra Pradesh, Telangana, Kerala, Tamil Nadu, and Karnataka) responded against the pro-BJP national trend in the 2014 election. Their response has been consistent with what they have been resisting since last five decades or so, beginning with the 1962 general election. The electoral landscape in the south, according to the author, reveals that the 'federalisation' of politics recognised in the 1990s continues to characterise the ongoing political trends. On the one hand, the BJP as a national alternative has failed to displace the parties those who replaced the Congress earlier in various southern states. The BJP's ambition to expand Hindutva politics has its limits and the formula that has worked so well in the north and other parts of India has failed in the south.

Arendt Michael's contribution, 'India's foreign policy and Hindutva: the new impact of culture and identity on the formulation and practice of India's foreign policy 2014–2017', addresses the foreign policy dimensions of the 2014 election. One key question raised here is this: what are the frames that animate Modi's foreign policy and how are they located in the larger historical and strategic dimensions of the frames? Examining various speeches that Modi delivered during the campaign leading to the 2014 election, and the BJP's manifestoes, the author evaluates various foreign policy developments and their implementation. Modi's foreign policy, argues the author, is derived and influenced by the Hindutva cognitive frame, and it has been a break with the past.

Charu Gupta's contribution, 'Allegories of "love jihad" and *ghar wapsi*: interlocking the socio-religious with the political' analyses how the political environment shaped by the 2014 election results has created incentives for various Hindutva groups to launch their programmes such as 'love jihad' and '*ghar wapsi*'. It is a major marker, she argues, signifying the shift of India's politics towards the right. She further argues how discourse of religious othering and hatred has gained a new lease of life. *Ghar wapsi*'s language is not intended to promote religious values and spirituality instead it is driven by strong anti-Christian and anti-Muslim overtone. The reconversion campaign – like 'love jihad' – is dominated by violent practices given that the Ghar wapsi movement asks to avenge past humiliation and historical wrongs of conversion, regain courage and become warriors of a proud Hindu race. This chapter introduces us to various operational details of non-state actors in Hindutva politics and the mechanism to promote their ideological objectives.

The chapter by Sudha Pai and Avinash Kumar titled 'Understanding BJP's victory in Uttar Pradesh' endeavours to explain the factors behind the BJP's 2014 spectacular success in Uttar Pradesh, which they view more as a Modi victory, not that of the BJP's victory. According to them, the Modi-Shah duo was able to revive the BJP's organisation in various parts of Uttar Pradesh, and convert it into an election machine. In the face of a lacklustre campaign by key opposition parties such as the Congress(I) party, Samajvadi Party (SP) and Bahujan Samaj Party (BSP), it was relatively easy for the BJP to unleash its own brand of campaign, a mix of Hindutva and development. Branding the BJP campaign as communal, they present a detailed discussion of the political strategy behind such a large-scale victory in UP's Muzaffarnagar. They appear doubtful about the future of the Congress party and also durability of the BJP's electoral success. Also, my chapter titled 'An inquiry into the causes and consequences of the saffron whirlwind that swept Uttar Pradesh in the 2017 Assembly election' in which I argue that the rise of Hindu right in Uttar Pradesh could be better understood if it is seen more as a continuity of a political tradition that could be traced to as early as 1930s or even before. It is not an abrupt political development. I also suggest that Muslim politics would remain within the framework of nationalist secular politics despite the offensive from the Hindutva forces.

Harsh Mander's chapter, 'Election 2014 and the battle for India's soul', presents the discussion of Gujarat violence in 2002 in the context of the 2014 election. Given that background, it is not that easy for Modi to emerge as a moderate national leader for which erasure of his past culpability is essential. Describing this election as a battle for India's soul, the author recognises a decisive ideological shift that has accompanied the victory of the BJP and Modi in the 2014 election. This shift poses a major threat, not just to what India has achieved in past few decades, but also concerning the mortal danger to India's religious minorities, especially Muslims and Christians. The chapter by Zoya Hasan, 'Collapse of the Congress party', recounts various dimensions of the issues pertaining to the Congress party and its decline. It explores issues concerning its leadership, and its unwillingness to take measures to revive the party. It presents a comprehensive view on its failure to respond to Modi's political challenge during the 2014 campaign. As the title suggests, the collapse of the party is self-inflicted, according to Zoya Hasan.

My other chapter titled 'Explaining the inconvenient truths of Indian political behaviour: Hindutva, Modi, and Muslim voters in 2014' explores the question of India's Muslim voters and their attitude towards Hindutva and Modi. Ever since the Gujarat riot 2002, a global perception has been built about Modi being an anti-Muslim Indian leader. But Modi made efforts to reach out to Muslims and his efforts seem to have borne fruit to some extent in 2014 election. Using the survey data, I demonstrate that Muslims voted for Modi in few states such as Gujarat, Karnataka, and Uttar Pradesh in significant numbers. I also argue that only the argument of secularism is not enough to keep Muslim flocks together, instead, the idea of secularism needs to be supplanted with development to be more effective. The chapter reflects on Modi's campaign in Benaras. At the end, it offers some explanation of the Muzaffarnagar violence and how it needs to be contextualised to make sense of the reception as well as the threat that Hindutva politics poses. Rudolf C. Heredia's contribution, 'The dance of democracy: election 2014 and the marginalised and minorities', expresses deep concern for the future of religious minorities (particularly Christians) in India in the context of a Modi-led BJP. He explains how the neoliberal development model has created conditions for the rise of Hindu Rightwing politics. These forces present challenges for the religious minorities even if they are granted many rights and safeguards in India's Constitution.

Out of the two chapters on the Aam Admi Party (AAP) and its politics, Pritam Singh's chapter, 'Aam Admi party's electoral performance in Punjab: implications for an all India political scenario', endeavours to present a comparative perspective of two varied types of success that the AAP accomplished in the 2014 Parliamentary and 2017 Assembly elections. The latter is far less spectacular owing to various blunders that the AAP leadership committed in the post-2014 period. The noteworthy factor, according to Singh, that resisted the Modi wave is what he describes as *political specificity* of Punjab. The rise of the sikh militant movement in the 1980s, and its suppression, and the rise of the Maoist and Naxalite movement in the late 1960s, and its suppression in the 1970s, constitute two prominent aspect of Punjab's political specificity. Despite all the setbacks, the AAP remains a key player in Punjab politics, according to Singh. The other contributions on the AAP is by Nissim Mannathukkaren. It is titled 'The "people" and "political": Aam Aadmi and the changing contours of the anti-corruption movement'. Mannathukkaren makes a compelling argument by cautioning the readers that the notions such as *people* and *political* should not be viewed in reductionist terms. And it is crucial to reflect and analyse the political conditions which led to the formation of the Aam Aadmi Party (AAP) to form a comprehensive understanding of its roots as an anti-corruption movement, and its later phase party activities. Deliberating at length about its origin, various competing ideological struggles, the party split, and its role when in power in Delhi – particularly its policy orientations – the author suggests that the AAP's positioning as a centrist party with some left characteristics and its opposition to the Hindu rightwing party the BJP is its most noteworthy development. However, at present, he notes that the party is at crossroads.

Uday Chandra's chapter, 'The 2014 national election from the margins of modern India', seeks to explain how Indian politics looks from the margins after the 2014 election. Using his fieldwork in various parts of India, especially in Chattisgarh and Jharkhand, Chandra argues for a possible distortion to enter into India's democratic path that would appropriate what he considers the gains of a second democratic upsurge and also that of the Nehruvian consensus. The Modi coalition, according to Chandra, combines organic social unity, political stability, economic growth, and a powerful state, but it rests on a complex coalition of social groups and interests, 'which gives Hindu fascism today its vitality even as it threatens to fragment its carefully crafted ideological consensus'. In the margins of modern India, negotiations with Hindu fascism take multiple forms and a measure of mass support for the BJP there cannot be understood without acknowledging the compromises that anchor these cross-caste alliances.

Maidul Islam's chapter, 'Big national parties in West Bengal: an exceptional outcast?', attempts to explain why two major national parties, the Congress(I) and the BJP, are outcast in West Bengal. The political dynamics at this time is characterised by the limited presence of the Congress party, and the attempt of the BJP to emerge as the main opposition party. Also, there is a sustained decline of the Left parties, and further consolidation of the ruling Trinamool Congress (TMC) party in West Bengal, creating a unique political milieu and ideological competition. Looking into various historical factors, the author compares the political trends based on the 2014 Parliamentary election and 2016 Assembly election. He concludes that the dominance of the regional parties would continue. At the same time, he expresses deep worries about the possible rise of the Hindu right party, particularly because it would change the political discourse from development to religious identity, of which some signs are already noticed.

Cornelia Guenauer's chapter, 'National elections in a tribal state: The 2014 Lok Sabha election in Meghalaya', seeks to reflect on the broader political developments in the northeast region through the analysis of the 2014 election in Meghalaya. The political discourse in Meghalaya was dominated by two major factors: one was a feeling of alienation from the Indian state, and the other was the concern over the influx of outsiders. She delves into historic factors that have led to particular conditions, and then examines the specific factors pertaining to 2014 election. Despite the BJP's success in some regions in the northeast, she argues, any attempt to present the BJP's success as a saffron wave in the northeast could be misleading, given that the Congress party continues to retain many of its strongholds.

The chapter by Ritu Khosla, 'Lok Sabha elections in (un)divided Andhra Pradesh: issues and implications in Telangana and Seemaandra', explores myriad factors that led to the victory for Telangana Rashtiyasangharsa Samiti (TRS) in Telangana and also Telugu Desam Party (TDP), an old ally of Bhartiya Janata Party in Seemandra. In both the states, Andhra Pradesh's bifurcation became a key issue along with the development-related issues. What is important to note is that in these southern states, both national parties BJP and the Congress(I) had little appeal in this election. The results were against the national trend. The author discusses in detail not only the campaign, manifestoes but also how various leaders were perceived during the campaign. It offers useful insights to the party politics in this region. The chapter by Aijaz Ashraf Wani, 'Electoral politics in Jammu and Kashmir (J & K) and the problem of communal polarisation', argues that though problems of communalisation in the state could be traced to the pre-1947 era – but the 2014 election took it to a new height. His analysis goes beyond the 2014 election and incorporates the analysis of the following Assembly election in 2015, and by doing so, he advances his analysis of communalisation in the larger context of both the elections.

In conclusion: how close are we to Hindu Rashtra?

Very close or we are almost there.

These two possible answers could be most agreeable on the Hindu Rashtra. Comments made by a few prominent public personalities such as Rajinder Sachar, Nayantara Sehgal, and others direct us to such a conclusion. For instance, Rajinder Sachar said, 'In 2019, India will be declared as Hindu Rashtra'.[82] Likewise, Nayantara Sehgal has said in an interview, 'RSS wants a Hindu Pakistan'.[83] The political developments since the 2014 election have created the necessary conditions for the Indian state to reorganise its organs to function more as a majoritarian Hindu state. Its most animating evidence has been witnessed in various statements and views of many ministers, Chief Ministers, and governors serving under the Modi government, and has also been also corroborated by their activities.

Two events are, however, crucial to make sense of the direction of Indian democracy: the first one is from 6 December 1992: the day of the demolition of Babri Masjid. The other is Indira Gandhi's *Emergency* (1975–1977). Apparently, the Hindu right, particularly the BJP, wants India to remember only *Emergency*, and would like the demolition of Babri Masjid to be remembered as an inspiration for an attempt to correct a historic injustice, instead of a tragic event that gave a blow to India's secular edifice. This is echoed in Prime Minister Modi's speech on 6 November 2016 at the Ramnath Goenka award in New Delhi, hosted by the *Indian Express*, in which he urged everyone not to forget *Emergency*.[84] There is also a substantive difference in the manner the mainstream media recalls the *Emergency* and the demolition of the Babri Masjid, the former is recalled with great enthusiasm, and the remembrance of the latter is rather lukewarm in the past few years.[85]

Furthermore, the rise of saffron power has the potential to subvert India's present political system, giving rise to what I describe as a *saffron system*. While the BJP's uninterrupted electoral expansion may appear to be swallowing/gulping down the social bases of various political parties like the CPM in West Bengal; the Congress(I) in Odisha; the Bahujan Samaj Party (BSP), the Samajwadi Party (SP), and the Congress in Uttar Pradesh; or National Conference (NC) in J&K; Assam Gano Parishad (AGP), and the Congress(I), among others, in Assam; or even Shiv Sena (SS) in Maharashtra, there is no guarantee that there would be no setback to this trend. Indeed, tremors, convulsions, or setbacks in the BJP's onward march are expected sooner or later as the history of evolution of India's party politics suggests.

The saffron system that is replacing the populist secular Congress system and its successor coalition politics may have its own pathology. This single majority Modi government, it is probable, could lapse into a new cycle of unstable coalition governments in the post-2019 era, but the ideological shift that India has witnessed, I argue, could be irreversible. Mainly because various outfits promoting Hindu Right *agendas*, such as love jihad, *ghar wapsi*, ban on cow slaughter, or cow vigilante groups, etc., would remain active in different shapes and forms regardless of the BJP's electoral setbacks at the Centre or in states. For instance, many of the agendas of love jihad or *ghar wapsi* took place in Uttar Pradesh during Akhilesh Yadav's Samajwadi Party (SP) government (2012–2017); the killings of many journalists and rationalists like Gauri Lankesh occurred under the Congress government in Karnataka. Often seen as strategic outfits, these so called fringe organisations are extracted from more organised Hindu right organisations such as Rastriya Swayam Sevak Sangh (RSS), Vishwa Hindu Parishad (VHP), Bajrang Dal, and others. They would push the Hindu right's ideological agenda. The future work of the Hindu Rashtra would be advanced on what could be already achieved under the Modi regime. Therefore, the source of inspiration and legitimacy could always be attributed to the political developments of the 2014 election. Dhirendhra K Jha's *The Shadow Army* (2017) presents fascinating details about the roles of these organisations.

Research on the evolution of political parties indicates fragmentation or decline, owing to multiple reasons (such as ideological or personality clash, etc.), of a growing party is as natural to its life as to its growth. Indeed, evolutionary history of the Indian National Congress (INC) and Communist Party of India (CPI) is a good example. These parties went through multiple divisions and mergers over the years, leading to various kinds of political formations. Such things would happen with the BJP in future.[86] The former Karnataka Chief Minister from the BJP B.S. Yeddyurappa's decision to form his own party, Karnataka Janata Paksha (2012–2014), is a good example. What is however crucial to note is that these newly formed parties coming out of the BJP's womb, big or small, would pursue Hindutva politics. Some of these new parties would be more extreme and others a little more moderate in their ideological outlook or programmes, but they would operate primarily within the framework of majoritarian politics with a different mix of violence and exclusion towards minorities and Dalits in India. Hence, the overall framework of Indian party politics thus would move from the populist secular kind to the Hindutva variety. Consider how some of the splintered groups like the Trinamul Congress party (TMC) in West Bengal or National Congress Party (NCP) in Maharashtra have emerged from the womb of the Congress party; but retained the populist secular ideological framework as part of their official ideology. Similar trends of fragmentation could be expected from the growing rise of the BJP. This fragmentation or division would derail the evolving consensus towards the inclusive and democratic politics and replace it with majoritarian/Hindutva political discourse.

What kind of challenges could India's saffron system face? The saffron system's future could be challenged internally, owing to fragmentation in the BJP or other similar political formations, and externally, owing to resistance from the political parties opposed to the BJP's Hindutva ideology. In its few decades of rather fast-growing electoral rise of the BJP since 1980,[87] the most serious ideological challenge to the BJP until now took place in 1996. As a result, the party under Atal Vihari Vajpayee failed to garner requisite support to form a national coalition government, which lasted only 13 days (16–29 May 1996) despite being the largest party with 161 seats in Lok Sabha. The party stood completely isolated in India's Parliamentary politics: this was echoed in the famous words of irrepressible Somnath Chatterjee, who uttered them while interrupting Vajpayee's closing confidence motion speech on 27 May 1996. Such a well-coordinated effort among secular political parties, national or regional, to isolate the BJP is unlikely to happen today or in future. Interestingly, the task of putting together the anti-BJP coalition in 2014 or 2019 should have been easier owing to Narendra Modi, one of the most polarising political figures in modern Indian history.

Three factors that could possibly prevent the 1996 type resistance by secular parties against the BJP in future are the following:

> First, the political elites of India's regional parties, mostly dynastic, barely see India's national character as diverse and plural, as central to their existence, unlike the older generations of leaders associated with national movement or national politics. A few leaders, who claim to be product of the Jai Parakash (JP) movement of the 1970s, have become staunch supporters of Modi like Ram Vials Paswan. Or have joined the NDA under Modi as was the case with Nitish Kumar. Other leaders who claim to be opponents or critics such as Lalu Yadav or Mulayam Yadav are woefully discredited. Needless to say, their shameless use of the JP to promote their political ambitions must have deeply embarrassed JP had he been alive. Moreover, for these regional parties, the idea of a region as a polity (that only their territory or what could be described as their social base matters), and the ideological shape of India's national polity is a secondary concern, which is why no serious enthusiasm for a national coalition is seen. Thus, their concern for secular India is more of a lip service.[88]

Second, having led the NDA, the BJP coalition since 1998 has created enough opportunities for leaders of various secular parties – such as National Conference (NC), Telugu Desam Party (TDP), JD(U), etc. – to attain a comfort level through political socialisation, diluting their anti-Hindutva politics/anti-BJPism. The decision to return to the NDA fold by Nitish Kumar in 2017 could be attributed partly to this socialisation.

And, finally, the Modi-Shah leadership's willingness to skillfully accommodate their political adversaries. For instance, its endorsement of Nitish Kumar, despite their bitter clash and separation, or the warm embrace for opposition leaders such as the Congress party's Rita Bahuguna in Uttar Pradesh or Assam's Himanta Biswas Sharma, a key leader of the Tarun Gogoi's Congress, or S.M. Krishna, former foreign minister of the UPA[89] are some of the examples.[90] By opening spaces for these adversaries, the Modi-Shah leadership has diluted ideological resistance towards their political project.

Why is an ideological party like the BJP willing to practice opportunistic co-option? These co-options are strategic as well, partly to weaken the opposition parties, mainly the Congress party, which works as a hub for opposition activities. In the process, these co-options will dry the opposition parties out of their political resources, create a leadership vacuum, ramshackle the network of opposition parties, and help accumulate inside information of the Congress or other parties more effectively. In the literature of war studies, there is a strategy called *strategy of annihilation*, which is what seems to be employed by the Modi-Shah BJP in India today.[91] In addition, the major political party, the Congress, is also deeply compromised owing to the fact that it is saffronised in many parts of India. For instance, Gujarat Congress is seen as a mirror image of the BJP. All these contribute not just to the dilution of resistance, but also facilitate the movement towards the Hindu Rashtra. That is why when the Congress leader Salman Khurshid said that good RSS men have been with the Congress, he indeed alluded to some of the hidden characters of the Congress party.[92]

While it is not easy to predict the evolving nature of the Modi wave in forthcoming elections (including the 2019) – the fact remains that Modi has established himself as an enduring player in India's national politics for the time being. If L.K. Advani has shaped the BJP's mass character during the 1980s and later, then Modi would be credited for making the BJP India's largest political party and giving it its hegemonic character as a dominant governing party at the Centre and also in many states.

Introduction 31

Ever since he has become India's Prime Minister, Modi has been frequently compared with Indira Gandhi.[93] In an op-ed in the *Hindu* (27 May 2017), 'Rewriting of Nehru', I have argued Modi and Nehru as the most ideological Prime Ministers of India in the history of modern India. Martha Nussbaum and Zoya Hasan have compared Modi with Donald Trump.[94] German scholar Brita Ohm has compared Modi with Turkish President, Erdogan (Ohm 2015). Interestingly, no one compares Modi with Vajpayee.[95] No doubt, Modi will remain a contentious political figures in Indian politics, but his contributions in laying down a durable social base and turning India towards the Hindu right will remain unparallel. By doing this, he will also be blamed for setting off India on the path of de-democratisation. Consequently, the politics that emerges will challenge the liberalism, an ideology embedded in a bundle of rights (including human rights and minority rights) that American philosopher John Rawls so powerfully argued in *Political Liberalism* (2005).[96]

Notes

1 On 8 November 2016, Indian Prime Minister Narendra Modi declared Rs 500 and Rs 1000 invalid as legal tender from midnight: it is now recognised as India's demonetisation policy. While the objective was to curb black money, the Reserve Bank Of India (RBI) Report (2017) suggests very little achieved to this end. It caused great deal of hardships to people of all classes, and the poor suffered the worst. And yet, the BJP had a landslide in Uttar Pradesh Assembly Election, and won civic elections in Maharashtra and New Delhi handsomely held in the post-demonitisation period. It is bad economics, but as an act of vigilantism it served Modi politically very well, argued Maitresh Ghatak in an op-ed in *the Wire*, 13 March 2017. Oxford economist Barbara Harris White argued that demonetisation had damaged India's growth story in an interview published in *the Wire*, 25 January 2017. Pro-reform economists like Kaushik Basu remained deeply critical of it in a series of op-eds and interviews. See Basu (2017); for a comprehensive picture on this, see Patnaik, Ghosh and others (2017).
2 Considerable amount of scholarship has emerged on the 2014 election till date; some of the scholarly ones are Wallace (2015); Palshikar, Kumar and Lodha (2017). Also, there are extended journalistic accounts such as Sardesai (2014), Khare (2015), Prashant Jha (2017). Further, there are several major academic journals that have published special issues on Indian elections, say, for instance, *Journal of Democracy* (USA), *Contemporary South Asia* (UK), and *Television and New Media* (USA).
3 Some recent accounts on *India's Emergency (1975–1977)* are by Kapoor (2016), Bhusan (2017). For more detailed analysis, see works by Nayar (1977), Nayar (2014), Dhar (2001); and for alternative account of the JP movement, see Chandra (2017)
4 However, Adnan Farooqui and E. Shridharan (2014) argue that the NDA would not be able to attain Rajya Sabha majority even if it does

remarkably well in Assembly Elections between 2014–2018, even by the late 2018. Though this was the dominant thinking among South Asianists, but the results of recent elections and Nitish Kumar's decision to return to the NDA has changed all of that.
5 The key players of the BJP are from the RSS, including Amit Shah and Narendra Modi.
6 For a nuanced understanding of the RSS and its activities, see the following works: Anderson and Damle (1987), Jaffrelot (2007), Sharma (2003), and Jha (2017)
7 'Historian Irfan Habib Compares RSS With IS, Faces Criticism', 3 November 2015, www.quint.com (accessed 24 September 2017).
8 There is a great deal of enthusiasm among the leaders in Modi government to promote the works of Deen Dayal Upadhyaya. For instance, Maharashtra Chief Minister Devendra Fadnavis ordered his Hindi literature works for the public library. See the report 'The Art of Immortalising: RSS Icon Deen Dayal Upadhyaya Hold Sway in BJP States', *The Hindustan Times*, 10 August 2017.
9 In 1984, the BJP had only two seats, which grew to eighty-six in 1989; it then moved further in the 1990s and the BJP began to lead the NDA coalition.
10 For a thoughtful analysis on coalition politics, see Adeney and Saez (2006) and Shridharan (2014).
11 Rajni Kothari published major formulation on the notion of the Congress system in an article in *Asian Survey* in 1964. Kothari expanded this formulation in some of his more widely read books; two of which are worth looking at: Kothari (2012) and Kothari (1989). A short but interesting commentary on this after the 2014 election was written by Ramachandra Guha (2014). For a more nuanced understanding of party politics in India, see Frankel, Hasan and others (2002), Hasan(2004), and De Souza and Sridharan (2007).
12 The Congress party found its roots and grew under colonial conditions of the British India with a singular objective to end British rule, which made it relatively easy for the party to allure people of diverse backgrounds from different corners of India. On the contrary, the Hindutva ideology around which the BJP seeks to create a political consensus has inherent exclusionary forces, and is incompatible to India's diverse political conditions, which makes it hard to flourish at a speed the BJP would like. Hence, the historical and political conditions are distinctly different for both the parties. The political environment in which the two parties operate today are also different.

Set up in 1885, the Congress party became the most representative of Indian political movement to fight the British colonial rule, but the party went through churnings resulting in multiple fragmentations both before and after 1947. It was Mahtma Gandhi who gave the party a mass character. For a preliminary account of the Congress party's life prior to independence, see Chandra Bipan and Mridual Mukherjee (2016). For a rich account concerning what happened to the Congress party in recent years, see Hasan (2012); for other important research on party politics, see Frankel, Hasan, Arora and Bhargava (2002).
13 'Gau rakhyakas' means protector of cows.

Introduction 33

14 For contemporary analysis of cow vigilantism, see Taseer (2017), Jha (2016), and Deka (2017). For a historical understanding of the place of cow in Hinduism and beef eating practices, see Dharamal and Mukundan (2002) and Jha(2009). The book by Dharampal and Mukundan (2002) was based on the findings of a report prepared by a Commission on the protection of cows (2001). The Commission was set up by Vajpayee government, and Dharmpal served as its Chairman.

15 On 5 May 2017, Dalit–Thakur violence erupted in Saharanpur, Uttar Pradesh. The reason: on that day Dalits objected to a procession carried out by Thakurs and Rajputs to celebrate King Maharana Pratap, which led to a clash in which one young man from the Thakur caste died. In retaliation, fifty Dalit homes were torched, triggering a Thakur–Dalit riot that took several forms of protest. Shaharanpur is 20 per cent Dalits and 40 per cent Muslims. Between 2010 and 2016, there were 544 communal flare ups, the highest in the state.

One organisation that has played a key role in making the protest national is the Bhim Army. Set up sometime in 2015 by a charismatic lawyer, Chandrasekhar Azad (Ravan), the Bhim Army has somewhere around 20,000 followers in the Shaharanpur area. Its ambition seems to be 'direct action based on confrontation to preserve or restore the dignity of Dalits'. See a report titled, 'The Lowdown on the Bhim Army', *The Hindu*, 10 June 2017.

16 Syama Prasad Mukherjee was the founder of Bhartiya Jana Sangh (BJS) party set up in 1951 – mainly because the RSS wanted a political party to pursue its ideological goals. For a comprehensive account of the BJS politics, see Graham (2007).

According to Amit Shah, the current President of the BJP, Mr.Mukherjee should be remembered for three major achievements: (1) ensuring West Bengal remains in India; (2) integrating J&K with India; (3) for founding the BJS. He said this at an event to launch a book titled, *Syama Prasad Mukherjee: His Vision of Education* (2017). See a report, 'Syama Prasad Mukherjee Integrated J and K with India Says Amit Shah', *The Indian Express*, 16 July 2017. A research foundation is now devoted to promote his works and contributions based in Delhi by name, Syama Prasad Mukherjee Foundation, New Delhi (www.spmrf.org) (accessed 24 September 2017). However, it is Deen Dayal Upadyaya, who is seen as the far more important thinker to Modi- Shah led BJP today.

17 Political leaders like Lalu Yadav, Sharad Yadav, Sonia Gandhi, and others are making efforts to put together opposition coalition against the Modi-Shah-led BJP, but they appear quite half-hearted. Also see footnote 22 for further details.

18 This *mahagath bandhan* was stiched together between Nitish Kumar's JD(U), Lalu Yadav's Rastriya Janata Dal(RJD), and Indian National Congress (INC) prior to the Bihar election in 2015 with a clear objective to prevent the BJP from coming to power. The *mahagath bandhan* achieved a spectacular success in the 2015 Assembly election. With RJD 80 seats, JD(U) 71 seats, and INC 27 seats together, the mahaganthbandhan managed to wrest 178 seats in Bihar and stemmed the Modi wave from resurfacing in Bihar after the 2014 election.

19 See, 'No One Can Beat Modi in 2014 Lok Sabha Polls" Says Nitish Kumar', *The Times of India*, 1 August 2017.
20 See Adam Robert, 'Modi's Strongman Economics', *The New York Times*, 9 July 2017.
21 Lalu Yadav was served an Income Tax notice to explain the massive expenditure in putting together the "BJP Bhagao, Desh Bachaho" according to a report in the *Times of India* on 2 September 2017. No such notices were ever served to the BJP or for Modi's rally all over India since 2013.
22 The Chennai gathering was attended by fifteen parties, Sharad Yadav's New Delhi gathering was attended by sixteen political parties, and Lalu Yadav's Patna rally on 27 August was attended by fifteen political parties.
23 Biju Patnaik was the Chief Minister, Odisha in 1996, and was CM in the 1960s. He was a national leader with considerable contributions to national politics. Among other things, it was he who gave the idea to manipulate V P Singh's election as India's Prime Minister after the 1989 election against the challenge posed by Chandrasekhar. Biju Janata Dal (BJD), the party that rules Odisha now is named after him and is led by his son, Naveen Patnaik. It needs to be noted that Biju Patnaik should not be accused of pursuing dynastic politics because he did not encourage his children to join politics. Naveen Patnaik entered politics after the death of Biju Patnaik. See 'Biju Patnaik, 81, Daring Pilot-Patriot of India' *The New York Times*, 21 April 1997.
24 I attended this 1996 Election campaign meeting in Bhubaneswar, Odisha as part of my research on 1996 elections.
25 For a good understanding of the 2009 election, particularly the failure of the BJP, see Wallace and Roy (2011).
26 For a nuanced understanding of the 2014 elections, see Wallace(2015); Sardesai (2014); Khare (2015); Price (2015); Palshikar and others (2017).
27 During the *Emergency* era, it was a coalition of opposition parties led by Jai Prakash Narayan (JP) that challenged Indira Gandhi and in 1989 it was another coalition of opposition parties again led by V.P. Singh that challenged Rajiv Gandhi. No such possible challenge is seen against Modi in the foreseeable future, particularly in 2019.
28 For a close look at Modi's life, see Mukhopadhaya (2013).
29 During the 2012 Gujarat election, I had a chance meeting with the BJP MP and former spokesman, Shahnawaz Hussain at Delhi Airport. I asked him about the impending Gujarat election. He replied sarcastically, 'Which election you are alluding to? there is no election at all'. It showed how confident the BJP was, and how not-serious the Congress party was about the Gujarat election that was won by Modi.
30 Gandhis here imply Sonia Gandhi and Rahul Gandhi, leaders of the present Congress party.
31 Muslims belonging to Ghanchhi caste celebrated Modi becoming India's Prime Minister. See the report 'Ghancchi Muslims Plan to Felicitate Modi', *The Times of India*, 21 May 2014.
32 For a critical look into Modi's life, see Mukhopadhaya (2013) and Marino (2014). Also see a report, 'Emperor Uncrowned: The Rise of Narendra Modi', *The Caravan (New Delhi)*, 1 March 2012.
33 Aakar Patel, 'Everything You Need to Know About Narendra Modi', www.livemint.com, 29 September 2011 (accessed 14 May 2017). Having

Introduction 35

known Modi for several years, Patel categorically certifies that Modi has an anti-Muslim mindset.
34 Ibid.
35 However, one wonders had Modi not been born in Gujarat, or if he were from Nagaland or Puducherry, what kind of political career he would have had enjoyed? Born to Ganchhi caste, a caste of oil pressers, he barely had a caste base in Gujarat.
36 'Narendra Modi Anointed Chairman of BJP National Election Campaign Committee', *The Times of India*, 9 June 2013.
37 'Its Official: Modi Is BJP's Choice', *The Hindu*, 14 September 2013.
38 On Advani's resistance, the only argument that was made was that Modi is an authoritarian figure and would consume the BJP. My sense is there were deeper reasons behind Advani's resistance, and that they had been simmering for many years. Other than L.K. Advani, Yaswant Sinha, Yaswant Singh, Satrughna Sinha, and Uma Bharti were some of the prominent faces who chose to stay away from Goa's national executive meeting, signalling their resistance to Modi's elevation to head its campaign committee in June 2013. See the report, '*BJP's Goa Meet: House Divided Over Naming Modi as Head of Campaign Panel*', 9 June 2013. www.firstpost.com (accessed 24 May 2017).
39 'New Look BJP, BJP Drops Advani, Joshi From Parliamentary Board', 27 August 2014, www.livemint.com (accessed 24 September 2017).
40 'PM Modi, Amir Shah Lay Foundation for New BJP Headquarter in New Delhi', *The Indian Express*, 18 August 2016.
41 The Gujarat 2002 riot is the most devastating incident that happened to Modi's political career. One of the most widely discussed riots ever, it would have destroyed the political career of any other politician, but Modi used it to his advantage by converting it in favour of his ideological posture, and by hardening his Hindutva convictions. For a critical reflections on this, see Varadharajan (2002); Ayub (2016); Lokhande (2016).
42 Noted feminist, Madhu Kiswhar, a scholar working with the Centre for the Developing Studies (CSDS), New Delhi, for many years contributed significantly in combatting the anti-Muslim image. She published a series of articles challenging Modi's anti-Muslim image in *Manushi*, a magazine of which she is the founding editor. She also published a book titled, *Modi, Muslims and Media: Voices From Modi's Gujarat* (Manushi 2014). Its *Foreword* is written by noted script writer Salim Khan, the father of Bollywood star, Salman Khan.
43 My favourite interview during the campaign took place on 9 November 2013 in Lucknow. An autowalla while giving me a ride to a guest house said he would vote for Modi Sahab. When I asked him for reason, he replied, '*Modi sahab nei Gujarat Ko Chamka Diya Hei*' (Gujarat is dazzling because of Modi Sahab). It so happened that he was a Muslim voter from Rai Bareli, Uttar Pradesh, Sonia Gandhi's Constituency. This eerie coincidence of a Muslim, Rai Bareli, Modi voter made me realise that the election was heading for the BJP and there was a Modi wave.
44 Vote mobilisers are the voters who not only vote a particular party, but also raise funds, do door-to-door campaigning, etc.
45 For instance, Omar Abdullah said, 'Modi Has No Courage to Come to Kashmir', 28 April 2014, www.zeenews.com (accessed 24 September 2017);

Salman Khurshid called Modi 'impotent', see report in the *Times of India*, 20 February 2014; Derek O Brien, spokesman of Mamata Banerjee's TMC party called Modi, 'Butcher of Gujarat'. See reports on 28 April 2014; Lalu Yadav remarked that even a butcher will be a better PM than Modi on 29 April 2014.

46 Hardik Patel (b. 1993–) is a young political activist who launched the Patidar agitation in October 2015. The Patidar or Patel agitation exploded the myth of the Gujarat model of development. He was later arrested and is now accused of sedition charges. The agitation was so powerful that it not only shook up the BJP rule in Gujarat, there were even protests in the USA of the Patel community against Modi during his visit to the USA.

47 It means mother-son government (here the mother is Sonia Gandhi and the son is Rahul Gandhi).

48 It means 'Good Days'. This slogan clearly denounced the UPA days as bad days.

49 This directly refers to the accomplishments that Gujarat had made under his leadership as its Chief Minister.

50 It means tea seller.

51 It means fifty-six-inch Chest. This was Modi's way of describing himself as the bravest of the brave politicians of our time.

52 In the larger context, Ravinder Kaur does a very incisive analysis of the idea of *Acche din*. See Kaur (2015).

53 Amit Shah had served as minister under Modi till he was arrested. He was one of Modi's trusted Cabinet members, and the most powerful man under Modi's Gujarat government. I first heard of him in a conversation with Mallika Sarabai in 2004. She was targeted for her work to bring justice to the victims of the 2002 riots.

54 'Shah's of BJP's Game Plan Who Wants to Alter India's Political Culture', *The Hindustan Times*, 16 July 2016. Mr. Patrick French, author of several books, has now joined as Dean the Ahmedabad University located in Gujarat.

55 *The Week*, 2 July 2017. Amit Shah now figures in the cover page of many leading magazines. Recently, *The Open* magazine also has carried him as a cover story.

56 Sohrabuddin encounter took place on 26 November 2005.

57 'Things You Need to Know About BJP's President Amit Shah', www.dnaindia.com, 9 July 2014 (accessed 24 April 2017). It is reported here he first met Modi in 1982 in the RSS circles in Ahmedabad, Gujarat.

58 'Ex Solicitor General in a Letter Vents Air', 26 June 2014, www.Deccanchronicle.com (accessed 24 September 2017).

59 See the report, 'Amit Shah's Assets Grew Threefold in Five Years', 31 July 2017, www.Firstpost.com (accessed 24 September 2017).

60 Court packing is a very important political strategy in the ideological warfare in American politics. Various Presidents from both parties, Democratic Party and Republican Party, often take great interest to nominate people of their ideological and party preference in order to tilt the ideological balance of the Supreme Court. Robert G. Maclosky's *American Supreme Court* (2016) is one of the most influential books on the relationship between American Court and American politics. With regard to the Indian case, Upendra Baxi's *Indian Supreme Court and Politics* (1980) will be perhaps the closest to such kind of research. However, a lot more

61 The extension given to Dr Mahesh Rangarajan was supposed to last till 2024. It means the end of his extended term would have coincided with Modi's end of second term as India's Prime Minister.
62 Modi appeared in a recent front page advertisement of Reliance Company, a first of its kind by the Indian Prime Minister. It is another evidence of his proximity to big capital. See *The Hindustan Times*, 2 September 2016. This appearance has invited great deal of criticism.
63 Pramod Mahajan was rumoured to be a politician working as intermediary between the party and the big capital for the BJP during the Vajpayee era, and in the case of Congress party, there were several names.
64 Anandiben Patel was chosen by Modi as his successor as Gujarat CM.
65 Nilanjana Mukhopadhaya (2017).
66 See the report, 'RSS Drops Its Veil, Prepares Blueprint to Get Ready for 2014 Polls', *India Today*, 12 July 2013.
67 'BJP's 2014 Win Was Not a One-Man Show', *The Times of India*, 11 August 2014.
68 Some of the state elections were the following: New Delhi in which Aam Admi Party (AAP) won in February 2015; the victory of the now disintegrated *mahaganthabandhan*, Janata Dal (U), Rastriya Janata Dal, and the Congress party coalition that won Bihar in November 2015; Trinamool Congress (TMC) in West Bengal in May 2016; and All India Dravidra Munetra Kazagam (AIDMK) in Tamil Nadu again in May 2016.
69 There were a few state elections that BJP did win after the 2014 victory. For instance it won state elections in Haryana and Maharashtra, and it was able to put together coalition governments in two border states, Kashmir and Assam.
70 'Top (BJP) Ministers Attend RSS Meet: Opposition Questions Government Accountability', *The Indian Express*, 3 September 2015.
71 Yaswant did not however mention the RSS's adversarial role in his removal as India's finance minister in his book. See Yaswant Sinha (2007). He lost his finance portfolio to Yaswant Singh in a reshuffle as Mr Singh was seen more trustworthy by Vajpayee. Yaswant Sinha was seen as Chandrasekhar's man. In a rather candid interview with me, Sinha blamed the RSS and Indian Left as being mainly responsible for holding back the country.
72 Walter Anderson to the author in an e-mail communication on 20 September 2017. He is currently working on a book on the RSS.
73 'Kerala RSS Worker's Murder: Data Reveals Record of Political Killings', 4 August 2017, www.ndtv.com (accessed 24 September 2017).
74 'Only India Can Save the World From the Clutches of Capitalism: Mohan Bhagwat', *The Indian Express*, 5 August 2017.
75 Jairam Ramesh, '"Sultanate has gone, but.." Admits Jairam Ramesh Congress Is in Deep Crisis', 10 August 2017, www.ndtv.com (accessed 24 September 2017).
76 There is a considerable discussion on how letting Hemant Sharma leave the Congress party contributed to its dismal results in Assam Assembly elections that led to the formation of the BJP government.

77 See Shaikh Mujibur Rehman, 'Review of Democratic Dyansties: State, Party and Family in Contemporary Politics' of Kanchan Chandra's (2016) book, published in 2016. *The Hindustan Times*, 8 October.
78 See Christopher Jaffrelot and Gilles Veniers (2016).
79 See the analysis, 'Left Gets in Right', *The Frontline*, 10 June 2016.
80 Rajiv Kumar has not taken charge as Vice Chairman of NITI AYOG, the body that replaced the Planning Commission, in September 2017.
81 *South Asia Multidisciplinary Academic Journal* (SAMAJ).
82 'In 2019, India Will Become a Hindu Rashtra', 17 April 2017, www.rediff.com (accessed 24 September 2017).
83 Interview of Nayantara Seghal, Indiacultural Forum, 27 April 2017.
84 *Indian Express*'s Editor-in-Chief, Rajkamal Jha, as part of his vote of thanks, underlined the importance of a dissenting voice in media against the state, but did not mention 6 December 1992 as the dark day in Indian history as much as the *Emergency* is as reminded by Prime Minister Modi. The fact that 6 December is either forgotten or slighted indicates how casual the approach has been in media to fight against the Hindutva.
85 For an analysis on this, see my Introduction in Rehman (2016).
86 Both the Congress party and the Communist Party of India (CPI) went through split for varied reasons.
87 In 1984, the BJP won only two seats. One was by Advani and the other was by Atal Bihari Vajpayee.
88 Consider this statement by Sharad Pawar who urged the Congress to ally with satraps to stop the BJP, 14 April 2017. Sharad Pawar is a veteran Indian politician with a mass base of his own. It is expected of him to play a key role in building the anti-BJP coalition for 2019 instead of simply making statements, which barely give hints for a serious conviction for secularism.
89 S.M. Krishna joined the BJP in May 2017. Rita Bahuguna Joshi, former party chief of the Congress in Uttar Pradesh joined the BJP in October 2016, and her brother Vijay Bahuguna, who had served as the Congress Chief Minister in Uttarakhand, had joined the BJP earlier. The Uttar Pradesh election took place between 11 February and 8 March 2017; Himanta Biswa Sharma, who was the most influential confidante of Tarun Gogoi, Congress Chief Minister of Assam, joined the BJP in August 2015. On the day of his joining, Mr Sharma did a roadshow, driving in an open vehicle from the airport to the BJP party office in Guwahati, that lasted for five hours. The Assam election took place in April in 2016. These former Congress leaders were given a warm welcome by the BJP, and both Bahuguna and Sharma are rewarded with ministerial berths in the BJP governments in Uttar Pradesh and Assam respectively. No national party/government in the past ever approached leaders of opposition parties as the BJP has been doing under the Modi-Shah leadership.
90 In August 2017, six rebel Trinamool Congress MLAs join BJP in Tripura.
91 For a fascinating discussion on this, see Hew Strachen (2007). This book is a commentary on Carl von Clausewitz's classic *On War*.
92 See the report, 'There Are "good" RSS People in the Congress, Says Salman Khurshid', *The National Herald*, 9 July 2017.
93 There are several very interesting books on Indira Gandhi. For a good reading on this subject, see Malhotra(2014), Gupte(1992), Katharine(2007), and Ghose (2017).

94 Martha Nussbaum and Zoya Hasan, 'India and US: Spot the Difference', *The Indian Epxress*, 24 July 2017.
95 For a nuanced understanding of Vajpayee's life and politics, see Ullekh, N. P. (2017).
96 For a comprehensive analysis of the notion of political liberalism that John Rawls theorised, see Michel Sandel's review of Rawls's *Political Liberalism*. 1994. *Harvard Law Review*, Vol 107, 1765–1794. The expanded edition of John Rawls's book was published in 2005.

Bibliography

Adeney, Katharine and Lawrence Saez. 2006. *Coalition Politics and Hindu Nationalism*. London: Routledge.
Ananth, V. Krishnan. 2016. 'The Decline of the Left: A Causality of Ideological Contradictions', in *Making Sense of Modi's India*. New Delhi: Harper Collins.
Anderson, Walter and Shridhar Damle. 1987. *Brotherhood in Saffron: The Rashtriya Sevak Sangh and Hindu Revivalism*. New York: Westview Press.
Arendt, Hanna. 2017. *The Origins of Totalitarianism*. London: Penguin.
Ayub, Rana. 2016. *Gujarat Files: Anatomy of a Cover Up*. Mumbai: Rana Ayub.
Banerjee, Mukulika. 2014. *Why India Votes? Exploring the Political South Asia*. London: Routledge.
Basu, Amrita. 2015. *Violence Conjectures in Democratic India*. New York: Cambridge University Press.
Basu, Kaushik. 2017. 'Look at the Facts on Demonetization, But Not Politics', *The Indian Express*, May 11.
Baxi, Upendra. 1980. *Indian Supreme Court and Politics*. New Delhi: Eastern Book and Co.
Bhusan, Prashant. 2017. *The Case That Shook India: The Verdict That Led to Emergency*. New Delhi: Penguin Random House.
Bilgrami, Akeel. 2011. *Democratic Culture: Historical and Philosophical Essays*. London: Routledge.
Brita, Ohm. 2015. 'Organizing the Popular Discourse with and against the Media: Notes on the Making of Narendra Modi and Recep Tayyip Erdogan as Leaders –without- Alternative'. *Television and News Media*. 16(4): 370–377.
———. 2016a. *Marx, Gandhi and Modernity: Essays Presented to Javeed Alam*. New Delhi: Tulika Books.
———. 2016b. *Secularism, Identity, Enchantment*. New Delhi: Permanent Black.
Calhoun, Craig. 1994. *Social Theory and Politics of Identity*. London: Wiley-Blackwell.
Chandra, Bipan. 2017. *In the Name of Democracy: JP Movement and the Emergency*. New Delhi: Penguin Random House.
Chandra Bipan, Mridula Mukherjee, Aditya Mukherjee, Sucheta Mahajan and K. N. Panikkar (eds.). 2016. *India's Struggle for Independence*. New Delhi: Penguin Random House.

Chandra, Kanchan. 2016. *Democratic Dynasties: State, Party and Family in Contemporary Indian Politics*. New Delhi: Cambridge University Press.

Chatterjee, Partha and Ira Katznelson. 2012. *Anxieties of Democracy: Reflections on Toquevillean Reflections on India and the United States*. New Delhi: Oxford University Press.

Chibber, P. K and S. L Ostermann. 2014. ' The BJP's Fragile Mandate: Modi and Vote Mobilizers in 2014 General Election'. *Studies in Indian Politics*, 2(2): 137–151.

De Souza, Peter D. and E. Sridharan. 2007. *India's Political Parties*. New Delhi: SAGE Publications.

Deka, Kaushik. 2017. 'How Cattle Slaughter Rules Threaten Economy, Revolt in South India', *India Today*, June 1.

Dhar, P. N. 2001. *Indira Gandhi, the Emergency and Indian Democracy*. New Delhi: Oxford University Press.

Dharampal and T. M. Mukundan. 2002. *The British Origin of Cow Slaughter in India: With Some British Documents on the Anti-Kine Killing Movement 1880–1894*. Mussourie: Society for Integrated Development of Himalayas.

Farooqui, Adnan and E. Shridharan. 2014. 'Is the Coalition Era Over in Indian Politics?' *The RoundTable: The Commonwealth Journal of International Affairs*, December 6: 1–13.

Frank, Katharine. 2007. *Indira: Life of Indira Nehru Gandhi*. London: Harper Perennial.

Ghose, Sagarika. 2017. *Indira: India's Most Powerful Prime Minister*. New Delhi: Juggernaut.

Graham, Bruce. 2007. *Hindu Nationalism and Indian Politics: The Origins and Development of the Bhartiya Jana Sangh*. London, Cambridge: Cambridge University Press.

Guha, Ramachandra. 2014. 'The Past and the Future of the Congress Party', *The Hindustan Times*, August 3.

———. 2016. *Democrats and Dissenters*. New Delhi: Penguin.

———. 2017. *India After Gandhi*. London: Pan Macmillan.

Gupte, Pranay. 1992. *Mother India: A Political Biography of Indira Gandhi*. New Delhi: Penguin.

Hasan, Zoya. 2004. *Parties and Party Politics in India*. New Delhi: Oxford University Press.

———. 2009. *Politics of Inclusion: Caste, Minorities and Affirmative Action*. New Delhi: Oxford University Press.

———. 2012. *Congress After Indira: Policy, Power and Political Change (1984–2009)*. New Delhi: Oxford University Press.

Hasan, Zoya, Francine Frankel, Rajeev Bhargava and Balveer Arora (eds.). 2002. *Transforming India: Social and Political Dynamics of Democracy*. New Delhi: Oxford University Press.

Jaffrelot, Christophe. 1998. *The Hindu Nationalist Movement in India*. New York: Columbia University Press.

———. 2007. *Hindu Nationalism: A Reader*. Princeton: Princeton University Press.

Jaffrelot, Christophe and Gilles Veniers. 2016. 'The Resistance of Regionalism: BJP's Limitations and the Resilience of State Parties', in Paul Wallace (ed.), *India's 2014 Elections: A Modi-Led BJP Sweep*, pp. 28–45. New Delhi: SAGE Publications.
Jehanbegloo, Ramin. 2016. *The Decline of Civilization*. New Delhi: Aleph Book Company.
———. 2017. *Letters to Young Philosophers*. New Delhi: Oxford University.
Jha, D. N. 2009. *The Myth of Holy Cow*. New Delhi: Navayana.
Jha, Dhirendra K. 2017. *Shadow Armies: Fringe Organizations and Foot Soldiers of Hindutva*. New Delhi: Juggernaut.
Jha, Prashant. 2017. *How BJP Wins*. New Delhi: Harper Collins.
Jha, Prem Shankar. 2016. 'Cow Vigilantism Is Tearing Apart India's Social Fabric', October 14. www.thewire.com (accessed on September 14, 2017).
Kapoor, Coomi. 2016. *The Emergency: A Personal History*. New Delhi: Penguin.
Kaur, Ravinder. 2015. 'Good Times, Brought to You by Brand Modi', *Television and News Media*, 16(4): 323–330.
———. 2016. 'I am India Shining: The Investor- Citizen and the Indelible Icon of Good Times', *The Journal of Asian Studies*, 75(3), August: 1–28.
Khare, Harish. 2015. *How Modi Won It*. New Delhi: Hacchette India.
Kiswhar, Madhu. 2014. *Modi, Muslims and Media: Voices From Modi's Gujarat*. New Delhi: Manushi.
Kothari, Rajni. 1988. *State Against Democracy*. New Delhi: South Asia Books.
———. 1989. *Politics and People* (Vol. 1). New Delhi: New Horizon Press.
———. 2012. *Politics in India*. New Delhi: Orient Blackswan.
Lokhande, Sanjeevini B. 2016. *Communal Violence, Forced Migration, and the State: Gujarat Since 2002*. Cambridge: Cambridge University Press.
Maclowsky, Robert. 2016. *American Supreme Court*. Chicago: The University of Chicago Press.
Malhotra, Inder. 2014. *Indira Gandhi: A Personal and Political Biography*. New Delhi: Hay House.
Marino, Andy. 2014. *Narendra Modi: A Political Biography*. New Delhi: Harper Collins.
Mukhopadhaya, Nilanjan. 2013. *Narendra Modi: The Man, the Times*. New Delhi: Tranquebar Press.
———. 2017. 'Gujarat Muslims Will Quietly Join Those Critical of BJP and Let the Fingers Do the Talking', *The Economic Times*, November 29.
Nayar, Kuldeep. 1977. The Judgement: Inside Story of the Emergency in India. New York: Asia Book Corporation of America.
———. 2013. *Emergency Retold*. New Delhi: Konark Publishers.
———. 2014. *Between the Lines*. New Delhi: Konark Publishers.
Nussbaum, Martha. 2007. *The Clash Within*. New Delhi: Permanent Black.
Palshikar, Suhas, Sanjay Kumar and Sanjay Lodha (eds.). 2017. *Electoral Politics in India: The Resurgence of Bhartiya Janata Party*. New Delhi: Routledge Publications.
Pashikar, Suhas, K. C. Suri and Yogendra Yadav (eds.). 2011. *Party Competition in Indian States: Electoral Politics in a Post-Congress Politics*. New Delhi: Oxford University Press.

———. 2014. *Party Competition in Indian States: Electoral Politics in a Post-Congress Polity*. New Delhi: Oxford University Press.

Patnaik, Prabhat, Jayati Ghosh and C. P. Chandrasekhar. 2017. *Demonetization Decoded: A Critique of India's Currency Experiment*, kindle ed. New Delhi: Routledge.

Paul, Wallace. 2015. *India's 2014 Elections: A Modi -Led BJP Sweep*. New Delhi: SAGE Publications.

Price, Lance. 2015. *Modi Effect: Narendra Modi's Campaign to Transform India*. London: Hodder and Stroughton.

Rawls, John. 2005. *Political Liberalism*. New York: Columbia University Press.

Rehman, Mujibur. 2016. *Communalism in Postcolonial India: Changing Contours*. London and New Delhi: Routledge.

———. 2018. *Rise of Saffron Power: Reflections on Indian Politics*. London and New Delhi: Routledge.

Reserve Bank of India, *Annual Report* (2017), Mumbai: Publications Division, Government of India.

Rudolph, Sussane and Lyod Rudolph. 2010. 'An Intellectual History of the Study of Indian Politics', in Niraja Gopal Jayal and Prata Bhanu Mehta (eds.), *Oxford Handbook on Indian Politics*. New Delhi: Oxford University Press.

Rupalia, Sanjay. 2015. *Divided We Govern: Coalition Politics in Modern India*. New Delhi: Oxford.

Sandel, Michael. 1994. 'Review of Political Liberalism', *Harvard Law Review*, 107: 1765–1794.

Sardesai, Rajdeep. 2014. *Election That Changed India 2014*. New Delhi: Viking.

Sen, Amartya. 2006. *Argumentative Indian: Writings on Indian History, Culture and Identity*. London: Penguin.

———. 2007. *Identity and Violence: Illusions of Destiny*. London: Penguin.

Sharma, Jyotirmaya. 2003. *Hindutva: Exploring the Idea of Hindu Nationalism*. New Delhi: Viking (Penguin).

Shastri, Sandeep, K. C. Suri and Yogendra Yadav (eds.). 2009. *Electoral Politics in Indian States: Lok Sabha Elections in 2004 and Beyond*. New Delhi: Oxford University Press.

Shridharan, E. (ed.). 2014. *Coalition Politics in India: Selected Issues at the Centre and States*. New Delhi: Academic Foundation.

Sinha, Yaswant. 2007. *Confessions of a Swadeshi Reformer: My Years as a Finance Minister*. New Delhi: Penguin.

Strachen, Hew. 2007. *Clausewitz's on War: A Biography*. New Delhi: Atlantic Books.

Tachil, Tariq. 2014. *Elite Parties, Poor Voters: How Social Services Win Votes in India*. Cambridge: Cambridge University Press.

Taseer, Aatish. 2017. 'Anatomy of a Lynching', *The New York Times*, April 16.

Tawa Lama- Rewal, Stephanie. 2009. 'Studying Elections in India: Scientific and Political Debates', *South Asia Multi- Disciplinary Academic Journal*

(SAMAJ), (3): 1–15, online. http://samaj.revue.org (accessed on November 25, 2017).
Taylor, Charles. 1997. *Philosophical Arguments*. Cambridge: Harvard University Press.
Thapar, Romila, Sundar Sarukkai, Dhruv Raina, Peter Ronald Desouza, Neeladri Bhattacharya and Jawed Naqwi (eds.). 2015. *The Public Intellectuals in India*. New Delhi: Aleph Book Company.
Ullekh, P. N. 2016. *The Untold Vajpayee: Politician and Paradox*. New Delhi: Penguin Random House.
Vaishnav, Milan. 2017a. 'Modi's Victory and the BJP's Future: Will Modi Remake the Party?', *Foreign Affairs*, 15. www.foreignaffairs (accessed on November 25, 2017).
———. 2017b. *Why Crime Pays*. New Delhi: Harper.
Vajpayi, Ananya. 2012. *Righteous Republic: Political Foundations of Modern India*. Cambridge: Harvard University Press.
Varadharajan, Siddarth. 2002. *Gujarat: The Making of a Tragedy*. New Delhi: Penguin.
Vinaik, Achin. 2017. *Hindutva Rising: Secular Claims, Communal Realities*. New Delhi: Tulika Books.
Wallace, Paul (ed.). 2015. *India's 2014 Elections: A Modi-Led BJP Sweep*. New Delhi: SAGE Publications.
Wallace, Paul and Ramashray Roy (eds.). 2011. *India's 2009 Elections: Coalition Politics, Party Competition and Congress Continuity*. London: SAGE Publications.
Wilkinson, Steve. 2004. *Votes and Violence: Electoral Competition and Communal Riots in India*. New Delhi: Cambridge University Press.
———. 2010. 'Data and the Study of Indian Politics', in Niraja Gopal Jayal and Prata Bhanu Mehta (eds.), *Oxford Handbook on Indian Politics*. New Delhi: Oxford University Press.

1 'Yes, but not in the South'
The BJP, Congress, and regional parties in South India[1]

James Chiriyankandath

> 'Yes, but not in the South', with slight adjustments, will do for any argument about any place.
> Stephen Potter, *Some Notes on Lifemanship*, London: Rupert Hart Davis, 1950, p. 14

The aphorism coined by Stephen Potter (1900–1969), the British writer and BBC radio producer, seems apt in referring to many countries and continents, from the USA or Brazil, or the Americas as a whole, to England or Italy or Europe, Nigeria, or Sudan. It is certainly so when we analyse electoral politics in India and especially how the main national political parties, the Indian National Congress and the Bharatiya Janata Party (BJP), have fared in the south relative to the rest of the country. This was again starkly evident in the results of the 2014 Lok Sabha elections.

The five states of south India (Andhra, Telangana, Karnataka, Kerala, and Tamil Nadu) have behaved differently in Lok Sabha elections for more than half a century. Figures 1.1 and 1.2[2] show how – from the third general election in 1962, the second following the linguistic reorganisation of states – parties classified as 'national' by the Election Commission[3] have consistently won a smaller proportion of seats in the south than nationally, while regional parties (mostly classified as 'state parties') have correspondingly performed better in the south. Parties qualifying as national and winning seats in the south in 2014 were Congress, the BJP, the Communist Party of India (Marxist) (CPIM), and the Communist Party of India (CPI); the Bahujan Samaj Party (BSP) and the Nationalist Congress Party (NCP) contested but won no southern seats.

The overall trend shown conceal significant state-level differences. National parties have been marginalised in Tamil Nadu since the

'Yes, but not in the South' 45

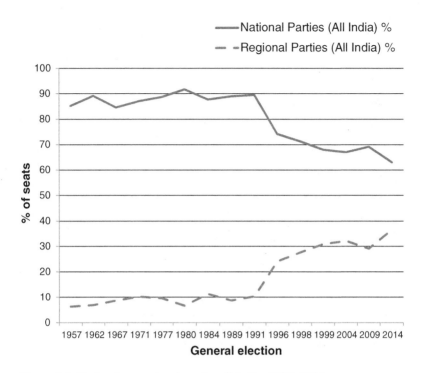

Figure 1.1 National vs. regional parties all India: 1957–2014

Dravida Munnetra Kazhagham (DMK) displaced Congress as the ruling party in the state in 1967, and Congress and their Communist opponents have always needed local allies in neighbouring Kerala, unique in being the only notable state where the BJP has still to register a presence on the electoral map in terms of winning a Parliamentary seat, only gaining one in the state Assembly for the first time in 2016. However, in united Andhra until the advent of the Telugu Desam (TDP) in the early 1980s, and in Karnataka, where the BJP emerged as a significant contender in the 1990s, the main national parties have been stronger. It is therefore also possible to discern a difference between north and south within the southern region as a whole.

What are the historical antecedents and the wider political significance of the divergence? What explains the relative weakness of national parties in the south?

The peninsular south with its Dravidian languages has long been distinguished by social and cultural differences from the north,

46 James Chiriyankandath

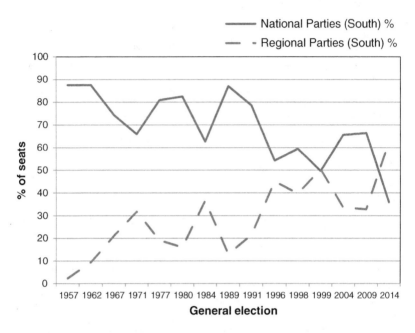

Figure 1.2 National vs. regional parties in the south: 1957–2014

west, and east of India despite sharing a common Indian civilisational heritage. Historically, the Hindu empires and kingdoms of the south maintained their independence until relatively late in the Mughal period with the far south – the south of what is now Tamil Nadu, as well as Kerala – never coming under the dominion of the Mughals or their Muslim offshoots. Visible even in the landscape of towns and cities in the south that contrasts with the Islamic architectural styles that predominate in many of their counterparts in the north, this background maybe what has given its politics less of the fraught communal (i.e. Hindu-Muslim) edge evident in the Hindi-speaking states and in both western and eastern India. It has been an important factor in limiting the appeal of the Hindu nationalism, shading into chauvinism, espoused by the BJP and the Rashtriya Swayamsevak Sangh (RSS) *sangh parivar* (associational family) to which it belongs. In addition, coterminous to the development of the Congress nationalist movement in the south, the early social and political mobilisation of lower castes in Kerala and the Tamil Dravidian movement also imparted a distinct regional character to politics.

Tamil Nadu: Dravidian bastion

The first southern state to march to a different political drumbeat was Tamil Nadu, the heart of the pre-independence south, first the Madras Presidency and then the Madras province of British India until its partition to create Andhra in 1953 in response to the Telugu-speakers demand for separation. This became evident as early as the 1920s, following the introduction of limited provincial self-government under the Montagu-Chelmsford dyarchy reforms. It had its roots in the growing assertiveness of educated sections of numerically significant commercial and agricultural castes, including Tamil Vellalas, Chettis and Nadars, Telugu Reddis and Kammas, and Malayali Nairs and Ezhavas, against the dominance of the small minority of Brahmin castes. In particular, Tamil Brahmin Iyers and Iyengars not only possessed ritual supremacy in a rigorously hierarchical and discriminatory Hindu social order, but also dominated administration and the judiciary and were prominent in the nascent modern forms of political activity emerging under British rule from the late nineteenth century.

Consequently, the largely Brahmin-led Indian National Congress in Madras faced powerful opposition from social reform movements among lower castes, most notably the Self-Respect Movement led by the radical rationalist E.V. Ramaswamy Naicker (1879–1973), pioneer of Dravidian identity politics, and the non-Brahmin Justice Party which dominated Madras politics for two decades until defeated in 1937.[4] Congress, under the astute leadership of Mahatma Gandhi's closest southern associate, Brahmin C. Rajagopalachari (1878–1972), re-established its primacy in the 1937 provincial elections. Yet unlike in western India and the Hindi-speaking states of the centre and north, the post-independence Congress continued to face strong opposition, both from the new Dravida Munnetra Kazhagham, which broke away from the Dravida Kazhagham (the successor to the Justice Party established by Naicker) in 1949, and the Communists who had especially established themselves in the regions of Malabar, in the Malayalam-speaking southwest, and Telangana, in inland Andhra to the north. The Communist challenge disappeared with the creation of the states of Andhra and Kerala as a result of the linguistic reorganisation of states in the1950s.

The Madras Congress was able to keep the Dravidian threat at bay, in part due to the rise to the leadership of the state party of Kumaraswami Kamaraj (1903–1975), a skillful political operator from the Backward Class Nadar caste (their traditional occupation had been tapping toddy from coconut trees) who ended the run of Brahmin Congress leaders and maintained a well-organised state-wide Congress machine. Congress was also temporarily aided by a split in the Dravidian movement resulting in the ascendancy of the DMK, led by C.N. Annadurai (1909–1969). Nevertheless, through the 1950s and 1960s, Dravidian politics gained powerful traction through its growing dominance in the expanding Tamil film industry and the controversy generated in the mid-1960s by anxiety that English would be discontinued as a language of government business and state institutions and Hindi would become established as the sole national language.[5]

The language agitation, that even aroused fears of a potential secessionist movement, was defused by a compromise that effectively meant the indefinite retention of a three-language (Hindi, English, and the respective state languages) formula. Yet the passions unleashed by the agitation over the issue contributed to the DMK's stunning victory in the 1967 state Assembly election. The repercussions of the national Congress split in 1969 that left Kamaraj opposing Prime Minister Indira Gandhi's Congress (R) also helped the DMK retain Madras, renamed Tamil Nadu, in the subsequent elections in 1972. With another split, this time in the DMK, bringing the Anna DMK (ADMK) of Tamil film superstar turned politician M.G. Ramachandran (MGR) (1917–1987) to power in 1977, Congress was relegated to the position of a marginal actor in Tamil Nadu politics, a position it has remained in ever since. Weakened in the mid-1990s by a temporary state-level breakaway (the Tamil Maanila Congress), its value as a junior electoral ally for either of the rival Dravidian parties has declined. In 2014, contesting all thirty-nine constituencies on its own for the first time since 1967, it won none with just 4.4 per cent of the total vote. Learning from this mistake, it renewed its alliance with the DMK in the 2016 state Assembly elections and did better, winning eight of the forty-one seats it contested.

If through the course of the twentieth century the pre-eminence of different flavours of Dravidian identity politics in Tamil Nadu eroded the appeal of Congress, reducing it to a bit player, its effect was even more pronounced when it came to the failure of Hindu nationalism to make inroads in the state. That the politics of Hindu identity were promoted by organisations such as the Hindu Mahasabha and the RSS, generally perceived as north Indian, aggressively pro-Hindi, and dominated by Brahmins and other upper castes, were hugely negative factors. Their local branches, insofar as they existed at all, tended to bear out these stereotypes, dependent as they were on people from north Indian trading castes and Tamil Brahmins alienated by Dravidian politics. It was only in the early 1980s that the RSS sought to extend their social base beyond such groups and the state capital, Chennai, and other urban commercial centres. In Kanyakumari, the southernmost district in the state, the RSS offshoot, the Vishwa Hindu Parishad (World Council of Hindus), which had built a complex of Hindu nationalist establishments on Vivekananda Rock just off the southern tip of India, fueled controversy over the alleged induced mass conversion in 1981 of low caste Hindus to Islam in the village of Meenakshipuram.

Handicapped by its Hindi, north Indian and upper caste associations, the BJP, and the sangh parivar have struggled to overcome the image of being eccentric and anti-Dravidian, not helped by the idiosyncrasies of the BJP's best-known Tamil politician, Subramanian Swamy, a Brahmin maverick with little local following. The BJP's success in winning Parliamentary representation from the state came as a result of its national strength which enabled it to attract first the DMK and then the ADMK into the National Democratic Alliance (NDA) that it led to power in the late 1990s.[6] As a junior partner of one or other of the rival Dravidian parties, it won three and then four seats in successive general elections in 1998 and 1999. However, allied to neither in 2014 the BJP was only able to win in the Kanniyakumari constituency, one of the few in the state where it had established a presence over decades. It fared worse in the 2016 state Assembly poll when it contested all 232 seats and drew a blank with under three per cent of the vote.

Kerala: politics of the Left and communal accommodation

It is unsurprising that the politics of Kerala, India's southernmost state, are exceptional. Cochin and Travancore, two of the most advanced of the pre-independence princely states, made up two-thirds of the Malayalam-speaking state when it was created in 1956; the Malabar district of Madras providing the other third. Muslim and Christian communities, the oldest in India with histories stretching back well over a thousand years, constitute over forty-five per cent of the population with the Backward Class Ezhava caste the largest Hindu group. The state has also been unusual in terms of its social development with a strong tradition of matriliny among not just the Nairs, the largest caste Hindu group, but also sections of Ezhavas and Mappila Muslims; it has the highest rates of life expectancy (76.9 female, 71.5 male) and literacy (93.91 per cent) in the country,[7] and a relatively high overall average standard of living with little extreme poverty.

Two factors above all have shaped Kerala's distinctive politics. First, from the late nineteenth century, widespread caste and religious social reform movements spearheaded a sustained struggle against the region's rigorously conservative, hierarchical, and discriminatory social practices (e.g. on the Malabar coast the untouchability of the Hindu caste system expression had even become interpreted as unapproachability). These movements channeled nascent political activity into influential caste and communal organisations that, aided by the peculiar communal demography, came to develop sophisticated patterns of communal accommodation. And second is the rise from the 1920s of a formidable Communist movement, especially strong in Malabar, that by 1957 was powerful enough to defeat Congress in the first elections for the Kerala Legislative Assembly, the first time an opposition party did so in a state in post-independence India.

For a quarter of a century after 1957 Kerala witnessed significant social and economic changes including the introduction of radical programmes of land reform and social provision punctuated by intense political flux featuring frequently shifting coalitions and changes of government (there were eleven changes of Chief Minister) interrupted by periods of President's rule. From 1982 there has been greater stability with politics having developed to reflect the translation of class interests, and the plurality of Hindu castes, and Muslim and Christian sectarian and communal identities, into a complex party system based on rival coalitions, or fronts, centred respectively on the Congress Party and the CPIM – the United and Left Democratic Fronts (UDF and LDF). The two fronts have now alternated in power for over three decades.

In this context, the Congress Party in Kerala came to represent a range of political interests, notably politicians and businessmen from the more affluent and conservative sections of the Nairs and other 'forward' Hindu castes or belonging to the various Syrian Christian denominations, as well as socially progressive non-communist youth leaders emerging through the Youth Congress from the late 1950s. In 1964 some of the former broke away to launch the Kerala Congress, itself in subsequent years subject to successive splits. To successfully oppose the Communists, also divided from the mid-1960s between the CPIM and the smaller, pro-Moscow CPI, the Congress in Kerala had to learn the art of coalition building nearly half a century before it did so successfully in national politics. The LDF has traditionally enjoyed the support of a majority of Ezhavas and other Hindu lower castes, as well as many poorer Latin Christians and Muslims and some Namboodiri Brahmins, Nairs, and Syrian Christians with left sympathies. So crucial for the Congress-led UDF in winning power has been the support of the Muslim League and the main Kerala Congress factions, especially strong in Christian centres in central Kerala.[8]

Behind these alignments lie a century of political engagement by caste and communal organisations and churches that even the Communists could only afford to disregard to their cost (since the 1960s Communist-led governments have generally depended on support from at least factions of the Kerala Congress and Muslim League). In such an environment the Hindu nationalist politics of the BJP and its predecessor, the Bharatiya Jana Sangh (BJS), attracted very few.[9] Despite the very considerable effort put in by the RSS and the sangh parivar over decades, Kerala remains the only state of any size in the country where the BJP has still to win a Parliamentary seat. Since 1987 it has come second in a handful of Assembly and Parliamentary constituencies in elections and recorded occasional surges in votes, especially in Lok Sabha elections (it gained over ten per cent of the vote in 2004 and again in 2014), without, until the 2016 Assembly polls, being able to build on its gains from one election to the next.

Recognising the reality of the state political environment, the BJP has sought to win allies among the traditionally influential Hindu caste organisations in particular, most recently wooing the leadership of the Sree Narayan Dharma Paripalna Yogam (SNDP Yogam), the main Ezhava body. In alliance with the Bharatiya Dharma Jana Sena, a new party backed by the SNDP, it made significant gains in the 2016 state Assembly elections, winning its first ever seat as the ruling UDF went down to expected defeat by the opposition LDF. The NDA won 14.6 per cent of the vote, more than doubling the BJP's vote share in the previous (2011) elections. Supported by a third of Nair voters, it supplanted the UDF as their second choice, also claiming nearly a fifth of the Ezhava and the rest of the Other Backward Class vote, and just under a quarter of the votes of the Scheduled Castes.[10] As long as the BJP remains shunned by the parties belonging to both the main fronts in Kerala, it will only be able to advance from being the perennial third party in two front politics by building on these gains among the state's Hindus exponentially to eventually displace one of the fronts. Although not as inconceivable as it seemed a few years ago, that remains a daunting challenge, given how entrenched the LDF and the UDF have been in state politics.

Andhra and Telangana: Telugu regional identity and sub-regional politics

If Tamil Nadu and Kerala maybe regarded as the 'south of the south', Karnataka and pre-2014 undivided Andhra Pradesh can be seen as the 'north of the south'. The difference has certainly been evident in their politics. Up until 1983 both states were Congress strongholds, remaining in the Congress fold even when the party suffered severe reverses elsewhere in 1967 and defeat nationally in 1977 in the wake of Indira Gandhi's *Emergency* rule. In the past three decades Congress has alternated in power with the Telugu Desam Party (TDP) in Andhra and the Janata Party/Janata Dal and then the BJP in Karnataka. However, in 2014 it recorded its worse ever performance in elections to what became the assemblies of the newly bifurcated states of Andhra and Telangana, drawing a blank in Andhra and barely hanging on to a distant second place in Telangana.

In the years immediately after independence Prime Minister Jawaharlal Nehru's Congress government faced several of its biggest challenges in the Andhra region. In 1948 an attempt to resist integration into the new Indian Union by Hyderabad, the largest of the princely states where the Muslim Nizam ruled over largely Hindu subjects, was bloodily suppressed as was a Communist peasant uprising in Telangana. Then the demand for a state for the Telugu-speaking population in the northern districts of Madras began the process that culminated in the linguistic reorganisation of states. The fast unto death of Potti Sreeramulu (1901–1952), a veteran Gandhian Congressman, was followed by Nehru conceding the demand for Andhra which came into being in 1953 with the Congressman 'Andhra Kesari' (Lion of Andhra) Tangutari Prakasam (1872–1957), who had previously served as the Chief Minister of Madras, becoming the first Chief Minister of the new state.

Unlike in the Tamil region of Madras where pre-independence non-Brahmin politics morphed into radical Dravidian identity politics, in Andhra Congress' recognition of Telugu identity enabled it to retain widespread support. In 1956 Andhra Pradesh came into being with the integration of the Telangana part of erstwhile Hyderabad. Thereafter a succession of able Chief Ministers (Sanjiva [1913–1996], Brahmananda [1909–1994] and Chenna Reddy [1919–1996], and P.V. Narasimha Rao [1921–2004]) pursued strategies of accommodation that helped Congress maintain its hold despite intense competition for power and influence within the party, not least between leaders from the dominant landowning castes, the Kammas and the Reddys, and the repercussions of splits at the national level in 1969 and 1978.[11] In the early 1970s the first major agitation for recognition of the needs of poorer and less developed (except for the capital, Hyderabad) Telangana was also defused with some of the demands of the leaders of the separatist Telangana Praja Samiti, who included Chenna Reddy, being accommodated.

However, with the appointment by Indira Gandhi of a series of weak, inept, and short-lived Chief Ministers and the launch of the TDP by the idolised Telugu cine superstar N.T. Rama Rao (NTR) (1923–1996), three decades of Congress' dominance came to an end in 1983 with the TDP sweeping to a landslide victory, holding office until 1989 and then again from 1994 to 2004. The TDP was particularly supported by Kammas, resentful of the traditional Reddy dominance in Congress, with the hugely popular NTR, a Kamma, supplanted in 1995 by his son-in-law, N. Chandrababu Naidu, also a Kamma. Naidu proved himself a singularly skillful politician, acquiring a reputation for efficient, tech-savvy governance and an influential voice at the centre as a leading partner of the BJP in A.B. Vajpayee's NDA government from 1998 to 2004.

Although Congress returned to power in 2004 with Y.S. Rajasekhar Reddy (1949–2009) (widely referred to as 'YSR'), a formidable campaigner, at the helm, his death in a plane crash shortly after winning a second term in 2009 set off a steep decline in the party's fortunes. YSR was, like Naidu, a skillful political operator, but the Congress High Command under Sonia Gandhi, the party's longest serving president, clumsily spurned a hasty bid for power by his son, Jagan Mohan. He then formed a breakaway YSR Congress that seriously undermined support for the party in the Reddy-dominated areas of Rayalaseema. This misstep was compounded by an egregious miscalculation in response to the surging support for the long simmering campaign for a separate state in the Telangana region. At the end of 2009, within days of a fast to death being proclaimed by K. Chandrasekhar Rao (popularly nicknamed 'KCR'), the leader of a revived Telangana Rashtriya Samiti (TRS), seeking to take advantage of the political vacuum created by Rajasekhar Reddy's demise, the UPA government at the centre announced that a new state would be created. However, the move was ill-prepared and, following a furious backlash in the rest of Andhra Pradesh, the government then vacillated, only confirming the decision in 2013 after four years marked by mass resignations from the legislature and popular protests and strikes for and against.

By the time the legislation to create the two new states of Telangana and Seemandhra (comprising coastal Andhra and Rayalaseema) was signed into law in February 2014, Congress, bereft of local leadership, had lost much ground in aggrieved Seemandhra to the breakaway YSR Congress and an uneasy, cobbled-together revival of the former alliance between its main national opponent, the Bharatiya Janata Party (BJP) and the regional Telugu Desam (TDP) of former Chief Minister Chandrababu Naidu. Yet its prevarication also harmed it in Telangana where, despite Congress seeking to credit party president Sonia Gandhi for the creation of the new state, the TRS that had spearheaded the movement for separation garnered most of the seats. The consequence was that Congress was humiliated in the Andhra districts in 2014, where it won no Lok Sabha or Assembly seats with just 3 per cent of the vote; the TDP emerged victorious with the breakaway YSR Congress led by Jagan Mohan Reddy as the main opposition. In Telangana Congress could claim only two of seventeen Lok Sabha seats and twenty-one of the 109 Assembly seats to eleven and sixty-three respectively for the TRS.

If the Congress trajectory in Andhra since 1983 has taken it from dominance to bi-party competition for power to being threatened with irrelevance, over the same period the BJP has moved from the political periphery to emerging as a notable electoral factor in the 1990s and, since the end of that decade, coalition with the TDP during the NDA's periods of government at the centre. Rather than local reasons the BJP's advance in the 1990s can largely be ascribed to the impact of the sangh parivar's Ram Janambhoomi agitations in the late 1980s and early 1990s and the profile enjoyed by the BJP as the official opposition at the centre from 1991. Until then, despite three centuries of Muslim rule in the Hyderabad region, the BJS and BJP had failed to make any appreciable inroads. Although the headquarters of the RSS lay across the border in Nagpur in Maharashtra, and neighbouring Madhya Pradesh represented one of the main strongholds of the BJS/BJP, this had not resulted in gains for Hindu nationalism in Andhra Pradesh. While perhaps not as handicapped by their image as a Hindi Hindu party as in Tamil Nadu, for long their Hindu nationalist message clearly failed to resound.

However, in 1991 the BJP gained the Lok Sabha constituency of Secunderabad, notably predominantly Hindu and adjoining Hyderabad, the old Muslim capital and a stronghold of the local Majlis Ittehadul Muslimeen. More significantly, the party almost quintupled its share of the vote state-wide to just under ten per cent. After a blip in 1996, when it contested alone, this rose to four seats and an 18.4 per cent vote share in 1998, benefitting from growing support from especially the urban Hindu business and middle classes and an alliance with the faction of the TDP led by NTR's widow, Lakshmi Parvathi. This was very much a consideration for Chandrababu Naidu in deciding to take the TDP into the NDA. Since then the state BJP's electoral fortunes have risen and fallen in tandem with that of the TDP; in 2009 when it contested on its own, running candidates in all but one constituency, it recorded a measly 3.8 per cent of the vote.

Karnataka: the Southern 'national' exception?

Karnataka is the one state in the south that stands out in terms of the dominant role played in its politics by national parties, whether Congress, the BJP, or the Janata party and the Janata Dal in the 1980s and 1990s. Part of the reason for this lies in the integration of Kannada and Tulu-speaking districts of the old Bombay state with the erstwhile princely state of Mysore in 1956 as a result of the linguistic reorganisation of states. Another historical factor is that the development of a distinct regional identity based on the Kannada language was arguably less pronounced than with Tamil, Malayali, or even Telugu identity. However, the role of local political actors in post-independence Karnataka and their relationship to national politics should not be discounted – political agency must form a substantial part of the explanation for the state's 'exceptionalism'.

The two most numerous landowning caste groups in Karnataka, the Vokkaligas and the Lingayats, a distinct Shaivite sect peculiar to the region, have loomed large in the political life of the state, constituting around a third of the population and providing fifteen of its twenty-two Chief Ministers. The first three Congress Chief Ministers before the expansion of the state in 1956 were all Vokkaligas, reflecting their concentration in the erstwhile princely state of Mysore in the state. Thereafter the Lingayats, much more numerous in the northern erstwhile Bombay districts, became the largest grouping, providing the next four Congress Chief Ministers until, in the 1970s, Devraj Urs (1915–1982) upset the traditional Lingayat–Vokkaliga political dominance.

Belonging to the Arasu, a smaller aristocratic caste associated with the old Mysore ruling family, Urs, unlike most of the main Lingayat and Vokkaliga Congress leaders, supported Indira Gandhi after the 1969 party split. Leading Mrs. Gandhi's wing of Congress to victory in four successive Lok and Vidhan Sabha elections between 1971 and 1978, as Chief Minister he introduced radical programmes such as land redistribution and rural debt forgiveness. Urs's Congress won strong support from Dalits, a quarter of the population, and Other Backward Classes' poor; the party also enjoyed strong backing from Muslims, another tenth of the population. This broader ruling coalition was not sustained by the 'grossly incompetent' R. Gundu Rao (1937–1993), a crony of Indira Gandhi's younger son, Sanjay, after Urs abandoned the Congress fold, thus affording scope for the Janata opposition to win power in the 1983 elections.[12]

The 1983 elections also provided the BJP with the opportunity to make a notable debut in state politics through an alliance with the Janata Party that gave the Hindu nationalists an unprecedented eighteen of 224 Assembly seats. In the wake of the *Hindutva* agitations of the late 1980s and early 1990s, the BJP made significant inroads especially among the Lingayats, Brahmins, and the growing population of north Indian Hindi speakers drawn to the rapidly growing state capital and metropolitan centre of Bangalore, the premier hub of India's burgeoning computer software industry. Even without a particularly impressive state leadership, by the mid and late 1990s, the party was in a position to exploit disarray in Congress and divisions in the perennially fractious Janata camp. It achieved second place in the 1994 and 1999 state Assembly polls, won the most Karnataka seats in four out of the five Lok Sabha elections from 1998, and emerged as the largest party in the 2004 and 2008 Vidhan Sabha elections.[13] In 2007 B.S. Yeddyurappa, a Lingayat politician, became the first BJP Chief Minister in the south, only to be forced to resign – and even briefly jailed – in 2011 following charges of involvement in illegal land dealing and mining. Two years later Congress returned to power after seven years in opposition, no party having retained office in the state for more than a six-year stretch since 1983.

The 2014 election in the south and its aftermath

In the 2014 election the contrast between the south and the rest of the country was particularly stark, made so by the fact that unlike on two of the three previous occasions when it had lost power nationally – in 1977 and 1989 – the blow to Congress was not cushioned by

Table 1.1 INC, BJP, and CPI/CPM share of seats from the south in Lok Sabha elections: 1989–2014

Year	INC	BJP	CPI/CPM	Aggregate
1989	109 (83.2%)	0	3 (2.3%)	112 (85.5%)
1991	91 (69.5%)	6 (4.6%)	5 (3.8%)	102 (77.9%)
1996	36 (27.5%)	6 (4.6%)	12 (9.2%)	54 (41.3%)
1999	41 (31.3%)	20 (15.3%)	18 (13.7%)	79 (60.3%)
2004	47 (35.9%)	18 (13.7%)	21 (16.0%)	86 (65.6%)
2009	62 (47.3%)	19 (14.5%)	6 (4.6%)	87 (66.4%)
2014	19 (14.5%)	21 (16.0%)	6 (4.6%)	46 (35.1%)

Source: Based on Election Commission of India data accessed at http://eci.nic.in/eci_main1/ElectionStatistics.aspx (01/03/2017)

success in the region. As for the BJP, neither the media blitz of the presidential-style campaign focused on Narendra Modi nor the party's edge over Congress in forming useful alliances in Andhra and Telangana (with the Telugu Desam of new Andhra Chief Minister Chandrababu Naidu, an erstwhile partner in the NDA) and Tamil Nadu (with five smaller parties, most notably the Desiya Murpokku Dravida Kazhagham of film star Vijayakanth) helped it achieve a breakthrough in the south. Although it managed its highest tally of seats in the south, for the first time winning more than Congress (see Table 1.1), this was only because of the Congress's total decimation in Andhra in the aftermath of the signal mishandling of the creation of the separate state of Telangana. It is telling that in nearly half – sixty-one of the 131 – southern constituencies, no national party was able to come either first or second. In addition to the twenty-one seats the BJP won, it was Runner-up only in fifteen while Congress, which won nineteen, came second in forty-one.

In the past, the five southern states and two union territories (Puducherry and Lakshadweep) returning 131 of the 543 members of the Lok Sabha had been crucial to the survival in adversity of India's grand old ruling party: in four of the five general elections after Congress was first ejected from power in the extraordinary post-*Emergency* rule poll of 1977, the party won seventy per cent of southern seats; southerners formed a majority of Congress MPs in both 1977 and again when it was defeated in 1989. However, in 2014 Rahul Gandhi was not able to emulate his father, Rajiv, and grandmother, Indira, in maintaining a southern prop.

Congress's eventual tally even fell short of the measly twenty-five seats forecast by the final opinion poll completed for the NDTV network before the first phase of voting commenced on 7 April. It was the party's worst-ever performance in the region and a sharp drop from the sixty-two it managed in 2009, the consequence of two miscalculations by the Congress leadership, one serious and the other disastrous. The serious, albeit perhaps unavoidable mistake, was finding itself having to go it alone in Tamil Nadu following the withdrawal of its ally, the Dravida Munnetra Kazhagham (DMK), from the United Progressive Alliance in 2013. In the five decades that the state had been ruled by one or other of the two rival Dravidian parties – the DMK of nonagenarian five-time former Chief Minister M. Karunanidhi and the ADMK of the late Chief Minister J. Jayalalithaa (1948–2016) – Congress had never succeeded electorally without being allied to one or the other. However, what proved even more significant for the party's southern fortunes was its mishandling of Andhra Pradesh, precipitating the collapse of its southern bulwark (Congress had returned the largest number of Andhra MPs in all but one of the seven elections since 1989).

In the two other southern states the 2014 election followed a familiar pattern. In Kerala, where power has generally alternated between rival coalitions led by either Congress or the Communists and the incumbents have tended to suffer losses in Parliamentary elections on their watch, the ruling Congress-led UDF of Chief Minister Oommen Chandy retained a majority (twelve) of the twenty seats despite losing four to the Communist Party of India (Marxist)-led LDF. As in the 2011 state Assembly elections the LDF's campaign, despite the defection of one of its junior constituents, the Revolutionary Socialist Party, to the UDF, was energised by the redoubtable ninety-year-old former Chief Minister K. Achuthanandan.

Karnataka was the only state in the south where the Congress found itself pitted against the BJP as its main opponent. Going against the national dip in its popularity, Congress had succeeded in ousting the BJP, badly split and discredited by corruption allegations, from power in the 2013 state Assembly elections, and the new Chief Minister, K. Siddaramaiah, hoped to benefit from an extended political honeymoon. The BJP in the state counted on a patch up of the differences within the state unit and the national presidential-style campaign of Narendra Modi to retain the two-third's share of the state's twenty-eight seats that it had garnered in the last two general elections. In the event both the main parties increased their share of the vote at the expense of the third party in the state, the Janata Dal (Secular), and other minor parties and the BJP share of the state's twenty-eight seats was only cut by two to seventeen.

Apart from in Karnataka, across the rest of the region, the BJP remains far behind Congress, and even the CPI(M), in terms of state Assembly seats (as previously noted it only won one in Kerala in 2016 and is unrepresented in Tamil Nadu). Of course, national parties tend to perform better in national elections – in 2014 they won sixty-three per cent of Lok Sabha seats, having taken only 54.3 per cent of the 4,120 Assembly seats in the preceding elections in the twenty-nine states and two territories (the respective figures for the south were 35.9 per cent and 31.8 per cent) – but the current dichotomy between the national position and that in the south is unprecedented (see Figures 1.3 and 1.4). Although it attracted relatively little attention in analyses of the sixteenth general election, it presented a challenge to Narendra Modi and the new NDA government that the BJP's remarkable achievement in gaining an overall majority in the Lok Sabha obscured.

It was perhaps in acknowledgment of this that the Presidential address on 9 June 2014 setting out the government's programme

'Yes, but not in the South' 59

highlighted Cooperative Federalism,[14] mentioning reinvigorating federal bodies like the National Development Council and the Inter-State Council in order to actively engage states on national issues. Yet how far these stated intentions could be realised greatly depended on how accommodative and responsive Prime Minister Modi showed himself to be in addressing the needs and demands of parts of the country that had proved largely impervious to his electoral appeal. It also depended on how he dealt with regional leaders, whether within the NDA (Chandrababu Naidu) or outside – the rival Dravidian party leaders vying for power in Tamil Nadu following the death of Chief Minister Jayalalithaa in 2016, Chandrasekhar Rao in Telangana, the Congress Chief Minister of Karnataka and, since 2016, his CPIM counterpart in Kerala. Three years into his premiership, opposition-controlled state governments remained doubtful about how real the centre's commitment to 'cooperative federalism' actually was.[15]

Despite Modi's national triumph providing the headline of the 2014 general election, this survey of the electoral landscape in the south reveals that the 'federalisation' of politics recognised in the 1990s remains a central feature of the political scene. First set in train by the dismantling of the post-independence Congress system theorised by Rajni Kothari (1928–2015) close to half a century ago, this process has found clearest expression in the steady shrinkage of the electoral and representative space occupied by Congress, with the emergence of the BJP as its national rival not compensating for the expanding influence of primarily regionally focused caste and identity-based parties. That this should be especially evident in the south should not surprise any student of the history of the subcontinent. We can still say: 'Yes but not in the South'.

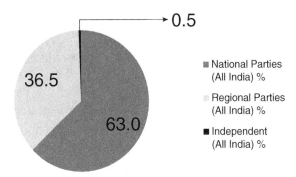

Figure 1.3 All India share of seats for national and regional parties – 2014

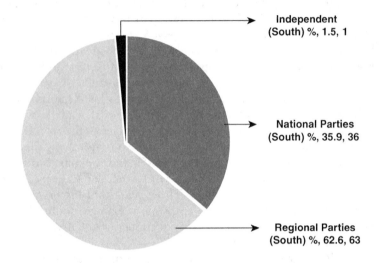

Figure 1.4 National and regional parties' share of seats in the south – 2014

Notes

1 This chapter had its origins in a paper presented at a round table discussion of the 2014 Lok Sabha elections organised by the South Asia Institute, School of Oriental and African Studies, University of London, on 10 June 2014, and a workshop at the King's India Institute, King's College, University of London, on 11 June 2014, and I'd like to thank the respective conveners, Gurharpal Singh and Louise Tillin.
2 All figures and tables are based on data derived from the Election Commission of India, http://eci.nic.in/eci_main1/ElectionStatistics.aspx (accessed 4 June 2014). Thanks are due to Joseph Chiriyankandath for his assistance.
3 For the qualifications to be defined as a 'National Party' or to be recognised in a state see http://eci.nic.in/eci_main/ElectoralLaws/OrdersNotifications/ElecSym19012013_eng.pdf (accessed 7 November 2013).
4 C.J. Baker, *The Politics of South India 1920–1937* (Cambridge: Cambridge University Press, 1976); D.A. Washbrook, 'Caste, Class and Dominance in Modern Tamil Nadu. Non-Brahmanism, Dravidianism and Tamil Nationalism' in Francine R. Frankel and M.S.A. Rao (eds.), *Dominance and State Power in Modern India. Decline of a Social Order*, vol. 1 (New Delhi: Oxford University Press, 1989).
5 Narendra Subramanian, *Ethnicity and Populist Mobilization. Political Parties, Citizens and Democracy in South India* (New Delhi: Oxford University Press, 1999).
6 Andrew Wyatt, *Party System Change in South India. Political Entrepreneurs, Patterns and Processes* (London: Routledge, 2010).
7 Jean Dreze and Amartya Sen, *An Uncertain Glory. India and Its Contradictions* (New Delhi: Penguin, 2013), 300 (Table A.3: Selected Indicators

for Major Indian States, Pt. 2: Mortality and Fertility); Literacy Rate: National Commission on Population, Ministry of Health and Family Welfare, Government of India, http://populationcommission.nic.in/content/933_1_LiteracyRate.aspx (accessed 26 January 2016).
8 James Chiriyankandath, ' "Unity in Diversity"? Coalition Politics in India (with special reference to Kerala)' in Subho Basu and Suranjan Das (eds), *Electoral Politics in South Asia* (Calcutta: KP Bagchi and Co., 2000).
9 James Chiriyankandath, 'Bounded Nationalism: Kerala and the Social and Regional Limits of Hindutva' in Thomas Blom Hansen and Christophe Jaffrelot (eds), *The BJP and the Compulsions of Politics in India* (New Delhi: Oxford University Press, 1998).
10 J. Prabhash and K.M. Sajad Ibrahim, 'Changing Voting Behaviour in Kerala Elections', *Economic and Political Weekly*, Vol. 52, No. 5 (4 February 2017), 64–68.
11 G. Ram Reddy, 'The Politics of Accommodation. Caste, Class and Dominance in Andhra Pradesh' in Frankel and Rao, *op. cit.*
12 Atul Kohli, *Democracy and Discontent. India's Growing Crisis of Governability* (Cambridge: Cambridge University Press, 1990), 96.
13 James Manor, 'Letting a Winnable Election Slip Away: Congress in Karnataka', *Economic and Political Weekly*, Vol. 43, No. 41 (11 October 2008).
14 The term was applied to the Indian context by Granville Austin, *The Indian Constitution. Cornerstone of a Nation* (Oxford: Oxford University Press, 1966), 187.
15 Louise Tillin, 'Federal Faultlines', *India Today*, 4 January 2017, http://indiatoday.intoday.in/story/narendra-modi-centre-state-relations-reformations/1/849645.html (accessed 10 March 2017).

2 India's foreign policy and Hindutva
The new impact of culture and identity on the formulation and practice of Indian foreign policy 2014–2017

Arndt Michael

> We will build a strong, self-reliant and self-confident India, regaining its rightful place in the comity of nations.
> (Bharatiya Janata Party 2014: 40)

> I am confident my Hindutva face will be an asset when dealing with foreign affairs with other nations.
> Narendra Modi, 23 April 2014 (Kuber 2014)

> This is a country that once upon a time was called 'the golden bird'.
> Narendra Modi, 22 September 2014 (*The Hindu* 2014f)

Introduction

In International Relations theory and especially constructivist scholarship, the intricate relationship between culture, identity, and foreign policy has become an important and fertile field of research (Hudson 1997). In his seminal study on culture, strategy, and foreign policy change, Michael Barnett employed the trinity of concepts of identity, narratives, and frames to analyse 'how cultural resources, the underlying norms, values and symbols of society, are part of the arsenal available to actors to press their policies' (Barnett 1999: 8). More specifically, Barnett expounded on the concept of frame and claimed that this

> concept of frame is central for understanding the conversion of cultural resources into foreign policy actions. Actors deploy frames to help fix meanings, organize experience, alert others that

their interests and possible their identities are at stake, and propose solutions to ongoing problems.
(Barnett 1999: 25)

The notion of frame sheds lights on the importance of e.g. symbols, specific metaphors, symbolic representations, or cognitive cues which are used by actors (in a strategic manner) in order to achieve particular goals. These can used, for instance, by applying frames to organise experience, fix meaning to or situate events, or they are used to render or cast behaviour and such events in an evaluative mode. The underlying objective is to attain a particular outcome and a particular objective; actors guide political or social mobilisation towards that objective. For Barnett, framing – as one part of his analytical trinity – is 'critical for understanding the cultural foundations that make possible and desirable certain actions' (Barnett 1999: 9).

More concretely, there are two specific dimensions ascribed to frames. First, there is a strategic dimension and 'principled purpose' (Barnett 1999: 15): it can be expected that there will be 'conscious strategic efforts by groups of people to fashion shared understandings of the world and of themselves that legitimate collective action' (McAdam, McCarthy and Zald 1996: 6). This is the result of a genuine competition of actors involved to frame the event. The manner in which the event will be understood will eventually be of crucial importance for ultimately mobilising action (and furthering actors' interests). All this can be understood as a 'strategic framing process' (Barnett 1999: 15). In such cases, one can expect political elites to take recourse to 'cultural symbols that are selectively chosen from a cultural toolchest and creatively converted' (Tarrow 1994: 119) into frames for mobilisation or action. This particular cultural toolchest can include certain symbols whose deployment is geared towards mobilising sentiment and guiding action.

Second, there is a historic dimension. Collective mobilisation is part of the objective of frames, but there are specific historical moments – especially when cultural contradictions and competing future visions between political agents surface – when frames are of utmost importance. Mayer Zald (1996: 268) notes: 'Political and mobilization opportunities are often created by cultural breaks and the surfacing of long dormant contradictions that reframe grievances and injustices and the possibilities for action'. It can become a necessity for political or social entrepreneurs to actually construct frames that are able to reconcile these aforementioned contradictions, and to situate these events in ways that are in accordance with the cultural foundations. In a way, there can be a cost-benefit calculation regarding the relationship between particular policies and the actual conditions at moments of cultural breaks.

Clearly, the 2014 Indian general election was as much about Indian political parties vying for political power as they were about opposing worldviews, differences in identity, and understanding of what constitutes Indian culture. Still, foreign policy is never an election game-changer, and the Indian elections that were conducted from 7 April to 12 May 2014 were no exception to that rule. Foreign policy played a subordinated role before and during the elections, a fact that was best illustrated by the timing of the Bharatiya Janata Party (BJP) election manifesto which expounded on the strategies and objectives of the BJP, but only came out on the day of the beginning of the elections and dedicated but one single page to foreign policy issues. After ten years of a Congress-dominated foreign policy, new foreign policy behaviour and strategic priorities were to be expected from the Prime Minister's Office (PMO), especially with a view to starkly differing identity, worldviews, and attitudes between the former secular Congress government and the new BJP one. Modi and the BJP as political entrepreneurs have given specific cognitive cues on the extent and parameters and new direction of India's foreign policy.

Building on the approach taken by Barnett, I expand his concept of framing by adding an additional historic dimension, which I term 'pre-framing'. While the trinity as employed by Barnett was instrumental in providing answers to research lacunae (see Barnett 1999: 7–8), analysing Modi's foreign policy as a foreign policy essentially 'in the making' necessitates to give special meaning to the period before the elections as the 'event' that signalled the beginning of a new era. While at first glance, it might appear that the pre-foreign policy statements were of lesser importance, their inherent cultural – as well as strategic – significance necessitates a much closer look, and especially an analysis of how pre-framing has affected foreign policy behaviour.

What, then, are the frames that animate Narendra Modi's nascent foreign policy, and how are these located in the wider context of the strategic and historic dimension of frames? This chapter looks at the months leading to the elections and the three years after the elections, focusing on how identity and attitudes as expressed in documents and speeches were framed, and then on how these frames were implemented in actual foreign policy behaviour. The present chapter thus uses the concepts of pre-framing and framing to locate the BJP's foreign policy culture and looks at their implementation. I argue that the foreign policy of Narendra Modi is, in fact, a clear emanation of BJP-specific/Hindutva cognitive frames. I also argue that assessments of Modi's foreign policy being 'shorn of ideology, with pragmatism being its hallmark' (Chellaney 2014) do not factor in the existence and impact of (cognitive) frames, and that the opposite if the case, i.e. that ideology and its ramifications are a direct result of such cognitive frames.

Considering these points, the chapter is structured as follows. The first section examines the stage of pre-framing including the BJP manifesto; the second section analyses the foreign policy of Modi's government by looking at the regional, bilateral, and multilateral level. The concluding third section uses the findings of the preceding sections to locate Modi's nascent foreign policy frames in a wider context.

As regards methodology, the article relies on primary data (especially speeches by Narendra Modi, BJP leaders, and the BJP manifesto) and content analysis of secondary sources, especially leading English Indian newspapers such as *The Hindu*, the *Times of India,* and the *Hindustan Times.*

Pre-framing: Narendra Modi in Gujarat and pre-election foreign policy statements

The gradual process of pre-framing identity, culture, and preferences of a nascent foreign policy before the elections has two distinct dimensions: the special role of the states and the intricate relationship between a strong economy and foreign policy influence.

The first dimension of pre-framing was a focus during Modi's term as Chief Minister. As the long-serving Chief Minister of Gujarat from 2001 to 2014, Modi was principally concerned with strengthening the economy of his state and garnered a reputation for being pro-business and enabling investments. In the wake of the communal riots in Gujarat in February–March 2002, Modi was banned from entering the USA and the European Union (EU), and hence his ability to travel abroad was severely constrained, a situation that only began to change when the United Kingdom (UK) ended the boycott of Modi in October 2012 and Modi subsequently met with the British high commissioner. The EU eventually followed suit in February 2013 (*India Today* 2013), and Modi afterwards met individually with several European business leaders, lawmakers, and ambassadors, including those from Germany, France, Italy, and Sweden, enabling him to continue with his agenda for attracting investments, though with a considerable time lag.

During his tenure, Modi visited a number of economically important countries several times in his capacity as Chief Minister, despite the geographic travel constraints: he travelled to Japan twice, China four times, and to South Korea with the aim of receiving investments for his state. He was, e.g. highly successful in cultivating a personal rapport with Japanese Prime Minister Shinzo Abe. Although other Chief Ministers of Indian states have also been going abroad in order to invite and increase investments to their respective states, Narendra Modi was probably the first leader to impart an almost 'diplomatic profile' to his overseas visit. His international visibility and the relationship between a BJP-run state and select influential and highly industrialised states in the Asia-Pacific were hallmarks during his tenure. More specifically, the Japanese government received him with a protocol appropriate for a Cabinet-ranking Minister of the Union, which in the Order of Precedence is higher than that of a Chief Minister outside the state. This result and these experiences of Modi's efforts towards strengthening the relationship between an individual state and other countries as a Chief Minister confirmed an important focus in a nascent BJP foreign policy, namely the crucial role of states and that states by themselves can be important actors outside the centre in Delhi.[1]

Foreign policy or foreign policy experience in itself played no direct role during the selection process of the BJP candidate for the elections in 2014. As far as direct statements by Modi and other BJP leaders are concerned, there have been only scarce statements at India's foreign policy trajectory under a new, BJP-led government. Still, three important signposts can be subsumed under the second dimension of the pre-framing concept, with important repercussions for the future trajectory of foreign policy:

In July 2013, then-BJP president Rajnath Singh commented on fears of a potentially different BJP foreign policy and explicitly ruled out any fundamental shift in India's foreign policy if his party was voted to power.

> As far as changes in the foreign policy is concerned, there is not likely to be a basic change in its fundamental principles. But whenever the other party comes, we are having our own perspective and we decide accordingly. [. . .] Our foreign policy would be to have cordial relationship with our neighbours, It would be our full effort to improve relationship with Pakistan. At the same time we expect from Pakistan to respond similarly. But till today, I can say, that Pakistan has not responded in the manner we have taken

the initiatives to have a cordial relationship with them. [. . .] We are always in favour of good relationship with Pakistan.

(*The Hindu* 2013)

These statements already show that the party tried to keep a low foreign policy profile and assuage any fears about a volte-fact foreign policy, while Modi constantly reiterated his economic successes in Gujarat.

All in all, Modi himself gave just one landmark foreign policy speech during his campaign for the general election in 2014, delivered in Chennai on 18 October 2013. There, he demanded a greater role for states in India's economic diplomacy (Iyer 2013) and argued that India's inherent economic strengths of her different states would have to be factored in for an effective foreign policy, essentially referring to the concept of para-diplomacy. In consonance with his experiences as a Chief Minister and the investment schemes of foreign countries in Gujarat, he stated that 'I believe a strong economy is the driver of an effective foreign policy. [. . .] We have to put our own house in order' (Jaishankar 2014).

Both statements framed the idea that the economy is paramount for domestic and international success. Apart from this speech, Modi practically refrained from raising foreign policy issues. He did explicitly refer to the unsatisfactory situation in Arunachal Pradesh in a speech on 23 February 2014 and China's 'mind-set of expansion' (Mandhana 2014), and on 11 March 2014 he discussed the problem of 'illegal immigration' from Bangladesh to eastern states like Assam and West Bengal (Gosh 2014). For the concept of pre-framing it is important to note Modi's focus on the role of states and the economy as influencing foreign policy. Both pre-frames mark important signposts for the BJP.

Framing a Hindutva foreign policy for India: the BJP election manifesto and BJP attitudes

The process of ideational foreign policy framing took a great leap forward in April 2014, with two landmark events, i.e. the BJP election manifesto and an interview by Modi with an Indian newspaper in which he outlined crucial elements of his foreign policy vision:

On 7 April 2014, coinciding with the first day of India's national elections which were to last five weeks, the BJP finally released their 2014 election manifesto (Bharatiya Janata Party 2014), a forty-two-page document outlining the party's roadmap on economic, political, social, and foreign policy issues. Only three pages in the entire manifesto are devoted to perspectives towards external security, defence, and foreign relations, with the latter section coming at the very end, taking up but one page. The manifesto states in its preface:

> India is the most ancient civilization of the world. [. . .] Before the advent of Britishers, Indian goods were internationally recognized for their quality and craftsmanship. India had a much bigger role and presence in industry and manufacturing than any nation in Europe or Asia.
>
> (ibid: 1)

In this emphasis on India as an ancient trading power, the manifesto differs to a certain degree from 2009 BJP manifesto (Bharatiya Janata Party 2009) which focused especially on the achievements of Indian civilization in agriculture, science and technology, medicine, and education. However, the introduction also frames India's premier position in the world, and in subsequent sections establishes the important frame of an Indian civilizational continuity with several parts of the world.

In the section titled 'Foreign Relations – Nation First, Universal Brotherhood' (ibid: 39–40), the BJP addresses foreign policy and India's place in the world. The general introduction to the section on foreign policy establishes the link between culture, identity, and foreign policy:

> [The] BJP believes a resurgent India must get its rightful place in the comity of nations and international institutions. The vision is to fundamentally reboot and reorient the foreign policy goals, content and process, in a manner that locates India's global strategic engagement in a new paradigm and on a wider canvass, that is not just limited to political diplomacy, but also includes our economic, scientific, cultural, political and security interests, both regional and global, on the principles of equality and mutuality, so that it leads to an economically stronger India, and its voice is heard in the international fora.

The BJP promises to be 'guided by our centuries old tradition of *Vasudeva Kutumbakam*'.[2] The foreign policy will 'be based on best National interests. We will create a web of allies to mutually further our interests. We will leverage all our resources and people to play a greater role on the international high table'. This marks another, if not the most important, new frame of foreign policy, namely the objective to enter into alliances. As one of its major guiding principle for foreign policy, the document notes that 'equations will be mended through pragmatism and a doctrine of mutually beneficial and interlocking relationships, based on enlightened national interest'.

The manifesto in particular stresses Indian soft power, noting that

> India has long failed to duly appreciate the full extent and gamut of its soft power potential. There is a need to integrate our soft power avenues into our external interchange, particularly, harnessing and focusing on the spiritual, cultural and philosophical dimensions of it.

The country has always undercapitalized its 'ancient wisdom and heritage' which continue 'to be equally relevant to the world today in today's times of Soft Power'.

In the section on foreign policy, there is one sentence which seems to be directed at the USA: '*Instead of being led by big power interests, we will engage proactively on our own with countries in the neighbourhood and beyond*'. With regard to the neighbourhood, the BJP will 'pursue friendly relations' but 'where required we will not hesitate from taking strong stand and steps'. Relations through regional fora, like the South Asian Association for Regional Cooperation (SAARC) and Association of Southeast Asian Nations (ASEAN), along with the Asia Europe Meeting (ASEM), the BRICS (Brazil-Russia-India-China-South Africa), G20, IBSA (India-Brazil-South Africa), and the Shanghai Cooperation Organization (SCO) are explicitly mentioned. The United Nations (UN), however, is not mentioned.

Regarding defence, the BJP wants to strengthen India's indigenous arms industry, including improving India's defence research and development capabilities by strengthening the Defence Research and Development Organization (DRDO) and wants India as a 'global platform for defence hardware manufacture and software production'.

The manifesto notes that the BJP would follow a 'two-pronged independent nuclear program, unencumbered by foreign pressure and influence, for civilian and military purposes'. While the BJP manifesto of 1998 pledged to 'Re-evaluate the country's nuclear policy and exercise the option to induct nuclear weapons', the BJP now pledges to update India's nuclear doctrine to 'make it relevant to challenges of current times'. The party will maintain India's policy of a credible minimum deterrent 'in tune with changing geostatic realities'. This statement could be interpreted as drop of India's no first use nuclear doctrine (Keck 2014) and is a significant departure from the Congress manifesto, which uses the word 'nuclear' only once in the context of civilian nuclear energy.

Regarding international economic policy, the BJP wants to make India 'globally competitive', (ibid: 34) and promotes a 'Brand India built on quality' (ibid: 'Pledges'). In this context, the Indian diaspora receives special mention as an asset in developing 'Brand India'. The BJP manifesto also talks of reviving 'Brand India with the help of our strengths of 5 T's: Tradition, Talent, Tourism, Trade and Technology'. The BJP likewise promises to provide states a 'greater role in diplomacy; *actively building relations with foreign countries to harness their mutual cultural and commercial strengths*'.

On matters of national security and foreign policy, the BJP manifesto talks about 'zero tolerance' on terrorism. The document notes that the BJP would deal with incursions 'with a firm hand' and will maintain Kashmir as 'an integral part of the Union of India' (ibid: 8).

Essentially, the BJP manifesto frames crucial aspects of Hindutva ideology in its foreign policy trajectory, namely the idea of alliances, cultural soft power, civilizational linkages with other countries, and the significance of India's national interest, especially with a view to its nuclear doctrine.

In consonance with certain statements of the manifesto, in an interview with *The Indian Express* on 23 April 2014, Modi said:

> I believe in Hindutva which is based on the age-old concept of *Vasudeva Kutumba*. I believe mutual respect for one another and cooperation should be the basis for relationships with foreign nations. And I am confident my Hindutva face will be an asset when dealing with foreign affairs with other nations. [. . .] I will follow the (foreign) policies of the Vajpayee-led NDA government. [. . .] And that also applies to relationship with the United States. I don't think a decision taken by any individual or one event should impact the overall policy.
>
> (Kuber 2014)

In this interview, in the middle of the elections, a broad vision of foreign policy was thus framed, a vision that fused ideology, culture, and national interest. Modi referred to the idea of Vasudeva Kutumbakam, just as the BJP manifest did. More importantly, he stressed that he would base his foreign policy on 'Hindutva' or 'Indian-ness'. Modi thus framed his ideas on foreign policy in terms of Hindu nationalism.

Even though he did not elaborate on the exact extent of what Hindutva meant for foreign policy, this nonetheless signified a break clear with ten years of a Congress-led governments whose ideas on foreign policy were in essence guided by the parameters of Nehruvian determinants.[3]

Transferring frames into practice

The regional and bilateral dimension

The cognitive frames of Modi's foreign policy were put in practice following his election victory. India's central role in the subcontinent was the first public display of Modi's foreign policy. Modi invited the SAARC heads of state or government (and Mauritius) to his swearing-in ceremony on 26 May 2014 (Panda 2014) and held bilateral talks with each of them on his first day in office, including Pakistani Prime Minister Nawaz Sharif. Modi also invited Tibetan leader Lobsang Sangay to the ceremony. Just days after assuming office Modi declared in a speech at the BJP party headquarters on 1 June:

> We have never thought beyond the country's frontiers. We are a big country, we are an old country, and we are a big power. We should make the world realise it. Once we do it, the world will not shy away from giving us due respect and status.
> (*Siasat Daily* 2014)

In June, Modi visited Bhutan as his first foreign policy destination, and in August he travelled to Nepal, the first Indian Prime Minister in seventeen years. Modi offered a US$1 billion line of credit for economic linkages, assistance infrastructure development and energy projects. He praised the Nepalese efforts to prepare a constitution and promised to provide the interim government all possible help in its journey towards democracy. In the case of Bhutan, Modi highlighted the similarities between the countries and spoke about the peaceful transition to democracy. Modi stressed that 'the stronger India will be, the better it is for Bhutan and other SAARC nations' (Jacob 2014). Following the example of Modi, Minister of External Affairs Sushma Swaraj also chose South Asian countries as her first official visits and travelled to Bangladesh and Nepal.

As a first concrete result of Modi meeting Sharif, foreign secretary level talks were agreed upon between India and Pakistan (Barry and Raj 2014), but these were cancelled just a week before they were scheduled. The reason was that Pakistani High Commissioner to India, Abdul Basit, had met with Kashmiri separatists in August (Haidar 2014a). While such talks had taken place in the past, they were actually silently tolerated by the Congress government, a behaviour that the Modi government did not condone.

Subsequently, on Monday June 9, the President of India Pranab Mukherjee formally opened Parliament and outlined Modi's economic and foreign policy agenda, stressing that Modi intended to 'engage energetically' with neighbouring countries (Agarwal 2014).

The first country outside South Asia to be visited by Modi was Japan, with his visit lasting five days and resulting in a 'special global strategic partnership', with both an economic and military dimension. Japan pledged US$35 billion in investments and promised that it would double its FDI within the next five years. Japan also agreed to provide bullet trains. The military relationship was strengthened with both countries agreeing to institutionalise 'two plus two' security arrangements between foreign and defence ministers, to work on common maritime exercises on a regular basis and to continue with Japanese participation in the ongoing Indo-US exercises. Modi also emphasised that his motivation for deepening linkages with Japan were common (democratic) values.

In addition, Modi and Japanese Prime Minister Abe discussed greater linkages between cities of economic and cultural importance. A memorandum of understanding was signed between Kyoto and Varanasi, which is in consonance with Modi's desire to make Varanasi a so-called smart city (*The Hindu* 2014a). The ideational frame of historical and cultural linkages that is part of the BJP's and Modi's ideational foreign policy frame also received a prominent position: Japanese Prime Minister Abe was given a book by Modi about Japan and Swami Vivekananda ('*Vivekanda and Japan*') (Maini 2014).

Next to Japan, China has been a focus of Modi's foreign policy. The current Indo-Chinese relationship suffers from problems of an uneven balance of trade and territorial disputes, principally two of Modi's main foreign policy frames. Consequently, on 9 June 2014, Modi met the Chinese foreign minister and stressed old 'civilizational contacts' between the countries (Agarwal 2014) as the bedrock of India-Chinese relations, while problems about Chinese border crossings in the Mimalyayn region of Ladakh, Tibet were discussed. It was again Modi's focus on trade that led Modi to delay his Japan tour by several weeks to first meet Chinese President Xi Jinping on the sidelines of the BRICS summit on 15 July.

On September 17 (Modi's sixty-fourth birthday), the Chinese president Xi Jinping visited Modi's hometown of Ahmedabad in Gujarat (*The Hindu* 2014d). Ongoing border incursions were criticised on the day of meeting (*The Hindu* 2014e), showing that the aspect of 'engaging' was meant in earnest. These issues notwithstanding, Modi invited Chinese investment for modernising India's infrastructure, especially railroads, power stations, and industrial parks. While China had roughly invested US$400 million between 2004 and 2014 in India, the Chinese president pledged to now invest up to US$20 billion in the sectors of manufacturing and infrastructure in the next years (*The Hindu* 2014c). Besides, the building of high-speed rail links and two industrial parks were agreed (*Hindustan Times* 2014b).

Engaging the ASEAN region has become another key objective for India, especially considering the economic possibilities in the region, but also the geostrategic relevance. Sushma Swaraj visited Myanmar and then Vietnam: while in Nay Pyi Taw, she participated in the East Asia Summit, the ASEAN Regional Forum, and India-ASEAN foreign ministers' meetings. On the sidelines, she met with the foreign ministers of Australia, Brunei, Indonesia, Japan, New Zealand, Philippines, South Korea, Thailand, and Vietnam (Varghese 2014). Swaraj also spoke with Burmese leaders. When she visited Vietnam, she held meetings with the heads of the Indian missions in East and Southeast Asia. In this context, Swaraj highlighted the importance of India not just 'looking east', but 'acting east' as well (Madan 2014; *Times of India* 2014). More specifically, engaging Vietnam has received an economic and military dimension: on 15 September, India purchased seven new oil and gas blocks from Vietnam in the South China Sea, and in terms of defence cooperation, India has promised to modernise Vietnamese defence forces (Haidar 2014c).

With regard to the Indo-US relationship, Modi was received by then US President Barack Obama at the White House on 30 September 2014 and later spoke at Madison Square Garden. An agreement was reached for the extension of the existing defence cooperation for another ten years and an expansion of trade and investment in India's defence sector (Chaudhuri 2014; *The Hindu* 2014g; Economist 2014; Varadarajan 2014; Subramanian 2014). And with regard to Australia as another major player in the Asia-Pacific, Modi and Australian Prime Minister Tony Abbot signed a civil nuclear energy deal on 6 September.

Modi's trip to Sri Lanka on 13–14 March 2015 became the first in twenty-eight years by an Indian Prime Minister. Four agreements were signed, among them an agreement regarding exemption from visa for holders of diplomatic passports as well as cooperation in mutual assistance in customs. India also offered a new line of credit of US$ 380 million to the Sri Lanka's railway sector. India also committed itself to making Trincomalee a petroleum hub with Sri Lanka's state-run Ceylon Petroleum Corporation (CPC) and the local subsidiary of Indian Oil Corporation agreeing to develop a strategic oil storage facility in Trincomalee. Modi also became the first Indian Prime Minister to visit Jaffna in the war-ravaged Northern Province. There, he handed over houses that had been built with Indian assistance. He also assured Colombo that India stood with Sri Lanka 'to build a future that accommodates all sections, including Tamils, for peace, justice and equality in Sri Lanka' (*Economic Times* 2015). Modi also visited the memorial to the Indian Peace Keeping Force (IPKF) outside Colombo.

Shifting Indian foreign policy to a new level of assertiveness, during Modi's visit to China in May 2015, he stressed 'the need for China to reconsider its approach on some of the issues that hold us back from realizing full potential of our partnership' and 'suggested that China should take a strategic and long-term view of our relations' (Areddy and Mandhana 2015). Afterwards, in a speech at Tsinghua University, Modi pointed out the need to resolve the border dispute and to 'ensure that our relationships with other countries do not become a source of concern for each other' (MEA 2015). These two remarks show the shift in Indian defensiveness vis-à-vis China and underscore a policy recalibration by pointing towards China as the responsible for the stalemate in bilateral ties. Modi's subsequent visits to Mongolia and South Korea after China in May 2015 signalled that New Delhi remained keen on also expanding its profile in China's periphery. In the realm of soft power, the Indian government was successful in 2015 in having the United Nations declare an international yoga day (June 21).

From Pakistan to the USA, from Africa to the ASEAN region – bilateral relations with countries, regions, and institutions received a great deal of foreign policy attention. A major success of the Modi government certainly became the intensive nurturing of major power relations: until 2017, the Modi government upheld a robust relationship with the USA, while stabilising its ties with Beijing and Moscow. New Delhi's outreach to countries such as Japan, Australia, Vietnam, Singapore, Philippines, and Malaysia all grew drastically. India's footprint in Africa, Latin America, and the Middle East also deepened. In the South Asia region, India's ties with Bangladesh markedly improved, and the two countries managed to resolve their long-pending disputes.

Relations with Sri Lanka also showed signs of improvement. Additionally, India enhanced its security role in Afghanistan.

With regard to the USA, in 2016 Narendra Modi met then US President Barack Obama five times either in the frame of bilateral or multilateral meetings. Modi was also invited to address the US Congress – a great honour which showed the significance of India to the USA –, and the USA designated India a major defence partner.

India was less successful in its bid to gain membership in the Nuclear Suppliers Group (NSG) in 2016, due to Chinese resistance. While Modi met Chinese president Xi Jinping three times in 2016 (at the SCO, the G-20, and BRICS summits), the Indo-Chinese partnership did not progress. Conversely, India showed a new foreign policy assertiveness by allowing pro-democracy Chinese dissidents to meet in Dharamsala in April 2016, the Tibetan Buddhist Karmapa to visit the US ambassador in Delhi in October and Tawang in November 2016. The Dalai Lama even visited Arunachal Pradesh in April 2017, despite vocal Chinese protests.

One of the foreign policy milestones of the Modi government was Modi's visit to Pakistan on 25 December 2015 (Haidar 2015). However, the positive political fallout soon disappeared. A terrorist attack against the Pathankot air base in January 2016 and against military camps in Uri in September 2016 and Nagrota in November 2016 marked low points in Indo-Pak relations. Modi publicly announced 'surgical strikes' across the Line of Control (LOC) in retaliation for the Uri attack, a new and, for some, unexpected foreign and security policy behaviour. Modi also announced India's intention to exercise full rights under the Indus Waters Treaty for which the first inter-ministerial meeting was convened. Conversely, the regular meetings of the Indus Waters Commissioners were then cancelled.

Modi made successful visits to Saudi Arabia and Qatar in 2016, with the Qatar Prime Minister returning the visit in December and the invitation extended to the UAE Sheikh to be Chief Guest at the Republic Day in January 2017. Modi's visit to Iran in May 2016 at the occasion of the signing by Iran, India, and Afghanistan of the geopolitically important Chabahar port agreement was central in terms of expanding Indian outreach to the region. India's announced 'act east' policy was implemented with a successful India-Japan summit in November 2016. During that summit, a civil nuclear agreement was signed. With regard to India's outreach to Africa, following the Third India-Africa Forum Summit in New Delhi in October 2015 Modi went on a lengthy trip to Africa and visited Kenya, Mozambique, South

Africa, and Tanzania in July 2016. And regarding Russia, the 17th India-Russia summit in October 2016 in Goa led to the announcement of major defence- and energy-related agreements.

The multilateral and para-diplomacy dimension

Following the frame and idea of new 'alliances' outlined in the BJP manifesto, Modi travelled to Brazil to participate in the BRICS summit. At the summit, it was decided to found a New Development Bank (NDB) with US$100 billion and a contingency fund to deal with financial crises (Acharya 2014).

In terms of global economic multilateralism, India took a strict stance at the World Trade Organization on negotiations for a Trade Facilitation Agreement. The government blocked the deal because of food security concerns (*The Hindu* 2014b). Modi cited national interest as the main reason, which is in consonance with his perspective on India First, but was in a way a recourse to an unrelenting and uncompromising position that India used to have taken in the past and was thought to have been overcome (Narlikar 2006). Modi's was heavily criticised for his actions, especially with a view to the fact that the vast majority of the countries present had negotiated the whole package deal at the WTO meeting in Bali in December 2013 where the Manmohan Singh government had negotiated a transition phase for India, which Modi did not accept. With regard to SAARC, after participating in 2014, India decided to boycott the SAARC summit in Islamabad in November 2017, with other SAARC member states also declaring their boycott. At the time of writing, no date for the next SAARC summit had been agreed upon.

As far as Modi's pre-frame of the role of states is concerned, Modi gave a speech in Mumbai on 16 August 2014 in which he did call for a more prominent role of the states. This demand was strengthened when Minister of State for External Affairs and Minister for the North Eastern Region, V.K. Singh, visited Bangladesh. During this visit, a number of high officials accompanied him from states sharing a border with Bangladesh. In particular, there were the Chief Minister of Meghalaya state, Mukul Sangma, and the industry minister of Tripura state, Tapan Chakraborty. Just days after Modi's speech on 16 August, Mukula Sangma discussed the necessity for greater connectivity between Meghalaya and Bangladesh at an Investor's Conclave in Dhaka on 24 August. Prior to his visit to Bangladesh, V.K. Singh met Chief Ministers from northeastern states. In a first move towards strengthening the position of the states, the MEA was tasked to coordinate foreign investment in States (Haidar 2104b). The idea of para-diplomacy had been regularly demanded by Modi as part of the pre-framing process of foreign policy, and thus its announced implementation was straightforward.

Conclusion: does the 'golden bird' start to fly again, and when?

While the BJP publicly stresses the trinity of nation, identity, and culture, the latter has certainly influenced the foreign policy approaches of both Congress and BJP, but to different degrees. The earlier sections have shown how pre-frames and frames of a specifically BJP-influenced novel foreign policy developed and were subsequently put into practice. All of this shows a new direction of India's foreign policy: cultural identity and nationalist values play a much more prominent role in foreign policy now. It does not come as a surprise that Modi took his oath of office in Hindi, a first in the history of the office and a public break with the tradition of his predecessors. After Indian civil servants were instructed to use only Hindi in their social media statements, Modi, however, had to change his stance quickly and included only Hindi-speaking states (*Hindustan Times* 2014a). All this, in a way, reflects major cultural differences between the previous Congress Party–led government and Modi's BJP. Internationally, the international yoga day became the latest element in Indian soft power.

In terms of foreign policy behaviour, Amit Shah, BJP President, stated on 9 July 2014 'Narendra Modi has made it clear that there is nothing above the interest of our border or country. If the country's interests are not served, there can be no talks' (*Economic Times* 2014a). This nationalist perspective on foreign policy is in consonance with Modi's professed wish to have India called 'the golden bird' again (*The Hindu* 2014f), a term which has not been used for India in a long time. Modi has long and frequently referenced India's ancient glory and former global role, so he is likely to drive the country's geopolitical ambitions forward, particularly in Asia.

By the end of 2017, Modi's foreign policy behaviour has been a break with the past. He hosted the SAARC leaders when he was sworn in in May 2014; he immediately, after assuming office, visited India's close neighbours Nepal and Bhutan; he went to the BRICS summit in Brazil and agreed to participate in the NDB; he received promises of large-scale investments from both Japan and China; and he spoke at Madison square garden in front of a frenetic crowd. In sum, he managed to put a personal stamp on foreign policy issues to a much faster and a much more far-reaching degree than any former Prime Minister, except for Nehru. 'Buy India', 'India First', 'Brand India', and 'Make in India' have become household economic mantras for India. In terms of military spending and upgrading, the Indian military companies are already heavily upgrading their factories (Wilkes 2014) in anticipation of large orders from the Indian military.

At the same time, the BJP's professed search for 'alliances' is also a novel element, leaving behind classic Nehruvian concepts of non-alignment. An alliance denotes a close relationship between countries, including regular consultations and even obligations, a position very different from non-alignment. In terms of geopolitics, Modi's focus has so far been the neighbourhood, then the 'act east' maxim, followed by Japan and China. Modi intends to continue with the project 'Mausam', a project that will stretch from East Africa to Indonesia and will extend India's zone of influence over the Indian Ocean (Parashar 2014). It is, in a way, a response to Chinese plans for the region, particularly regarding the Maritime Silk Route and the One Belt One Road (OBOR) initiative that would link Europe to China via the Indian Ocean. The Prime Minister's plan of para-diplomacy ultimately aims at giving states more say in foreign policy, an emanation of Modi's own experiences. This will further increase the role of cultural identity: Bengali identity will influence Bangladesh policy; Tamil Nadu identity will influence Sri Lankan policy.

While Modi has received mostly positive assessments (Chellaney 2014; Madan 2014) about his pro-active and pragmatic leadership (and style), some analysts have pointed out several problems that Modi has not addressed properly, e.g. in the neighbourhood (Muni 2014).

At the time of writing, after almost three years in in office, it has become clear that India is projecting a much more robust profile on the global stage, compared to its behaviour over the previous decade. But still: Modi's foreign policy actions are a clear indicator of Hindutva pre-frames and frames put into concrete action, and these show that Modi's foreign policy is based upon Hindutva ideology, cultural nationalism, and a desire to return India back to her former position as a great civilization and power, a role which, in the eyes of the BJP, it currently no longer possesses.

Notes

1 The stakeholder opportunities and potential role of states in India's neighbourhood policy has been critically analysed by Pattanaik (Pattanaik 2014).
2 A Sanskrit term translated as 'the world is a family' or 'universal brotherhood'.

3 See for determinants, norms, contradictions, and key drivers of India's Foreign policy e.g. Sahni 2007; Mitra 2009; Ogden 2010; Michael 2013; for an assessment of BJP foreign policy ideology and approach, see especially Chaulia 2002.

Bibliography

Acharya, Amitav. 2014. 'Move Over, Big Brother', *The Hindu*, July 21. www.thehindu.com/opinion/op-ed/move-over-big-brother/article6231205.ece (accessed on July 22, 2014).

Agarwal, Vibhuti. 2014. 'India's Modi Holds Talks with Chinese Foreign Minister', *Wall Street Journal*, June 9. http://online.wsj.com/articles/indias-modi-holds-talks-with-chinese-foreign-minister-1402333538 (accessed on June 10, 2014).

Areddy, James T. and Niharika Mandhana. 2015. 'India's Modi Prods China to Change Tack on Strategic Issues', *Wall Street Journal*, May 15. www.wsj.com/articles/indias-modi-urges-china-to-put-aside-differences-1431689382 (accessed September 21, 2015).

Barnett, Michael. 1999. 'Culture, Strategy and Foreign Policy Change: Israel's Road to Oslo', *European Journal of International Relations*, 5(1): 5–36.

Barry, Ellen and Suhasini Raj. 2014. 'India and Pakistan in "Common Agenda"', *The New York Times*, May 27. www.nytimes.com/2014/05/28/world/asia/india-pakistan.html (accessed on May 28, 2014).

Bharatiya Janata Party. 2009. *Election Manifesto 2009*. www.bjp.org/images/pdf/election_manifesto_english.pdf (accessed on December 12, 2009).

———. 2014. *Election Manifesto 2014*. http://bjpelectionmanifesto.com/pdf/manifesto2014.pdf (accessed June 10, 2014).

Chaudhuri, Rudra. 2014. 'Putting People Before Politicians', *The Hindu*, September 30. www.thehindu.com/opinion/op-ed/modi-us-visit-new-york-public-speechescentral-park-madison-square-gardens-putting-people-beforepoliticians/article6458585.ece (accessed on July 10, 2014).

Chaulia, Sreeram S. 2002. 'BJP, India's Foreign Policy and the "Realist Alternative" to the Nehruvian Tradition', *International Politics*, 39: 252–234.

Chellaney, Brahma. 2014. 'Narendra Modi's Imprint on Foreign Policy', September 2. www.livemint.com/Opinion/Rx9Waq6uNG6yHJaSJMurTL/Narendra-Modis-imprint-on-foreign-policy.html (accessed on September 4, 2014).

Economic Times. 2014a. 'India Has Got Government With a Strong Foreign Policy: Amit Shah, BJP President', July 9. http://articles.economictimes.indiatimes.com/2014-09-07/news/53653027_1_amit-shah-bjp-president-narendra-modi (accessed July 10, 2014).

———. 2014b. 'PM Narendra Modi's Japan Visit: 10 Key Takeaways', September 2. http://articles.economictimes.indiatimes.com/2014-09-02/news/53479892_1_india-and-japan-bullet-trains-pm-narendra-modi (accessed September 4, 2014).

———. 2015. 'India seeks a life of peace and dignity for Tamils in Sri Lank', March 2015. https://economictimes.indiatimes.com/news/politics-and-nation/india-seeks-a-life-of-peace-and-dignity-for-tamils-in-sri-lanka-pm-modi/articleshow/46554674.cms (accessed October 10, 2015).

Economist. 2014. 'India and the United States: Charming, Disarming', October 4, p. 34.

Gosh, Palash. 2014. 'India's 2014 Elections: Narendra Modi Says Some Illegal Immigrants From Bangladesh Are Better Than Others', *International Business Times*, March 11. www.ibtimes.com/indias-2014-elections-narendra-modi-says-some-illegal-immigrants-bangladesh-are-better-others (accessed on April 15, 2014).

Haidar, Suhasini. 2014a. 'Hurriyat Has No Stake in Peace Process, India Counters Pakistan', *The Hindu*, August 20. www.thehindu.com/news/national/hurriyat-has-no-stake-in-peace-process-indiacounters-pakistan/article6335531.ece (accessed on August 22, 2014).

———. 2014b. 'MEA to Oversee Foreign Investments in States', *The Hindu*, October 25. www.thehindu.com/news/national/mea-to-oversee-foreign-investments-instates/article6530956.ece (accessed on October 26, 2014).

———. 2014c. 'India to Modernise Vietnam's Defence Forces', *The Hindu*, October 29. www.thehindu.com/news/national/indiavietnam-bilateral-ties-india-to-modernisevietnams-defence-forces/article6542138.ece (accessed on October 30, 2014).

———. 2015. '3 Minutes That Changed Indo-Pak Ties', *The Hindu*, December 26. www.thehindu.com/news/national/3-minutes-that-changed-indiapak-ties/article8029441.ece (accessed December 29, 2015).

The Hindu. 2013. 'BJP Rules Out Major Foreign Policy Shift, If Voted to Power', July 25. www.thehindu.com/news/national/bjp-rules-out-major-foreign-policy-shift-if-voted-to-power/article4952138.ece (accessed on August 8, 2013).

———. 2014a. 'India, Japan Sign MoU to Develop Varanasi Into "Smart City"', August 30. www.thehindu.com/news/national/india-japan-sign-mou-to-develop-varanasi-into-smart-city/article6365189.ece (accessed on September 2, 2014).

———. 2014b. 'India Not Blocking Rule-Based Global Trade: Narendra Modi', September 9. www.thehindu.com/news/national/india-not-blocking-rulebased-global-trade-narendra-modi/article6394311.ece (accessed on September 9, 2014).

———. 2014c. 'A Historic Opportunity', September 17. www.thehindu.com/opinion/editorial/xi-jinping-in-india-a-historicopportunity/article6416555.ece (accessed on July 10, 2014).

———. 2014d. 'China, India Should Take Strategic Ties to Higher Plane: Xi', September 18. www.thehindu.com/news/national/china-india-should-take-strategic-ties-tohigher-plane-xi/article6422179.ece (accessed on September 20, 2014).

———. 2014e. 'Under Sangh Pressure, Modi Takes Hard Line on Incursions', September 18. www.thehindu.com/news/national/modi-raises-issue-of-chinese-incursions-withxi/article6422103.ece (accessed on September 20, 2014).

———. 2014f. 'Modi: India Can Rise Again as Global Power', September 22. www.thehindu.com/news/national/modi-india-can-rise-again-as-globalpower/article6432851.ece (accessed on October 5, 2014).

———. 2014g. 'Forward and Together in Progress', October 1. www.thehindu.com/opinion/op-ed/narendra-modi-and-barack-obama-forwardand-together-in-progress/article6462523.ece (accessed on October 2, 2014).

Hindustan Times. 2014a. 'Modi Govt Softens Stand on Hindi Diktat After Row', June 20. www.hindustantimes.com/india-news/ensure-english-is-used-on-social-media-jaya-to-pm/article1-1231522.aspx (accessed on June 22, 2014).

———. 2014b. 'Modi Talks Tough With China's President Xi on Border Row', September 18. www.hindustantimes.com/india-news/asiantigers-meet/modi-talks-tough-with-china-s-xi-on-border-row/article1-1265628.aspx (accessed on September 20, 2014).

Hudson, Valerie M. 1997. *Culture & Foreign Policy*. Boulder: Lynne Rienner Publishers.

India Today. 2013. 'After the UK, Other European States Set to Join the Modi Line', February 8. http://indiatoday.intoday.in/story/eu-ends-embargo-against-narendra-modi/1/249495.html 8 (accessed on February 12, 2013).

Iyer, Shekar. 2013. 'States Should Have Larger Say in Foreign Policy: Modi', *Hindustan Times*, October 19. www.hindustantimes.com/india-news/allaboutnarendramodi/states-should-have-larger-say-in-foreign-policy-modi/article1-1137265.aspx (accessed on November 24, 2013).

Jacob, Jayanth. 2014. 'Stronger India Will Be Better for Bhutan, SAARC Nations: PM Narendra Modi', *Hindustan Times*, June 16. www.hindustantimes.com/india-news/allaboutmodisarkar/pm-modi-lays-stress-on-india-bhutan-ties-says-strong-india-will-be-helpful-for – neighbours/article1-1229918.aspx (accessed on June 18, 2014).

Jaishankar, Dhruva. 2014. 'Eeny, Meeny, Miney, Modi', *Foreign Policy*, May 19. www.foreignpolicy.com/articles/2014/05/19/does_narendra_modi_have_a_foreign_policy_india_pakistan_china (accessed on May 22, 2014).

Keck, Zacharya. 2014. 'Is India About to Abandon Its No-First Use Nuclear Doctrine?', *The Diplomat*, April 9. http://thediplomat.com/2014/04/is-india-about-to-abandon-its-no-first-use-nuclear-doctrine/ (accessed on April 10, 2014).

Kuber, Girish. 2014. 'My Hindutva Face Will Be an Asset in Foreign Affairs', *Indian Express*, April 23. http://indianexpress.com/article/india/politics/my-hindutva-face-will-be-an-asset-in-foreign-affairs/ (accessed on April 25, 2014).

Madan, Tanvi. 2014. 'Indian Prime Minister Modi's Foreign Policy: The First 100 Days', August 29. www.brookings.edu/research/opinions/2014/08/28-modi-100-days-foreign-policy-madan (accessed on September 2, 2014).

Maini, Tridivesh Singh. 2014. 'Narendra Modi's Foreign Policy – Too Early to Judge?', *East Asia Forum*, September 6. www.eastasiaforum.org/2014/09/06/narendra-modis-foreign-policy-too-early-to-judge/ (accessed on September 20, 2014).

Mandhana, Niharika. 2014. 'India's Modi Talks Tough on China', *Wall Street Journal*, February 24. http://blogs.wsj.com/indiarealtime/2014/02/23/indias-modi-talks-tough-on-china/ (accessed on February 26, 2014).

McAdam, Doug, John McCarthy and Mayer Zald. 1996. 'Introduction', in D. McAdam, J. McCarthy and M. Zald (eds.), *Comparative Perspective on Social Movements: Politcial Opportunities, Mobilizing Structures and Cultural Framing*. New York: Cambridge University Press.

MEA. 2015. 'Address by Prime Minister at the Tsinghua University Beijing', May 15. www.mea.gov.in/Speeches-State-ments.htm?dtl/25242/Address_by_Prime_Minister_at_the_Tsinghua_University_Beijing_May_15_2015 (accessed on May 20, 2015).

Michael, Arndt. 2013. *India's Foreign Policy and Regional Multilateralism*. Basingstoke: Palgrave Macmillan.

Mitra, Subatra K. 2009. 'Nuclear, Engaged and Non-Aligned: Contradiction and Coherence in India's Foreign Policy', *India Quarterly: A Journal of International Affairs*, 65(1): 15–35.

Muni, S. D. 2014. 'Modi's Neighbourhood Initiative', *Economic and Political Weekly*, 49(38): 28–30.

Narlikar, Amrita. 2006. 'Peculiar Chauvinism or Strategic Calculation? Explaining the Negotiating Strategy of a Rising India', *International Affairs*, 82(1): 59–76.

Ogden, Chris. 2010. 'Norms, Indian Foreign Policy and the 1998–2004 National Democratic Alliance', *The Round Table: The Commonwealth Journal of International Affairs*, 99(408): 303–315.

Panda, Ankit. 2014a. 'Modi Reaches Out to SAARC Leaders Ahead of Swearing-In as Prime Minister', *The Diplomat*, May 22. http://thediplomat.com/2014/05/modi-reaches-out-to-saarc-leaders-ahead-of-swearing-in-as-prime-minister/ (accessed on May 24, 2014).

Parashar, Sachin. 2014. 'Narendra Modi's "Mausam" Manoeuvre to Check China's Maritime Might', *Times of India*, September 16. http://timesofindia.indiatimes.com/india/Narendra-Modis-Mausam-manoeuvre-to-check-Chinas-maritime-might/articleshow/42562085.cms (accessed on September 19, 2014).

Pattanaik, Smruti S. 2014. 'Federalising India's Neighbourhood Policy: Making the States Stakeholders', *Strategic Analysis*, 38(1): 31–48.

Sahni, Varun. 2007. 'India's Foreign Policy: Key Drivers', *South African Journal of International Affairs*, 14(2): 21–34.

Siasat Daily. 2014. 'World Should Realize the Strength of India's Democracy: Narendra Modi', June 2. www.siasat.com/english/news/world-should-realize-strength-india%E2%80%99s-democracy-narendra-modi (accessed on June 3, 2014).

Subramanian, Nirupama. 2014. 'Interview With U.S. Ambassador to India Kathleen Stephens', *The Hindu*, October 21. www.thehindu.com/news/national/interview-with-us-ambassador-to-indiakathleen-stephens/article6524198.ece (accessed on October 22, 2014).
Tarrow, Sidney. 1994. *Power in Movements*. New York: Cambridge University Press.
Times of India. 2014. 'Sushma Tells Indian Envoys to "Act East" and Not Just "Look East"', August 26. http://timesofindia.indiatimes.com/india/Sushma-tells-Indian-envoys-to-act-east-andnot-just-look-east/articleshow/40931866.cms (accessed on July 10, 2014).
Varadarajan, Tunku. 2014. 'Modi's Operandi', *TIME*, October 6, p. 17.
Varghese, George K. 2014. 'Modi Diplomacy Proactive, Strong and Sensitive: Minister', *The Hindu*, September 8. www.thehindu.com/news/national/modi-diplomacy-proactive-strong-andsensitive-external-affairs-minister-sushma-swaraj/article6391938.ece (accessed on September 9, 2014).
Wilkes, Tommy. 2014. 'Indian Firms Tool Up for Defense Orders on Modi's Buy India Pledge', *Reuters*, August 20. http://in.reuters.com/article/2014/08/21/india-defence-idINKBN0GL02P20140821 (accessed on August 30, 2014).
Zald, Mayer. 1996. 'Culture, Ideology, and Strategic Framing', in D. McAdam, J. McCarthy and M. Zald (eds.), *Comparative Perspective on Social Movements: Political Opportunities, Mobilizing Structures, and Cultural Framing*. New York: Cambridge University Press.

3 Allegories of 'love *jihad*' and *ghar wapsi*[1]
Interlocking the socio-religious with the political

Charu Gupta

The unprecedented victory of the Bhartiya Janata Party (henceforth BJP) in 2014 has left scholars and analysts grappling for its multifaceted layers. If corruption of UPA-II, the corporate parading of 'development', and the overpowering Modi largely marked 2014, it was also the year of a perceptible shift to the Right, with politicised Hindutva's socio-religious cries against 'love *jihad*' and for *ghar wapsi* (return to home). The unabashed political use of Hindu religious symbols in communal riots of Muzaffarnagar saw overt and widespread manifestation in such idioms. It has been noted that one of the critical aspects of 2014 elections was 'that for the very first time in the history of our Republic, a political party explicitly based on religious identity . . . secured more than 50% of the seats in our Parliament'.[2] Immediately after the general elections of 2014, a section of confident and elated Hindutvavaadis felt they could play communal politics in much more aggressive ways by deploying such metaphors, which became particularly visible in the context of the by-polls in Uttar Pradesh (henceforth UP), held immediately after the general elections. 'Love jihad' was alleged to be a movement to forcefully convert vulnerable Hindu women to Islam through trickery and marriage. Ghar wapsi signalled a synchronised vocabulary of anti-conversion by the BJP and of reconversion by the VHP and Dharm Jagran Samiti, an affiliate of the Rashtriya Swayamsevak Sangh (henceforth RSS).

This chapter examines the larger politics of such constructed campaigns. It highlights how both these drives were charged with a moral and communal fervour, adopting an unrestrained anti-Christianity and anti-Islamic polemic, and implicitly attempting to influence the larger politics and elections of 2014. At the same time, the outcome of UP by-polls reflected that such idioms did not particularly transform into an electoral vote bank. It may also be argued that the corporate media and big capitalists, while conservative in their economic outlook, and all-out supporters of the 'developmental' model of Modi, were uncomfortable with cries of 'love jihad' and *ghar wapsi*, seeing them as antithesis of development paradigms. It has thus been stated that BJP's success in the 2014 elections had less to do with the victory of Hindutva, and more to do with weak and jobless economic growth, alongside the corruption and rudderless quality of the incumbent UPA regime. In other words, BJP's success had less to do with its Hindu-ness and more to do with the desperate desire – especially amongst the huge cohort of new and young voters – for inclusive economic growth and improved prospects for employment.[3] However, while the BJP's national face has officially largely kept away from concoctions of 'love jihad' and *ghar wapsi*, these continue to operate at a subterranean level, with attempts being made to make them a part of our 'common sense'. The chapter argues that such constructed idioms reflect complex, contradictory grids. In some ways they signal the triumph of Hindu majoritarianism, of politicised Hinduism, whereby segments of groups have felt emboldened. But it may also be contended that the relative 'failure' of such lingos underline their limitations. While 'love jihad' and *ghar wapsi* signal the interlocking of the social and the religious with the political, they also reflect deep-seated anxieties of Hindutva politics regarding female free will, subversive potential of love, pliable and ambiguous religious identities, and syncretic socio-religious practices, which continue to exist in different forms. The chapter explores these various meanings of 'love jihad' and *ghar wapsi* amidst the background of the tumultuous 2014.

Love jihad: a jihad against love

The Lok Sabha results of 2014, with BJP getting a thumping majority, in spite of polling only 31 per cent of votes, in certain ways spelled a confident Hindu majoritarian mindset, whereby it was felt that covert propagandas could now be engaged with in a forefront manner. The most visible manifestation of it was immediately after the Lok Sabha elections in the UP by-polls the same year. There was a widespread and systematic campaign around 'love jihad' in various villages, *mofussils*, and towns of western UP by Hindutva organisations like the Dharma Jagran Manch, the Vishwa Hindu Parishad, and the Bajrang Dal in the months of August and September 2014, just prior to the by-poll elections. 'Love Jihad' was an attempt at political and communal mobilisation in the name of women. It was alleged by Hindu hardliners that 'love jihad' was an organised conspiracy, whereby Muslim men were forcefully converting vulnerable Hindu women to Islam through trickery and marriage. In actual practice, 'love jihad' was an emotive mythical campaign, a 'delicious' political fantasy, a lethal mobilisation strategy, and a vicious crusade – a jihad against love – for political gains in elections. RSS's *sarkaryawah* Suresh Bhayyaji Joshi stated in a press conference as late as 20 October 2014 that the 'Hindu *samaj* (society) has been facing the shame of love jihad since long', and the UP government should take a 'serious view' of it, as it 'hurts the dignity of women'.[4] The 7 September 2014 issues of RSS's mouthpieces, *Panchjanya* and *Organiser*, had their cover stories on 'love jihad'. They urged people to raise the slogan 'love ever, love jihad never!' *Panchjanya*'s cover had an illustration of a man wearing a *kaffiyeh* or traditional Arab headdress, a beard in the shape of heart, and sinister sunglasses in which red hearts were reflected. The magazine asked on the cover, 'pyar andha dhandha' (love blind or trade) (see Figure 3.1).[5]

The idioms, language, and symbols invoked during the 'love jihad' campaign were not only meant to draw sharper lines between Hindus and Muslims, but were also thought to reap rich political harvest in the election landscaping of 2014. The figure of the Hindu woman became central to this orchestrated campaign. Besides the politics of vote bank and elections, this violent movement against love had multiple layers as it simultaneously attempted to invoke Hindu male prowess, promote images of an 'evil' and 'licentious' Muslim male, fabricate fears of declining Hindu numbers, construct a homogenous Hindu identity and Hindu nation over a sharply caste-class divided society, and reinstate familial patriarchies. At the same time, it also exposed grave anxieties and fears over women's independent and individual expressions of love, desire, and intimacy. While this chapter specifically focuses on the implications of the campaign in the context of 2014 elections and its aftermath, it is significant to note that in certain ways 'love jihad', and the various issues it harped on, had an uncanny resemblance to the 'abduction' and conversion campaigns launched by the Arya Samaj and other Hindu revivalist bodies in the 1920s in UP, at a time when there was a spate of Hindu-Muslim riots in the region. Similar idioms have been repeatedly conjured in diverse ways, for example in 2009, revealing the larger continuities of such fabricated metaphors, which I have discussed elsewhere.[6] Particularly in times when religious identities are sharpened, such idioms take more overt forms. For example, in the 1920s, according to British commentators, UP witnessed more riots than any other province in India.[7] The Hindu Mahasabha and the Arya Samaj attained a new importance in the region, challenging conversions in an organised manner through *shuddhi* (purification; Hindu movement in the late nineteenth and twentieth century to reclaim those who had converted from Hinduism to other religions)

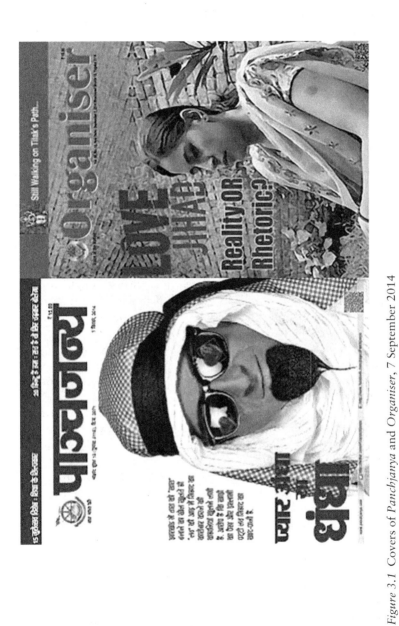

Figure 3.1 Covers of *Panchjanya* and *Organiser*, 7 September 2014
Source: *Panchjanya*, 7 September 2014; *Organiser*, 7 September 2014

and *sangathan* (an organisation launched by Hindu organisations in defence of 'Hindu' interests).[8] In 2014, we saw something similar happening. I discuss in this section why and how the 'love jihad' campaign worked in the year, and its various repugnant measures.

Through 'love jihad', some of the Hinduvaadis tried to evoke Hindu male prowess, and they gave a call for a united Hindu community and nation. Through invocations and related concerns with Hindu female purity, Hindu male virility attempted to reassert itself in a public-political domain in more forceful ways. Through the motif of 'love jihad', Hindus were being constantly asked to be brave, to avenge past wrongs, and to be the warriors for a strong Hindu race. Further, Hindu publicists felt that while the Ramjanmabhoomi movement had lost its steam, this issue could be even more emotive, as it entered our most intimate, domestic spaces, and could potentially carry the 'fear' of Muslim into every Hindu home, and shift mentalities at an everyday, mundane level. It was believed that it could also provide a cohesive Hindu unity, camouflaging deeper social tensions around caste, and thus be extremely beneficial in the vote bank politics. These politicised entanglements generated an 'intimate politics', an embodied struggle, in which threatened patriarchal familial structures and Hindu communal agendas reformulated themselves through women. Propagating myths of 'love jihad' through pamphlets, meetings, conversations, rumours, and the everyday conversations fed by them, it was sustained as an active cultural, and therefore political, issue. The year 2014 thus saw orchestrated propaganda campaigns and popular inflammatory and demagogic appeals by a section of Hindu publicists against 'love jihad', against supposed 'abductions' and conversions of Hindu women by Muslim men, ranging from allegations of rape and forced marriages, to elopement, love, luring, and conversion. Drawing on diverse sources like small meetings, handbills, posters, myths, rumours, and gossip, the campaign against the mythical 'love jihad' operated in a public-political domain and attempted to monopolise the field of everyday representation. In UP, as well as to an extent in Bihar and some other regions, attempts were made to make 'love jihad' an important determinant of Hindu identity and consciousness in 2014, providing a section of Hindu publicists with a common reference point. For example, giving a clarion call to Hindus of western UP, BJP MLA Sangeet Singh Som announced a *mahapanchayat* to protest against 'love jihad' in his Assembly constituency of Sardhana in Meerut district.[9] Invoking Hindu male prowess, 'Hindu brothers' were specifically appealed through posters taken out by an outfit called 'Anti Love-Jihad Front', to protect their 'Hindu sisters' (see Figure 3.2).

Allegories of 'love jihad' and ghar wapsi 89

Figure 3.2 'An Appeal to Hindu Brothers'

Awake Hindus Awake. Beware of Love Jihad!

> Keeping Hindu names, tying the sacred thread on their hand and putting the sectarian mark on their forehead, Muslim boys rope in Hindu girls in their love net, convert them, marry them, have a child with them, exploit them physically and mentally and then leave them.

Source: www.youthkiawaaz.com/2014/09/politics-love-jihad-damaging-secular-fabric-country/, accessed on 5 September 2014

In more forceful ways than before, stereotypes of 'lustful' and 'licentious' Muslim men were strengthened, with new contours added in 2014. Some Hindutva spokespersons stated that 'love jihad' was a characteristic Muslim activity and constructed the Muslim male as a rapist and an abductor. Lecherous behaviour, luring Hindu women through false promises, high sexual appetite, a life of luxury, and religious fanaticism were portrayed as dominant traits of Muslim characters.[10] It was further claimed that almost all young Muslim men were indulging in such practices. Before 2014, in 2009 also the bogey of 'love jihad' had been raised, when Shahan Sha of Kerala was charged with forcibly abducting and converting Methula, a Hindu girl. The year 2014 saw similar allegations being repeatedly made. BJP's UP President Laxmikant Bajpai pronounced, 'Have they got certificate to rape girls because they belong to a particular religion?'[11] He went on to enunciate that 90 per cent of all rapes were committed by Muslims! Of course, there was no data given to back such preposterous claims. 'Love jihad' was predicated on exclusionary principles, and it drew inspiration through constant and repetitive references to the aggressive and libidinal energies of the Muslim male, creating a common 'enemy other'. Often there were not just particular cases; there was a ready move from the particular to the general and the abstract. Representation, performance, and events fed into each other, providing one of the primary sources of communal power. The motif of 'love jihad' added new dimensions to the stereotype of the Muslim male. In the wake of terrorist threats and Muslim fundamentalism, anxieties were created of a global Islamist conspiracy and foreign hand in 'love jihad'. It was even professed that Muslim youth were receiving funds from abroad for purchasing designer clothes, vehicles, mobile phones, and expensive gifts to woo Hindu women and lure them away. Dr Chandramohan, spokesperson of the UP state BJP stated: 'This is part of global love jihad that targets vulnerable Hindu girls'.[12] It was further alleged that beautiful, well-dressed young Muslim men were posing as Hindus. With red *puja* threads on their wrists and with ambiguous nick-names, they were hanging around girls' schools and colleges. It was further stated that this was a conspiracy hatched in Deoband![13] In the process, the centre of sexual violence moved from men in general and Hindu men in particular towards the Muslim male.

In the bogey of 'love jihad' the 'fear' that was constantly expressed by Hindutva forces was that Hindu women were being converted to Islam in the 'false' name of love. I will talk more about conversions in the next section. Suffice to state here that feminists have repeatedly argued that while each case of fraud, violence forcible conversion, abduction, and rape must be probed as an act of crime against women, which is structured by larger patriarchal structures within and outside a community, the problem arises when separate incidents, many of them constructed, are viewed with the same lens, when every love, romance, and inter-religious marriage is rewritten as deception. In this context, as stated, 'Are BJP leaders MJ Akbar, Mukhtar Abbas Naqvi, Shahnawaz Husain, and even the late Sikhandar Baksht, guilty of love jihad because they married Hindu women? How about Subramaniam Swamy's own daughter who is married to a Muslim? That's "love jihad" too?'[14] Hindu organisations also argued that if one is marrying for love, why should conversion follow? However, conversion is a matter of personal choice, and is very much allowed by our constitution. Moreover, the Special Marriage Act, under which such marriages can take place, requires one month notice, which an eloping couple is afraid to give, as they are already facing a lot of opposition. Conversions provide a way out. It is important to understand the procedural impediments in the Special Marriage Act because if a young couple in love would like to legalise their relationship in the teeth of parental opposition, the Special Marriage Act is a difficult and imperfect option. Campaigns like 'love jihad' privilege moral panic and public morality over constitutional morality, whereby the converted Hindu woman is portrayed as a potential site of outrage of family order, patriarchal authority, and religious sentiment, strengthening the drive for a restoration of family and community honour. The intermeshing of romance, marriage, and conversions produce increasing worries, deeply politicised representations and everyday violence, framed around the bodies of women.

The 'love jihad' campaign, while focusing its anger on the Muslims, received its emotional bonding from the 'victimised' Hindu woman. The Hindu woman has often been regarded as an exclusive preserve of the Hindu man, and safeguarding her virtue is identified as his exclusive prerogative. In the name of protecting 'our' women, which they have never asked for, they justify all violence. What was involved in 'love jihad' was a self-image of a community at war. The abducted and converted Hindu woman was metamorphosed into a symbol of both sacredness and humiliation. Simultaneously, images of passive victimised Hindu women at the hand of inscrutable Muslims attempted to silence and erase female subjectivity and desire. It is significant that even before the term 'love jihad' was coined, the Bajrang Dal ran a 'Bahu Betiyon ki Izzat Bachao' (Save the Honour of Daughter-in-Laws and Daughters) campaign.[15] Ram Sena leader Pramod Muttalik launched a 'Beti Bachao Andolan' in Karnataka. He was instrumental in coining the term 'love jihad' and claims it first featured in discussions in Hindutva groups from around 2005, where there was a spike in terrorist activities across the country. According to a magazine – *Bharat: Darool Harab Darool Islam* – printed and circulated by some BJP and RSS workers in western UP after the Muzaffarnagar riots, incidents of girls falling prey to love jihad in western UP between 2008–2011 numbered 1,611. An organisation called Meerut Bachao Manch was thus floated in Meerut in 2014 to fight the 'menace' of love jihad.[16] Posters appealed to Hindu men to protect their daughters and sisters from becoming 'victims' of love jihad (see Figure 3.3).

Figure 3.3 'Hindus Beware: Love Jihad'

Love-Fraud-Marriage-Conversion-Pain

Make your sisters, daughters aware of 'love jihad' and save them from becoming its victim!

Join a huge demonstration against love jihad.

Nationalist Shiv Sena and United Hindu Front hold a huge demonstration against Love Jihad.

Date: 23 September 2014

Time: 10.00 am

Venue: Jantar Mantar, New Delhi

Source: Photo taken by me of the Poster

Allegories of 'love jihad' and ghar wapsi 93

The 'love jihad' campaign overwhelmingly represented the woman as 'foolish', 'lured', and 'brainwashed' into the 'trap', with no mind or heart of her own. She was perceived as a menace for Hindutva, and as a danger to constructs of Hindu nation. Armed with peacock feathers and blessed water, godman Baba Rajakdas continues to sell a love 'cure' in Saharanpur to save Hindu girls, who according to him, get easily carried away by Muslim boys as they do not understand that they are being exploited. He claims to have an 'expertise' in this field, and to have 'cured' more than 200 girls in Saharanpur alone and over 500 in neighbouring Muzaffarnagar and Shamli.[17] It is impossible for Hindu groups to conceive that Hindu women can voluntarily elope or convert. Any possibility of women exercising their legitimate right to love, choice, and conversion is marginalised. In convoluted ways women are thus told that inter-religious marriages are undesirable for the good of women themselves. It is also assumed that the mere act of marrying and staying with a Muslim ensures that the woman is leading a dreadful life and her unhappiness is ensured. There appears to be a consensus among Hindu groups against any exercise of women to convert as individuals, sans familial and community approval. Perhaps, therefore, it might be better to see these women not so much as 'vulnerable victims', but as 'risk taking subjects'.

It is alleged by Hindu organisations that Muslim fundamentalism is being ignored in India. It is of course true that Muslim fundamentalism is equally vicious and patriarchal, and its dictates have imposed umpteen restrictions on women. Concerns about 'contamination' and 'conquest' can be found in most closed ethnic or racial groups. Thus states Maulana Ameeruddin, who runs a *madarsa* in Meerut, 'We need strict laws against adultery and pre-marital sex'.[18] Moreover, patriarchies are so deeply entrenched in our society that Muslim families get equally worried when their daughters marry Hindu men. In fact, inter-religious marriages are opposed by many Hindu and Muslim families, which further exposes the bogey of 'love jihad' as being some organised conspiracy. It is also to be noted, as stated by historian Tanika Sarkar, that 'communal stereotypes abound in all communities, but those of the majority community enjoying state power carry far greater import',[19] and this became all the more visible in 2014.

Hindu organisations also claim that while Hindu women have married Muslim men, the reverse has not really happened. However, there is a long list of celebrated Hindu husbands with Muslim wives, to name a few: Sunil Dutt-Nargis, Atul Agnihotri-Alvira Khan, and Urdu author Krishan Chander-Salma Siddiqui. Former sheriff of Mumbai, Nana Chudasama is a Hindu Gujarati Rajput married to Munaira

Jasdanvala, a Muslim. Actor Aditya Pancholi is married to Zarina Wahab. Cricketer Ajit Agarkar, a Maharashtrian Brahmin, is married to Fatima Ghadially. Congress MP Sachin Pilot is married to Sarah Abdullah. Nayyara Mirza, Miss India finalist of 1967, converted to Hinduism after marriage and became Nalini Patel. However, when a Hindu man marries a Muslim woman, it is always portrayed as 'romance' and 'love' by Hindu organisations, while when the reverse happens it is depicted as 'coercion'.

I think the most critical aspect of 'love jihad' was not just linked to election politics, but was an attempt by Hindutva forces to penetrate into the everyday lives of women. Hindutva's cry for segregation expresses a geography that maps power and hierarchy through bodies, by denying free movement to Hindu women. It uses threats of physical, emotional, and religious harm to women's bodies as powerful weapons of social control. In various meetings held in UP, detailed instructions were given to Hindu women, including 'not to wear green clothes', 'not to go to Muslim tailors and barbers', and 'not to go to any grave of Muslim saints'. Everyday public spaces like schools, colleges, theatres, ice cream and juice parlours, mobile charge shops, and private spaces like television and Internet were identified as sites where Hindu girls were 'wooed'.[20] Pramod Muttalik wrote a book *Love Jihad: Red Alert for Hindu Girls*, which devised 'preventive' measures and gave instructions on how to prevent Hindu women from 'becoming victims' (see Figure 3.4). It had instructions like the following:

> Be cautious about her wearing a head-scarf since it becomes difficult to recognize a girl who wears a headscarf and sits behind a two-wheeler. . . . Since some cases of love jihad have taken place with help of mobile phones, check incoming calls. Remember that saved numbers may be under a false name. . . . To get help from Hindus in a difficult situation, apply kumkum on the forehead.[21]

Muslim men were banned from *garba* celebrations (see Figure 3.5).[22]

Such minute instruction showed the need felt not so much to protect the 'Hindu *kanya*', but to facilitate the penetration of disciplinary regimes over a woman's actions and choices. The language of protecting Hindu women from being lured or misled by Muslim men actually means that they have to be kept on watch on a daily basis – whom they meet and where they go. All public spaces then need to be patrolled and if the so called love jihadists take on Hindu names to 'fool' women, then, as a writer states, 'all love affairs are presumptively suspect, since an apparently Hindu boy may actually be a love-toting jihadist. Which

Figure 3.4a and Figure 3.4b Front and back covers of Ram Muttalik's book *Love Jihad: Red Alert for Hindu Girls*

Source: www.loonwatch.com/2012/06/muslim-youths-again-targeted-with-love-jihadhate-campaign-in-kerala/, accessed on 26 August 2014

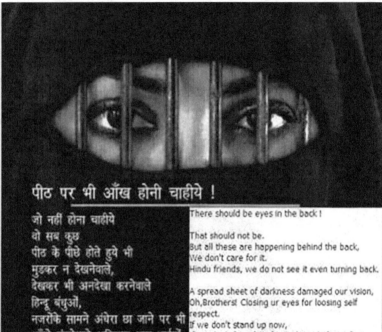

Figure 3.4a and Figure 3.4b (Continued)

Allegories of 'love jihad' *and* ghar wapsi 97

in turn means that the only way that "love jihad" can be thwarted is by launching a jihad against love',[23] thus blurring the distinction between love jihad and love marriages. Women's actions are producing daily policing and everyday violence, along the alliance model of sexuality, where through the arrangement of marriages, relations and boundaries of religion are policed. Campaigns like 'love jihad' attempt to underwrite an exclusivist grammar of 'difference' in intimate regimes of love and marriage. However, they also reveal deep-seated fears and anxieties against female free will, against the subversive potential of love, and against threats to traditions.

'Love jihad' rests on a series of lies, whereby reckless and venomous generalisations have been made, without concrete proof, of abductions and conversions of Hindu women. Wild claims have been made that 30,000 to 300,000 thousand women have been converted till now. The concrete stories and examples narrated to establish 'love jihad' have repeatedly been falsified. Through investigations in many cases, the fallacy and fantasy of 'love jihad' has been exposed. The phrase 'love jihad' first made an appearance around 2007. In Kerala, Karnataka, and Gujarat, various allegations were made, with even posters appearing, showing men dressed in green clothes standing outside colleges and roaming in public spaces to 'lure' Hindu women. Turning love marriage on its head, the ogre of 'love jihad' became a public citation of Hindu communalists in BJP-ruled Karnataka in August 2009 when eighteen-year-old Silija Raj ran away with twenty-four-year-old Asgar Nazar from Chamarajnagar, a small Karnataka town around 180 km

Figure 3.5 Poster stating that 'Garba Venues' should only allow Hindus

from Bangalore. A division bench of the court ordered a CID probe in October 2009 to investigate cases of 21,890 'missing' girls between 2005–2009 and found that 229 girls had married men of other faith, but conversion had occurred only in sixty-three cases. Cases of inter-religious marriages were reported from across the board. In its report on 31 December 2009, then CID DGP D.V. Guruprasad told the high court: 'There is no organised attempt by any group of individuals to entice girls/women belonging to Hindu or Christian religions to marry Muslim boys with the aim of converting them to Islam'. Not only did the Karnataka high court finally close the investigations into 'love jihad' in November 2013 after no evidence of any such conspiracy was found, the high court said Silija Raj was free to go anywhere she wished. She chose to go with her husband.[24] In 2012, the Kerala police categorically declared that 'love jihad' was a 'campaign with no substance', and instead brought legal proceedings against the website hindujagruti.org for spreading religious hatred and false propaganda.

The notorious Meerut gang-rape and forced conversion case, which became the headlines in 2014, took a complete U-turn.[25] The case of shooter Tara Sahdev appeared as a complex family story where her husband claimed he was born of a Sikh father and a Muslim mother and himself a late convert. In a case reported from Muzaffarnagar, the police gave a clean chit to a youth named Pervez on 7 September 2014, who was accused of kidnapping and forcibly converting an eighteen-year-old girl. The girl gave her statement in a local court stating that she had gone with Pervez of her own free will. The two had eloped on 25 August 2014, allegedly because of opposition from their families to their relationship.[26] News was spread by Hindu Rightwing organisations in Meerut on 5 September 2014 that a minor Hindu girl has been forcefully abducted for 'love jihad' by a Muslim boy. Roads were blocked, and two shops of Muslims – one a beauty salon and the other a hair dressing shop – were vandalised and robbed. The two were soon arrested, and the Hindu organisations promptly labelled it as a case of 'love jihad'. However, the girl recorded her statement with the police, in which she categorically stated that she had gone with the boy of her own free will, and the boy did not take any advantage of her. She had gone with him, thinking of making a career for herself in Mumbai.[27] So far thus there is no hard empirical evidence of 'love jihad'. If 'love jihad' is really an organised conspiracy, then is it not amazing that the CID, the courts, the police, and the governments where BJP has been in power have found no basis for such a planned 'crime'? If there is any conspiracy here, it is a conspiracy of the Hindu Right to polarise

Allegories of 'love jihad' and ghar wapsi 99

communal passions. While the poor performance of BJP in the UP by-polls made the rhetoric of 'love jihad' take a backseat, it continued to resurrect in 2015. The beginning of 2015 thus saw *Himalaya Dhvani*, a magazine of Durga Vahini, the women's wing of VHP, have on its cover the image of Kareena Kapoor, half covered in burqa (see Figure 3.6).

But there are various crack and fissures in such rhetoric, which I will discuss in the last section of the chapter.

Figure 3.6 Cover of the Magazine: *Himalaya Dhvani*

Love Jihad: From Conversion to Change of Country. . . .
Source: www.indiatvnews.com/entertainment/bollywood/kareena-kapoor-morphed-image-on-vhp-magazine-19814.html, accessed on 10 January 2015

Double speech of Hindutva: anti-conversion and *ghar wapsi*

Besides 'love jihad', the other rhetoric that gained momentum in the Hindutva parlance at the end of 2014 was that of *ghar wapsi*. Religious conversions and reconversions, two sides of the same coin, acquired political colours in more contentious ways. The end of 2014 saw Christmas Day attaining a different meaning for the Hindutva brigade. More than Christmas, it came to signify the birth anniversaries of Madan Mohan Malaviya, one of the stalwarts of the Hindu Mahasabha, and Atal Bihari Vajpayee, the eminent BJP leader. Equally critically, on 23 December 1926, Swami Shraddhanand, the leading ideologue of the shuddhi movement was assassinated by a Muslim fanatic, and on 25 December, a condolence motion was moved at the Guawhati session of the Congress. This day was given new political shades in 2014, when the Dharm Jagran Samiti declared that on that day it would 'reconvert' 4,000 Christians and 1,000 Muslim families in Aligarh. However, it was forced to drop it due to pressures from a Parliament in session as well as other protests. The twin strategies of anti-conversion and *ghar wapsi* have had a long history and past. Through such moves Hindu organisations state that they wish to reclaim the 'victims' and protect the 'faithful'. Just as shuddhi became an instrument for Hindu communal mobilisation in the early twentieth century, attempts were made at the end of 2014 to make *ghar wapsi* fulfil the same role in the present political scenario.

The combination of anti-conversion rhetoric with that of *ghar wapsi* at the end of 2014 and in the beginning of 2015 has powerfully invoked metaphors of exile and home. Ghar wapsi has been flaunted as a return to the authentic origin, the starting point, the abode of birth. It produces and enforces notions of a primordial religious identity, whereby all and everyone are declared Hindus. Thus states Praveen Togadia of the VHP: 'At a point of time, the entire world was Hindu. There were 700 crore Hindus, and now there are just 100 crore'.[28] The shift from the whole world to the Hindu nation is swift, as *ghar wapsi* denationalises Islam and Christianity, facilitating their 'othering'. In the name of a home, a nation, a boundary, it adopts a language where all other religions are seen as anti-national, as falling in the domain of an exile. Anti-conversion combined with *ghar wapsi* thus signals for the Hindu Right a shift from anti-national to national, from exile to home, from forced to voluntary, from people to citizens, from false to truth, from constructed to original, from unnatural to natural, from outsider to insider. Since one is returning to one's origins, all other 'deviations' are declared null and void. The invocation of metaphors of enemies and robbers on the one hand and brothers, sons, and home on the other has been a hallmark of such reconversion and anti-conversion campaigns. Ghar wapsi resonates with nostalgia – a homecoming, a cocoon, an insulated space that protects and shelters by taking one to his/her supposed roots. It is indeed ironical that while Hinduism too has carried on conversions, it is shown as totally unacceptable by using the euphemism of reconversion. Through such an analogy, even while propagating conversion, the Hindu Right escapes its charge, and easily insists simultaneously on anti-conversion laws.

However, the claim of 'origins' and of 'home' was powerfully challenged historically by various Dalit and anti-caste ideologues, like Phule, Periyar, and Ambedkar,[29] and in UP by Achutanand, Chandrikaprasad Jigyasu, and Swami Bodhanand Mahasatveer.[30] In various ways they rejected Vedic Hinduism and constructed a pre-Aryan identity of Dalits as the original inhabitants – Adi Hindus – of India. They claimed that not only were they the original inhabitants, and thus had prior rights over its land and territory, but also that there was a glorious history of Adi Hindu monarchy without caste, which was destroyed by Brahmanical Hinduism. They further stated that Dalits had been conquered by upper caste Hindus through chicanery and cunningness. While examining *adivasi* conversions in Orissa, Biswamoy Pati pointed out that we need to seriously question if they were 'born as Hindus'.[31] These put a serious question mark over the supposed primordial religious identity of India's inhabitants.

Related to this is another paradox in the anti-conversion/reconversion rhetoric. Arguments of lure, force, fraudulence, and material gains have been constantly made in anti-conversion laws and by the Hindu Right when opposing conversions. This is also one of the chief arguments in the 'love jihad' rhetoric, where it is stated by Hinduvaadis that while they have 'no objection' to voluntary conversion, they are explicitly opposed to 'forced' conversion. Reconversion, however, is claimed as a voluntary return, by choice. In the same breath, conversion is upheld as illegitimate in one case and legitimate in another, forcible in one case, voluntary in another. But how can a religion, which one is born in, without any choice in the matter, be regarded as voluntary? And how do we define force or material gains? If one is converting in the hope of a better life, education and dignity, and material progress, what is wrong with that? Religious conversions have traditionally been and continue to be one of the common expedients of those who are on the margins of Hinduism to reject hierarchies and reconfigure social boundaries.[32] Historically, when Dalits, or others who have been on the margins of Hindu society (widows, low caste women, sex workers), have converted, it is often because they have felt 'lured' by the fact that it can signal some dignity, education, clothing, employment, and *roti-beti* ties for them, along with the right to inhabit unmarked bodies.[33] This radical dissent against caste discipline and writing oneself into modernity through better education and clothes – can it be called a 'luring', an implicit 'forcing'? Dilip Menon shows how 'the attraction of the lower castes for Christianity in colonial India was partly prompted by the need to move away from the cycle of oppression and inequality and also because the religion allowed for their entry into a wider public sphere, as individuals'.[34] Conversion has also been explained by historians like Gyan Pandey to refer to Dalit conversion to full formal citizenship. It also, according to him, meant a conversion to the 'modern', signified by a certain sensibility, particular kinds of dress and comportment, and particular rules of social and political engagement.[35] Asking what is so fraudulent about religious conversions, Nivedita Menon states:

> But why is religious conversion essentially different, in a democracy, from other kinds of conversion? When rival companies bid for candidates offering higher salaries and better perks, inducing them to convert from one employer to another, why is that not fraudulent? When political parties attempt to convert voters by wild promises, when Naxalites are wooed back into mainstream society by the State, when political ideologies – of the market or of Marxists, of feminists or of the Hindu Right – attempt to convert with promises of redemption and threats of various kinds, both material and spiritual – why are all these not fraudulent?[36]

She goes on to argue that the possibility of change, in this case brought through religious conversion, is central to democracy. However, conversions from Hinduism have been an anathema to Hindutva, which has come out in potent ways both in the rhetoric of 'love jihad' and *ghar wapsi*. It appears that when confronted with the phenomenon of conversion from Hinduism to Islam, especially by Hindu women, certain kinds of Hindus lose their logical faculties. The politics of cultural virginity and a myth of innocence are combined with a perceived 'illegitimacy' of the act, leading to rants of violation, invasion, seduction, and rape, which become more volatile when combined with election politics. Religious conversion may work and may not work for someone, but let anyone who is converting decide for herself/himself that. Moreover, if reconversion is indeed so 'voluntary', then why, as per a pamphlet of the VHP, does a *karya karta* require Rs 2 lakh per year to 'work on a Christian' and as much as Rs 5 lakh for a 'Muslim problem'?[37] Or what does one make when Adityanath purportedly stated in a video: 'Why are Hindu girls marrying Muslim men? It should have been probed. . . . We have decided that we will convert 100 girls of their religion if they convert one Hindu girl'.[38] The Dharma Jagran Manch stated that on 23 December 2014, the martyrdom day of Swami Shraddhanand, who was the leader of the shuddhi movement in late nineteenth–early twentieth century, they will convert Muslims to Hinduism in at least fifty locations in West UP.[39] As succinctly states Kumkum Sangari, 'The anti-conversion discourse teeters between an authenticated primordialism and an aggrandised voluntarism, and it oscillates between the two because neither can singly sustain a Hindutva agenda'.[40]

The language of *ghar wapsi* is not motivated by a desire to promote spirituality and religious values, but by a strong anti-Christian and anti-Muslim overtone and passion. Charged with a moral and communal fervour, it adopts an unrestrained anti-Christianity and anti-Islamic polemic. Simultaneously, the reconversion campaign, just like 'love jihad', is characterised by a creed of violence and Hindu masculinity. Today, with a shift in power, the political energies of Hindutva have been harnessed for even a more militant and martial public expression. The *ghar wapsi* movement repeatedly asks Hindus to avenge supposed past humiliation and historical 'wrongs' of conversion, regain courage, and become warriors of a proud Hindu race. Physical prowess is seen as a remedy for surrender, loss, and defeat. Addressing the *sant samagam* called by the Dharm Jagran Manch of the RSS at Vaishali in Bihar, BJP MP Yogi Adityanath (and now the CM of UP) gave the *mantra* of '*mala ke saath bhala*' (pray and fight) and '*shastra ke saath shaastra*' (weapons along with scriptures).[41] While conversion from Hinduism is represented as a loss of power, weakness and misery, *ghar wapsi* is imagined as a reversal of this loss and a restoration of masculine power to Hindu men.

Another common thread between 'love jihad' and *ghar wapsi* is its obsession with the numerical strength of Hindus. Numbers game, and constructed fears around it, has been central to the modern politics of Hindutva. Numerical alignments, in the name of caste or religion, are pivotal in elections as well. Religious conversions have been regarded as not only challenging an established community's assent to religious doctrines and practices, but also altering demographic equations and producing numerical imbalances. In the evocation of 'love jihad', one of the arguments given by Hindu groups has been that the conversions of Hindu women are linked with enhancing Muslim numbers.[42] Pro-Hindu organisations in 2014 claimed that forced conversions of Hindu women in the name of love were part of an international conspiracy to increase Muslim population. 'Love jihad' not only constructed a picture of numerical Muslim increase, but also lamented and mourned the potential loss of child-bearing Hindu wombs due to conversions of Hindu women to Islam, and the loss of greater control over women's reproductive capacities to enhance Hindu numbers. It is perceived by the hardliners within Hindu polity that both 'love jihad' and *ghar wapsi* can become rallying points for aligning Hindus, while also invoking fears of increasing Muslim numbers. RSS thus describes 'love jihad' as a movement to convert vulnerable Hindu girls to Islam, to decrease the population of Hindus and increase Muslim numbers in the country. The underbelly of everyday life before and after elections has tried to harp on a weird arithmetical equation, with Hindutva forces invoking their notorious slogan, which had gained momentum during the Ramjanmabhoomi campaign in the 1990s as well:

> *Ek Hindu ka Nara Hai – Hum Do, Humare Do;*
> *Jabki ek Muslim ka Nara Hai – Hum Panch, Humare Pacchis.*[43]
> (The family planning motto of a Hindu is we two, i.e. husband and wife, and our two, i.e. children. While that of a Muslim is we five, i.e. husband and his four wives, and our twenty-five, i.e. children.)

In this lament of constantly declining Hindu numbers, the twin devices of anti-conversion and reconversion are seen to increase Hindu numbers. Thus the RSS local unit in Aligarh has proudly claimed that it has carried out approximately 40,000 'reconversions' in and around Aligarh.[44] There are, however, various contradictions in such contentions. First, various statistical studies and surveys have debunked theories of declining Hindu numbers. Second, many tribal and Dalit groups have objected at various points of time to their accounting as Hindus. Third, Hindutva rhetoric conveniently includes Buddhists and Jains as part of Hinduism. Fourth, even if in some distant, remote future, Hindu numbers do decline, how is religious identity in any way going to alter our basic constitutional and democratic fabric? What is significant however is that how, through a constant harping of declining numbers, a demographic and dominant majority can portray itself as an 'endangered' minority. The number-crunching politics of Hindutva is also seen as signalling unity and consolidation among a Hindu community and nation, brushing under the carpet caste hierarchies and tensions. The twin strategies of anti-conversion/reconversion are also attempts to harden religious identities and boundaries, while undermining syncretic cultural practices and religious pluralities in our everyday life. The anxieties of the Hindu Right and a section of Hindu men have coalesced around threatened religious collectivities as well as intimate matters of family and the individual.

Fissures in Hindutva rhetoric

Both 'love jihad' and *ghar wapsi* acquired significant colours in the panorama of 2014. At the same time, fragmentary instances give us some hope, and I wish to end this chapter with three such examples. First is linked to the issue of conversions. The leading historian Richard Eaton, who has extensively worked on the subject, has effectively shown that conversions here (as elsewhere too) do not signify a passive acceptance of a monolithic, outside essence.[45] Rather, conversion to Islam and Christianity in India has entailed a creative and selective adaptation, and constant translation, whereby these religions have themselves been indigenised and 'vernacularised' according to people's needs and desires. Christian and Islamic doctrines have interacted with Dalit and tribal cosmologies, and have been molded by them. There is no fixed or unchanging essence of any religion here. Conversions have often signified mobility, flexibility, and plurality. Many in India carry within them hybrid religious identities, where burial practices, for example, coexist with Hindu marriage customs. Such pliable and ambiguous religious identities challenge campaigns like *ghar wapsi* and pronounce the continuation of syncretic practices and plural religious customs. Conversions are important expedients to reject hierarchies and refigure boundaries and must continue for our religious freedom. Islam and Christianity have as much roots in India as Hinduism, where each has been creatively molded and indigenised (and rejected) by various communities. Those who have lived for centuries with syncretic religious practices – they too are as much at 'home' as any other.

The second example I wish to take is from a completely different plane. Another happening amidst the cries of 'love jihad' and *ghar wapsi* in 2014 itself, at the level of popular cultural space, was the launch of *Zindagi*, an Indian entertainment television channel, on 23 June 2014, which began telecasting cross-border serials from Pakistan. The channel captured our imagination, and Fawad Khan, a Pakistani Muslim male, became an endearing and enduring metaphor, a fascinating icon, the new heartthrob and fantasy of Indian girls and women. Fan mails for Fawad Khan poured over websites. One of them said:

> You have to be living under a rock if you have not heard of Fawad Khan yet. . . . Did your mother just tell you she has a crush on Fawad Khan? Your female colleagues are probably head-over-heels in love with him too. . . . Women maybe have more photos of Fawad Khan in their phones than their own.

Describing the film *Khubsoorat*, in which Fawad Khan starred, Shobhaa De articulated: 'So, who is the real "khubsoorat" in the movie. . . . Any guesses? You've got it! It's a slim, bearded bloke from across the border. . . . He's as yummy as those irresistible Lahori kebabs, and *desi* ladies want him'.[46] The juxtaposing of disjunctive phenomena of Fawad Khan with cries of 'love jihad' and *ghar wapsi* can be a stimulating endeavour to expose the fissures in the Hindutva rhetoric. While the 'love jihad' and *ghar wapsi* hysterics have been crying themselves hoarse, trying to draw sharper religious and national boundaries, the phenomenon of Fawad Khan to an extent signifies a religious and national liminality that can stump the hysteria over such constructed bogies. The representation of Fawad Khan on the one hand, and the construction of 'love jihad' and *ghar wapsi* on the other, in very different ways are part of fictive imaginations, myths and rhetoric, spectacles, and obsessions. At the same time, they undercut each other, reflecting desires on the one hand and Hindu fears on the other. Love for Fawad Khan personifies allegories of intimacy and romance, while the 'love jihad' and *ghar wapsi* campaigns embody hatred and anxieties. One contests power, the other attempts to reinstate it. The metaphor of Fawad Khan discursively bridges the conventional physical and psychological distance between Hindu/Muslim, Indian/Pakistani, signifying a mobility which defies any tantrums of the Hindutva brigade. It also hints that there are Indians who are nonchalant and apathetic to the delusional constructions of the 'evil' and 'monstrous' Muslim male, manufactured by 'love jihad' and *ghar wapsi*. Khan as a Muslim male idol defies stereotypes of Muslim men or any negative–positive binaries. The contrasts here between the romantic and the pathological, the hero and the villain, the icon and the devil, the defender and the predator bring out the paradoxes of our society.[47]

My third example draws from the substantial increase in inter-caste and inter-religious romances, bonding and marriages, particularly in the past few decades, in spite of several adversities, which implicitly challenge certain customs and norms and reveal indifference among a section of Indian women and men to pressures of conforming to community and family expectations. Inter-communal couples question the authority of family and religious communities in determining their life and upset relentless communal polarisation.[48] These localised and embodied practices require great social courage and have deep social ramifications as they show how some people, particularly women, have taken control over their lives. Such women and men implicitly place themselves between two worlds, deftly dealing with both of them and not giving a damn about the shouts of 'love jihad' and *ghar wapsi*. It is their

Allegories of 'love jihad' and ghar wapsi   107

ambiguous and ephemeral existence, and their 'instability' as defined and fixed religious and national beings that is a source of hope. In spite of all threats and campaigns against inter-religious and inter-caste love, and against conversions, such couplings have continued to increase in number in India. As Nivedita Menon says, 'Young men and women *are* falling in love, across caste and religious divides, and this is rocking the foundations of caste and religious identity'. She further states succinctly: 'Even in these terrible times, every single day, another young woman decides to risk her very life on the strength of a glance, another young man defies death for a smile. Subversive youthful desire – it's enough to cheer up the most jaded of middle aged anti-romantics!'[49] Moreover, as Janaki Nair says, 'Indian women have taken control of their lives at a much faster pace than expected' and they are 'no longer passive bearers of caste, religious, ethnic or other meaning – but the makers of meaning'.[50] Ambedkar upheld inter-caste marriages as one way to annihilate caste, since it produced fissures in maintenance of caste purity and control of women's sexuality. Inter-religious marriages too perhaps can be a way to produce cracks in orthodox Hindu mandates, create ripples in codified definitions and ruptures in a certain Hindu logic. Such an exercise of choice, even when partial, can perhaps also aid a transformative and transgressive politics of intimate religious rights. The recalcitrance of love, inter-religious marriage, and desires to improve one's position can throw up emancipatory possibilities of rights, where highly ritualised acts of conversion and marriage could at times become a metaphor for a new vocabulary of body, of interiority, of subjectivity.

Conclusion

Campaigns like 'love jihad' and *ghar wapsi* signify a shift of electoral politics to the Right and the marginalisation of non-communal forces, whereby discourses of religious 'othering' and hatred have persisted and gained a new lease of life. However, it is not just the ascent of Hindu Right in Indian politics that tells us the full story of 2014. The continuation of hybrid and syncretic religious–cultural practices, our love for Fawad Khan, and the openness of a section of people to inter-religious romances show that in spite of all campaigns, religious divisions have become muddier and more fluid, as a section of Indians are discarding binary categories and fixed identities. They also remind us of the precariousness of Hindutva designations, and suggest that dominant investments of Hindutva in asserting the primacy of Hindu men and the mastery of Hindu masculinity are under threat from within. A politics that imposes sexual prescriptions and designates which partners are appropriate and legitimate, or a rabble rousing campaign against conversion and for reconversion, is no longer tenable. Certain aspects of popular culture, our everyday practices, and, above all, love can dismantle the wild allegations of 'love jihad' and *ghar wapsi*. Such markers and spaces need to be taken seriously for what they tell us about our society. The dynamics of heterogeneities are knocking on our doors, whereby processes of exclusion, and by implication inclusion, which define homogenous identities, have developed many cracks and fissures. The links between sex and segregation, between control of women and Hindu supremacy are being subverted in our everyday lives and actions. Our syncretic practices, our love for Fawad Khan, and our inter-religious romances symbolise religious crossings, transgressions of taboos, and flirtations with moral castigations, imperilling the Hindutva order and threatening their constructed religious and cultural 'purities'.

Notes

1 A version of the article was earlier published in *Archiv Orientalni*, Vol. 84, No. 2 (2016), 291–316.
2 Sankaran Krishna, 'A Chronicle of an Event Foretold?' 1 June 2014, Kafila, http://kafila.org/2014/06/01/a-chronicle-of-an-event-foretold-sankaran-krishna/, downloaded on 16 June 2015.
3 Krishna, 'A Chronicle of an Event Foretold?'
4 Atiq Khan, ' "Love Jihad" Hurts Women's Dignity: RSS', *The Hindu*, 21 October 2014.
5 *Panchjanya*, 7 September 2014; *Organiser*, 7 September 2014.
6 Charu Gupta, *Sexuality, Obscenity, Community: Women, Muslims and the Hindu Public in Colonial India* (New Delhi: Permanent Black, 2001), 222–320; idem, 'Hindu Women, Muslim Men: Love Jihad and Conversions', *Economic and Political Weekly*, Vol. 44, No. 51 (2009), 13–15.
7 4/1927, Home Political, National Archives of India.
8 For details: Gupta, *Sexuality*, 223–229.
9 Quoted in Lalmani Verma, 'BJP MLA Call for "love jihad" Mahapanchayat', *The Indian Express*, 8 September 2014, 1–2.
10 Construction of such stereotypes have had larger historical roots. For details, see Vasudha Dalmia, *The Nationalization of Hindu Traditions: Bharatendu Harischandra and Nineteenth-century Banaras* (New Delhi: Oxford University Press, 1997); Sudhir Chandra, *The Oppressive Present: Literature and Social Consciousness in Colonial India* (New Delhi: Oxford University Press, 1992); Meenakshi Mukherjee, *Realism and Reality: The Novel and Society in India* (New Delhi: Oxford University Press, 1985).
11 Quoted in Lalmani Verma, 'BJP Puts UP Campaign Into Gear, Asks, "Does religion give them licence to rape?"', *The Sunday Express*, 24 August 2014, 1.

Allegories of 'love jihad' *and* ghar wapsi   109

12 Quoted in Varghese K. George, 'BJP, Parivar Outfits to Intensify Campaign Against "love jihad"', *The Hindu*, 8 August 2014, 1.
13 Anjali Modi, '"Love Jihad": The Sangh Parivar's Sexual Politics by Another Name', *Caravan*, 29 August 2014, www.caravanmagazine.in/vantage/love-jihad-sangh-parivar-sexual-politics-another-name.
14 Sagarika Ghose, 'Ishq, ishq, ishq: Love Can Build a New Social Contract', *Times of India*, 7 September 2014, 10.
15 Modi, ' "Love Jihad": The Sangh Parivar's Sexual Politics'.
16 Lalmani Verma, 'Citing "love jihad", Sangh Groups in UP Unite to "fight"', *The Indian Express*, 31 August 2014, 1–2.
17 Vasudha Venugopal, 'The Monk Who Sold a Love "cure"', *Sunday Times of India*, 10 August 2014.
18 Quoted in Varghese K. George, 'Incongruity in Meerut Victim's Story', *The Hindu*, 8 August 2014, 11.
19 Tanika Sarkar, 'Love, Control and Punishment', *The Indian Express*, 16 October 2014, 11.
20 'Key Findings of the Voice of Justice Report', *Organiser*, 7 September 2014.
21 Quoted in T.A. Johnson and Lalmani Verma, 'Who Loves Love Jihad', *The Indian Express*, 7 September 2014, 13.
22 Also see Milind Ghatwai, 'After BJP MLA's Call for Ban on Muslim Men in Garbas, Orders Go Out: No ID Cards, No Entry', *Indian Express*, 20 September 2014, 1–2.
23 Santosh Desai, 'A Jihad Against Love?', *The Times of India*, 1 September 2014.
24 T.A. Johnson and Lalmani Verma, 'Who Loves Love Jihad', *The Indian Express*, 7 September 2014, 13.
25 Amit Sharma, 'Their "love jihad" Centrepiece in Tatters, Hindu Outfits See Plot in Meerut U-Turn', *Indian Express*, 14 October 2014, 1–2.
26 Staff Reporter, 'Love jihad: Girl Denies Conversion', *The Hindu*, 8 September 2014, 1.
27 Amit Sharma, 'BJP Men Beat Up Muslims Over Elopement', *The Indian Express*, 7 September 2014, 10; M. Kaunain Sheriff and Amit Sharma, 'Two School Students With Bollywood Dreams Versus "love jihad" Nightmare', *The Indian Express*, 11 September 2014, 1–2.
28 Quoted in Express News Service, 'VHP Presses for Anti-Conversion Law', *The Indian Express*, 15 December 2014.
29 Anupama Rao, *The Caste Question: Dalits and the Politics of Modern India* (New Delhi: Permanent Black, 2009); Eleanor Zelliot, *From Untouchable to Dalit: Essays of Ambedkarite Movement* (New Delhi: Manohar, 1992).
30 See Nandini Gooptu, *The Politics of the Urban Poor in Early Twentieth Century India* (Cambridge: Cambridge University Press, 2001); Ramnarayan S. Rawat, *Reconsidering Untouchability: Chamars and Dalit History in North India* (New Delhi: Permanent Black, 2012).
31 Biswamoy Pati, *Identity, Hegemony and Resistance: Towards the Social History of Conversions in Orissa, 1800–2000* (New Delhi: Three Essays Collective, 2003).
32 Gauri Vishwanathan, *Outside the Fold: Conversion, Modernity, and Belief* (Princeton: Princeton University Press, 1998); Sathianathan Clarke, *Dalits and Christianity: Subaltern Religion and Liberation Theology in*

India (New Delhi: Oxford University Press, 1998); John C. B. Webster, *The Dalit Christians: A History* (New Delhi: ISPCK, 1994), 2nd edn; Geoffrey A. Oddie, *Religious Conversion Movements in South Asia: Continuities and Change 1800–1900* (Surrey: Curzon Press, 1997); Charu Gupta, 'Intimate Desires: Dalit Women and Religious Conversions in Colonial India', *The Journal of Asian Studies*, Vol. 73, No. 3 (2014), 661–687.
33. Rao, *The Caste Question*; Gupta, 'Intimate Desires'.
34. Dilip Menon, 'Religion and Colonial Modernity: Rethinking Belief and Identity', *Economic and Political Weekly*, Vol. 37, No. 17, 27 April 2002, 1662 [1662–1667].
35. Gyanendra Pandey, 'The Time of the Dalit Conversion', *Economic and Political Weekly*, 6 May 2006, 1779–1788.
36. Nivedita Menon, '"The Meerut Girl", Desperate Hindutvavaadis and Their Jihad Against Love', 14 October 2014, Kafila http://kafila.org/2014/10/14/the-meerut-girl-desperate-hindutvavaadis-and-their-jihad-against-love/, downloaded on 26 October 2014.
37. Quoted in Pragya Kaushika, 'Wary Aligarh Christians, Muslims Seek Security', *The Indian Express*, 14 December 2014.
38. Quoted in Piyush Shrivastava, 'Video Stirs "love jihad" Controversy: BJP's Adityanath Filmed Saying Hindus Should Convert "100 Muslim girls" for Every One of Theirs', *Mail Online India*, 27 August 2014.
39. Varghese K. George, 'BJP, Parivar Outfits to Intensify Campaign Against "love jihad"', *The Hindu*, 8 August 2014, 1.
40. Kumkum Sangari, 'Gender Lines: Personal Laws, Uniform Laws, Conversion', *Social Scientist*, Vol. 27, Nos. 5–6, May–June 1999, 39 [17–61].
41. Quoted in Santosh Singh, 'Babri Demolition Was Show of Hindu Unity, Don't Stop ghar wapsi: Adityanath to Govt', *The Indian Express*, 15 December 2014.
42. For a powerful critique, see Mohan Rao, 'Love Jihad and Demographic Fears', *Indian Journal of Gender Studies*, Vol. 18, No. 3 (2011), 425–430.
43. Anon., *Chetavani-2: Desh Khatre Mein* [Pamphlet] (New Delhi: Vishwa Hindu Parishad, 1990).
44. Pragya Kaushika, 'Don't Want a Religion That Only Rejects Us, Say the Aligarh Dalits on RSS List', *The Indian Express*, 14 December 2014.
45. Richard Eatron, 'Comparative History as World History: Religious Conversion in Modern India', *Journal of World History*, Vol. 8, No. 2 (1997), 243–271.
46. Shobhaa De, 'Pakistan's Fawad Khan: India's Hearthrob', www.ndtv.com/opinion/pakistans-fawad-khan-indias-heartthrob-670680 (accessed 10 October 2014).
47. For details: Charu Gupta, 'Our Love for Fawad', *Indian Express*, 30 October 2014, 11.
48. Jyoti Punwani, 'Myths and Prejudices About "Love Jihad"', *Economic and Political Weekly*, Vol. XLIX, No. 42, 18 October 2014, 12–15.
49. Menon, '"The Meerut Girl"'.
50. Janaki Nair, 'Why Love Is a Four Letter Word', *The Hindu*, 6 October 2014.

4 Understanding the BJP's victory in Uttar Pradesh

Sudha Pai and Avinash Kumar

The 2014 Lok Sabha election introduced significant shifts in Uttar Pradesh (UP), a key state that reflects the sweeping political change in the country. UP was the electoral battleground from where two principal contenders – Narendra Modi and Rahul Gandhi – fought the election. The Bharatiya Janata Party (BJP) won a spectacular victory in all regions of the state, reducing the Congress and the Samajvadi Party (SP) to their family strongholds. It also penetrated deep into the backward and Dalit base of the two well-established and strong identity-based parties, the SP and the Bahujan Samaj Party (BSP).

This chapter seeks to understand the reasons underlying the spectacular victory of the BJP in UP. We propose that its victory was due to revival of its organisation and social base. A new leadership led by Narendra Modi and his selected aides with the support of the Sangh Parivar has been replacing the older leaders/founders of the party Atal Behari Vajpayee and L.K. Advani. Among the new generation leaders in the BJP, Modi was able to take control of the party due to his three successive victories in the Gujarat Assembly elections and his close association with the RSS. In fact, we argue that in 2014, it was *not so much a BJP as a Modi victory in UP* due to a two-pronged, well-organised and strategised campaign by him and his confidante Amit Shah, using both Hindutva and development. Modi stressed the lack of development under UPA-II and the ruling SP in UP and promised its rapid development based on the 'Gujarat Model'. The party cadres, following a different path, employed communal strategies – used at times by Modi himself – to create a broad Hindu vote bank encompassing the upper castes, the backwards, and also the Dalits.

The ideology of Hindutva under Modi has undergone change despite the changing socio-political context in the country in the wake of globalisation and the rise of a new and more demanding aspirational middle class. While under Vajpayee, development and economic reforms was prioritised over religious mobilisation, as evident during the 1999 and 2004 national elections. Modi, in addition to addressing the aspirations of the frustrated young generation of voters due to the lack of development in UP, also revived religious mobilisation on issues such as the Ram Mandir in 2014. Further, towards the end, it was also realised that it was important to address in a more inclusive manner development of all sections of the population, not only the Hindus.

However, an equally important factor affecting the election was the changed political context in UP skilfully harnessed by Modi. The weakening of the two well-established, state-level parties are particularly important. The ruling SP suffered from slow development, poor governance, and failure to control communal riots, while the BSP's popularity fell due to its Sarvajan experiment leading to its defeat in the 2012 Assembly elections. Decline of the two major state parties provided Modi room to mount his campaign. Hence, we argue that two factors were responsible for the victory of the BJP: first, longer term factors such as the continuing decline of the Congress and, second, weakness of state-level parties visible in their lacklustre campaigns. However, the victory of the BJP also lies more importantly in the ideological and organisational changes introduced by its new leadership and their long, well-organised and planned campaign. Thus it is through the lens of the new 'avatar' of the BJP that we attempt to understand its phenomenal success vis-à-vis the poor performance of other parties in UP.

Analysing the results

Victory of the BJP in UP

The magnitude of the victory of the BJP was surprising as the party has been in decline in UP from the mid-1990s after the Babri Masjid issue lost importance following its destruction. As Table 4.1 shows, its seats in Parliament dropped from fifty-seven in the 1996 to twenty-nine in the 1999 and ten in the 2009 Lok Sabha elections. In the 2012 UP Assembly elections, the party had won only forty-seven seats (with barely 15 per cent of the total votes polled) and was forced to forfeit deposits in 229 seats. In contrast, in the 2014 election the BJP obtained seventy-one seats with 42.3 per cent of the votes and its ally Apna Dal (AD) won two seats in eastern UP. It also stood second in all the seven constituencies that it lost (Figure 4.1). In terms of Assembly segments, together with the AD, it gained the highest number of votes in 337 out of 403 Assembly constituencies and finished as the trailing party in another sixty-three seats (Figure 4.2). Together they swept nearly 84 per cent of the Assembly segments of UP.

Table 4.1 Position of parties in the Lok Sabha elections in up since 1989

Name of the party	2009 Won (Contested) Vote %	2004 Won (Contested) Vote %	1999 Won (Contested) Vote %	1998 Won (Contested) Vote %	1996 Won (Contested) Vote %	1991 Won (Contested) Vote %	1989 Won (Contested) Vote %
BSP	20 (80) –	19 (80) 24.67%	14 (85) 22.08%	4 (85) 20.9%	6 (85) 20.61%	1 (67) 8.7%	2 (75) 9.93%
BJP	10 (71) –	10 (77) 22.17%	29 (77) 27.64%	57 (82) 36.49%	52 (83) 33.44%	51 (84) 32.82%	8 (31) 7.58%
INC	21 (69) –	9 (73) 12.04%	10 (76) 14.72%	0 6.02%	5 (85) 8.14%	5 (80) 18.02%	15 (84) 31.77%
SP	23 (75) 23.25%	35 (68) 26.74%	26 (84) 24.06%	20 (81) 28.7%	16 (64) 20.84%	JD 22 (73) 21.27% Janata Party 4 (81) 10.84%	Janata Dal 54 (69) 35.9%

Source: Election Commission of India (*henceforth referred as ECI*)

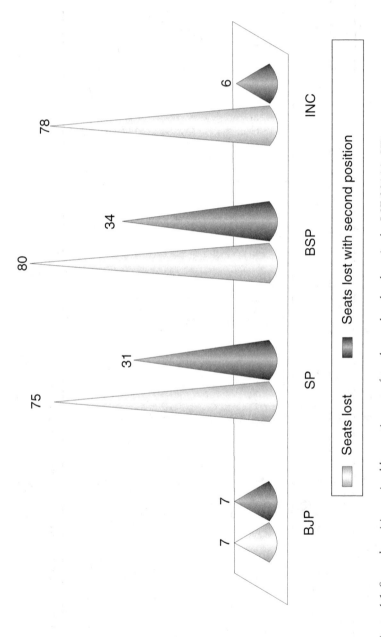

Figure 4.1 Second position gained by parties out of total seats lost by them in the LSE 2014 in UP

Source: Compiled from the data of the State Election Commission, UP

Understanding the BJP's victory in UP 115

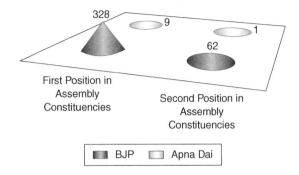

Figure 4.2 Position of BJP and its ally (Apna Dal) in the Assembly segments during the LSE 2014 in UP

Source: Compiled from the data of the State Election Commission, UP

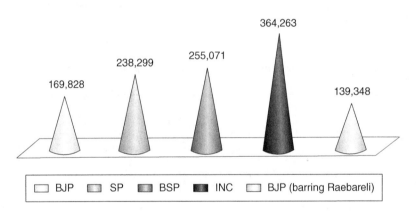

Figure 4.3 Average loss margin

Source: Compiled from the data of the State Election Commission, UP

Moreover, as Figure 4.3 shows, the BJP had the lowest average margin of loss (169,828 votes). This declines sharply if we leave the disproportionate margin of loss for BJP candidate (more than 3.5 lakh votes) contesting against Sonia Gandhi, from Rae Bareli.

The BJP gained, as the Lokniti-CSDS NES in Table 4.2 reveals, substantial votes from all caste groups over the 2009 elections – over

70 per cent of the Brahmins and other upper castes, 60 per cent of the OBCs, 53 per cent of the Kurmis, and 45 per cent of the other Dalits – cutting into the vote share of all parties (Verma, Beg and Kumar 2014). The study points to no clear class factor. Voters of all ages, educational backgrounds, economic statuses, and genders supported the BJP and its prime ministerial candidate Modi. The highest support (47 per cent) came from the first-time voters (18–22 years) (ibid).

Defeat of other parties in UP

The Congress party, which had obtained twenty seats and 12.04 per cent in the 2009 Lok Sabha elections, reached a historic low in 2014 winning only two family seats, Rae Bareli and Amethi, held by Sonia Gandhi and Rahul Gandhi, respectively. It finished at second position in less than 10 per cent of the seats (Figure 4.1) and gained only 7.5 per cent of the total votes polled. Its average margin of loss (364,263 votes) was the highest (Figure 4.3) and it was confined to only forty-five

Table 4.2 Support to various political parties across castes/communities in 2014

Castes/Communities	Congress +RLD 2014	Swing from 2009	BJP+AD 2014	Swing from 2009	BSP 2014	Swing from 2009	SP 2014	Swing from 2009
Brahmins	11	−20	72	28	5	−4	5	0
Rajputs	7	−9	77	33	5	−2	8	−4
Other Upper Castes	9	−16	76	20	3	−8	7	−1
Yadavs	8	−2	27	21	3	−2	53	−20
Kurmis/Koeis	16	−12	53	35	4	−14	17	−1
Other OBCs	8	−9	60	32	11	−8	13	−12
Jatavs	2	−2	18	14	68	−16	4	−1
Other Dalits	4	−12	45	37	29	−35	10	0
Muslims	11	−14	10	7	18	0	58	28
Others	10	−8	51	31	20	−3	17	−2

Source: NES 2014 conducted by Lokniti-CSDS (Verma, Beg and Kumar, 2014)

Note: Sample size 2324. Votes in per cent and swing in percentage points. Figures rounded off

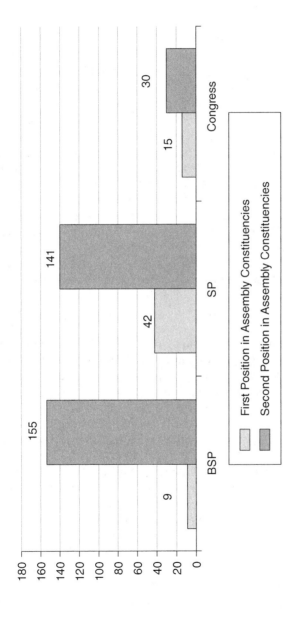

Figure 4.4 Position of non-NDA parties in the Assembly segments in UP in LE 2014

Source: Compiled from the data of the State Election Commission, UP

Assembly segments (Figure 4.4). Congress candidate in Varanasi, pitted against Modi, finished a distant third, forfeiting his deposit. The party lost the confidence of all sections that had supported it during the 2009 Lok Sabha elections (Table 4.2, column 3).

The reasons for the collapse of the Congress lie in the deep decline of the organisation and social base of the party in UP since the late 1980s. Efforts made first in 1998 by Sonia Gandhi and in the 2000s by Rahul Gandhi to revive the party in UP have yielded little success (Pai 2013). They faced an uphill task as the party had no social base or structural linkages between grassroots workers and the state leadership. Massive organisational changes were attempted to infuse young blood, reduce endemic factionalism, build disciplined cadres, and identify key constituencies where it could concentrate its strength in elections. However, rebuilding its Brahmin-Muslim-Dalit base proved difficult as these groups had shifted to newer parties in the state.

In the 2014 elections apart from the anti-incumbency against UPA-II, Rahul Gandhi, and his select team in UP failed to provide leadership and direction. The selection of candidates was poor, the campaign remained lacklustre, and the party's unwillingness to declare Rahul Gandhi as the prime ministerial candidate also proved unpopular. The attempt to form a national alliance with the BSP in January 2014 did not materialise with Mayawati preferring to contest the elections alone. Nor did the decision to provide reservation to Jats in UP and neighbouring states help the party in western UP. In fact, in Amethi, a stronghold of the Gandhi family, Modi's belligerent campaign was able to swing votes towards the BJP candidate Smriti Irani, a new entrant into politics, reducing Rahul Gandhi's victory margin from 370,198 in 2009 to 107,903 votes.

With both the Congress and BJP in decline in the 1990s, it was the SP and BSP, two strong identity-based, parties that dominated UP politics in the 2000s (Table 4.1). Until the 2012 Assembly elections, people had showed faith in the larger backward class leadership, and had rejected the manifestations of both the national parties (Kumar 2012). SP and BSP together won over 300 seats (i.e. 75 per cent) in first position and nearly two-third (BSP at 210 seats and SP at 77) even at the second position, leaving only marginal space for all others. However, both performed badly in 2014. The SP obtained only five family seats, all by narrow margins.[1] Out of total seats lost (seventy-four), it finished as the trailing party in thirty-one Parliamentary seats and its average margin of loss was significant (see Figures 4.1 and 4.3). In Assembly segments, despite being the ruling party in the state with 226 MLAs, it gained the highest number of votes in only forty-two seats and remained the trailing party in 141 (see Figure 4.4). It could gain only 53 per cent of its core Yadav vote which was 20 per cent less than 2009 and lost considerable support among all other sections of the backwards (Table 4.2).

Mulayam Singh Yadav formed the SP in 1992 by uniting socialist groups, agrarian interests, and the BCs combined with supported by the Muslim community unhappy with the Ram Mandir movement. By the early 2000s the SP faced decline due to its inability to homogenise all sections of the backwards and its internal decay into a family fiefdom with criminal links and numerous factions. More recently, there has been disappointment with Akhilesh Yadav appointed as Chief Minister after the victory in 2012, as soft and inexperienced, unable to maintain law and order, provide clean governance or development, or maintain control over an internally divided party (Pai 2014). Consequently the SP lost the confidence of both the Muslims and the Hindus who, disliking the support given by the SP to the former, moved towards the BJP. It's increased support among the Muslims could not get translated into seats.

The BSP despite gaining almost 20 per cent of the votes in UP could not win even a single seat. Its average margin of loss was over 250,000 votes (see Figure 4.3). It gained 7.22 lakh more votes in 2014 compared to the 2009 polls, spread over forty-six seats across the state. Its vote share fell primarily in the western UP and some parts of Bundelkhand.

By securing second position in thirty-four constituencies, as shown in Figure 4.4, the BSP was the biggest challenge to the 'Modi wave' in UP. It also performed well in all the reserved constituencies, increasing its vote share in fourteen out of seventeen and was the trailing party in eleven seats (Figure 4.5). In five districts, which have over 30 per cent Scheduled Caste population (Kaushambi, Sitapur, Hardoi, Unnao, and Rai Barely), BSP increased its absolute votes in all by significant margins except Rai Bareli, won by Sonia Gandhi (Figure 4.6). Yet, there was a significant shift of the BSP's Dalit vote base over the 2009 national elections towards the BJP: 16 per cent of the Jatavs and 35 per cent of the other Dalits. It also lost the support of all other social groups particularly the MBCs and its Muslim vote base remained almost the same as in 2009. But detailed analysis would show that the party's Dalit base remains secure despite some drop in votes. The party could not translate votes into seats due to multi-cornered contests in a first-past-the post system (Pai 2014).

The defeat of the BSP in the 2014 elections is mainly due to the manner in which the party's mobilisational/electoral strategies have evolved in recent years. In the 1990s the BSP attempted to widen its social base by giving tickets to the backwards and upper castes (Pai 2002). After the mid-2000s, based on its *Sarvajan* strategy, it began to directly mobilise the Brahmins and upper castes, Muslims, and MBCs to vote for the party, promising them a share in positions of power and the benefits of economic development, which provided it a majority in the 2007 elections.

Once in power, Mayawati attempted to implement an inclusive agenda covering the needs of all social groups, instead of solely Dalit-oriented policies, as in the past. Since the party had captured power alone after many years of struggle, Dalits expected that their needs would be given priority. But the government's inability to fulfil the developmental needs and aspirations of all sections of Dalits led to unhappiness among them. In fact, balancing the aspirations and providing equal distribution of resources between upper and lower castes and between Dalit sub-castes became difficult for Mayawati. Subsequently, there developed anger against the BSP among some sections of the Dalits and they started moving towards the BJP.

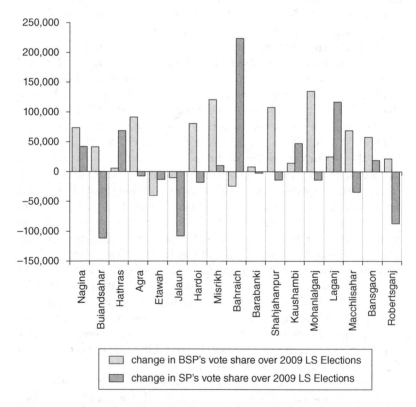

Figure 4.5 Change in BSP's and SP's Votes Share in LSE 2014 over LSE 2009

Source: Compiled from the data of the State Election Commission, UP

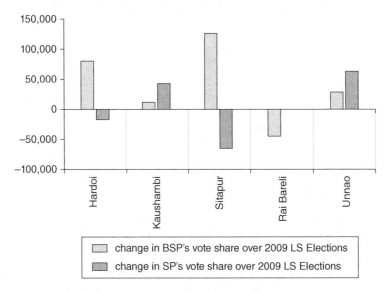

Figure 4.6 Change in absolute vote share of BSP and SP in constituencies with more than 30 per cent of the SC population

Source: Compiled from the data of the State Election Commission, UP

Analysing the BJP's victory

The BJP, aware of the importance of UP if it was to capture power at the centre in 2014, began preparations in the state over a year in advance. The electoral campaign began with the shifting of Amit Shah from Gujarat to UP to be in charge of party campaign in early May 2013.[2] This was followed by the announcement of Narendra Modi as the BJP's prime ministerial candidate in September 2013, and closer to the elections his decision to contest from Varanasi. The spectacular performance of the BJP in UP, according to Shah, was the 'cumulative effect of a host of factors'.[3] However, it can be traced to reorientation of the Hindutva ideology and revamping of its organisation which enabled a well-planned campaign on the ground.

Ideological underpinnings: Hindutva redefined

In the early 1990s, during the Babri Masjid/Ram Janma Bhoomi dispute, Hindutva was conceived as a largely religious ideology used for political mobilisation and identified with mainly upper caste

Hindus. But during the 2014 electoral campaign, Modi seemed to have redefined this ideology by including rapid economic development to create a strong and stable nation and greater inclusiveness through improving the lives of all castes and communities. This does not mean that the BJP abandoned or did not use its strategy of communal mobilisation to secure the Hindu vote, but it was combined with a discourse of development, which appealed to a larger section of the electorate.

During the campaign, Modi, on several occasions criticised the role of caste in politics and countered it with his pan-India plans. This idea emerged both from his belief that in UP caste-calculations would not suffice; addressing the developmental aspirations of the electorate, particularly the younger generation, was required. Most of his speeches at rallies dealt with issues of corruption, slow growth, and poor governance, both nationally by the Congress-led UPA-II and the SP in UP. While speaking about the latter, he pointed out that availability of jobs in Gujarat attracted large number of migration workers from UP. At a rally in Bahraich on 8 November 2013 he held, 'There is no district, tehsil of UP, whose youth don't stay in Gujarat. When they can do wonders for Gujarat, UP can also utilise their skills'.[4] With development projected as the prime agenda, Modi assured them of being their 'sevak' (servant) and the nation's 'chowkidaar' (guard). Reports about development in Gujarat were also brought home by the migrant workers.[5] In this way he focused on arousing the frustrations and aspirations of voters, especially the unemployed youth in UP.

However, this does not mean that Hindutva in 2014 became free of communal and caste mobilisation. At the RSS-BJP meeting held on 9 September 2013, it became clear that the core agenda of Hindutva – the Ram Temple, Common Civil Code, and Article 370 – would be used. Unable to create state-wide communal polarisation as in 1991, the BJP-RSS cadres, which had started working on the ground much earlier, attempted to orchestrate Hindu-Muslim tension prior to the elections by taking advantage of the numerous low-key communal symbols:

- The slogan *Jai Shri Ram* was used in most of Modi's rallies.
- The choice for Modi to contest in the holy city of Varanasi was significant.
- Modi's campaign in western UP was organised by the RSS-managed Vidya Bharati educational institutions.[6]
- RSS cadres circulated magazines that held the SP responsible for the riots creating unhappiness among the Yadavs (Verma 2014).[7]

Equally important was the stage-managed confrontation over the Chaurasi Parikrama Yatra, organised by the VHP, between the SP and the BJP in August 2013, with the former banning it and the latter supporting the efforts of the VHP. The Muzzafarnagar riots provided the BJP an opportunity to mobilise all Hindus, particularly the backward castes and Dalits, who had moved following decline of the BJP and the Congress towards the SP and BSP. Amit Shah held small, quiet meetings in remote villages largely directed at Hindus to take 'revenge'. Addressing the Jats during his campaign on 4 April 2014 in Shamli village, the epicentre of the Muzaffarnagar riots, Shah reportedly said that the election, especially in western UP was 'one of honour . . . an opportunity to take revenge and to teach a lesson to people who have committed injustice'.[8] An FIR was filed by the district election officers of Shamli and Bijnor against Shah for spreading enmity based on caste and religion and a notice by the Election Commission for violating of the model code of conduct.[9]

The impact of the communal campaign on the election can be understood from the fact that all BJP leaders who were implicated in the Muzaffarnagar riots and were given tickets won their seats with large margins. The riot-affected areas that went to poll in the first phase registered the highest polling and provided the highest victory margin for BJP in the state (Figure 4.7).

For the first time in UP, no Muslim candidate was elected from the state. The BJP won all the seats where the Muslim population is more than 20 per cent and the victory margin of the party, although significant in all these seats, was the highest in constituencies with Muslim population between 20 and 30 per cent (Figure 4.8).

At the same time, Shah did not ignore the caste factor and devised strategies to reach out to the Dalit and backward caste voters. The party gave twenty-eight tickets to OBCs and importance to OBC leaders such as Kalyan Singh, Uma Bharti, Satyendra Kushwaha, Rameshwar Chaurasia, and Rajveer Singh. The party's decision to field Modi from Varanasi, projecting him as a backward caste 'chaiwala' (tea seller) and the first OBC Prime Minister helped BJP obtain OBC votes. To obtain Dalit votes, especially that of non-Jatavs (Balmiki, Pasi, Dhobi, Koris, etc. who constitute 9 per cent of the total population of UP), the BJP decided to appropriate the legacies of B.R. Ambedkar and other Dalit icons. Shah organised meetings in several Dalit villages and promised Bharat Ratna for the BSP founder, Kanshiram. Modi addressed his second 3D rally, telecasted live at several locations across India on 14 April 2014, with garlanding the statue of B.R. Ambedkar. However, the prime focus was on obtaining the support of the Most Backward Castes (MBCs), which led to the alliance with

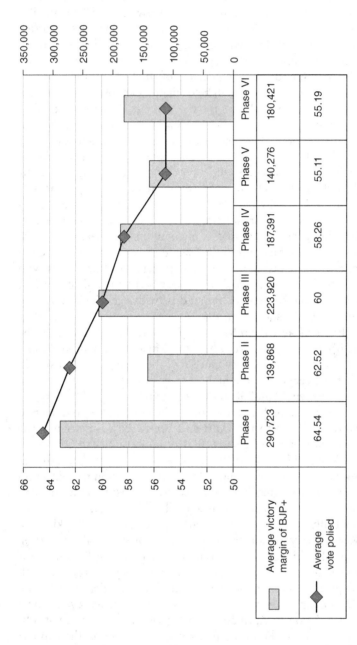

Figure 4.7 Phase-wise total vote percentage and victory margin of BJP in UP

Source: Compiled from the data of the State Election Commission, UP

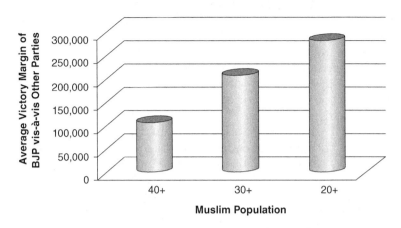

Figure 4.8 Average victory margin of BJP vis-à-vis other parties in constituencies with more than 20 per cent Muslim population in UP

Source: Compiled from the data of the State Election Commission, UP

the Apna Dal, and provided a base for Modi in Varanasi and in some other Poorvanchal seats with high BC voters.

Revamping the organisation and the campaign

The revival and redefinition of Hindutva enabled Modi to take firm control of the BJP with the help of the RSS, revamp the organisation and mount a well-planned, highly competitive and aggressive campaign organised by Amit Shah. Shah took a number of steps that considerably strengthened the organisation and improved the BJP's readiness for the election. An outsider, based on consultation with local leaders he established a core team that analysed the reasons for earlier electoral defeats. Meetings with party candidates who had lost elections enabled him to make decisions that set aside vested interests of state leaders and reach out to loyalists. Shah decided to replace veteran leaders from secure seats with new leaders loyal to Modi, and shifted the former to new constituencies; this reshuffling increased the party's chances of winning additional seats.[10] It also helped ensure that ticket distribution was based purely on a candidate's winnability factor. No candidate, except in a few places (Chandouli and Ghosi), was awarded a party ticket who had lost elections more than twice. Defunct district units were revived and committees were formed for over 80 per cent of the booths in the state.

Certain features of the campaign in UP contributed to the BJP's excellent performance. It covered the state extensively, was tightly controlled by Modi and Shah with excellent funding, and was technology driven with good media coverage. The campaign covered the state at two levels. The first organised forty massive rallies led by Modi with high media coverage across the state over a period of six months. Beginning with the *Vijay Shankhnaad* (Victory Declaration) rally at Kanpur on 19 October 2013, he addressed twelve rallies before the first phase of the election began on 10 April 2014, followed by another twenty-eight rallies spread over the next month. His campaign concluded with the *Bharat Vijay* (Conquering India) rallies at four constituencies in eastern UP, Kushinagar, Ballia, Deoria, and Robertsganj on 10 May 2014. At the end of all Modi's rallies, groups of RSS-recruited volunteers were found approaching people to gain their feedback which was then sent directly to the district RSS office (Narayan 2014).

Second, Amit Shah extensively toured the state planning Modi's campaign. He divided UP into eight zones, comprising of twenty-one clusters, of three to five seats, devising distinctive strategies for each. Young volunteers from 13,000 college campuses were recruited. For each rally people were brought from a radius of 175 km with a target set of ten people per booth. Good crowd management helped Shah consolidate the perception in the media of a 'Modi wave'. For areas beyond media's reach, classifying them as 'dark zones', Shah's team arranged more than 400 GPS-installed 'Modi-vans' with campaign material and a fourteen-minute video on his personality, speeches, and BJP's manifesto that traversed more than 100,000 villages across the state (Singh 2014). Social media such as SMS, WhatsApp, e-mail, Facebook, and Twitter were used to create a 'Modi Brand'[11] through a 'Social Media War Room' at the BJP's Lucknow headquarter manned by young volunteers from IT institutes under Sunil Bansal, a full-time RSS functionary and ABVP's national co-organisation secretary. In sum, Modi ran a hi-tech, US presidential-style, plebiscitary campaign, with extensive media coverage, in which the focus was mainly on him, leaving out the party and other senior leaders.

Conclusion

The 2014 Lok Sabha elections in UP have introduced highly significant changes in the state's politics. The election has witnessed the return of communal mobilisation and violence, largely absent since the early

1990s. Following the destruction of the Babri Masjid and the decline of the BJP, although the Ram Mandir issue was raised during elections, the two lower caste parties the SP and the BSP were able to contain the BJP and communalisation of state politics throughout the 2000s. However, numerous low-intensity, communal incidents since 2012 and the Muzaffarnagar communal violence in particular, show that political parties particularly the SP and BJP have attempted to revive/ strengthen and use their Muslim and Hindu vote banks, respectively, to create tension and win seats. An important reason for the victory of the BJP has been the communal campaign by the BJP–RSS cadres, Amit Shah and at times by Modi himself. That the chasm polarising the religious communities in UP is widening every day has been exemplified by the continual riots in sites such as Moradabad and Saharanpur (in July 2014) even after the elections. The absence of Muslim MPs from UP, a state with 18 per cent Muslim population, is itself a matter of grave concern for the democratic functioning of the state.

In keeping with the changed ideological outlook, the promise of rapid development and good governance was a central feature of Modi's campaign, contributing to the victory of the BJP. It also has its roots in the gradual weakening of identity politics in the Hindi heartland and importance being accorded to developmental aspirations of the people. There is a growing frustration and unhappiness among the youth and middle classes as they see themselves left behind compared to other states. Consequently, the two issues of identity and development now seem to coexist along a political spectrum, with both being used at different points of time by the BJP depending on need during the election campaign. The humiliating defeat of the SP and the BSP, which have strong identity bases, points in the same direction. For such parties, dependence on caste alone, ignoring development, may no longer remain an option.

The revival of the Congress party given its crushing defeat in UP seems difficult in the absence of a strong organisation, social base, and effective leadership. The low margin of victory in the Gandhi strongholds demonstrates that dynasty can no longer substitute for performance. Following the decline of the Congress and the BJP in the 2000s there was a bipolar contest and turnover of power between the two state-level parties, the SP and the BSP. Failure of the BSP's experiment of Sarvajan, the SP's poor record of governance, and Congress's inability to revive provided room for the BJP to sweep the state using a combination of both communal mobilisation and development.

However, UP has been a volatile state experiencing endemic political instability during the 1990s due to two competing strategies of caste and communal mobilisation under the BJP, the BSP, and the SP.

In contrast, during the 2000s, the electorate has chosen to give its mandate to a different party over successive elections each with its own ideology and agenda. In the 2007 Assembly elections, the state witnessed a break from the past as the BSP was voted to power with a full majority and the party completed its full term. In the 2012 Assembly elections, the SP defeated the BSP and formed the government. The 2014 national election has witnessed the defeat of both these parties and the emergence of a rejuvenated BJP under Modi.

Consequently, this has introduced a change in the state party system. While earlier the state-level parties with their specific social bases dominated state politics, in 2014, a national party, the BJP, has been able to sweep the election. The 2014 election witnessed very high levels of contestation between political parties to gain control over state politics and thereby control the centre. However, given the record of volatility that the state has witnessed over the past few decades, it remains to be seen if the BJP translates the 2014 victory into domination over state politics or if it remains short-lived.

Notes

1 Two won by Mulayam Singh Yadav, one by his daughter-in-law, and two by his nephews.
2 Modi and Shah worked together in early 1990s under the then Chief Minister of Gujarat, Keshubhai Patel. It is widely believed that Shah was instrumental in Modi's effort to dethrone Patel from Gujarat in 2001. When Modi became the Chief Minister in 2002, he appointed Shah as MoS (Home) and gave him ten portfolios, the most for any minister.
3 At the Idea Exchange programme organised by the Indian Express group on 13 May 2014. See http://indianexpress.com/article/india/politics/50-55-for-bjp-bsp-second-in-up-amit-shah/.
4 modi-charms-baharaich-vijayshankhnadrally. www.india272.com/2013/11/08/ (accessed 27 June 2014).
5 Gujarat is the third preferred destination of the migrant workers from UP after Delhi and Maharashtra (Bhagat and Mohanty 2009).
6 See 'RSS takes charge of Modi's Meerut rally', *Indian Express*, last updated on February 6, 2014. http://indianexpress.com/article/cities/mumbai/rss-takes-charge-of-modis-meerut-rally/.
7 These were *Muzaffarnagar Danga* and *Faisla Aapka? Bharat: Darool Harabya Darool Islam*.
8 He also reported to have claimed that 'When Modi becomes PM, Mullah (Muslim cleric) Mulayam's government in UP would fall on its own the very next day' (TNN 2014).
9 Ibid.
10 Rajnath Singh shifted to Lucknow, vacating the Ghaziabad seat for former Indian Army chief General V.K. Singh; Murli Manohar Joshi vacated Varanasi for Modi and shifted to Kanpur; Kalraj Mishra was sent to Deoria, while Kesarinath Tripathi, former Assembly speaker was asked to work for the party.

11 From Modi T-shirts to cups, from masks to sweets, *chai pe charcha* campaigns, and, the most impressive of all, the 3D Hologram rallies were a few of these tools.

Bibliography

Bhagat, R. B. and S. Mohanty. 2009. 'Emerging Pattern of Urbanization and the Contribution of Migration in Urban Growth in India', *Asian Population Studies*, 5(1): 5–20.

Kumar, Avinash. 2012. 'Understanding the UP Mandate', *The Hindu Business Line*, March 8.

Narayan, Badri. 2014. 'Modi's Modus Operandi in the 2014 Elections', *Economic and Political Weekly*, XLIX(20), May 17: 12–14.

Pai, Sudha. 2002. *Dalit Assertion and Unfinished Democratic Revolution: The Bahujan Samaj Party in Uttar Pradesh*. New Delhi: Sage Publications.

———. 2013. 'The Congress Party in Uttar Pradesh: Dominance, Decline, and Revival?', in Sudha Pai (ed.), *Handbook of Politics in Indian States: Region, Parties, and Economic Reforms*. New Delhi: Oxford University Press.

———. 2014. 'Uttar Pradesh: Competitive Communalism Once Again', *Economic and Political Weekly*, XLIX(15), April 12: 16–19.

———. 2014. 'Understanding the Defeat of the BSP in Uttar Pradesh National Election 2014', *Studies in Indian Politics*, 2(2):153–167.

Singh, Rohini. 2014. 'Election Results 2014: How Amit Shah Swept Uttar Pradesh for BJP', *Economic Times*, May 17.

TNN. 2014. 'EC Issues Notice to Amit Shah for Poll Code Violation', April 8.

Verma, A. K., Mirza Asmer Beg and Sudhir Kumar. 2014. 'A Saffron Sweep in Uttar Pradesh, *The Hindu*', *The Hindu*, May 23.

Verma, Lalmani. 2014. 'RSS Magazine Defends Jat Youths, Blames Akhilesh Government', *The Indian Express*, New Delhi, January 6.

5 Election 2014 and the battle for India's soul

Harsh Mander[1]

When the dust settled after the general elections of 2014, it was apparent that this had been no ordinary poll. What had been waged was no less than a battle for India's soul. No election in free India's history has left the moral, social, and political landscape of India so profoundly divided.

In India's puzzling first-past-the-post election system, less than two out of five voters backed the winning side, which was led charismatically and energetically by the leader of the Rightwing Bharatiya Janata Party (BJP), Narendra Modi. More than three out of five voted against the BJP and its allied parties. Just one in three voters supported the BJP. Yet the BJP earned a decisive majority in Parliament (even without its allies), the political support it received having surpassed all expectations. A wide range of parties retained loyal support in specific regions, but the Indian National Congress which, in a previous distinct avatar, had led India to freedom was reduced to its lowest seat tally and vote share since it was constituted 129 years ago. The Bahujan Samaj Party led by the feisty Dalit leader Mayawati Kumari won the third-highest vote share but not a single seat in Parliament. The Left parties were humiliated in their erstwhile strongholds.

However, it is important to understand that the election of 2014 was not just the emphatic victory of one political party and the humiliating defeat of others. This has happened many times in the short history of the Indian republic – in 1967, 1977, 1980, 1989, 1999, and 2004 – and is indeed the stuff of democracy. What was more significant this time was the rapture, hope, and triumphant vindication which significant segments of the population experienced in the victory of Narendra Modi, the highly controversial former Chief Minister of Gujarat – there can be no doubt that it was significantly his personal victory more than that of the political party which he led, because it was his personality which spurred such adoration among his supporters; but he was buoyed up also by the extensive mobilisation effected by cadres of the Hindu nationalist organisation, the Rashtriya Swayamsevak Sangh (RSS). Equally stark was the collective sentiment of dread, gloom, and hopelessness, as well as a profound insecurity, among millions of Modi's opponents.

The real story of the 2014 elections is of the social, and not merely the political, winners and losers – one segment of people who felt that Modi's victory signified the glorious consolidation of their own economic and social ascendancy, and another segment who felt devastated by the result, seeing in it a crushing of their dreams for themselves, their communities, and their country. For the latter, it was not the parties they supported – which many recognised to have floundered and failed them spectacularly and unforgivably – but they themselves who had been vanquished.

Who were the social winners of the 2014 elections, the people who voted for the BJP and who celebrated its conquests as their own? They included not just large numbers of India's urban, overwhelmingly caste-Hindu middle and upper classes – the most influential cheerleaders – but also people Modi himself describes as the 'neo-middle class' – the new entrants to the middle class – and the aspirational class, those who had not yet entered the middle class but were hopeful and impatient to benefit from India's growth. Many among these were first-time voters between eighteen and twenty-two years of age. In addition, the BJP benefited hugely from a unified anti-minority Hindu vote bank – there was a striking blurring of most caste lines and a significant recruitment even from among the subaltern castes, including that of Dalits in Uttar Pradesh and Bihar, against the religious minorities, especially Muslims but also of people in tribal areas, many of whom are Christians.

Who were those who perceived themselves to be the social losers of this election, many among the three out of five voters who opposed the victorious party and its allies? There was first the mass of secular Indians. This secular electorate comprises not only people from the numerically small upper-class liberal elite, but millions of ordinary Indians in the small towns and villages of the country who – in the ways they live their lives – oppose ideologies of difference and divisiveness and uphold an intensely pluralist though, simultaneously, a highly unequal civilization. The second set of losers were India's minorities, especially Muslims but also Christians, who are stunned and frightened by the scale of majoritarian consolidation, unmatched even by the aftermath of Partition and the demolition of the Babri Masjid, the two lowest points in communal relations in independent India. Many Muslim friends confessed to having wept when they heard the results. Also in dread of backlash and persecution were India's sexual minorities.

The third and the largest set of social losers were India's very poor people – migrant workers, landless farm labourers, displaced forest dwellers, farmers driven to despair and suicide, weavers and artisans threatened by extinction, women in unpaid or under-paid work, over 200 million people who still sleep hungry, over 100 million people condemned to the squalor of slums, young people who had never had the chance to enter school or continue beyond primary school, and people whom each health emergency pushes further into catastrophic penury or kills outright. They are the twenty-first-century Indians who cannot even dream of one day entering the golden middle class; they are a people exiled from aspiration. One of India's greatest living writers, Mahashweta Devi, once remarked that the first fundamental right of all is the right to dream. These are people in permanent exile from dreaming.

The emphatic rejection of the outgoing Congress-led government by significant sections of India's voters is also hailed by the winners as a decisive rejection of the ideas of both secularism and the welfare state. But this would be a grave misreading of the message sent by the voters. It is the *performance* of the previous government on these two yardsticks which was rightly and understandably rejected by the electorate. The ideas themselves remain critical for the survival and well-being of a country of such immense diversity of belief systems and ways of life, and of so many million residents who still live in abject want and oppression.

I am convinced that the battle for India's soul will be won in the end by the ideas of justice, equality, solidarity, public compassion, and reason. The social losers of the 2014 election are ultimately on the right side of history.

~

The challenges of inequality in India are compounded by the powerful revival of the politics of difference, a new conservatism and the evidence of active social and state hostility towards minority groups and communities, reflected in grossly under-provisioned Muslim ghettoes, religious profiling in both terror-related and other crimes, and the extra-judicial killings of tribals, Muslims, and Dalits.

There is growing appeal among the middle classes for Rightwing politics that often combines market fundamentalism with hostility towards minorities and India's neighbours. In the general elections of 2014, this mood was best represented by Narendra Modi, who fought a blistering electoral battle deploying 'shock and awe' tactics against his adversaries – who included liberals, socialists, 'secularists', and minorities – whom he felled decisively to become India's sixteenth Prime Minister.

Of all the major political parties seeking votes in the 2014 elections, the BJP, through its prime ministerial candidate, offered the Indian electorate perhaps the most cohesive, if troubling, vision for the country. Modi offered a combination of three fundamentalisms. First, a market orthodoxy which guarantees unprecedented levels of subsidies to big business in the form of long tax holidays, soft loans, cheap land, and electricity, at the expense of public expenditure on education, health, social protection, and public infrastructure. Next was communal fundamentalism, constituting barely disguised hostility towards religious minorities, especially Muslims, which was the main rallying agenda on the ground in electorally crucial states like Uttar Pradesh and Bihar. And the third was a militarist fundamentalism, envisioning an aggressive foreign policy, including war with Pakistan. Modi's offer to the voters was a kind of 'buy one, get two free' political bargain, but one in which you cannot embrace one of the fundamentalisms without also accepting the others.

It is important to recognise that the political choice that approximately 40 per cent of India's voters made in the summer of 2014 by voting for the Modi-led BJP and its allies is not unique.

Indeed, many countries of the world today, most notably in Europe, even including Scandinavia, show a similar preference for a confident, resurgent, and aggressive Right over centrist and Left-of-centre formations that are increasingly defensive and uncertain, with shaky commitments to social welfare and protection. (There are important exceptions in some Latin American countries, like Brazil and, in 2015, Greece.) But in many of these countries, Rightwing politics is mainly about market economics and does not combine the same open hatred of minorities that we find in contemporary Indian politics (although there is a latent anti-minorityism and, indeed, almost an Islam-phobia in the anti-immigrant stances of many European and North American Rightwing parties). It is little wonder, then, that one of India's foremost thinkers, Amartya Sen, remarked at the Jaipur Literature Festival in January 2014 that, as someone on the Left of politics in India, his 'big political wish is to have a strong and flourishing Rightwing party that is secular and not communal'. Given his own Left-leaning politics, this sounds paradoxical, but he explained that 'there is an important role for a clear-headed pro-market, pro-business party that does not depend on religious politics, and does not prioritize one religious community over all others'.[2]

But in India, Rightwing market economics has remained – as Sen puts it – 'parasitical' on Rightwing religious sectarian politics, as exemplified by the politics of the BJP and even more dramatically in Modi's leadership of Gujarat for a dozen years. This carries today, after Modi's national triumph, the deeply worrying prospect of worsening inequality and social intolerance. There is no necessary convergence between Rightwing economic policies, Rightwing chauvinism, and Rightwing militarism. Rightwing economic policies can coexist with liberal and secular policies relating to minorities and restrained defence plans. But where these do converge – as they do in Indian politics today – I believe they constitute a grave threat to secular democracy. The result of the elections of 2014 would not have caused such extensive dismay among many people if it was a victory only of an economic Right formation. It was the convergence of the economic Right with majoritarian and militarist triumphalism, spurred by enormous corporate financing, which caused such disquiet.

~

Varied imaginations of what constitutes a good state competed in the national elections of 2014, especially in the prime ministerial candidature of Narendra Modi. There were some who believed that Modi was India's most capable leader; his influential cheerleaders included several captains of Indian industry, senior academics, serving and retired civil servants, professionals, and traders. There were others who were equally convinced that his continuing ascendancy would be profoundly dangerous for democracy, pluralism, and social and economic equity.

Both assessments were based on evaluations of the results of Narendra Modi's leadership of the state of Gujarat, where he was Chief Minister from 2002 to 2014. It was extraordinary that the same administration should be evaluated in such irreconcilably divergent ways. These oppositional assessments reflect the two diametrically contradictory ideas of good government. One view is that governments must, first and foremost, effectively facilitate market-led economic growth, and their success should be measured against this yardstick.

The contrary view is that the performance of governments should be assessed by what they deliver for the most disadvantaged citizens of the country. For people who adhere to the former imagination of government, Modi is the most successful administrator in the country; whereas for the latter, he is the most failed of our leaders.

Modi's leadership style is aptly described by social commentator Tridip Suhrud as 'hyper-masculine': divisive, pugnacious, authoritarian, and surgically efficient.[3] A report published by a research wing of the US Congress portrays Gujarat under his leadership as 'perhaps India's best example of effective governance and impressive development . . . where controversial Chief Minister Narendra Modi has streamlined economic processes, removing red tape and curtailing corruption in ways that have made the state a key driver of national economic growth'.[4] India's wealthiest man Mukesh Ambani described Modi's leadership as 'visionary, effective and passionate'.[5] His brother Anil saw in him a 'role model' for other states to emulate, and hyperbolically claimed that he is the best leader Gujarat has had after Gandhi. He declared that Modi makes him proud to be a Gujarati and an Indian. 'Imagine what will happen if he leads the country?' he gushed.[6] Ratan Tata lauded Modi's track record as an 'exemplary' leader: 'Today there is no state like Gujarat. Under Mr Modi's leadership, Gujarat is head and shoulders above any state.'[7] Telecom giant Sunil Mittal likewise endorsed Modi's elevation as the CEO of the entire nation. These men, who own some of the largest business empires in India – and indeed, the world – chose to leave no doubt who their national icon was.[8]

Modi also has many supporters among the country's intellectuals. One of the best-known Indian economists, Jagdish Bhagwati, crossed swords with Amartya Sen as he celebrated the Gujarat model. He declared that 'Modi has the vision to take India to the next level'.[9] 'The Gujarat model', Bhagwati said, 'was not just about "creating prosperity". It (the Gujarat model) is also about using the wealth that is created, to increase social spending'.[10] Arvind Panagariya, who was appointed by Prime Minister Narendra Modi in 2015 to head the official policy think-tank, Niti Aayog, which replaced the Nehruvian Planning Commission, summarised Amartya Sen's rejection of Modi's model of development and his very public differences with Bhagwati.[11] Amartya Sen was critical of the Gujarat model because he felt that Modi laid much higher stress on physical infrastructure than on health or education.[12] 'Sen thinks', according to Panagariya,

> that the starting point for achieving the desired goal (of battling poverty) must be an immediate massive attack on illiteracy and ill health. This would not only directly contribute to better education and health, it would also bring about faster growth by producing

a healthier and more literate workforce. Higher growth would in turn yield larger revenues, allowing further attack on illiteracy and ill health.[13] A virtuous cycle will thus emerge. In this story, growth automatically follows improved literacy and health.

Bhagwati and Panagariya countered Sen by suggesting that Modi was on the right track in accelerating the liberalisation of foreign trade and investment, facilitating private players in infrastructure. 'Our view on development policy', Panagariya explained,

> is almost the opposite of Sen. Track-I reforms provide the true starting point for any poor country. On the one hand, rapid growth directly empowers the citizens through increased incomes that they can use to buy high-quality education and health in the marketplace. On the other hand, it gives the government ever-rising revenues to further enhance public expenditures on health and education.[14]

The twentieth century saw the massive expansion of the growth of the state in most parts of the world. In diverse political systems, the state derived its legitimacy mainly from what it pledged to its ordinary and, especially, to its impoverished citizens. What states actually delivered to them was very often paltry and deceitful, but they still continued to accept the political and ethical premise that the primary duty of governments was to deliver services, or protect the rights, of common people. This changed dramatically from the last decade of the twentieth century, when agencies like the World Bank and many economists influentially propagated the view that a good government was one that facilitated the functioning of private markets, and not one that directly provided to its dispossessed and socially oppressed peoples.

It is by this measure that Modi's administration in Gujarat could be arguably elevated to a model of good (the best?) governance (even though its glittering claims of double-digit growth and millions of dollars in investment were possibly exaggerated). If the yardstick of successful governance as creating a business and investment-friendly environment is accepted, Modi's government in Gujarat seemed, at least on the surface, to have performed creditably.

Gujarat achieved double-digit growth at rates higher than most other states. With just 5 per cent of India's population, it contributed 21 per cent to India's exports and 13 per cent to its industrial production in 2009. Yet, as Lyla Bavadam in *Frontline* observes, nearly thirty years before Modi's dispensation, Gujarat was among the three fastest growing states in the country in 1980. Since then it has more or less occupied that position, as Economist Atul Sood also reminds us.[15] This suggests that Modi's policies were not decisively responsible for this good performance. It is also pertinent that growth rates were higher in states like Maharashtra and Tamil Nadu. Gujarat's performance as the most attractive destination for private investment is also overstated. Its share in FDI in 2102–2013 was 2.38 per cent, placing it at a distant sixth position among the states of India. In contrast, Maharashtra's share was just under 40 per cent.[16] Economist Atul Sood also reminds us that of the total memoranda of understandings (MOUs) signed at successive high-profile investor summits, the proportion of projects actually realised fell precipitously from 73 per cent in 2003 to 13 per cent in 2011.[17]

Even more pertinent are the terms on which Gujarat attracted private investment. Its sterling reputation as an investor-friendly government derived greatly from the alacrity with which it provided land in Sanand to Tata Motors to set up a factory to manufacture the Nano, the company's small car, after the company had publicly failed to set up a manufacturing unit in Singur, West Bengal. But much of the land handed over to Tata Motors was already controlled by the Gujarat Industrial Development Corporation, while a small chunk owned by farmers was bought at above-market rates with little opposition.

The government gifted unprecedented tax concessions to the Tatas and other big business houses. Paranjoy Guha Thakurta, based on an internal document of the Gujarat state government, reported that the total subsidies given by the Gujarat government to Tata Motors added up to more than 300 billion rupees.[18] A Right to Information application revealed that Tata Motors invested 29 billion rupees while the state government awarded it a loan of 95.7 billion rupees at an incredible 0.1 per cent rate of interest, repayable on a monthly basis after twenty years. All the charges which are normally levied when transferring land from agricultural to non-agricultural purposes were completely waived. Registration fees, too, were not charged. The state government met the entire infrastructure cost of developing roads, provided electricity and gas supply, and allotted an additional 100 acres of land on the outskirts of Ahmedabad to build a township for Tata Motors employees. The Gujarat government also met the cost of shifting the project to the tune of seven billion rupees – this amount included expenses for bringing machinery and equipment from Singur to Sanand. The Centre for Science and Environment calculates that the total subsidy element of the 'cheap' car is half its total market price.[19]

This is all an astonishing exercise in turning on the head the principle of equity that it is the rich who must always subsidise the poor. What we saw in Gujarat was the exact reverse: contributions made by the ordinary taxpayer – which, because of a significant proportion of indirect taxes, includes payments by the poor – subsidising the super-rich. It is no wonder that Ratan Tata went on record to say that it would be stupid not to invest in Gujarat. From his perspective as a businessman, of course it would be. In an interview to a news channel, Tata praised Modi's capacity to deliver what he promised, such as land, which his peers were unable to accomplish. 'We are in a democracy', said Tata, and other elected heads of government 'do not have the capacity to make things happen' in the way that Modi does. In other words, Modi in his stewardship of Gujarat demonstrated the capacity to deliver state support for market-led economic growth *without dissent*. This is his major selling point to attract private capital investment, along with astounding tax benefits, which amounts to the subsidising of large industry by the ordinary taxpayer.

Those who oppose Modi's Gujarat model of development advocate an alternate, if you like, more feminine idea of good government, which is nurturing and caring. In terms of this alternate touchstone for assessing a government's worth by its success in battling poverty, discrimination, and want, the Gujarat administration dramatically slips from leading the country to being a conspicuous laggard. Between 2005 and 2010, poverty in Gujarat fell by 8.6 per cent; well behind states like Odisha (19.2 per cent), Maharashtra (13.7 per cent), and Tamil Nadu (13.1 per cent).[20] The International Food Policy Research Institute (IFPRI) found the Hunger Index of Gujarat 'alarming', the lowest among all high-income states, and below even Odisha which is notorious as India's hunger epicentre, and impoverished and poorly governed Uttar Pradesh.[21] Forty-five per cent of the children below the age of five in Gujarat were malnourished.[22] Infant mortality among girls, at fifty-one per 1,000, is higher than the national average of forty-nine.[23] The sex ratio fell from 920 to 918 females for 1,000 males between 2001 and 2011, well below the national average of 940.[24] Hirway concludes that 'the growth story of Gujarat is not inclusive, sustainable, equitable or environment-friendly', and that 'there is a disconnect between economic growth and developmental growth'.[25]

While the state gave unprecedented incentives to large businesses, there was a marked decline in investments in the social sector. In 2011–2012, Gujarat ranked seventeenth among Indian states in development expenditure as a proportion of total public expenditure.[26] Only 1.09 per cent of public expenditure in Gujarat was on education and health, well behind states like Rajasthan (3.09 per cent); a trend which dismayed and worried Amartya Sen.[27]

From the benchmark of social equity, the gravest culpability of the Modi government was its openly hostile relationship with its minorities. I will return to the question of the alleged complicity of Modi and his government in the slaughter of Muslims in 2002 later.

What is less noticed is the administration's refusal to extend equitable development services to the minorities. Muslim ghettoes are conspicuously under-serviced with roads, sanitation, drinking water, and electricity, compared to their glittering neighbours. Gujarat was the only state government in the country which, during the UPA years, refused to contribute its share to a centrally sponsored scheme of scholarships for children from minority communities, although 36 per cent Muslim children were out of school in that year.

Enough numbers of Indian voters voted in support of Modi's leadership, and pitched their hopes on the premise that the country would gain if it follows the Gujarat model of development as envisioned by Modi. But it is worth heeding the warning of Martha Nussbaum, the widely respected American philosopher. She observes that 'although the growth-based paradigm does indeed give Narendra Modi high marks, the Human Development paradigm, by contrast, shows his record as only middling, far worse than that of states such as Tamil Nadu and Kerala, which have been preoccupied, rightly, with the distribution of healthcare and education. Given the high economic status of Gujarat, one might conclude that Modi's record is not just middling but downright bad.'[28] She quotes distinguished economist Mahbub Ul Haq: 'The real wealth of a nation is its people. And the purpose of development is to create an enabling environment for people to enjoy long, healthy, and creative lives. This simple but powerful truth is too often forgotten in the pursuit of material and financial wealth'. She concludes:

> India will not shine without great strides in education and public health. More or less everyone knows this, even when they talk only about growth most of the time. A nation needs a healthy and educated work force if it is to do well into the future. But of course health and education are more than tools for business: they are also essential tools of democratic selfgovernance. A leadership with a bad record on these issues – and, what's more, with no shame about this record or public resolve to improve things – is likely to prove disastrous for India's future.

Although Modi greatly toned down his trademark divisive rhetoric and communal hectoring in his campaign, he still refused to apologise for the carnage of 2002 which occurred under his watch. In fact, after the carnage, Chief Minister Narendra Modi had led a triumphant Gaurav Yatra, March of Pride, across the state, referring to his now proverbial *chhappan-inch ki chhati*.[29,30] The subtext was that he alone was man enough to fell and tame the Muslims and to show them their actual place. This is why it took him until 2013 to express any regret for the carnage; and, even then, to only awkwardly say that were his car to run a puppy over, he would feel sorry![31]

~

Given Modi's own discourse – until he was chosen as the BJP's prime ministerial candidate eight months before the elections – of barely suppressed triumphalism surrounding the carnage of 2002, his transition to secular statesmanship required the erasure of his culpability. This erasure had been successfully accomplished earlier for the hawkish BJP leader Lal Krishna Advani to pave the way for his prime ministerial ambitions. The trail of blood which followed his *Rath Yatra* in 1989 and his robust contribution to the movement to violently pull down the Babri Masjid in 1992 were substantially expunged from public memory by a systematic campaign of his willing reinvention as a moderate statesman.

A similar exercise was undertaken in India's most expensive political campaign ever – in which the BJP reportedly spent close to what Obama spent in his election campaign, although the USA has a per capita income thirty times higher than that of India.[32] Except for his core Hindu nationalist constituency, Modi was reinvented as the avuncular messiah of market growth.

Given Modi's public position on the 2002 massacre, the obliteration of his role in it was even harder to accomplish than the reinvention of the two earlier prime ministerial candidates fielded by the BJP. But the leaders of industry, as much as large segments of the middle classes impatient to see his installation as the one man who could accelerate economic growth, rejected the idea that his ambitions to attain the highest post in national politics were disqualified by his alleged role in one of the most brutal communal massacres after Independence. They counselled that we should focus on the 'big picture' of growth, as though the violent suppression of minorities is but a minor blemish. Many European ambassadors lined up at his door in the hope of participating in Gujarat's growth story. All of them needed a fig leaf to cover the nakedness of their choices.

This fig leaf came was provided by the closure report filed by the Supreme Court–appointed SIT (Special Investigation Team) which absolved Narendra Modi of any role in the carnage, concluding there was no 'prosecutable evidence' against the Chief Minister. These findings were endorsed by the 'clean chit' given by the lower court which heard Zakia Jafri's petition of 15 April 2013, who had alleged that a high-level conspiracy had been hatched to manipulate the Godhra tragedy so that the carnage which followed could be organised and fuelled. The first name among the fifty-nine accused in Zakia Jafri's petition was that of Chief Minister Narendra Modi. Zakia's lawyer Mihir Desai argued in court that the political head of the state, the home ministry, and the administration had sanctioned the 'build-up of aggressive and communal sentiments, violent mobilisation, including carrying of arms, and a general outpouring against the minority community'.[33] Relying on documents collected by the SIT itself, Zakia's petition attempted to establish that there was a conspiracy at the senior-most levels of the state administration, not just to generate hatred against Muslims, but also to target Muslim people and their property and religious places and 'aid and abet this process by acts and omissions of persons liable under law to act otherwise'.[34]

How much does the SIT's closure report and the lower court's 'clean chit' to Modi really free him from taint? At best, they suggest that there is no irrefutable, *direct* evidence that, as Chief Minister, Modi actually directed that the slaughter of Muslims be allowed to continue, giving free rein to enraged 'Hindus' to violently vent their rage. The SIT chose not to give credence to the statements of one serving and one retired police officer that he indeed issued such instructions. But Manoj Mitta, in his carefully researched book, *The Fiction of Fact-Finding: Modi and Godhra*, writes that the SIT treaded carefully around the powerful politician. At no point did the SIT file an FIR against him. He was not held accountable for his uncorroborated, public statement, characterising the train burning at Godhra as a 'preplanned inhuman collective violent act of terrorism', which incited public anger and which continues to be used to justify the massacre.[35] It likewise did not question him about his claim that he first heard about the Gulbarg Society massacre, in which former Congress MP, Ehsan Jafri, lost his life at 8:30 p.m. – a timeline first established by Mitta in his book – on 28 February 2002, until many hours after the slaughter. By its own admission, the administration was monitoring events and Modi was holding a law-and-order review meeting even as the massacre unfolded, just a few kilometres away at the Circuit House Annexe.[36]

Senior advocate Raju Ramachandran, amicus curiae appointed by the Supreme Court to investigate allegations of Narendra Modi's complicity in the Gujarat riots, also disagreed with the conclusions of the SIT. His opinion, reported to the Supreme Court, was that 'the offences which can be made out against Shri Modi, at this prima facie stage, included promoting enmity between different groups on grounds of religion and acts prejudicial to (the) maintenance of harmony'.[37] He believed also that there were grounds to not dismiss the version of suspended police officer Sanjiv Bhatt out of hand by the SIT. According to Bhatt, on 27 February 2002, hours after fifty-eight passengers were set on fire in a train near the Godhra station, Modi held a meeting at his residence with senior police officers and told them that Hindus should be allowed to 'vent their anger'.[38] Ramachandran states: 'I disagree with the conclusion of the SIT that Shri Bhatt should be disbelieved at this stage itself. On the other hand, I am of the view that Shri Bhatt needs to be put through the test of cross-examination, as do the others who deny his presence'.[39]

Ramachandran also pointed to evidence that two senior ministers were placed in police control rooms on 28 February as riots raged in Ahmedabad and across the state. The SIT did not find evidence that they interfered with the police's independent functioning, but stated that 'there is the possibility that the very presence of these two ministers had a dampening effect on the senior police officials'.[40] He concludes:

> While there is no direct material to show how and when the message of the Chief Minister was conveyed to the two ministers, the very presence of political personalities unconnected with the Home Portfolio at the Police Control Rooms is circumstantial evidence of the Chief Minister directing, requesting or allowing them to be present.[41]

People who organised and actively participated in the massacre were rewarded. Chief Minister Modi appointed Maya Kodnani as his minister for women and child welfare, after she was charged with leading the mob which brutally killed more than a 100 people, including many women and children, in Naroda Patiya. Maya Kodnani was subsequently convicted and punished with imprisonment for her entire life for her part in the crimes.

However, Narendra Modi's culpability, as Chief Minister, for the carnage of 2002 should not hinge, in the end, on proving beyond doubt that he directed police officers to allow Hindus to 'vent their anger', or that his ministers and MLAs were obeying his commands by interfering in the independent functioning of the police force or leading murderous mobs. The fact that the carnage continued not just for days but for weeks should be evidence enough of the criminal complicity of senior state authorities, and so should Modi's intemperate statements, and the parading of the charred bodies of the people who died on the train in Godhra. Similar guilt should be attached to those who allowed other communal carnages to continue, whether on the streets of Delhi in 1984 and Mumbai in 1992–1993 or the killing fields of Nellie in 1983 and Bhagalpur in 1989.

The 'clean chit' given to Modi is, at best, a technical clearance in the absence of cast-iron evidence,[42] although even this is disputed by experts. But I believe that there can be no doubt of his grave culpability for inflaming sectarian passions by holding Muslims guilty for an offence without evidence, and for the conduct of his government which allowed, including through unconscionable inaction, the continuance of the carnage for many dark days and weeks in 2002.

~

Strident anti-Muslim rhetoric – dominant in his rallies in three successive election campaigns for the Gujarat Assembly in and since 2002 – was keyed low in his triumphant bid for the country's leadership. But still, many persistent undertones reflected his hostility towards India's minorities. He referred to the UPA government in the capital as the Delhi Sultanate and to Rahul Gandhi as the 'shehzada' – imagery which harked back to mediaeval domination by Muslim rulers. He donned every kind of headgear to build rapport with culturally diverse populations in all corners of the country, but refused to wear a skull cap. Even though Muslims form 10 per cent of Gujarat's population, Modi never put up a single Muslim candidate in successive polls in Gujarat. His policy was little different for the national elections, which is why the BJP does not have a single Muslim MP in the Lok Sabha – although Muslims constitute more than 14 per cent of the total population of India – a dubious first for any ruling government since Independence.

There is indeed no ambiguity in Modi's politics, no recourse to poetry and equivocality, unlike the last Prime Minister to be elected from the BJP, Atal Bihari Vajpayee. Through most of his vigorous and meteoric political career, Modi has worn no fig leaf of moderation, although during the run-up to the national elections, he did cover his majoritarian convictions with his promises that he would ensure miraculous economic growth.

One can speculate about how much of the middle class supported him for his promise of growth, his decisive leadership, or his communal hyper-nationalism. And even if we accept that there were many who backed him for his growth agenda, we must also accept that all these people were not uncomfortable with a leader who was openly hostile to India's constitutional pledge of equal citizenship to all persons regardless of their faith. This reflected at least a passive condoning of aggressive communalism, if not active support for his deeply divisive brand of politics. Journalist Javed Anand observes, 'The real secret of Modi's success lies in a happy coalition of those who adore him for what happened under his watch in Gujarat in 2002 and those who simply "don't care" what he did then because he promises unbridled growth'.[43] Filmmaker Saeed Mirza lamented at the Idea of India Conclave, held in New Delhi in July 2014, that 'a man vilified within the country and around the world for presiding over the mass slaughter of innocents ... uncompromising on the RSS's ideology and firmly grounded on its perception of history' was elected because

> it didn't matter to ... very large sections of the middle and upper-middle class because they had been either sufficiently polarised over the years or had been sucked into the world of consumerism and self-preservation. As for the youth from the middle and upper-middle class it also did not matter because to them history didn't matter.[44]

On the back of unprecedented and unimaginable levels of corporate funding, and fuelled by the media, both social and others, Modi's message reached almost every home. Academic Kanti Bajpai noted,

> The media has probably never been as one-sided as it was during this election campaign. So much for its role as the fourth estate; it acted more like the Modi estate. Media studies groups have already shown that Modi benefited from roughly three times the coverage of any other leader. A content analysis will also show that the media said almost nothing negative about Modi's record in Gujarat and almost nothing positive about Manmohan's record at the Centre.[45]

The battle for India's soul 145

Siddharth Mazumdar reported the unprecedented use of technology: approximately 200 out of 800 million people have access to the Internet, including via mobile phones, many of them young voters, and Modi was in touch with them continuously throughout his campaign.[46] Using 3D hologram rallies, Modi also managed to reach out to thousands of remote villages by addressing them simultaneously from a remote location. Similarly, through his now fabled 'Chai pe Charcha' or 'Discussion over Tea', Modi interacted with an incredible million people at a time, using a hybrid combination of broadcast and webcast.

But the real muscle of Modi's electoral success was in his sweep of seats in the Hindi heartland, especially Uttar Pradesh and Bihar. RSS volunteers shed all pretence of being 'distanced' from politics and joined hands with BJP workers to ensure Modi's victory. Most commentators agree that the dramatic resurrection of the BJP from being a distant fourth contender in 2009 in Uttar Pradesh, after the Bahujan Samaj Party, the Samajwadi Party, and the Congress, to the victor reflected a significant majoritarian consolidation. This same majoritarian storm swept neighbouring Bihar, where Nitish Kumar had to bite the dust even though it was perhaps he who was then offering a real model for inclusive growth to the country.

Many believe that this majoritarian consolidation was carefully and skilfully crafted by Modi's closest aide Amit Shah who, soon after the national triumph, was made president of the BJP. The tide turned decisively in favour of the BJP with the party's success in polarising Hindu voters across caste lines against Muslims by manufacturing hatred against them, beginning with Muzaffarnagar in Uttar Pradesh.

Both Uttar Pradesh and Bihar were embroiled in the throes of more than a hundred riots in 2013–2014, transforming – in the hearts and minds of Hindus – Muslims into hated 'others' who must be shown their place and taught a lesson.[47] There are many constituencies in which Muslims form a sufficient number of voters to be able to influence electoral outcomes. Amateur political commentators have long described this as the 'Muslim veto'. But almost all of these constituencies fell to the BJP wave. Neutralising the Muslim influence in these constituencies would have been possible only if *all* other castes and groups joined hands against the political choice of the Muslims. In Uttar Pradesh, Mayawati's loyal caste base of 20 per cent did not desert her; still, she won no seats despite capturing the third-highest vote share (both in Uttar Pradesh and the country as a whole). Even so, it is apparent that many Dalit voters and a larger number of OBC voters were drawn to the majoritarian consolidation represented by Modi and the BJP.

Jay Mazoomdar recounts a telling conversation he had with three young men in Varanasi after the elections:

> 'More than Muslims here, now Pakistan and China will be scared,' one of them said disarmingly. Why, was Modi going to fight a war? 'No, no, he need not. But they (neighbours) will know they cannot take us for granted anymore,' he explained quickly. His friend nodded in agreement before adding: 'And there will be riots no more. They (minorities) won't just dare'. Weren't they looking for jobs, development? 'Of course, there will be good work all around, also employment, and prices will go down. We will see better days,' assured the third friend. 'But how can one serve the country unless one serves one's own religion uncompromisingly?'[48]

Many more openly communal statements were made, not just by common people but also by Modi's aides. Modi himself said nothing of the sort but also, at the same time, never publicly reprimanded his aides or distanced himself from their comments. He was happy to reap the political benefits of majoritarian consolidation spurred by these remarks, but freed himself from taking responsibility for them.

Amit Shah said, openly, that the vote should be used for revenge in riot-ravaged Muzaffarnagar. Sangeet Som,[49] notorious for uploading a fake video, purportedly showing Muslims killing two Jat brothers in Muzaffarnagar, which fuelled the ensuing riots, was feted on the same political stage where Modi later addressed a rally.[50] Praveen Togadia exhorted his followers to violently prevent Muslims from buying houses in Hindu majority neighbourhoods in Gujarat. Bajrang Dal activists were protesting against a Muslim family which had bought a house in a Hindu-dominated residence in Bhavnagar in Gujarat. Togadia joined them, suggesting that the protesters should give the occupants forty-eight hours to vacate the house, and, if they did not do so, they should storm it with 'stones, tyres and tomatoes', spit on the house-owner when he walked out of the house, and put up a Bajrang Dal board in front of the residence.[51]

Modi himself allowed this thin mask of moderation to slip whenever he felt the need to personally stoke majoritarian sentiment. In his own unique fashion, he spoke, in the heartland of Bihar, of the 'pink revolution', alluding to the UPA government's alleged support for beef export by subsidising slaughter houses.[52] In Vadodara, he charged that secular opinion was in fact, divisive, and he declared that he would rather lose the election than fall to these strategies, trying to turn on its head the moral case for secularism.[53]

But even more damagingly, he stormed Assam with exhortations against Bengali Muslims, describing them as illegal immigrant Bangladeshis, ignoring the fact that more than nine out of ten Bengali Muslims in the state are legitimate Indian citizens.[54] He advised them to pack their bags after 16 May! On 1 May Assam witnessed one of the most brutal massacres since Nellie, targeting mostly Muslim women and children. Yet, a day after this massacre in the Baksa district, Modi thought nothing of reiterating his threats against Bengali Muslims in Bengal, declaring that those who did not worship the goddess Durga were not welcome in the state. Like every other statement in the campaign, this too received wide media notice, including *The Hindu* and *India Today*.

~

On 1 May 2014, forty-five women, children, and old men were slaughtered in a brutal shoot-out in Narayanguri village in Baksa in Assam. Their only crimes were that they were Muslim and spoke Bengali. Just a month earlier, the BJP prime ministerial candidate, Narendra Modi, addressing an election rally in Dhemaji, Assam, had been quoted by the Press Trust of India as saying,

> Aren't rhinos the pride of Assam? These days there is a conspiracy to kill them. I am making the allegation very seriously. People sitting in the government . . . are doing this conspiracy to kill rhinos so that the area becomes empty and Bangladeshis can be settled there.[55]

He also deplored what he called 'intrusions' from people in Bangladesh who he alleged were taking up jobs in India. He said it was time that these 'intrusions' stopped.

It is debatable if Modi's exclusionary election speech directly spurred the violence in Baksa. But in my many visits to Assam, I observed how Modi's rhetoric found many answering echoes in the deeply divided Assamese society. There is no doubt that indigenous groups like the Bodos have legitimate anxieties about the preservation of their land, forests, and way of life, all of which must be addressed.

But Bengalis have been lawfully migrating into the area from the nineteenth century, and scholars have established that not more than 10 per cent of Bengali Muslim residents in Assam could be illegal immigrants. And to the extent that India does indeed have an influx of economic refugees escaping hopeless poverty in their own countries, the country needs to debate if they should be purged and demonised, or whether it should keep its doors open for the needy of the world, as it has for centuries.

~

Half a decade is a long time for Modi's government to demonstrate and operationalise its worldviews and priorities and the direction it seeks to take the country. But these global trends suggest that his leadership will be marked by hard market economics, populism, and a changed relationship with India's minorities, especially the Muslims.

Some fear that the secular Constitution of the country will be formally altered on Modi's watch. But I feel it is unlikely that the word 'secular' will be formally excised, or that Section 25 of the Constitution, which guarantees freedom of religion, will be amended.

But, as historian Mukul Kesavan observes, the BJP's claim that it will ensure development for all but appeasement to none is not reassuring, because, in the BJP's lexicon, appeasement means special protections for Muslims.[56] It is to be seen if Modi will pull back on scholarships for Muslim children and development funds for Muslim settlements in the country, as he has done in Gujarat earlier. If he ends the subsidy for Haj travellers, I will not shed any tears; the subsidy does nothing to address the real material concerns of the ordinary Indian Muslim. My fears are graver – that his tough talk on terror will translate into even greater profiling of Muslims as terrorists and increase the soft-peddling of terror perpetrated by Hindutva organisations. But my deepest fear is that, in practice, the minorities of India will be made to accept second-class citizenship, and that this practice will be cumulatively embedded in new social, economic, and political relationships between India's religious communities. The chief patron of the Vishva Hindu Parishad (VHP) and senior RSS leader, Ashok Singhal – who, as noted by Prashant Jha of the *Hindustan Times*, had a front-row seat at Modi's swearing-in – declared ominously after the elections that the 'tables had turned' and the polls were a 'setback to Muslim politics' used by 'foreign and divisive forces to destroy our identity'.[57] The recent Lok Sabha polls had shown that an election could be won 'without Muslim support'. It was time for them to learn their lessons. 'Muslims will be treated as common citizens – nothing more, nothing less. And, they must learn to respect Hindu sentiments. If they keep opposing Hindus, how long can they survive?' Singhal elaborated that Muslims should give up claims over Ayodhya, Kashi, and Mathura and also accept a uniform civil code. 'We'll then give them love, and not claim any other mosque sites even though there are thousands built on the ruins of temples. But if they don't accept it, they should be prepared for further Hindu consolidation. It has happened at the Centre, it will happen in other states'.[58]

Gopal Krishna Gandhi, in an avuncular open letter to Modi, reminded him about his duties to India's minorities. 'In the olden days', he wrote to India's new Prime Minister:

> headmasters used to keep a salted cane in one corner of the classroom, visible and scary, as a reminder of his ability to lash the chosen skin. Memories, no more than a few months old, of the riots in Muzaffarnagar which left at least 42 Muslims and 20 Hindus dead and displaced over 50,000 persons, are that salted cane. "Beware, this is what will be done to you!" is not a threat that anyone in a democracy should fear. But that is the message that has entered the day's fears and night's terrors of millions.

He continues:

> No one should have the impudence to speak the monarchist language of uniformism to a republic of pluralism, the vocabulary of "oneness" to an imagination of manynesses, the grammar of consolidation to a sensibility that thrives in and on its variations. India is a diverse forest. It wants you to nurture the humus that sustains its great variety, not place before it the monochromatic monoculturalism of a political monotheism.[59]

But, 'If there is a message from Elections 2014 it is that India has been changing', Raghav Bawa observed in a perceptive commentary on the elections in the *Economic and Political Weekly*. 'It is becoming a society where those with a voice are becoming less tolerant, less compassionate and more aggressive towards those without a voice. This is just the atmosphere for an aggressive mix of religion and nationalism to find expression'.[60]

~

In drafting India's Constitution, Ambedkar laid great stress, not just on liberty and equality, but also on fraternity. He said, 'Fraternity means a sense of common brotherhood (and sisterhood) of all Indians – if

Indians are seen as being one people. It is the principle which gives unity and solidarity to social life. It is a difficult thing to achieve'.[61] He was convinced that 'without fraternity, equality and liberty will be no deeper than a coat of paint'.[62] Ambedkar dreamed of an India in which divisions of caste and religion would gradually fade away.

However, it is fraternity which has been most forgotten in our Constitution. It is forgotten not just by those chosen to uphold our Constitution, it is lost even in our public and social life, in which the aggressive use of oppositional identities remains for most political parties the most reliable instrument to harvest votes with, and prejudice and inequality are produced and reproduced in our hearts and homes. The idea of fraternity is closely linked to that of social solidarity, which is impossible to accomplish without public compassion; the daily, lived realisation that human beings who look different, wear different clothes, worship different gods, speak different languages, have different political persuasions, actually have exactly the same intrinsic human dignity, and experience the same emotions – dreams, hopes, despair, pain, happiness, anger, love, triumphs, and defeats – that we do.

Notes

1. This article substantially derives from my book *Looking Away: Inequality, Prejudice and Indifference in New India* (2015, Speaking Tiger).
2. Amartya Sen, 'Keynote Address', ZEE Jaipur Literature Festival, 2014, http://jaipurliteraturefestival.org/festival-inauguration-and-keynoteaddress-dr-amartya-sen/.
3. Tridip Suhrud, 'Modi and Gujarati "Asmita"', *Economic and Political Weekly*, Vol. 43, No.1 (2008), 11–13.
4. K. Alan Kronstadt, Paul K. Kerr, Michael F. Martin and Bruce Vaughn, 'India: Domestic Issues, Strategic Dynamics and U.S. Relations', *Congressional Research Service*, www.fas.org/sgp/crs/row/RL33529.pdf (accessed 19 January 2014).
5. Press Trust of India, 'Vibrant Gujarat 2011: India Inc All Praise for Narendra Modi', *The Economic Times*, 12 January 2011, http://articles.economictimes.indiatimes.com/2011-01-12/news/28423442_1_narendra-modi-vibrant-gujarat-vibrant-gujarat (accessed 19 January 2014).
6. Siddharth Varadarajan, 'The Cult of Cronyism', *Seminar*, April 2014.
7. Ibid.
8. Press Trust of India, 'Vibrant Gujarat 2011: India Inc All Praise for Narendra Modi'.
9. Interviews of Amartya Sen and Jagdish Bhagwati by, respectively, Subhabrata Guha and Surojit Guha, *The Times of India*.
10. Interviews of Amartya Sen and Jagdish Bhagwati by, respectively, Subhabrata Guha and Surojit Guha, *The Times of India*.
11. Arvind Panagariya, 'What Amartya Sen Doesn't See', *The Times of India*, 27 July 2013.

The battle for India's soul 151

12 Press Trust of India, 'Lessons to Be Learnt From Gujarat's Business Experience: Amartya', *The Times of India*, 23 July 2013.
13 Arvind Panagariya, 'What Amartya Sen Doesn't See'.
14 Ibid.
15 Lyla Bavadam, 'Going Beyond the Narmada Valley', *Frontline*, Vol. 17, No. 23 (2000), www.frontline.in/static/html/fl1723/17230400.htm (accessed 19 January 2014).
16 According to data provided by the Ministry of Commerce and Industry, Notes 390, http://dipp.nic.in/English/Publications/FDI_Statistics/FDI_Statistics.aspx (accessed 19 January 2014).
17 Atul Sood, *Poverty Amidst Prosperity: Essays on the Trajectory of Development in Gujarat* (New Delhi: Aakar Books, 2012).
18 Paranjoy Guha Thakurta, 'INDIA: Cheapest Car Rides on Govt Subsidies', *Inter Press Service*, 5 June 2009, www.ipsnews.net/2009/06/corrected-repeat-indiacheapest-car-rides-on-govt-subsidies/ (accessed 21 January 2014).
19 Paranjoy Guha Thakurta, 'INDIA: Cheapest Car Rides on Govt Subsidies'.
20 K.S. Chalam, 'Gujarat: Whose State Is It Anyway?', *Janata*, Vol. 67, No. 45 (2 December 2012).
21 'India Faces Urgent Hunger Situation', press release from the International Food Policy Research Institute, 2008 www.ifpri.org/pressrelease/india-faces-urgent-hungersituation? (accessed 14 January 2014) Print.
22 'Gujarat's Social Progress Yet to Match Economic Progress', *India* Notes 391 Spend, 30 October 2012 www.indiaspend.com/states/gujarats-economic-success-yet-to-matchsocial-progress (accessed 15 January 2014).
23 Ibid.
24 Ibid.
25 Indira Hirway, 'Selective Development and Widening Disparities in Gujarat'.
26 Harsh Mander, 'Worshipping False Gods in India', *Livemint*, 6 April 2014, www.livemint.com/Opinion/N3Pxc4L3QCOqe9TkYlFQeL/Worshipping-false-gods-in-India.html.
27 Reserve Bank of India, *State Finances: A Study of Budgets* (New Delhi: RBI, 2013).
28 Martha Nussbaum, 'Development Is More Than Growth', The Hindu Centre for Politics and Public Policy, 8 May 2014, www.thehinducentre.com/verdict/commentary/article5985379.ece.
29 'Modi Kicks off Gujarat Gaurav Yatra', *The Times of India*, 8 September 2002, http://articles.timesofindia.indiatimes.com/2002-09-08/ahmedabad/27299133_1_phagvel-postgodhra-bhathiji-maharaj (accessed 20 February 2015).
30 Ramachandra Guha, 'The Man Who Would Rule India', *The Hindu*, 8 February 2013, www.thehindu.com/opinion/lead/the-man-who-would-rule-india/article4390286.ece.114033100661_1.html (accessed 18 May 2014).
31 Amy Kazmin, 'Narendra Modi Rode Wave of Money to India Victory', *Financial Times*, 19 May 2014, www.ft.com/cms/s/0/ce68abf0-df3f-11e3-86a4-00144feabdc0.html#axzz34tAIuEZB (accessed 18 May 2014).
32 Ibid.
33 'SIT Report Contains Evidence on Conspiracy to Target Minorities', *The Hindu*, 10 July 2013 www.thehindu.com/news/national/sit-report-

contains-evidence-onconspiracy-to-target-minorities/article4899065.ece (accessed 20 February 2015).
34. Ibid.
35. Manoj Mitta, *The Fiction of Fact Finding: Modi and Godhra* (New Delhi: HarperCollins, 2014).
36. Manoj Mitta, 'Don't Ask, Don't Tell', *Outlook*, 17 February 2014 www.outlookindia.com/article/Dont-Ask-Dont-Tell/289455 (accessed 20 February 2015).
37. For full text of the report see, Raju Ramachandran, 'Report by the Amicus Curiae Dated 25.07.2011 Submitted Pursuant to the Order'.
38. Raju Ramachandran, 4.
39. Ibid.
40. Ibid.
41. Ibid.
42. 'SIT Clean Chit to Modi Challenged in Court', *Business Standard*, 16 April 2013, www.businessstandard.com/article/current-affairs/sit-clean-chit-to-modi-in-2002-riots-challenged-in-court-113041500420_1.html (accessed 14 January 2014).
43. Javed Anand, 'Why Modi Cannot Shake Off 2002', *The Indian Express*, 10 August 2012, http://archive.indianexpress.com/news/why-modi-cannot-shake-off-2002/986180/ (accessed 20 February 2015).
44. Saeed A. Mirza, 'The Age of Amnesia', unpublished paper presented at Idea of India Conclave, New Delhi, 4–5 July.
45. Arjumand Bano, 'Muslims Need Not Be Scared of Modi: Bajpai', The Times of India, 17 April 2014, http://timesofindia.indiatimes.com/india/Muslims-need-not-be-scared-of-Modi-Bajpai/articleshow/33872890.cms.
46. Siddharth Mazumdar, '2014 Heralds a New Era in Indian Politics', *Tehelka*, 24 May 2014 www.tehelka.com/2014-heralds-a-new-era-in-indian-politics/ (accessed 20 February 2015).
47. 'Communal Incidents Up 30% in 2013, UP Tops List', *Indian Express*, 4 February 2015, http://indianexpress.com/article/india/communal-incidents-up-30-in-2013-up-tops-list/ (accessed 20 February 2015).
48. Jay Mazoomdar, 'The Saffron Coup', *Tehelka*, 24 May 2014. www.tehelka.com/the-saffron-coup/ (accessed 20 February 2015).
49. 'Amit Shah Booked for "Revenge" Remark on Muzaffarnagar Riots', *India Today*, 6 April 2014, http://indiatoday.intoday.in/story/amit-shah-booked-muzaffarnagar-riotsmulayam-singh-yadav-narendra-modi/1/3539285.html (accessed 20 February 2015).
50. Ayeshea Perera, 'Modi Live: SP Made Congress' Vote Bank Politics Its Own', *Firstpost*, 21 November 2013, www.firstpost.com/politics/modi-live-sp-made-congress-votebank-politics-its-own-1241447.html (accessed 20 February 2015).
51. Vijaysinh Parmar, 'Evict Muslims from Hindus Areas: Pravin Togadia', *The Times of India*, 21 April 2014, http://timesofindia.indiatimes.com/india/Evict-Muslims-from-Hinduareas-Pravin-Togadia/articleshow/34017292.cms (accessed 20 February 2015).
52. Roshan Kumar, 'Modi Targets "Pink Revolution"', *The Telegraph*, 3 April 2014 www.telegraphindia.com/1140403/jsp/frontpage/story_18149409.jsp#.VNHMD52UdqU (accessed 20 February 2015).

53 Press Trust of India, 'Won't Appeal to Hindus or Muslims But to All; Ready to Face Defeat', *Hindustan Times*, www.hindustantimes.com/the-big-story/will-not-appealto-hindus-or-muslims-ready-to-face-defeat-modi/article1–1209629.aspx (accessed 20 February 2015).
54 See for instance, Nilim Dutta, 'The Myth of the Bangladeshi and Violence in Assam', *Kafila*, 16 August 2012, http://kafila.org/2012/08/16/the-myth-of-the-bangladeshi-andviolence-in-assam-nilim-dutta/ (accessed 20 February 2015).
55 Press Trust of India, 'People in Assam Govt Conspiring to Eliminate Rhinos: Modi', *Business Standard*, 31 March 2014, Notes 396, www.business-standard.com/article/pti-stories/people-in-assam-govt-conspiring-to-eliminate-rhinos-modi-114033100661_1.html (accessed 20 February 2015).
56 Mukul Kesavan, 'What About 1984? Pogroms and Political Virtues', *The Telegraph*, 26 July 2013, www.telegraphindia.com/1130726/jsp/opinion/story_17155627.jsp#.U4oMo_mSxvE (accessed 20 February 2015).
57 Prashant Jha, 'BJP Win Blow to Muslim Politics: Singhal', *Hindustan Times*, 17 July 2014, www.hindustantimes.com/india-news/bjp-win-blow-to-muslimpolitics-vhp-chief-patron-ashok-singhal/article1-1241242.aspx (accessed 20 February 2015).
58 Ibid.
59 Gopal Krishna Gandhi, 'An Open Letter to Narendra Modi', *The Hindu*, 19 May 2014, www.thehindu.com/opinion/lead/anopen-letter-to-narendra-modi/article6022900.ece.
60 'Anger Aspiration and Apprehension', *Economic and Political Weekly*, Vol. 49, No. 21 (24 May 2014).
61 Constituent Assembly of India Debates (Proceedings), Vol. 11, http://164.100.47.132/LssNew/cadebatefiles/C06121948.html (accessed 18 January 2014).
62 Ibid.

6 Collapse of the Congress party

Zoya Hasan

The 2014 general elections marked a tectonic shift in Indian politics. For the first time since independence, India elected a Rightwing party with a majority. Even though there have been bigger electoral landmarks in the past, this election stood out because Narendra Modi led the Bharatiya Janata Party (BJP) and the National Democratic Alliance (NDA) to a sensational win. Its victory was so complete that it captured all or most of the seats in some states and reduced the Indian National Congress to 44 of the 543 in the Lok Sabha – a shocking comedown for the party whose history is integral to India's founding narrative. Congress polled just 19.3 per cent of the votes, declining from 28.6 per cent in the 2009 election.

Election 2014 saw a shift in outcomes, processes, and personalities. This is the first time since 1984 that any party has won a majority for itself in the Lok Sabha. The BJP won 282 seats and 31 per cent of the national vote. Its main success came from the states of north and west India, with the party winning four of every five seats it contested. Its ability to garner a substantial Hindu vote in Uttar Pradesh and Bihar through communal polarisation paved its way to an absolute majority in the Lok Sabha. Never before had so much money been spent in fighting an election as in this one. The BJP received massive support from the corporate sector and easily outspent its rivals. This election also saw an extraordinary rise in media power with real politics done in TV studios and social media. It was the most personality-driven election with Modi deliberately turning a Parliamentary election into a presidential-style one.

Today, the Congress stands decimated. For more than three quarters of a century it dominated Indian politics. It is now without a strong base anywhere, having been completely wiped out in Tamil Nadu and Andhra Pradesh, made no headway in Telangana despite the decision to bifurcate Andhra, weakened in Karnataka, defeated in

Maharashtra, marginalised in Uttar Pradesh and West Bengal, and has drawn a near blank in most key states across the Hindi heartland. It did not win a single seat in Delhi, Gujarat, Goa, Himachal Pradesh, Odisha, Jharkhand, Rajasthan, Tamil Nadu, and Uttarakhand. It lost the Assembly elections in Haryana, Maharashtra, and Chhattisgarh held in October 2014. In Punjab, it is facing a serious threat from the Aam Aadmi Party (AAP). In Delhi, it has virtually disappeared. It failed to open its account in the 2015 Delhi Legislative Assembly elections perhaps for the first time in its history. It has lost its entire base to the AAP. Of the seventy candidates who contested elections to the Delhi Legislative Assembly, sixty-three lost their security deposits, including Ajay Maken, the chief of the campaign committee. More significantly, it is in no position to call the shots in the key states of Bihar, Uttar Pradesh, West Bengal, Tamil Nadu, Maharashtra, Andhra Pradesh, and Telangana.

The defeat of the Congress in the general elections in 2014 was far worse than anything in its long history. Indeed, its decimation everywhere in this election constitutes the most serious crisis for the party, worse even than the late 1970s after Indira Gandhi had suspended democracy. The Congress failure to win a single seat in Delhi only confirmed the existential crisis facing the party after it lost power at the centre. Congress leader Jairam Ramesh rightly observed: 'Our electoral debacle has been much deeper than we expected and the demoralization is increased because of the successive defeats we have had in the state elections'.[1] Yet, its top leaders have barely spoken after the defeat. Sonia Gandhi and Rahul Gandhi accepted personal responsibility for the defeat and offered to resign at the Congress Working Committee meeting immediately after the elections, but the party shielded them, rejecting their resignations.

The Congress faces a structural dilemma on several fronts: organisational weakness, ideological stagnation, and shrinking social support.[2] At one time, it was a democratic party with a formidable organisation that ran an effective political machine, distributing patronage in exchange for electoral support. From the 1970s onwards, party organisation in most states degenerated severely. This was mainly because Indira Gandhi, who had very little use for the institutional structure of the party, made systematic efforts to change it into a centralised and family-centred political organisation. From then on, no attention was given to the reorganisation and regeneration of the Congress. There is no evidence whatsoever that the party was able to use its stint in power to energise the organisation. Instead, for the last ten years, it has not allowed strong regional leadership to grow and consolidate. Even after the defeat, its leadership has done nothing to arrest the steep decline and hasn't initiated any mass mobilisation to revive the party or take up any issue that can truly galvanise an Opposition or demonstrated an interest in building alliances. The big question is whether the Congress can recover and reorganise its forces, ideas, and energies after this devastating defeat.

UPA's record

The BJP issued a booklet condemning United Progressive Alliance (UPA) Prime Minister Manmohan Singh's ten years as a 'Dark Decade in Governance',[3] and media commentators routinely described it as a 'wasted decade'[4] or 'India's lost decade'.[5] This has become so much a part of common discourse that we ignore some of the big ideas of the UPA, specially the UPA-I government, which enhanced the welfare of many. Despite economic slowdown and inflation, there was an enormous expansion of well-being over the last decade. The people are far better off than they were at the turn of the millennium.[6] Poverty declined faster than at any time in India's history.[7] The poverty ratio declined by at least 15 percentage points.[8] Between 2004–2005 and 2009–2010 – the initial years of UPA rule – the gap between rich and poor shrunk appreciably, as 40 per cent of the population experienced upward mobility.[9] Over these years, some 15 per cent of the total population or 40 per cent of the poor in India moved above the poverty line.

Even though neoliberal policies were never given up, the UPA-I did promote a range of social welfare measures and programmes. The government took advantage of high economic growth and the revenue it generated to pilot several welfare measures that enshrine a new set of socio-economic entitlements through legally enforceable rights. These rights were not abstract but extended to the day-to-day survival of marginal groups. Although the programmes' purpose was to compensate the poor for the deprivations they suffer under neoliberal policies, they do signify an emphasis on state as an instrument for redistribution and social change. Programmes like the Mahatma Gandhi National Rural Employment Guarantee Act (MGNREGA), Sarva Shiksha Abhiyan (SSA), Right to Education, National Rural Health Mission (NRHM), the Forest Rights Act, etc., tried to make overall economic growth more inclusive under UPA-I.

But the Congress failed to capitalise on the momentum of the change achieved under UPA-I. Its political support began to erode with the economic slowdown in the last two years of its second term. On the face of it, the UPA-II's problems on the economy were surprising, given that economic growth was at its strongest during the UPA's tenure, as compared to previous governments, though it declined significantly since 2010. Manmohan Singh, in his Independence Day speech as Prime Minister on 15 August 2013, blamed the global economic crisis for the domestic slowdown. But the government couldn't really blame external factors or internal political instability for the crisis which was actually a reflection of its own mismanagement.[10] While the global recession did slow down growth, most of the factors contributing to it were actually domestic in nature. In fact, the slowdown was linked to the neoliberal growth model itself which entails giving preference in everything from cheap credit to captive power to big business. It ended up promoting a crony capitalist system.

Economic expansion was driven by an investment boom helped by access to land and natural resources in return for payoffs to politicians. Elite capture was palpable in the sweetheart deals between political and economic elites in mining, land acquisition, and telecommunications. The investment subsidy implicit in underpricing of assets became unsustainable after the escalation of protests against the public acquisition of land for private purposes and corruption scandals.[11] The debate during the election indicated that the intrinsic relationship between crony capitalism and corruption was a major concern for the public. However, crony capitalism is not a new phenomenon, it has a long history in India and various parties and governments have promoted it, most notably the Congress in its previous stints in government. It was a striking feature of the Modi government in Gujarat as well, but these charges did not stick. In the case of the Congress, it was the sheer scale of corruption at the Centre for which the Congress had to take the blame. The resulting yearning for change due to this and other shortcomings in performance sealed the Congress's fate.[12]

Another major trigger for the Congress collapse was unrelenting inflation, the highest in twenty years, which turned the poor and the middle class against the party. This triggered people's anger and disenchantment and a strong desire for change. As the economic boom faded, the enthusiasm for welfare measures waned, leading to dilution in public support. The pullback on social sector programmes added to the deepening political crisis enveloping the Congress as it began losing the support of the poor who had helped it to rise from 141 seats in 2004 to 206 in the 2009 elections.

The implementation of rights-based programmes under UPA-II was very patchy. Strong attempts were made by the government to limit the scope of MGNREGA wages which were still not paid. It had become less important as its budgets were reduced in the name of targeted delivery, cash transfers and reducing subsidies. The Congress promised to enact legislation to ensure a minimum quantity of affordable food to all poor households in the country, if it was voted back to power. But the government took five years to enact the National Food Security Act (NFSA). It did push ahead with the food bill in the twilight of its second term, but it was not easy to do in the last six months what could have been done in the first six. Since it was passed by Parliament only in September 2013, the UPA could not implement it. As a result, it didn't get any political benefit out of it. Both these landmark programmes suffered because of differences within the government on coverage and quantum of support. The dithering and vacillation on some of these social legislations was certainly a factor in the failure to retain the support of the poor. Just as the increase in the spread of social programmes under UPA-I was a factor in the electoral victory of 2009, so it is likely that the poor showing under UPA-II added to public unhappiness with the government. This combined with a decade of jobless growth created eddies of discontent which was difficult to control.

As against the half-heartedness of the Congress on both the growth and redistributive fronts, Modi offered the electorate decisive action and the clarity of the Gujarat model which is as neoliberal as is possible in India: growth through private investment and good infrastructure and easy access to land and natural resources. Modi's image as a pro-business leader provided a clear alternative to the UPA's model driven by social policy.[13] He was the first leader in independent India who spelt out a vision for promoting prosperity rather than combating poverty. Needless to say, in his election campaign, the word 'inequality' wasn't heard even once. Instead, throughout the campaign, there was talk of spurring economic growth and facilitating ease of business which will do more to improve opportunities than more public spending on social welfare measures. This is just what the corporate sector and the aspirational middle class wanted to hear. This is perhaps why there was the near-unanimous condemnation of the right to food as profligate.[14] The NFSA was strongly attacked as an instance of irresponsible populism and frittering away of resources that will destroy the growth story forever. The idea that India cannot afford food security but can afford to give duty exemptions to keep gold imports out of the tax net illustrates the new politics which has come to dominate economic thinking.[15]

Turning point

The Congress party and its government lost control of the narrative in 2011, the year the anti-corruption movement took place, causing an eruption of public anger against the scam-tainted government. While the UPA government may have been able to disperse the crowds from the streets then, it could not really rid itself of the core charge that the protesters were making: that the Congress-led UPA-II government was perhaps the most corrupt in independent India. The explosion of revelations about corrupt practices pointed to the worst excesses of crony capitalism that underpinned the growth story. Yet, Manmohan Singh and Sonia Gandhi did not come out and assure the country that they would crack down on graft. Both of them hardly spoke to the public and the media. While the government kept silent, the BJP carried out a high-pitched political propaganda against the mega corruption of the UPA-II government. What's more, Singh's unwillingness to explain and communicate made the UPA come through as a regime that was not only corrupt and unaccountable but also arrogant and indifferent to feedback and criticism as well.

The anti-corruption movement hit the credibility of the government by questioning its legitimacy. In 2011, the Congress could have reached out to anti-corruption campaigners but didn't. This was a turning point in cementing hostility towards the Congress. While in 2011, the fallout of the movement was difficult to gauge as elections were still three years away, it was clear even then that the government had alienated vast swathes of voters across the social divide and had earned the wrath of the middle classes and young men and women voters of the future. It culminated in its colossal defeat at the hands of the BJP, and not the AAP, which was born out of the anti-corruption movement. However, AAP had a big hand in the BJP's win because its members played a central role in the movement that delegitimised the Congress. Furthermore, AAP had routed the Congress in the 2013 Assembly elections; the party never recovered from this rout. The BJP was undoubtedly the beneficiary of the bumper anti-Congress harvest that the India Against Corruption (IAC) movement and AAP sowed.

On the whole, both the government and the party were beleaguered throughout the five years of the second term. Manmohan Singh ran a government with multiple power centres. The leadership vacuum was such that no one's was the last word in the government or the party. An important reason for this was differences within the Congress and between the party and government. There were conflicting positions in the party and government on most issues – notably, the Indo-US nuclear deal, land acquisition, foreign direct investment in multi-brand retail, and, more generally, neoliberal economic reforms. The rift seems to have begun with the Women's Reservation Bill when Sonia Gandhi first goaded and then directed a reluctant government to ensure its passage in the Rajya Sabha, despite obvious political risks. This was followed later by her party leaders virtually stalling the Nuclear Civil Liability Bill, which was threatening to become a sensitive issue as it seemed more to protect American commercial interests than address Indian safety concerns.

The Congress remained deeply divided with regard to the strategy for economic growth. Two dominant positions were discernible on the way forward. One was a nebulous social democratic platform supported by Sonia Gandhi that shares misgivings with regard to neoliberal economic reforms, favours an accommodative approach towards the marginalised and the poor, and believes such a position helps to differentiate and distance itself from the BJP. The other side led by Manmohan Singh and P. Chidambaram, including many other senior leaders in the party, favoured the neoliberal position with its emphasis on high GDP growth, fiscal consolidation, and economic reforms to push growth. The core issue was the conflict between those who advocated speeding up economic reforms as a way of restoring high growth and those who swear by social welfare necessary for inclusive growth.

Leadership crisis

Leadership was a major issue for voters in the 2014 elections. Modern mass politics demands visible leadership from the front, not the assertion of authority by remote control. Voters believe strong decisive leadership can solve the country's numerous problems. The leadership issue became critical as the BJP made the election more personal with Modi continuously attacking 'family' politics, and the Gandhi family in particular. However, the Gandhi family was in decline long before the Modi attacks.[16] Be that as it may, it is difficult to separate the party from the Gandhis. The 2014 verdict made clear that leadership in India is not a family entitlement and voters are increasingly less deferential to family privilege. Moreover, Rahul Gandhi demonstrated his inability to generate support on the campaign trail. He said the right things but failed to connect with the voters; he did not address them in an idiom that holds much appeal for them. Evidently, he was diffident about power and position, and showed no appetite for a political fight.[17] Even within his own party there were 'doubts about the capability and willingness of Rahul Gandhi to provide a hands-on leadership to the party'.[18] He was 'the leader who won't lead', as one TV anchor put it,[19] in sharp contrast to Modi who was overeager to lead and dominate.

Rahul Gandhi was expected to assume a larger responsibility in the party's affairs after the electoral debacle. But he didn't. His reluctance was apparent from the Karnataka Congress leader Mallikarjun Kharge's appointment as the Parliamentary party leader in the Lok Sabha in the aftermath of the defeat. As the *Hindu* editorial, after the Congress party scored a zero in the 2015 Delhi Legislative Assembly elections, put it, 'He does not have what it takes: he has neither demonstrated the ability to sustain an idea or the hard work demanded of a full-time politician in a leadership role'.[20]

The failure of leadership in the Lok Sabha election and in a series of state Assembly elections before and after it is patently obvious; yet, the party's confidence in the Gandhis remains unchanged. Their authority and supremacy have not been seriously challenged within the party. Thus, despite repeated electoral failures, there is a demand for Rahul Gandhi's elevation as the president of the Congress party. But the challenges facing Gandhi appear far too numerous for any politician to tackle single-handedly.[21]

Ideological drift

Apart from the leadership crisis, two other issues were important. These pertained to the ideology and policies of the party, and reform and reorganisation of the party. The Congress never had a clear-cut ideology like most other catch-all parties. Yet, its identity is rooted in a Left-of-centre platform which it betrayed by flirting with neoliberalism and indulging in crony capitalism. Besides, as mentioned previously, the Congress kept moving back and forth between pro-poor distributive policies and neoliberal policies which left its supporters confused. This equivocation was apparent in December 2013 when Rahul Gandhi tried to placate big businesses and dispel the swelling criticism, from both industrialists and the Opposition, by highlighting the strong connect between the Congress and the Indian industry. He told a gathering at the Federation of Indian Chambers of Commerce and Industry (FICCI) that members of the industry are 'stakeholders of the Congress party', and that he had removed an obstacle to growth by changing the minister (Jayanthi Natarajan), who had in the perception of businessmen delayed environmental clearances.[22] However, a year later, in February 2015, he said: 'Let me make it very clear . . . I don't do politics for industrialists. I do politics for the poor and will continue to fight for their rights'.[23]

With each successive spell out of power, the party's ability to retain its supporters has dwindled. The rainbow started to fade from the early 1990s, especially in the post-Mandal period. By the late 1990s, the famous Congress system had all but vanished. While it once embraced a broad spectrum of social groups across the country under its capacious umbrella, the attempt to recreate a social coalition through inclusive development did not produce a sustainable social base. It has lost its wide appeal across the country, as powerful caste and community groupings have voted for regional and smaller parties. The problem is that the rich and the poor, the upper castes and the lower castes, and the minorities, all are angry with the Congress. Ironically, even as the party has lost ground with the middle classes, it has also lost the support of Dalits, Adivasis, and Muslims to regional parties. In short, the Congress is left with no distinct group to turn to for support. To regain its influence, it needs decentralisation and it needs to build broad-based social coalitions at the state level. Strong, locally rooted state leaders could improve its political prospects, which in turn can spread to national politics.

As for party reform, it is a well-known fact that the Congress is a much depleted grassroots organisation in need of a complete revamp. For nearly a decade, Rahul Gandhi has focused his political capital on the long-term project of trying to democratise the party organisation.[24] But his efforts have neither produced any discernible change in the organisation nor delivered a new crop of leaders. So far his efforts to introduce inner-party democracy have not worked either because he has not put his heart into it or is stymied by senior leaders because they fear that it will end up marginalising them.

A series of discussions after the massive election defeat has led neither to a plan of action, nor reorganisation of the party.[25] A committee, headed by former defence minister A.K. Antony, was appointed by Sonia Gandhi to investigate the causes of the defeat.[26] It absolved the party's top leadership of any blame.[27] The committee submitted its report to Sonia Gandhi which was not shared with the members of the party. While submitting the report, Antony said that 'the reasons for the Congress defeat were something else'.[28]

Botched campaign

As a final point, the Congress ran a lacklustre campaign which clearly failed to connect with the new generation of voters who are no longer bound by traditional affiliations to a family or an ideology. It was no match for the BJP's well-crafted nationwide campaign against UPA's misrule and Congress ineptitude, creating a public mood in favour of the BJP as the preferred agent of change. The Congress campaign appeared to be weak, directionless and disjointed, and constantly played catch-up rather than defining the political narrative. At the meeting just a few weeks after the defeat, Sonia Gandhi singled out the party's communications strategy as one of its major failures, saying that 'the message of Congress was lost in the din and dust raised by an aggressive and polarizing campaign by our opponents, which was backed by unlimited resources and a hostile media'.[29] But it is the Congress and the UPA parties who are to blame for this as they hardly publicised the welfare measures either because of a lack of conviction in them or because of the feeling that they had not lived up to their own promises.

The BJP's slick campaign, bankrolled by corporate India, was unprecedented.[30] The grassroots efforts of the nationwide branches of the RSS and its affiliated organisations, enthused by Modi who was one of their own, helped convert a groundswell of dissatisfaction with the Congress into a wave. But Modi, for his part, aimed his barbs at a single target: the Gandhi family, which he took to task for everything that had gone wrong in the country. By turning the campaign into a highly personalised one, he put them on the defensive.[31] That only lent greater credence to Modi's claim that to realise its full potential India had to get rid of the Gandhi dynasty and make India a 'Congress-mukt Bharat' (Congress-free India).

His ascent was undoubtedly powered by a pliant media which was deftly used by the BJP to create a 'Modi wave'. Its media blitzkrieg dominated electoral politics as the media became its main campaign platform. For weeks, any speech by Modi in any remote district ran live on several channels. A study by the Centre for Media Studies found that Modi dominated over a third of the prime-time news telecast on five major channels. From 1 to 11 May 2014, Modi's time crossed the 50 per cent mark. Over six times what Rahul Gandhi got. And ten times the share of AAP leader Arvind Kejriwal.[32] The phenomenon of paid news acquired a new dimension altogether with media houses under pressure to act as the wind in the sails of the Modi wave. Arguably, the media moved from 'manufacturing consent' to 'manufacturing dissent' against the UPA before it returned again to 'manufacturing consent' for Modi and his government.[33]

Rightwing resurgence

The fall of the Congress and Modi's arrival signals a shift of political landscape to the Right. The 2014 election verdict was not simply a defeat of the Congress; it was also a defeat of various progressive forces which were unable to provide any coherent alternative. The BJP's coming to power is, therefore, not just one party replacing the other but an indication of a significant shift in the ideological discourse of Indian politics. Modi's decision to disband the Planning Commission has to be seen in this context. Abolishing the Planning Commission within three months of coming to power marked a clear break from the economic policy tradition that Jawaharlal Nehru and the Congress under his leadership represented. Though the Planning Commission faltered in its developmental role, the decision to scrap rather than reform it indicates a systematic dismantling of checks and balances. It indicates that the role of the state would be minimal with regard to social welfare, and there will be much stronger adherence to markets, business, and entrepreneurship. Neoliberal policies have gained momentum as the BJP seeks to undo many of the progressive measures introduced by the UPA government of the last decade. An emphatic rejection of the Congress legacy with regard to these policies is further evident from the 2015–2016 budget which leans in favour of the corporates and taxpaying class at the expense of the poor. Reductions in allocations for Scheduled Castes and Scheduled Tribes and the Integrated Child Development Scheme (ICDS) can be cited as examples of the shift.

Modi's greatest success lies in his ability to refashion Hindu nationalism by adopting a developmentalist stance 'redefined as both aspirational and nationalist'.[34] The effort to dovetail religious nationalism with economic progress has led to a widespread belief that the BJP has gone beyond its communal agenda with its new emphasis on development and governance, when in fact 'development' and 'growth' have aligned with conservative social values and institutions to form the basis of Rightwing resurgence in the country.[35] Very many people have bought into this rhetoric; indeed, many see it as India's best bet for getting ahead. A large section of the electorate is not bothered about majoritarianism as long as it does not affect their personal domain, and as long as the government succeeds in delivering higher economic growth and jobs. Significantly, this current of conservative ideology sits comfortably with education, prosperity, and consumption.[36] It lacked electoral legitimacy previously but has gained wide acceptability, thanks to popular mobilisation efforts of the Modi campaign, which sought to justify it as an expression of the will of the majority.

The Congress's revival hinges on its ability to address its crisis of credibility, encouragement of state leaders, and functioning as a vigorous Opposition in Parliament, and outside. In the long road ahead, the Congress will have to rebuild itself as a credible alternative to Modi and the BJP which stand for both economic and social conservatism. Any attempt to reshape itself as pale saffron in a bid to mimic the winner will only help to legitimise the Rightwing political discourse, while failing to pick up the electoral dividends from this competitive wooing of the Hindu vote. It is, therefore, essential that the Congress leads a nationwide campaign to counter and negate the long-term social and political impact of Rightwing ideas and policies. A critique of and mobilisation against the BJP's change of emphasis from the path of social welfare and communal harmony charted by the UPA over the last decade to majoritarian neoliberalism should form the basis of its own political and organisational mobilisation for revival and survival.[37]

However, without a dynamic leadership, voters will not look to the Congress as a viable political choice. The real key to rejuvenation lies in mass contact, the kind of platform that it adopts, and the leadership's ability to communicate that to the people on the ground rather than the eternal verities of dynastic leadership.

Notes

1 Jairam Ramesh, 'Interview by Supriya Sharma', 24 February 2014, Scroll. in (accessed 24 February 2014).
2 Zoya Hasan, 'The Congress' Moment of Truth', *The Hindu*, 11 August 2014.
3 'Dark Decade in Governance: BJP's Chargesheet on Congress-Led UPA', www.bjp.org/ . . . /A%20Dark%20Decade%20in%20Governance%20Aaro. . . (accessed 10 February 2015).
4 Economic Times Bureau, 'UPA Presided Over a Wasted Decade: BJP', *The Economic Times*, 19 January 2014.
5 Anil Padmanabhan, '2004 to 2014: India's Lost Decade', *Livemint*, 10 January 2014.
6 Mint, www.livemint.com/trading-up.
7 Mihir Sharma, 'Farewell, a Golden Age', *Business Standard*, 11 May 2014.
8 Maitreesh Ghatak, Parikshit Ghosh and Ashok Kotwal, 'Growth in the Time of UPA: Myths and Reality', *Economic and Political Weekly*, No. 16, 19 April 2014.
9 Ibid.
10 Jayati Ghosh, 'Change the Policy Mindset', *Tehelka*, 22 August 2013.
11 Mritiunjoy Mohanty, 'The Growth Model Has Come Undone', *The Hindu*, 11 July 2012.
12 Kunal Sen, ' "It's the Economy, Stupid": How the Poor Economic Performance of the UPA Regime Is a Key Issue in the Indian Elections', *University of Nottingham Blogpost*, 8 May 2014.
13 Pradeep Chhibber and Rahul Verma, 'The BJP's 2014 Modi Wave: An Ideological Consolidation of the Right', *Economic and Political Weekly*, Vol. XLIX, No. 39, 27 September 2014, 50.

166   Zoya Hasan

14 Harish Khare, 'This Perverse Rage Against the Poor', *The Hindu*, 30 August 2013.
15 Jean Dreze and Amartya Sen, *An Uncertain Glory: India and Its Contradiction* (New York: Allen Lane, 2013), 254–256.
16 Hartosh Singh Bal, 'Family Ties', *Caravan Magazine*, 1 January 2015.
17 'My mother came to my room and cried . . . because she understands that power is poison', Rahul Gandhi had said in a highly emotional speech after taking over as the Vice President in the Jaipur session of the AICC in January 2013. Reported in 'My Mother Cried, She Understands Power Is Poison: Rahul', *The Hindu*, 20 January 2013.
18 Harish Khare, 'Can Rahul Be Reborn', *Open Magazine*, 13 June 2014.
19 NDTV anchor Barkha Dutt quoted in Sadanand Dhume, 'The Last Gandhi', *First Post*, 19 August 2014.
20 'Congress Zero', Editorial, *The Hindu*, 12 February 2015.
21 After his return from his fifty-day sabbatical in early 2015, Rahul Gandhi appears serious about shouldering greater responsibility in the party and assuming a leadership role. There is no doubt that his sustained campaign against the BJP government on several issues, especially the Land Acquisition Bill, has put the government on the back foot. It has helped the Congress occupy the Opposition space and put the NDA on the defensive. But he is yet to unveil a systematic long-term plan for reviving the party or rebuilding the party organisation which is in shambles.
22 'Rahul Gandhi Pushes for Middle Path in Development', *Sakal Times*, 21 December 2014.
23 'Rahul Gandhi Breaks Silence on Jayanthi's Charges', *The Hindu*, 5 February 2015.
24 Zoya Hasan, 'Rahul Revivalism: Rahul Gandhi's Elevation and the Congress's Future', *Caravan*, 1 March 2013.
25 Sonia Gandhi set up at least three major committees to review and reorganise the party. All the committees recognised the lack of internal democracy as one of the reasons for the growing disillusionment with the organisation and recommended ending the practice of selecting Pradesh Congress Committee chiefs by nomination. But these reports were shelved, for fear of stirring up the pot too vigorously and upsetting the status quo. See more at: www.caravanmagazine.in/perspectives/rahul-revivalism#sthash.FBdp0anq.dpuf
26 A.K. Antony, Mukul Wasnik, R.C. Khuntia, and Avinash Pandey were members of this committee. Previous to this one, two more committees were headed by A.K. Antony to look into various Congress debacles and had come to the same conclusion that top leadership was in no way responsible for Congress defeats.
27 'A.K. Antony Committee Blames UPA Govt for Poll Rout, Lets Rahul Gandhi Get Away', *Financial Express*, 17 August 2014.
28 'Rahul Gandhi Not Responsible for Congress Defeat in Lok Sabha Polls: A. K. Antony', *The Economic Times*, 15 August 2015.
29 'Sonia Gandhi, Rahul Gandhi Offer to Resign From Congress Posts After Defeat, Party Refuses', *The Economic Times*, 19 May 2014.
30 Analysis by Association for Democratic Reforms (ADR) and National Election Watch (NEW) found that BJP cornered about 69 per cent of total donations made to parties in 2013–2014 even though the party was not

in power at the centre when it gained the most. Kumar Vikram, 'BJP Coffers Bulged With Corporate Cash in Financial Year 14', *Mail Today*, 25 February 2015.
31 Harish Khare, *How Modi Won It: Notes From the 2014 Election* (New Delhi: Hachette, 2015).
32 Cited in P. Sainath, 'Many Waves, and a Media Tsunami', *NewsClick*, 21 May 2014.
33 Zoya Hasan, 'Manufacturing Dissent: The Media and the 2014 Election', *The Hindu Centre for Politics and Public Policy*, 2 April 2014.
34 Arvind Rajagopal, 'The Reinvention of Hindutva', *The Hindu*, 4 March 2015.
35 Varghese George, 'A Hindutva Variant of Neo-Liberalism', *The Hindu*, 4 April 2014.
36 Santosh Desai, 'Hope and Dread: 2014 Begins and Ends With It', *The Times of India*, 28 December 2014.
37 On this see, Editorial, 'On the Verge of Extinction', *Economic and Political Weekly*, Vol. L, No. 8, 21 February 2015.

7 Explaining the inconvenient truths of Indian political behaviour

Hindutva, Modi, and Muslim voters in 2014

Mujibur Rehman[1]

The dominant political commentaries on the election results have recognised the presence of Modi wave during the 2014 campaign and the further opportunity for Hindutva politics to expand and consolidate. No scientific evidence available at this stage points to an irreversible trend, or critical realignment towards the BJP; for the latter to happen, similar or more solid outcomes have to come out of Parliamentary elections in 2019 and in 2024. However, there is enough in the 2014 mandate to suggest that India has moved Rightward, ideologically showing signs of the deepening of the Hindutva project. Furthermore, the tone and tenor of the campaign as well as the majoritarian nature of the Hindutva project does raise questions about the future of minority rights, and the Indian state's approach to its religious minorities, particularly Indian Muslims. It is in this context that I intend to reflect on the relationship between the idea of Hindutva, the approach of Modi-led campaign towards Muslim voters and their response, and how their future relationship is likely to unfold.

Broadly, this chapter suggests that the post-2014 political moment in Indian democracy has become a moment of intense anxieties, deep concerns, and troubling dilemmas for Indian Muslims. Indeed, it is comparable to the post-1857 Sepoy mutiny political moment during the British Indian history. Therefore, this election is very unique compared to other elections in modern India.[2]

Bhartiya Janata Party (BJP) and Muslim voters in 2014

The Hindu Rashtra[3] project and its hardline electoral agenda, such as the Uniform Civil Code (UCC), ban on cow slaughter, removal of the Art 370, and the construction of the Ram Temple at the disputed site in Ayodhya, Uttar Pradesh, are some of the key issues that have formed basis of deep mistrust between the Bhartiya Janata Party (formerly the Bhartiya Jana Sangh) and Indian Muslims to the extent that Muslims have looked at the party as an anti-Muslim party.[4] Other sister organisations of the BJP such as Rastriya Swayam Sevak Sangh (RSS) and Vishwa Hindu Parishad (VHP) have been part of this agenda.[5] The writings of the founding fathers of these organisations, such as Hegdewar, Savarkar, and Gowalkar, present a very inimical approach towards Indian Muslims.[6]

The Hindutva politics inspired by this understanding of Indian history found expression in the Ayodhya movement during which Muslims were often described as 'Babar's Santan'.[7] The Ayodhya movement that eventually led to demolition of Babri Masjid on 6 December 1992 cemented BJP's anti-Muslim perception among Muslims and secular non-Muslims. The Ayodhya movement, thus far, remains the most powerful political movement of these organisations, which both catapulted the BJP into a major political force and transformed Indian polity to what L.K. Advani says 'bi-polarity'.[8] Broadly, two kinds of scholarly arguments have developed on the subject: first, that which views it as an Indian version of fascism;[9] and second, that which labels it as a Hindu nationalist force.[10]

According to the post-election survey conducted by the Centre for the Study of Developing Countries (CSDS) in 2014, as Table 7.1 shows, the national vote share of Muslim votes was 7 per cent in 1999 and 2004, but it declined to 4 per cent in 2009, and then rose to 8 per cent in 2014. At the national level, it remained within the statistically insignificant range, thus it is hard to argue for a national surge of Muslim votes for the BJP. What is significant, however, is that there are some states where there has been a significant rise of Muslim votes for the BJP. Some of these states are Karnataka (25 per cent), Gujarat (17 per cent), and Uttar Pradesh (10 per cent) (see Table 7.2).

Table 7.1 Muslim voting pattern in national elections, 1999–2014

	1999	2004	2009	2014
Congress	40	36	38	38
BJP	7	7	4	8
Others	53	57	58	54

Note: Figures are percentages.

Source: National Election Study conducted by the Centre for the Study of Developing Countries (CSDS) in 2014, 2009, 2004, and 1999

Table 7.2 Survey-based estimates on Muslim voting preference: 2014 and 2009 (in %)

States	2014 INC/INC+	2014 BJP/BJP+	2014 Other Major Party	2009 INC/INC+	2009 BJP/BJP+	2009 Other
Andhra** Pradesh	-	-	-	45	-	TDP-23
Assam	42	3	AIUDF-39	32	2	AIUDF-61
Bihar	64 INC+RJD	2	JD(U)-21	29	10	RJD-21
Delhi	38	2	AAP-56	78	BJP+JD(U) 15	7
Gujarat	66	17	17	67	12	21
Karnataka	68	25	JDS-5	68	11	JDS-14
Kerala	65 UDF	3	LDF-21	71 UDF	-	LDF-27
Maharashtra	85 INC+NCP	6 BJP+SHS	-	55 INC+NCP	12 BJP+SHS	-
Uttar Pradesh	11 INC+RLD	10 BJP+AD	SP-58 BSP-18	24	3	SP-30 BSP-18
West Bengal	24	2	Trinamool-40 Left-31	58 INC+Trinamool	1	Left-30

** In this case, the figures are disaggregated during the survey by Telangana and Seemandhra so they are not comparable for many reasons.
Source: National Election Study conducted by the Centre for the Study of Developing Societies (CSDS) in 2014, 2009, 2004, and 1999

Truths of Indian political behaviour 171

Reacting to the stunning electoral victory of the BJP in 2014 Parliamentary election, Maulana Mahmood Madani,[11] General Secretary of Jamait Ulema Hind, and an influential figure of Deoband (also a former MP), said, 'So-called secular parties have suffered at the hustings as people were annoyed with them. There should not be fear or anxiety or apprehension (in the minds of Muslims) people to come and go. This country is very strong. It will not bend or break.'[12] Welcoming Modi's emphasis on development Madani said Muslims should 'get the maximum benefit' as they are the most deprived. Muslims are the second largest community. 'The country cannot go forward without us. Muslims and Dalits will get maximum benefit from development', said Madani.

What is equally striking is that the BJP is seemingly convinced that it could attract Muslims to the Hindutva project. Over past several decades, the BJP has attacked secularism and its flawed interpretation. It has also accused the secular governments of both the Congress and the non-Congress ones at the centre and in the states for practicing appeasement policy towards Muslims in their practice of secularism.[13] Inspired by the unprecedented success in 2014, various organs of the BJP have begun mobilising Muslim voters in different parts of India. One such place is West Bengal, where the BJP did not do well in terms of winning the Parliament seats, but the rise of general vote share for the BJP was significant.[14]

Not just the BJP, even the RSS has been working hard to address this trust deficit with Muslims and sell the Hindutva project. To address this after the victory, the RSS made sure to invite some Muslims for Prime Minister Modi's oath-taking ceremony on 26 May 2014, in New Delhi in order to prove that the BJP has Muslim support. It had arranged for thirty Muslims from different parts of India to attend the swearing in ceremony.[15] The RSS runs a Muslim Rashtriaya Manch (MRM) unit, and this invitation was extended to Muslims connected with this manch. Some of the former RSS members, such as Girish Jayal, Golok Behari, and Mahiradhwaj Singh, were deputed to look after these Muslim guests.[16] The invitees included Faiz Khan and Dr Salim Raj, both from Raipur. Also included were S.K. Moinnuddin (Jabalpur), Tayyab Qureshi (Ghaziabad), Maulana Shamoom Kashmi and Maulana Shoen Kashmi (Bijnore), Dr Sadakar Ali (Roorkee), Mohd Ashraf Ashrafi (Bareilly), Imran Chaudhury and Mohammed Afzal (Delhi), Shezad Ali (Agra), Abbas Ali Vohra (Bangalore), Latif Maqdoom (Pune), Dr Shahid Akhtar (Ranchi), Engineer Gulam Ali (Srinagar), Abu Baqar Naqvi (Tonk), Reshma Hussain (Jaipur), Ghani Bhai Qureshi (Gujarat), Maulana Zahid, Zahangir Alam, and others.

The detailed list does not contain any star names, but names of ordinary Muslims and some professionals.

The controversy that ensued from the anointment of the Narendra Modi as the BJP's prime ministerial candidate (especially the resistance by L.K. Advani and his decision to resign) came as both a surprise and shock even to many BJP sympathisers.[17] In recent memory, the appointment of V.P. Singh as India's Prime Minister in 1989 in the National Front government would perhaps qualify for such a comparison (but it was a post-election incident).[18] While Nitish Kumar, the JD(U) leader, had made his opposition towards Narendra Modi clear, so the JD(U)'s decision to quit the NDA coalition was predictable.[19] The decision by the Janata Dal(U) and L.K. Advani's resistance are not just the reflection of the non-consensual nature of its decision; it also recognises how much Muslim voters count.[20]

Gujarat 2002 remained a matter of concern for the BJP's leadership. Mr Modi cited a clean chit from lower judiciary as the evidence of his innocence, and steadfastly declined to offer any apology for the carnage. Instead, he said in an interview to Sahid Siddiqui, then spokesperson of the Samajvadi Party (SP), that he would prefer to be hanged in a public square if he is found guilty.[21] These factors and perceptions of Muslims about Modi hung heavily on the minds of the BJP leadership during the campaign, including Rajnath Singh, who most staunchly endorsed Narendra Modi, and as party president anointed him as BJP's prime ministerial candidate. But at the event 'Modi for PM, Mission 272, Role of Muslims', even Rajnath Singh said, 'Please note that whenever, wherever, if there has been a mistake and shortcoming on our part, I assure you that we will apologize to you by bowing our heads'. Singh's remarks triggered speculation that the BJP chief was referring to events like the Babri Masjid demolition or the Gujarat riots. He further added, 'Modi's hand in riots is a Congress propaganda'.[22]

Though the JD(U) chose to move out in 2014, and gave clear signal it would return to the NDA if anyone other than Narendra Modi is fielded as the NDA's prime ministerial candidate, there are others who reluctantly caved in but laid out a careful campaign strategy in Muslim-dominated areas, excluding Modi from the campaign materials.[23]

Narendra Modi, his anti-Muslim image and Muslim voters

The BJP's decision to field Narendra Modi as the prime ministerial candidate made 2014 election campaign largely Gujarat centric in terms of key themes of public debate, almost unprecedented in Indian election history in which a state's politics was so central to a national campaign debate. It made the Gujarat model of development and the Gujarat carnage 2002, the twin pillars around which major debates revolved. All the violent memories and anti-Muslim images associated with the demolition of the Babri Masjid were obliterated, even if the issue remains alive and the key actors politically active.

The UPA and its coalition partners considered this decision of the BJP extremely convenient. They presumed Modi's candidature had made the task to win the election somewhat easier in a heightened polarised campaign milieu. Even easier, they thought, was to form the next coalition government because, for the BJP, finding post-election coalition partners under Modi's leadership could be a daunting task. The NDA's long-standing partner JD(U)'s decision to leave the coalition only raised the UPA's hopes for the formation of the next government even in the face of comparatively poorer electoral performance. However, the UPA leadership did not realise that the Modi-led campaign would turn it around so much that it would explode the myth of coalition politics.

The pro-BJP/NDA secularists recalled Vajpayee with such fondness, as if the Ayodhya movement that polarised Indian electorate for so long was a secular movement. Pavan Verma, spokesperson of the JD(U), wrote article after article in major media during the 2014 campaign saying how there was so much of secularism in the poetry and politics of Atal Vihari Vajpayee, though there was none. It was Vajpayee who gave blessings to his party to endorse and support the Ayodhya movement. He was also the one who rushed to the Indian president to withdraw support from the V.P. Singh government when Advani was arrested by Lalu Yadav, the then Bihar Chief Minister, during his infamous *Rath Yatra* leading to unprecedented cycles of ethnic violence in Indian history.[24]

But Modi's candidature presented opportunities to the opposition parties to employ the Gujarat riot as the key issue to mobilise votes, especially among Muslims and other secular voters. A concerted attempt was made by these parties to present Narendra Modi as the most dangerous communal face in modern India. Omar Abdullah said in an interview that Modi as Prime Minister would sever Jammu and Kashmir from India.[25] Rahul Gandhi warned, '22,000 will be killed if BJP wins'.[26] Trinamool Congress party (TMC) spokesperson, Derek O'Brion, called him the 'Butcher of Gujarat'.[27] Thus, the BJP's image as a communal party largely remained intact in Muslim minds, and some also perhaps got carried away by Modi wave. On 9 November 2013, a Muslim auto-driver from Rai Barelliy told me in Lucknow that he was going to vote for the BJP because 'Modi sahib Gujarat ko chamka diya hei (Gujarat shines because of Modi)'.[28]

On the other hand, Narendra Modi campaigned mainly on the issues of development and governance, though he did offer his own spin of religion and caste in his speeches occasionally. For instance, in campaign meetings at Mangaldal, Assam, on 19 April 2014; at Hoogly, West Bengal, on 21 April 2014; and then at Bankura, West Bengal, 4 May 2014 he repeatedly raised the issue of Bangladeshi migrants, and promised he would throw them away after 16 May. He also said on 6 May 2014 in Ayodhya, 'If you want to imagine an ideal state; then it must be Ram Rajya'.

Obviously, Modi gave mixed signals and used his caste and religious identity strategically to mobilise votes during the campaign. Almost no evidence was found in his campaign speeches with any inkling of his belief in multiculturalism and no evidence of recognition of the violence emanating from the practice of the Hindutva politics.

Indeed, Modi has been the most vocal and consistent critic of secularism, which he mocked and dismissed as a bogey, and minority rights, which he labelled as a vote bank politics. No other prime ministerial candidate in the history of modern India attacked secularism as consistently and passionately as Narendra Modi did during the campaign. On the first twitter message he sent as India's Prime Minister, he chose not to mention the word 'secular' instead he used the phrase, ' inclusive India'. After becoming Prime Minister, although he has vacillated on many other issues, he has been remarkably consistent in his commitment to criticise secularism. On 14 April 2015, at a party in Berlin hosted by the India's Ambassador to Germany, he spoke of how Sanskrit has suffered owing to India's so-called secular fever.[29]

Thus, more than the demolition of Babri Masjid on 6 December 1992, it was the Gujarat carnage of 2002 that determined the anti-Muslim face of the BJP campaign in 2014, and Narendra Modi became the iconic anti-Muslim face. The campaign for Gujarat victims, especially the interventions by higher judiciary (especially SIT), as well as campaigns by various civil society organisations, contributed to the greater awareness of the Gujarat violence over the years.[30] The decision on the part of Western governments such as the USA's decision to deny a visa to Narendra Modi in 2005 on the grounds of lack of religious tolerance in Gujarat during his rule, and of European governments to sever working relationship with the Modi government also contributed to his anti-Muslim image and religious intolerance at the global level.

As the possibility of the BJP-led NDA victory became relatively obvious, there were reconciliatory efforts by the Western governments, and resumption of a working relationship with Mr Modi, the then Gujarat Chief Minister. Although there was some resistance in terms of visa denial, Modi did keep in touch with the West, and even toured several countries. He was in touch with Gujarati diaspora in America and elsewhere through video conferences. As Gujarat Chief Minister, Modi had visited several countries such as Hong Kong, Malaysia, Singapore, Taiwan, and Thailand. He had gotten Japan and Canada as partners for his biennial Vibrant Gujarat Investors Summit. Modi had visited Russia with former Prime Minister Atal Bihari Vajpayee, also in the past. He also travelled to London and Switzerland and brought back the remains of Shyamji Krishna Verma, an Indian revolutionary.

He visited China thrice, the last time in 2011 as the Gujarat Chief Minister, during which he managed the release of twelve out of twenty-two diamond traders from Gujarat who had been arrested by Chinese custom officials. Modi had visited the USA a few times before he became Chief Minister in 2001 in Gujarat.[31] According to Walter Anderson, Modi had visited the USA several times as a State Department visitor in the early 1990s. Anderson recalled having met Modi in Washington, DC, but did not find him impressive. Clearly, Modi was not considered an international pariah, despite the US ban. It also suggests how divided the modern world is on the issue of human rights violations.

However, when it became evident that Modi was going to be the BJP's prime ministerial candidate, several European governments sought reconciliation with him and reached out to him. It was in 2008 that the two European diplomats, Ole Paulsen of Denmark and Lars Olof Lindgren of Sweden, defied the European Union (EU) visa ban and reached out to the Gujarat Chief Minister. In May 2011, Poulsen's successor Freddy Svaney met Modi at the inaugural event of a Danish company's Rockwool facility at Dahej, Gujarat. He was the first European Ambassador to meet him. Svaney said, 'I am really happy I opened up towards Modi. The EU boycott was wrong. In all my meetings with him, I have found him to be thoughtful, sincere, and result oriented'.[32] Svaney was of course invited to the 2013 Vibrant Gujarat Summit and found himself on the podium. In August 2012, British High Commissioner James Bevan travelled to Gandhinagar to meet Modi, and he said, 'Engagement is not endorsement'.[33] Soon after, German ambassador Michael Steiner reached out to Modi despite opposition from Berlin and other European capitals. Separately, French Ambassador Francois Richier opened communication with Modi at the same time.

Many scholars and op-ed columnists made a case of Modi's involvement in Gujarat carnage. During the election campaign, on 10 April 2014, several prominent citizens published an open letter in *The Guardian*, London, titled, 'If Modi is elected, it will bode ill for India's future'. This letter was signed, among others, by Salman Rushdie, Anish Kapur, Deepa Mehta, and British MPs such as Mike Wood, John MacDonnel, Fiona MacTaggart, and a few others. Such campaigns contributed to the crystallisation of the anti-Muslim image of Narendra Modi.

What also strengthened this anti-Muslim perception in particular were national stories of fake encounter cases such as the Ishrat Jahan encounter case and the Sohrabuddin encounter case, in which his trusted aide and former Gujarat Home Minister, Amit Shah, now the BJP's party President, was jailed for three months. Added to this is Narendra Modi's decision to ignore the Sachar Report (2006) that was about Muslim backwardness. He resisted the implementation of the Report's recommendations, especially the scholarships from the centre for Muslim students, for which the Modi-led Gujarat government went to the Supreme Court to get approval of his decision. His resistance to this central government scheme was based on the argument that all are equal and there are no 'majorities and minorities'.

Unlike other parties, he did not offer any tickets to Muslims to run for Assembly membership. As a result, Muslims from his party remained entirely unrepresented in the Assembly of Gujarat, and also in the Parliament, during his time. At a panel discussion in *India Today Conclave 2008* with Digvijay Singh, a key Congress party spokesperson, and others, Modi said Muslim leaders were coming up at the local level. He also challenged Mr Singh to explain why there was a decline of Muslim MLAs (from seventeen to four) in the Congress party in Gujarat, and why there was no representation of other minorities, such as Parsi or Sikhs etc.[34] Diversity in representative democracy as a key principle is clearly something he does not believe in, which also offers some evidence of his belief that in Hindu India only Hindus should be holding high places of political power and minorities should remain as subordinates.

The deliberate nature of Mr Modi's neglect and discrimination against Muslims becomes apparent by his decision not to respect a High Court ruling that asked his Gujarat government to give compensation for damaged shrines during the Gujarat violence in 2002. On the other hand, his Gujarat government's decision to give Rs 100 crore to build the statue of Sardar Patel, which Mr Modi wants to be taller than the Statue of Liberty, and his subsequent decision to give Rs 200 crore from the national purse for the same purpose, only perpetuates his anti-Muslim attitudes, and exposes the hollowness to his claim of equality for majorities and minorities.

After several years of silence, as he began to nurture the ambition to become India's Prime Minister, his Gujarat government in 2011 gave Rs 50,000 compensation for shrines damaged during the 2002 riots, which the Islamic Relief Committee (IRC) rejected, saying it was 'non-commensurate with the losses sustained'.[35] The religious organisations questioned the Modi government's sincerity as it has refused to formulate a policy to compensate the damaged shrines for nine years, despite the High Court's order in its affidavit filed before the Supreme Court. It described the award a pittance, and cited the 2002 High Court order to be evaluated on a case-to-case basis. But various trusts connected with the damaged shrines had moved to the concerned district judges, and, according to their estimate, the compensation amount had touched up to Rs 85 lakh following the High Court order.

The *Sachar Report*'s publication in 2006 that provided data of extreme Muslim underrepresentation brought Muslim welfare and discrimination to the central stage of India's public debate. Though the Congress party ruled India for the greater part of seventy years, the decision to publish this report in some ways helped the UPA, particularly the Congress Party, as a pro-Muslim/minorities party. The then Prime Minister Dr Manmohan Singh's statement that Muslims must have the first right to national resources after the publication of the *Report*[36] was fiercely denounced by the BJP. The BJP also dismissed the *Sachar Report* as an attempt to perpetuate an appeasement policy for Muslims, which further hardened its anti-Muslim image. During this period, Narendra Modi was largely a prominent state figure only as Gujarat Chief Minister, and had little do with the BJP's national politics or party position with regard to Muslims.

During the ensuing period of the post-2009 election, there were efforts by Modi showing signs of willingness to interact with Muslims. This became more frequent after his victory in the Gujarat Assembly election in 2012. One of the key figures in this strategy of Muslim outreach was a Muslim businessman, owner of Parsoli Corporation in Ahmedabad, an Islamic investment Company called Zafar Sareshwala.[37] Attempts were made for an image makeover on this issue. This led to several programmes and meetings with Muslim groups.

By 16 May 2014, according to Zafar Sareshwala, Mr Modi had met more than 200/250 small groups of Muslims to understand their problems.[38] The most prominent among these meetings were two: one in which he decided not to accept a skull cap offered to him creating further controversy of his anti-Muslim image. Nitish Kumar, the Bihar Chief Minister and JD(U) leader, was fiercely opposed to his PM candidacy and advised, 'In a country like India, if you aspire to govern, you have to learn to carry people of all kinds, and all faiths. Sometimes you have to wear skull cap, sometimes you have to put tilak on your head'.[39] The other was a small gathering of *Young Indian Leaders Conclave* organised by Citizens for Accountable Governance. Mr. Modi was closeted for the entire day with 150 young Indians, out of which thirty were from the minority communities.[40] In this gathering, Sayed Zafar Mehmood,[41] who had worked with the *Sachar Report* (2006), shared the data of Muslim backwardness. When Modi was requested by Mr Mehmood to offer scholarships to Muslim students like the BJP governments in Madhya Pradesh and Chattisgarh, he retorted forcefully that 'he does not believe in minority or majority category. Other BJP governments may be doing that, but there will be no special treatment for anyone under his dispensation'. What also created further controversy was his statement of 'puppy' while trying to explain his pain for the riot victims in an interview with *Reuters* on 12 July 2014 at his Gandhi Nagar residence.[42] In fact, he did not directly compare Muslims to puppies, but that is how it got interpreted by the media, making Muslim voters wary again about his attitudes towards Muslims. It is in this interview, he asserted, that he was a Hindu nationalist. That event was, in my view, a clear case of media distortion.

The Modi campaign was certainly aware of his anti-Muslim image and arguments. It prepared for a defence. The most spectacular defence came from a Delhi-based feminist and intellectual, Madhu Purnima Kiswar. She wrote a book titled, *Modi, Muslims and Media: Voices from the Narendra Modi's Gujarat* (Manushi 2014). The *Foreword* for this book is written by a prominent journalist from the south, Chao Ramaswamy, and its *Introduction* is written by Salim Khan, one of the legendary script-writers of Salim-Javed fame, and also father of Bollywood superstar, Salman Khan.

There was also an attempt to get an endorsement from actor Salman Khan, which he skilfully avoided by saying that the best man should become India's Prime Minister in the presence of Modi at a kite flying event. Subsequently, Salman Khan told the media his view on Prime Minister is inconsequential. But, he was one of the prominent Muslim invitees to the oath-taking ceremony on 26 May 2014; and he was found sitting adjacent to Zafar Sareshwala, the key interlocutor. In the foreword of *Modi, Muslims and Media*, Salim Khan writes, 'When I was climbing down the staircase of the theatre after watching Richard Attenborough's *Gandhi*, I felt that after seeing the film I was a better human being. The film that is being screened via this book in some ways has a similar impact' (Kiswhar 2014: 11). The book's main argument is that media and conflict entrepreneurs are mainly responsible for creating the anti-Muslim image of Modi. Twenty-two chapters in it cover themes from the Godra incident to Muslim support for Modi.

At this stage, I shall discuss Modi's position on two further cases and reflect on his anti-Muslim image and Muslim voters. The first is the Muzaffarnagar riot, and the second is his decision to run for the Varanasi parliamentary constituency.

Muzaffarnagar riots in August–September 2013 and Narendra Modi

Even if one is willing to give clean chit to Modi, as some claim, on the Gujarat riot in 2002; the Muzaffarnagar riots offer another opportunity to reflect on the issue of his anti-Muslim image. During August–September 2013, the Muzaffarnagar riots took place, in which more than fifty people died and, within days, thousands of people, particularly Muslims, became homeless. These victims had to take refuge in various relief camps.[43] It was argued that the riot that erupted was part of a larger conspiracy to polarise the voters across religious lines in Uttar Pradesh, and some even argue it had paid off during the last Parliamentary election.[44]

Central to the BJP strategy for election 2014 was to win Uttar Pradesh, for which Amit Shah, a trusted aide of Narendra Modi was given the charge. Mr Modi has remained tight-lipped about the violence ever since, as if nothing happened. Mr Modi did go to address a rally near Muzaffarnagar[45] (in a place called Bulandsahar, only 100 kilometres away), which was attended by scores of Muslims according to media reports. In his speech, Modi used data from the *Sachar Report* (2006) to argue that Muslims of Gujarat are better off than Uttar Pradesh. He mocked those who use secularism to deride him, and said the Congress brand of secularism has destroyed Muslims:

> Aaj Kal Fashion Ho Gaya hai, when Modi says Vikas,
> They say, 'secularism ko Kya Hoga?'
> When Modi says aparadh, 'Secularism ko kya Hoga?'
> Secularism, Secularism, Secularism. . . .
> I ask you: Do you want corruption, crime free development oriented government?

Referring to the *Sachar Report*, he said. 'PSUs in UP have 6% Muslim employees, in Gujarat PSUs it is 8.5%. Further in lower level, Gujarat employs 16% Muslims while UP employs only 5%'. It is in this meeting that some of the accused of Muzaffarnagar, also major leaders of the BJP in the locality, were honoured. In the beginning, there was a plan to honour these accused by Narendra Modi himself, but the plan was changed, and they were honoured before Mr Modi arrived at the same podium. One of the accused, Sanjeev Baliyan, now an elected MP from the BJP ticket, was made a member of Modi's Cabinet.[46]

Mr Amit Saha, on the other hand, gave several hate speeches during the campaign. He was reprimanded and a ban was on imposed on his campaign by the Election Commission. In one meeting he declared, 'Azamgarh is the base of terrorists'.[47] Prominent politicians from Uttar Pradesh such as Mayawati and Akhilesh Yadav condemned his statement.[48] Mr Shah had earlier been debarred from campaigning following his controversial statement at a poll meeting in Muzaffarnagar in April. Aligarh Muslim Teachers Association (AMUTA) demanded that the Election Commission to reimpose the ban on Amit Shah.[49] The occasion when Mr Modi mentioned the Muzaffarnagar riots was when he decided to attack Rahul Gandhi's statement about how Pakistan intelligence agencies (ISI) were working to brainwash young Muslim victims and were recruiting for terror activities.[50] Mr Modi expressed his anger on Rahul Gandhi for tarnishing the image of an entire community, and later attacked Mulayam Yadav for failing to help victims.[51]

After the riots, prominent leaders of the UPA government such as Dr Manmohan Singh, Sonia Gandhi, and Rahul Gandhi paid visits to camps and riot-hit areas. BJP spokesperson, Mukhtar Abbas Naqvi, made fun of these visits as acts of 'secular tourism',[52] adding new vocabulary to the discussion on secularism. After being elected as India's Prime Minister, Narendra Modi has yet to open his mouth about these victims. He has made many visits to several foreign capitals as Indian Prime Minister, but not one to the relief camps of Muzaffarnagar victims. These camps are still active and located less than hundred kilometres away. This is very similar to his conduct as Gujarat Chief Minister, when he chose to not visit relief colonies in Ahmedabad during his reign of more than a decade. The decision not to recognise these victims of violence, largely innocent citizens, belonging to Muslim community reflects an ideological aspect of his mindset.[53]

In addition, a group of Kashmiri students studying at a college hostel in Noida, Uttar Pradesh, were made to shout a pro-India, anti-Pakistan slogan during this campaign. They were roughed up and terrorised by men allegedly associated with Hindutva groups.[54] Modi, generally super-active in responding to political developments, chose to remain tight-lipped.

Narendra Modi, Varanasi, and Muslim voters

The decision to fight the Varanasi parliamentary seat by Narendra Modi was part of the larger plan to exploit the symbolic religious value of Varanasi. This was another crucial masterstroke that the BJP pulled off successfully in the 2014 election campaign. Given that there has been a loud claim that Modi's campaign was all about development, one wonders how Varanasi fits into that narrative. It was clearly aimed to deepen the Hindutva politics.

On the other hand, after the resounding success of the AAP party in the Delhi Assembly election in 2013, its leadership had developed ambition to expand nationally. As part of that strategy, hoping to make the party nationally relevant, the AAP had decided to fight against Modi in any seat outside Gujarat. According to a letter published by Manish Sisodia, it was Yogendra Yadav who had forced reluctant Arvind Kejriwal to fight from the Varanasi seat.[55] This decision also forced Narendra Modi to stand from a second seat, Vadodara, Gujarat, a place where he had spent quite a few years as a pracharak. Modi won the Varanasi seat by a margin of 3.37 lakh votes against Arvind Kejriwal who polled 179,739 votes against Modi's 516,593 votes. There was total polling of 10.28 lakh votes at the 12 May election.

Varanasi had a significant Muslim population and the BJP did make an effort to reach out to them. It is a place from where legendary musician, the late Bishmillah Khan, comes and the BJP made an attempt to rope in the family of Bishmillah Khan as one of the proposers for Modi's candidacy. The family of Mr Bishmillah Khan turned down the request saying that it did not want to take sides on politics. Ironically, some of family members played Sehnai when Rahul Gandhi had his roadshow in support of the Congress party candidate, Mr Ajay Rai, only a few days after Narendra Modi's roadshow.

After Modi's rally, Arvind Kejriwal organised a rally in Varanasi. According to a report, Kerjiwal started his rally from the Benares Hindu University (BHU), the same place from where Modi had started his show, and travelled to Lahuaabeer, covering six kilometres in three hours. 'The rally also had a substantial presence of Muslims, who walked with the crowd and also moved in the vehicles'.[56]

No doubt, the fight between Modi and Kejriwal became one of the most high-profile election fights in India's election history. Despite the defeat, Kejriwal was appreciated in various media outlets for fighting against Modi. Some reports with titles as follows appeared in the media such as, 'Kejriwal Waging Spirited Campaign'.[57] As it increasingly became clear that Modi was enjoying an advantage when reports like 'Modi Flying High, Kejri Lying Low' appeared.[58] Modi's major public meeting, which was organised closer to the Muslim residential area, was not allowed by the Election Commission as it could cause a law and order problem. On his second and last visit before the election, the BJP campaign committee managed to persuade Colonel Nizammudin, who had fought with Subha Bose's Azad Hind Fauz, to welcome Mr Modi, who offered his respect to the Colonel by falling at his feet, an act that earned some appreciation of local Muslims. Interestingly, according to a report, Modi spent less than a fifth declared by his Congress rival Ajay Rai and about a fourth of the cash-strapped AAP candidate Arvind Kejriwal, according to the data available on 1 May. While Modi spent about 5.83 lakhs, Kejriwal spent only 22 lakhs and Rai declared 32 lakhs on election-related activities.[59]

Narendra Modi won the Varanasi seat with a large margin owing to the support of Dalit voters. There were reports suggesting a shift of Dalit votes towards the BJP.[60] The Dalit vote in Uttar Pradesh is of two kinds. The bulk of these are known as Jatavs, also known as Chamars in the east. This caste, educated and predominant in government service, forms the core vote of Bahujan Samaj Party (BSP), not least because Mayawati herself was born into a Jatav family. The Pasis come in the second layer, and are followed, among others, by the Dhobis, Valmikis, Khatiks, and Dushads. The 2011 Census for UP lists sixty-six Dalit sub-castes. The Jatav/Chamar tops the population with a 55 per cent share of the state's Dalits. The Pasis are 15 per cent, a distant second. The Pasis shift has happened, is significant, and would be in keeping with the overall caste movement towards the BJP in this election. The Dalit castes outside the Jatav/Chamar core of the BSP are always susceptible to poaching by non-BSP parties. In his book, *Fascinating Hindutva*, Badri Narayan attributes this attraction to the BJP's conscious attempt at 'myth making' so as to add more and more caste groups to Hindutva's vote bank.[61]

Conclusion

There is not much evidence of a national trend among Muslim voters towards the BJP or Modi in the 2014 Parliamentary election. In the post-victory scenario, there seemed to be some enthusiasm among Muslims leaders, clergy class, and ordinary citizens for Modi/BJP, based on statements that have appeared in various media. The

Modi government has retained Ministry of Minority Affairs; and the Finance Minister has allotted Rs 100/00 crore for *madarsa* modernisation in 2014 budget. At the same time, new national programmes are launched in the name of Deen Dayal Upadhaya and Shyama Prasad Mukherjee, iconic names of the Hindutva project by the government. This sends mixed signals about the government's ideological orientation. Modi's silence on the Muzaffarnagar violence stands as a matter of concern. Ban on cow slaughter, cow vigilantism,[62] etc. have deepened Muslim mistrust towards the BJP and the RSS to such an extent that this mistrust is as high as if not more than the post–Babri Masjid demolition period.

In most Assembly elections that took place after 2014, particularly in Bihar, Uttar Pradesh, and Gujarat, the campaign rhetoric contributed significantly to religious polarisation. Prime Minister Modi's silence on the lynching of Muslims in various parts of India, and politics of 'love jihad', and *ghar wapsi* has created an anti-Muslim social and political climate and has created fertile ambience for the hate campaign against Muslims. Considering this, there are good reasons for savvy Muslim voters to be worried or concerned.

Unlike the post-1857 political moment, when Indian Muslims had to deal with only the colonial state, Muslim voters at this point have to deal with the BJP and non-BJP parties as well in their negotiation for their future and their rights together with the Indian state, thus facing broadly a triangular political world. Thus, there is some difference in the political context which makes the struggle for possibilities of minority rights and secularism particularly unique.

The Hindutva project's electoral future hinges on a number of factors, including the credibility of the Modi government to deliver on governance and development. After four years, there is little evidence that the Modi government is serious on delivery. More importantly, how are the non-BJP parties going to organise in various parts of India to challenge the BJP? At this point, there is little evidence of any credible anti-BJP anti-coalition. The fact remains that only 31 per cent voted for the BJP, and even in this 31 per cent, not all voted for the Hindutva project. There is a vast bulk of voters who should be the source of incentives for non-BJP political elites and for a non-Hindutva brand of politics, one that could be more responsive to development as well as to multiculturalism and minority rights.

Among the founding ideas, minority rights and secularism have emerged deeply wounded from the 2014 campaign. One wonders whether Muslim voters who are willing to strike a relationship with the Hindutva ideology are able to grasp the complexities associated with it. The argument that secularism finds its finest manifestation in the ever-expanding Hindutva project, and that its long history has no evidence of violence, and majoritarian usurpation of rights and resources are figments of imaginations of some vested interests has dangerous implications for Indian democracy. Clearly, voters have opted for development with Hindutva against secularism without governance or development as a political alternative in the 2014 Parliamentary election. For secularism and minority rights to find legitimate appeal, they needed to be combined with governance and development. The realisation of this fact could create real possibilities for providing credible alternatives to the fast-expanding Hindutva project.

Notes

1 I am thankful to scholars for their feedback on this chapter during its presentation at various Universities such as at the Wolfson College, University of Oxford, UK; European Association for South Asian Studies at Zurich, Switzerland (2014); Arnold-Bergstraesser-Institute, Frieburg, Germany, and a few other places.
2 There are many important works on this issue. See Hardy (1973); Hassan (1997); Robinson (2010); Hunter (2012)
3 Pandey (2007); Jaffrelot (2007); Ananya Vajpei (2012); Sharma (2016).
4 For an interesting analysis on the BJP, see Jaffrelot (1998); Hansen(1999); Wallace (2015).
5 There is a great deal of scholarship on the subject. Some useful works are Gopal (1992)
6 For an insight to the writings of Savarkar, Gowalkar, Hegdewar see, Sharma (2016); Jaffrelot (2007).
7 For a nuanced understanding of Ayodhya movement, see Gopal (1992).
8 See Advani (2010). By bi-polarity, Advani basically means that there is a challenger to the Congress party, and its most convincing evidence comes from the fact that India politics even today runs as a NDA and UPA coalition. Scholars, however, have argued that Indian polity has become multi-polar.
9 There are several works that look at it as Hindu fascism (Vinaik 2017).
10 Writing that examines it as Hindu nationalism, see Jaffrelot (2007); Adeney and Saez (2006).
11 Madanis are one of the most powerful Maulavi families in India, and have a major say in running the Deoband Madarsa for several generations. Once known for their proximity to the Congress party, some of the members of this family have changed loyalties.
12 'So Called Secular Parties Suffered as People Are Annoyed With Them', *The Economic Times*, 26 May 2014.
13 This argument of appeasement in fact goes back to the 1930s and 1940s. There are evidences in the letters Nehru wrote to Chief Ministers answering the question of appeasement.
14 If the Modi wave is to be judged based on its capacity to transform votes into seats, then West Bengal, Odisha, and Tamil Nadu are a few states that clearly fall into non–Modi wave states. Looking at the dramatic rise

of vote share of more than 10 per cent does indicate a massive surge of general votes for the BJP in West Bengal.
15 Similar invitations were extended to the Christian community.
16 'To Show Muslim Support, RSS Ensures Invites for Three Dozen', *The Indian Express*, 26 May 2014.
17 The major reason Advani cited was the possibility that Modi would swallow the BJP, and his concerns were how personal ambitions should not consume a party. But the truth is that no one perhaps has any clear idea why Advani opposed Modi. It is important to recall that Advani protected Modi from being sacked as Gujarat CM in 2002, if all the accounts about Vajpayee's comments are taken into consideration.
18 V.P. Singh-Chandrasekhar's story of power struggle is in some ways comparable to this, but there is difference between the relationship between these two with Advani-Modi case, where the relationship is of a master and disciple. Interestingly, no insider had any inkling about the Advani's resistance.
19 Nitish Kumar rejoined the NDA again in 2017.
20 Given that JD(U) was part of the BJP-led coalition even during Gujarat 2002, it is naïve to argue that the decision of JD(U) was purely driven by secularism, and was ideological in nature.
21 Samajvadi Party (SP) removed Siddiqui after this interview. See 'Samajvadi Party Disowns Siddiqui After His Modi Interview', *The Times of India*, 28 July 2013. The interview was conducted for *Naya Duniya*, which Siddiqui's family owns.
22 'Rajnath Woos Muslims With Offer of Apology for Mistakes', *The Indian Express*, 26 February 2014.
23 There are other places such as in Madya Pradesh where the campaign did not give much prominence to Modi, but it is certainly not owing to the Muslim factor.
24 Narendra Modi was little known in the public space but was a key organiser of Advani's *Rath Yatra*.
25 'Modi Will Sever J and K', *The Hindu*, 8 May 2014.
26 '22,000 Will Be Killed If BJP Wins', 10 May 2014, www.ndtv.com (accessed 14 September 2014).
27 'Blood Is Still Fresh in the Hands of the Butcher of Gujarat', 28 April 2014, www.ndtv.com (accessed 14 September 2014).
28 Interview with the author on 9 November 2013, Lucknow.
29 See my op-ed in *The Hindu*: Rehman (2016).
30 There are several activists who played key role in championing the human rights violation of Gujarat 2002. Some major names are Teest Setalvad, Mallika Sarabai, Sabnam Hashmi, Harsh Mander, and a few others.
31 'Modi Has Been to US', *The Times of India*, 26 May 2014.
32 'Denmark, Sweden Led the Way in Ending Modi's Global Isolation', *The Times of India*, 26 May 2014 (accessed 13 January 2018).
33 'Engagement With Modi Is Not an Endorsement: UK High Commissioner', 22 August 2013. www.firstpost.com (accessed 13 January 2018).
34 www.youtube.com, 29 August 2008 (accessed 14 September 2014).
35 'Muslims Reject Modi Govt Relief for Shrines', *The Times of India*, 22 January 2014.

36. 'Muslims Must Have First Claim on the National Resources: PM (Dr. Manmohan Singh)', *The Times of India*, 9 December 2006.
37. After the Modi government took power in New Delhi, Mr Sareshwala was rewarded with the post of Chancellor of Maulana Azad National Urdu University, Hyderabad, in 2015.
38. India TV show with Rajat Sharma, 28 May 2014.
39. 'Sometimes You Have to Wear Skull Cap, at Times Tilak', 20 September 2013, www.ndtv.com (accessed 14 September 2014).
40. 'Is This the 2014 Effect? Modi Sits Through the Presentation on 2002 Riots, Says It Will Consider It', *India Today*, 29 June 2013.
41. Sayed Zafar Mehmood, also brother of Tahir Mehmood, who served as the Chairman of the National Commission for the Minorities, New Delhi, during the NDA regime. The family has had connections with the BJP leadership for a long time.
42. 'Modi's Puppy Remark Triggers New Controversy Over 2002 Riots', 12 July 2014, in reuters.com (accessed 14 September 2014).
43. 'Muzafarnagar: Tales of Death and Despair in a Riot Hit Town', 25 September 2013, www.bbc.com (accessed 14 September 2014).
44. 'As Riot Hit Muzaffarnagar Votes, Religious Divide favours Modi', 10 April 2014, www.reuters.com (accessed 14 September 2014).
45. 'To Muslims, Modi Hard Sells Graft-Free Government', *The Indian Express*, 27 March 2014.
46. 'Muzaffarnagar Accused Makes It to the Modi Cabinet', 27 May 2014 www.Firstpost.com (accessed 14 September 2014).
47. 'Azamgarh Is the Base of Terrorists" Amit Shah', *The Times of India*, 4 May 2014.
48. 'Mayawati Slams Amit Shah's Remarks on Azamgarh', *The Times of India*, 6 May 2014. Akhilesh Yadav also condemned the Shah's statement.
49. 'Reimpose Ban on Amit Shah', *The Times of India*, 6 May 2014.
50. 'Youth in Muzaffarnagar Contacted by ISI: Officials Deny Rahul's Claim', *The Hindustan Times*, 26 October 2013.
51. 'Narendra Modi Refers to Muzaffarnagar Riots to Attack Mulayam', *The Indian Express*, 18 April 2014.
52. 'Manmohan, Sonia's Visit to Muzaffarngagar Is Secular Tourism: BJP', *The Indian Express*, 16 September 2013. The statement came from BJP spokesperson, Mukhar Abbas Naqvi.
53. For a nuanced understanding of this violence, see my essay, 'The Consequences of Playing With Fire in Uttar Pradesh', 2016, www.thehinducentre.com (accessed 13 January 2018).
54. 'Omar Cautions Modi Against Sending Henchmen to Intimidate Kashmiri Students', *The Times of India*, 6 May 2014.
55. 'AAP vs AAP: Full Test of Manish Sisodia and Yogendra Yadav's Letter', *The Times of India*, 9 June 2014.
56. 'Kejriwal's Show of Strength in Varanasi', *The Times of India*, 10 May 2014.
57. 'Kejriwal Waging Spirited campaign', *The Economic Times*, 10 May 2014.
58. 'Modi flying High, Kejri Lying Low', *The Economic Times*, 9 May 2014.
59. 'Man Leading BJP From Front Last in Varanasi Spending: Modi Spent Less Than a Fifth of the Amount Declared by Cong's Ajay Rai and Just About a Fourth of That Incurred by Arvind Kejriwal', *The Economic Times*, 7 May 2014.

60 Vidya Subramanium (2014).
61 Badri Narayan (2008).
62 For a detailed discussion on cow vigilantism, see Mujibur Rehman's 'Cow Vigilantism and Lynching of Muslims: Making Sense of New Face of Hindutva Politics' (unpublished), presented at Centre for South Asian Studies (CEIAS), Paris, 10 October 2017.

Bibliography

Adeney, Katharine and Lawrence Saez. 2006. *Coalition Politics and Hindu Nationalism*. London: Routledge.
Advani, L.K. 2010. *My Country, My Life*. New Delhi: Rupa Publications.
Anderson, Walter and Shridhar Damle. 1987. *Brotherhood in Saffron: The Rashtriya Sevak Sangh and Hindu Revivalism*. New York: Westview Press.
Banerjee, Mukulika. 2014. *Why India Votes? Exploring the Political South Asia*. London: Routledge.
Basu, Amrita. 2015. *Violence Conjectures in Democratic India*. New York: Cambridge University Press.
Bilgrami, Akeel. 2011. *Democratic Culture: Historical and Philosophical Essays*. London: Routledge.
———. 2016. *Secularism, Identity, Enchantment*. New Delhi: Permanent Black.
Calhoun, Craig. 1994. *Social Theory and Politics of Identity*. London: Wiley-Blackwell.
Chandra, Kanchan. 2016. *Democratic Dynasties: State, Party and Family in Contemporary Indian Politics*. New Delhi: Cambridge University Press.
Chatterjee, Partha and Ira Katznelson. 2012. *Anxieties of Democracy: Reflections on Toquevillean Reflections on India and the United States*. New Delhi: Oxford University Press.
De Souza, Peter D. and E. Sridharan. 2007. *India's Political Parties*. New Delhi: SAGE Publications.
Gopal, Sarvapalli (ed.). 1991. *Anatomy of a Confrontation: Ayodya and Rise of Communal Politics in India*. New Delhi: Penguin.
Graham, Bruce. 2007. *Hindu Nationalism and Indian Politics: The Origins and Development of the Bhartiya Jana Sangh*. London, Cambridge: Cambridge University Press.
Guha, Ramachandra. 2017. *Indira After Gandhi*. London: Pan Macmillan.
Hansen, Thomas Blom. 1999. *The Saffron Wave: Democracy and the Hindu Nationalism in Modern India*. Princeton: Princeton University Press.
Hardy, Peter. 1973. *The Muslims of the British India*. Cambridge: Cambridge University Press.
Hasan, Mushirul. 1997. *Legacy of a Divided Nation: Indian Muslims Since Independence*. New Delhi: Oxford University Press.
Hasan, Zoya. 2004. *Parties and Party Politics in India*. New Delhi: Oxford University Press.
———. 2009. *Politics of Inclusion: Caste, Minorities and Affirmative Action*. New Delhi: Oxford University Press.

———. 2012. *Congress After Indira: Policy, Power and Political Change (1984–2009)*. New Delhi: Oxford University Press.

Hasan, Zoya, Francine Frankel, Rajeev Bhargava and Balveer Arora (eds.). 2002. *Transforming India: Social and Political Dynamics of Democracy*. New Delhi: Oxford University Press.

Hunter, W.W. 2012. *Indian Mussalmans*. New Delhi: Rupa Publications.

Jaffrelot, Chrsiptophe. 1998. *The Hindu Nationalist Movement in India*. New York: Columbia University Press.

———. 2007. *Hindu Nationalism: A Reader*. Princeton: Princeton University Press.

Jha, D. N. 2009. *The Myth of Holy Cow*. New Delhi: Navayana.

Jha, Dhirendra K. 2017. *Shadow Armies: Fringe Organizations and Foot Soldiers of Hindutva*. New Delhi: Juggernaut.

Jha, Prashant. 2017. *How BJP Wins*. New Delhi: Harper Collins.

Kaur, Ravinder. 2015. 'Good Times, Brought to You by Brand Modi', *Television and News Media*, 16(4): 323–330.

———. 2016. 'I am India Shining: The Investor- Citizen and the Indelible Icon of Good Times', *The Journal of Asian Studies*, 75(3), August: 1–28.

Khare, Harish. 2014. *How Modi Won It*. New Delhi: Hacchette India.

Kiswhar, Madhu. 2014. *Modi, Muslims and Media: Voices From Modi's Gujarat*. New Delhi: Manushi.

Kothari, Rajni. 1988. *State Against Democracy*. New Delhi: South Asia Books.

———. 1989. *Politics and People* (Vol. 1). New Delhi: New Horizon Press.

———. 2012. *Politics in India*. New Delhi: Orient Blackswan.

Lokhande, Sanjeevini B. 2016. *Communal Violence, Forced Migration, and the State: Gujarat Since 2002*. Cambridge: Cambridge University Press.

Marino, Andy. 2014. *Narendra Modi: A Political Biography*. New Delhi: Harper Collins.

Mukhopadhaya, Nilanjan. 2013. *Narendra Modi: The Man, the Times*. New Delhi: Tranquebar Press.

Narayan, Badri. 2008. *Fascinating Hindutva: Saffron Politics and Dalit Mobilization*. New Delhi: SAGE Publications.

Palshikar, Suhas, Sanjay Kumar and Sanjay Lodha (eds.). 2017. *Electoral Politics in India: The Resurgence of Bhartiya Janata Party*. New Delhi: Routledge Publications.

Pandey, Gyanendra. 2007. *Routine Violence: Nation, Fragments and Histories*. Stanford: Stanford University Press.

Pashikar, Suhas, K.C. Suri and Yogendra Yadav (eds.). 2011. *Party Competition in Indian States: Electoral Politics in a Post-Congress Politics*. New Delhi: Oxford University Press.

———. 2014. *Party Competition in Indian States: Electoral Politics in a Post-Congress Polity*. New Delhi: Oxford University Press.

Paul, Wallace. 2015. *India's 2014 Elections: A Modi-Led BJP Sweep*. New Delhi: SAGE Publication.

Price, Lance. 2015. *Modi Effect: Narendra Modi's Campaign to Transform India*. London: Hodder and Stroughton.

Rehman, Mujibur. 2016. *Communalism in Postcolonial India: Changing Contours*. London and New Delhi: Routledge.
———. 2018. *Rise of Saffron Power: Reflections on Indian Politics*. London and New Delhi: Routledge.
Robinson, Francis. 2010. *Islam in South Asia*. Oxford: Oxford University.
Rupalia, Sanjay. 2015. *Divided We Govern: Coalition Politics in Modern India*. New Delhi: Oxford.
Sandel, Michael. 1994. 'Review of Political Liberalism', *Harvard Law Review*, 107: 1765–1794.
Sardesai, Rajdeep. 2014. *Election That Changed India 2014*. New Delhi: Viking.
Sen, Amartya. 2006. *Argumentative Indian: Writings on Indian History, Culture and Identity*. London: Penguin.
———. 2007. *Identity and Violence: Illusions of Destiny*. London: Penguin.
Sharma, Jyotirmaya. 2003. *Hindutva: Exploring the Idea of Hindu Nationalism*. New Delhi: Viking
Shastri, Sandeep, K.C. Suri and Yogendra Yadav (eds.). 2009. *Electoral Politics in Indian States: Lok Sabha Elections in 2004 and Beyond*. New Delhi: Oxford University Press.
Shridharan, E. (ed.). 2014. *Coalition Politics in India: Selected Issues at the Centre and States*. New Delhi: Academic Foundation.
Subramanium, Vidya. 2014. 'Chasing the Dalit Vote in UP', *The Hindu*, May 9.
Tachil, Tariq. 2014. *Elite Parties, Poor Voters: How Social Services Win Votes in India*. Cambridge: Cambridge University Press.
Tawa Lama-Rewal, Stephanie. 2009. 'Studying Elections in India: Scientific and Political Debates', *South Asia Multi-Disciplinary Academic Journal* (SAMAJ), (3): 1–15, online. http://samaj.revue.org (accessed on November 25, 2017).
Taylor, Charles. 1997. *Philosophical Arguments*. Cambridge: Harvard University Press.
Ullekh, P. N. 2016. *The Untold Vajpayee: Politician and Paradox*. New Delhi: Penguin Random House.
Vaishnav, Milan. 2017a. 'Modi's Victory and the BJP's Future: Will Modi Remake the Party?', *Foreign Affairs*, 15. www.foreignaffairs (accessed on November 25, 2017).
———. 2017b. *Why Crime Pays*. New Delhi: Harper.
Vajpayi, Ananya. 2012. *Righteous Republic: Political Foundations of Modern India*. Cambridge: Harvard University Press.
Varadharajan, Siddarth. 2002. *Gujarat: The Making of a Tragedy*. New Delhi: Penguin.
Vinaik, Achin. 2017. *Hindutva Rising: Secular Claims, Communal Realities*. New Delhi: Tulika Books.
Wallace, Paul (ed.). 2015. *India's 2014 Elections: A Modi-Led BJP Sweep*. New Delhi: SAGE Publications.

Wallace, Paul and Ramashray Roy (eds.). 2011. *India's 2009 Elections: Coalition Politics, Party Competition and Congress Continuity*. London: SAGE Publications.

Wilkinson, Steve. 2004. *Votes and Violence: Electoral Competition and Communal Riots in India*. New Delhi: Cambridge University Press.

———. 2010. 'Data and the Study of Indian Politics', in Niraja Gopal Jayal and Prata Bhanu Mehta (eds.), *Oxford Handbook on Indian Politics*. New Delhi: Oxford University Press.

8 The dance of democracy[1]
Election 2014 and the marginalised and minorities

Rudolf C. Heredia

The national election for the Lok Sabha in April–May 2014 was a watershed in India's democratic polity. The Baratiya Janta Party (BJP) made a quantum leap over the threshold of coalition politics, winning 282 seats out of 543, a clear majority on its own, while their coalition, the National Democratic Alliance (NDA) coalition, won 336 seats, an almost two-thirds majority. The Indian National Congress is a poor opposition with just forty-four seats, and sixty with its allies in the United Progressive Alliance (UPA). What would these results now mean for the minorities and the marginalised? Was this a negative anti-incumbency vote against the Congress and the UPA?

The election marks a quantum leap in the rise of saffron power committed to a Savarkarite Hindu Rastra (Savarkar 1964, 1989), which is authoritarian and majoritarian as well. With no credible national political party in the opposition as yet, there already is a severe suppression of dissent and little tolerance for minority communities, like Muslims and Christians, or for marginalised peoples, like Dalits and tribals. All this can only drastically undermine the Constitutional 'idea of India' as a socialist, secular democracy, which is ominously unravelling, leaving especially the marginalised and minorities insecure and fearful. Here the focus is on the Christians as a very small and vulnerable community, in particular tribal Christians.

Winners' surprise, losers' shock

For the winners, the general election of 2014 was an undeserved surprise, for the losers, an unexpected shock. Neither anticipated such extreme results. The largest two national parties, the BJP and the Congress, found themselves at the two opposite extremes: with their highest and the lowest tally, respectively, in the Lok Sabha to date. Those regional parties with a strong regional identity in their states and with a weak presence of a national party there did well: the TMC in Bengal, the BJD in Odisha, the AIDMK in Tamil Nadu. The others without any supporting alliance faired disastrously: the SP and the BSP in Uttar Pradesh, the JDU and the RJD in Bihar. In Punjab, Gujarat, Maharashtra, and across the states in the Hindu belt, the NDA made a near clean sweep.

The failure of the UPA and the Congress to heed the alarming early warning of the nine state legislative elections results in 2013, and to begin gearing up for the Lok Sabha elections in time, proved disastrous for them in 2014. It turned out to be its worst performance ever. And even now there are few indications that appropriate lessons have been learnt or remedial action initiated. The Congress, in particular, seems to be on a path to self-destruction.

On the other hand, once Narendra Modi had been appointed to lead the BJP election campaign and later was anointed to be its prime ministerial candidate, he led, single-mindedly, relentlessly pursuing his goal, constantly supported by the media-owned corporations and generously funded by corporate business. The media unashamedly went on 'flogging the Modi mythology until all the elements of it congealed into common sense, so much so that, for TV-watching India, way before 16 May arrived, the idea of Modi's Prime Ministership had acquired an aura of inevitability' (Sampath 2014). Supported by

> the process of catapulting him to this high pedestal has been one of the costliest in the world (estimated at Rs 10,000 crore), . . . The electoral process involved Modi addressing rallies at 5,800 locations, travelling a blistering 3,00,000 km, which included 1,350 locations covered by rallies using 3D holographic projection technology through which more than 100 places could be addressed simultaneously. . . . and, of course, backed by an army of lakhs of Rashtriya Swayamsevak Sangh (RSS) cadres, who ensured that, if required, specific places could be duly lubricated with blood, as in Muzaffarnagar in Uttar Pradesh and Kokrajhar in Assam.
>
> (Teltumbde 2014: 10)

Big business will now expect a huge payoff from Modi's Gujarat model of development, which has already done so well by them in the home state and which he insistently projected as the answer for the country's growth. Were the Lok Sabbha elections a majoritarian mandate for the Gujarat model of development and its Hindutva inspiration so successfully marketed by Modi and his supporters? Was it a vote against political corruption, that the Congress and the UPA were accused of, or a vote for good governance that the BJP was campaigning on? Whatever the mix of motivations, the victors are using their mandate to implement a majoritarian saffron neoliberalism.

The Congress loss

The Congress loss would seem like a self-filling death-wish: a listless campaign, overly dependent on the Gandhi family and senior leaders distancing themselves from the electoral fray. Little wonder then that it never really took off. This was so very different from the way Congress fought the general elections of 2004 and 2009. This time the party began their campaign with an air of defeat. Many leaders did not contest. There was no inspiring message, nothing to rally its voters. They never seemed to get their act together. In these circumstances the most recent economic woes of declining growth and increasing inflation, the weakening Rupee and the growing deficit were all successfully exploited by the opposition to gain convincing credibility. There was no vigorous counter-attack, no energetic defence or persuasive explanation made. The then Prime Minister's silence was deafening.

Yet much of the more recent economic decline from an earlier high was also a reflection of the weak global economy still struggling to recover from its earlier meltdown. Moreover,

> compared to the National Democratic Alliance regime, the UPA period has been characterised by faster growth, higher savings and investment, growing foreign trade and capital inflows, and increased infrastructure spending in partnership with private capital.
>
> (Ghatak et al. 2014: 34)

In fact, the overall performance of the United Progressive Alliance (UPA over ten years at the centre was better than that of the National Democratic Alliance (NDA) over its six:

> Indians started saving and investing more, the economy opened up, foreign investment came rushing in, poverty declined sharply and building of infrastructure gathered pace. . . . Measures of human development – nutrition, educational attainment, life expectancy, etc – continued to record slow improvement even as poverty was at its lowest and fell quite sharply. . . . Real GDP grew at nearly 6% per year under the NDA, which has increased to 7.6% during UPA's rule.
>
> (Ghatak et al. 2014: 34)

Its populist and welfare schemes were expected to yield rich returns at the hustings: the National Rural Employment Guarantee Act (NREGA), 2005, the Right to Information (RTI), 2005, the (Recognition of Forest Rights) Act, 2006, the Right to Education Act, 2009, the National Food Security Act, 2013, the Land Acquisition Act, 2014, and the Lokpal And Lokayukta Act, 2014. In actuality, 'it presided over a decade that saw the highest ever annual GDP growth, and the fastest ever reduction in poverty in the history of independent India' (Sampath 2014).

But the Congress electoral campaign did not really emphasise these genuine achievements to their own advantage. They raised expectations in their first term and then fell way short of them in their second one. However, the electoral payoff from such popular schemes in UPA-I (2004–2009) were effectively neutralised by corruption charges against the UPA, begun with the selective targeting by the Anna Hazare movement and finessed by the BJP. Congress did not and could not effectively counter this. They seemed to assume the charges would not stick against their record of real achievements. The 'family' would work its magic and see them through. But before the law could take its course the elections made a decisive judgement! The party had learnt little from the Bofors scandal which had brought down the Rajiv Gandhi government in 1989.

Moreover, UPA-II (2009–2014) was unable to manage the unintended consequences of the positive performance of UPA-I and so paradoxically fell victim to its own success: 'corruption, inflation, rising unemployment, and heightened aspirations and expectations' (Sampath 2014). Land acquisition for development generated severe conflicts with those who were being dispossessed; the expansion of education without a corresponding increase in quality led to a shortage of skilled man-power; the low quality of services to the ordinary citizen and the failure to tackle corruption, which inevitably accompanies the rapid creation of new wealth, alienated the people, particularly the neo-middle class, whose expectations were raised during UPA-I and who then felt betrayed by UPA-II and so abandoned the party.

In the context of a global economic slowdown, the heightened aspirations and expectations of a new generation of first-time voters, the increasing violence against the marginalised and the minorities, and the atrocities against women, against all this and more, even populist welfare measures could not retain the core voter base on which the party had always relied. It was finally caught between the Right, where impatient business lobbies eager to see the economy return to the path of high growth, regardless of the implications for equity, accused the Congress of 'popularist welfarism' at the cost of growth and inflation;

and the Left, which oppositely charged it with succumbing to vested business interests and crony capitalism. And so for different and quite opposed reasons, both sides, big business and the Left, agreed that Congress and its allies were now a disaster for the country.

The media played up the incompetence and crony capitalism of the UPA. The timid, tepid response of their government only encouraged charges of governmental paralysis, which in fact was more the result of an outrageously unruly Parliament and an unconscionably aggressive opposition led by the BJP, which, more often than not, was now opposing what it once promoted when in government, the most obvious being the civil nuclear agreement with the USA, and FDI in retail. Sadly whoever wins or loses, the people always pay the price of such political opportunism.

Furthermore, the Congress does suffer from a serious dynastic problem, which is part of the burden of its history. Unless it addresses this with vigorous urgency it will be unable to reinvent itself and recover its credibility and relevance in a new and changed situation. They hung together with the 'family' that kept them together. Perhaps the shock of this election will disabuse them of their illusions. The authority of the Nehru-Gandhi family has been drastically eroded and their ability to deliver patronage and motivate party workers is severely compromised. As a mass-based party without a cadre, it needs charismatic leadership to mobilise the masses to their cause. With the family failing to provide such leadership, and the party unable and/or unwilling to look outside the dynasty to find such a leader, it could well implode. For too long party leaders outside the family with a mass base have been cut to size and marginalised. Now none are left in the party to revive it.

Moreover, in this election, the new generation of young first-time voters had little memory of the Nehru-Gandhi legacy and like many others do not feel indebted to it any more. Unfortunately, in this amnesia, the Gandhi-Nehru (the Mahatma and the Pundit) idea of India is also lost. Already with the Emergency of 1975–1977 the authoritarian high-jacking of that vision had begun. This election in 2014 could well signal its irreversible loss. This would be tragic, not just for the Congress party but for the 'socialist, secular, democratic' Indian Republic that we as a people proclaimed in 1950, for there is no national political opposition party or leader in place as yet.

BJP win

It would seem then that the rejection of the Congress for its evident corruption and perceived non-performance is a mandate for good governance and developmental growth as promised by the BJP in it election campaign. The election rhetoric of the Congress was secularism versus communalism; that of the BJP was governance versus incompetence. However, we need to go beyond the rhetoric and unpack these terms. Obviously there was a huge spin put on the terms and they must be read in context. The real decider seems to have been the anti-incumbency, which worked against the Congress, the inadequacy of the Congress campaign, and most especially opportunistic corporate interests. Moreover, the corporate media owned by big business pursued a grossly one-sided bias:

> the Narendra Modi persona, for good or for bad has been largely a television media construction, amplified by saturation-point coverage of the leader, spread out over more than six months – staggering and almost unprecedented, even by global standards. Only Barack Obama's campaign, which officially began in April 2011, for a second term in 2012, eclipses it.
>
> (Bhushan 2014)

In India, secularism has come to mean more than state neutrality on religious matters (*sarva dharma nirapekshata*). To be real and effective in the Indian context it must extend further to an equal respect for all religions (*sarva dharma sambhava*). Regrettably, this more contextual understanding has been hollowed out by aggressive liberal-secular rationalists who have no stake in any religious belief. Put on the defensive, popular religious traditions responded with an even more aggressive fundamentalism. This politicised religion, the very thing the secular rationalists intended to prevent.

In all this the tragic casualty was religious tolerance, without which the pluri-religious richness of India is politically unsustainable. In the final analysis, aggressive religious fundamentalisms targeting each other become more strident. They get locked into relationships, which one can neither negate nor escape; the protagonists represent their own rejected, yet still threatening 'other'. This is a scene set for continuing confrontation in which secular rationalists have no credible or effective response.

The BJP had once played on Hindu victimhood to mobilise and consolidate their hold on the Hindu community. Threatened religious minorities on the defensive now fear the threat of victimisation and with more reason too. Their leaders have used this to project themselves as protectors and consolidate their support with their rallying cry: religion in danger. Now Hindutvawadis use Hindu pride for the same purpose: say with pride I am a Hindu (*garva se kaho, hum Hindu hai*). This has polarised the civil society and politicised the religious community divides. These then spills over into intolerance, conflict, and violence. A small spark ignites a huge conflagration.

The BJP and the RSS

The BJP strategy that succeeded at the hustings was fine-tuned, projecting the image of their leader to meet the local situation:

> a backward state will get the vikas purush [development leader], the more urbanised states will get a rashtra purush [national leader] or lauh purush [the iron man], key states of the north and west, more prone to Hindutva, will get the 'Hanuman' of Lord Ram.
>
> (Palshikar 2013)

Thus the 'vikas purush' creates inequalities and inequities that will marginalise the poor and undermine the unity of the rastra, which will then have to use nationalism as a hegemonic ideology. Moreover, in this 'Hindu rastra' the minorities will be further alienated and unity further undermined. Moreover, even among Hindus, Hanuman is not the most important deity in much of the subcontinent.

There will be many other anomalies and contradictions and blaming all uncomfortable difficulties as inherited from an earlier UPA is already wearing thin. The BJP had been constantly accusing the Congress of 'appeasing' minorities. In this election campaign, the BJP, from the party president to the cadre on the ground, made insistent appeals to minorities to trust them and vote for the promised development. However, such appeals were not really credible to Muslims. The communal polarising in the northeast over the supposed Bangladeshi immigrants to precipitate conflict there and the cynical engineering of the Musaffarnagar riots were used to polarise the electorate with huge electoral returns for the BJP in Uttar Pradesh (UP). But it did little to assuage minority fears and only succeeded in alienating them further.

Hindu pride strikes a chord with the neo-middle class Hindus looking for their place in the new emerging social order. These are readily co-opted to aspire to the free-market neoliberal Gujarat model and its supposed promise of rapid progress and higher standards of living. Corporate business used the media they controlled to promote this unashamedly, and personalised their appeal in the promises of an authoritarian leader who would get things done and brook no opposition. The Gujarat model already presaged huge advantages for them there, supposedly with a vibrant Gujarat.

The mentor of the BJP, the Rashtriya Seva Sangh (RSS), has its disciplined cadre out in the field mobilising voters for their party. A decade ago, Mr Vajpayee's free-market policies were staunchly opposed by Sangh affiliates such as the Swadeshi Jagran Manch, which also vocally opposed globalisation in the Congress era. The Hindu right with is based of petty merchants and manufacturers that once rejected modernisation and pro-market liberalism is now invisible and inaudible. In the present context, under the pressure of big business interests, the BJP soft pedals their indigenous pretentions to a Hindu model of development it had once projected with its mentor's guidance. Now it favours a more globalised one. The Swadeshi Jagran Manch has gone silent, banished from Gujarat, which is projected as a neo-middle class utopia: *ache din aane wale hai* (good days are coming).

As a Right-leaning party the BJP can best be described as pursuing a neoliberal capitalist development with Hindu characteristics! This is very much like the socialist model of development with Chinese characteristics in the People's Republic of China. We can wonder how much of the 'Hindu' will be left in this development once it is globalised, very much as we can wonder how much of the old 'socialism' is left in the Chinese model of rapid economic growth. The authoritarian structures are common to both, but civil liberties and democratic rights are not. In India with its formal democracy, any development process will have to factor this in.

However, without real substantive democracy, we could well have a democracy controlled not by the inclusion and participation of people through their representatives but by vested business interest through their lobbies. The USA is the prime example of this. When corporate interests co-opt populist politics of resentment, they can trump any opposition even with an otherwise perceived incompetent, unfit leader. This has happened in the USA in the 2016 presidential election. In this country, the 2014 election were decisively influenced by powerful neo-conservative business elites, selling the myth of the free market as the promised land of development.

Perhaps least of all can a country be governed by exploiting the negative feelings towards a defeated opponent, who now cannot be an excuse for failure. 'Anti-Congressism' sat well with the non-Congress, non-UPA parties and the NDA allies. It was aggressively and repeatedly used to contrast the Congress performance with the BJP promise. And this successfully mobilised an already Congress-weary electorate to their side. A successful leader with a large majority might chose to suppress dissent in the party and outside, that is, until this success begins to sour. Surely, this is the lesson authoritarian leaders, as also dynastic rulers too, must learn. The BJP's electoral success and its projection of its leader might turn out to be its Achilles's heal, and its enemies will be waiting to exploit this, just as the dynasty politics in the Congress party has become its blind spot, so successfully exploited by the BJP.

In the meta-narrative of a 'Hindu superpower' or even a 'majoritarian-secular nation', 'the resources and labour of the poor are used as collateral in nation-making. Terror and penalization are enacted on the bodies and aspirations of minorities and others vulnerable' (Chatterji 2009: 363). In this hyper-nationalism, as Samuel Johnson cautioned, patriotism is the last refuge of scoundrels. Certainly, we have no lack of these. An empowered civil society and alert human rights activists to monitor the political agenda are better at bringing justice to oppressed victims than governments, whose first priority is getting re-elected.

Moreover, the transition from running a campaign and governing a country is a delicate and difficult one. A government cannot be run on promises to a people, as in a campaign mode for the electorate. To be credible it must begin to deliver and to stay relevant; it cannot default on this. And there's the rub! Nor can good governance be premised on a sectarian nationalism in a multicultural, multilingual, pluri-religious country as diverse as India. Gandhi and Tagore rejected a narrow aggressive nationalism, for a broad inclusive patriotism:

> in this ideology of patriotism rather than of nationalism, there was a built-in critique of nationalism and refusal to recognize the nation-state as the organizing principle of the Indian civilization and as the last word in the country's political life.
>
> (Nandy 1994: 2)

Implications for minorities

Since the Partition, collective violence against minorities has increased in frequency and intensity. With the rise of the saffron brigade, it has led to an immense loss of life and property, and always the weaker groups come off by far the worst. In 1992, the demolition of the Babri Masjid communal riots escalated across the country, reaching a climax with the pogrom of 2002 in Gujarat. Atrocities against Christians are frequent and far-flung: the Dangs in Gujarat, Kota in Rajasthan, Mangalore in Karnataka, and Kandhamal district in Odisha. To add to all this, random local attacks have only further escalated this politics of hate and revenge, of fear and mistrust.

The role of communal polarisation for electoral returns cannot be gainsaid (Berenschot 2011). Thus in 1984 the pogrom against the Sikhs that followed in the ground-shake after 'a big tree' fell helped Rajiv Gandhi to consolidate his hold on the party. The Shiv Sena–BPJ combine defeated the Congress in the election after the 1992–1993 riots in Mumbai. In 2002, the Godra incident provide an action-reaction sequence with the massacre of Muslims to establish the dominance of the BJP in the Gujarat and Modi's pre-eminence in the party thereafter. The BJP has benefitted most by such inter-religious communal violence.

However, no party is above such a cynical use of communal violence when there are electoral returns to reap, for some the use of the communal card is more programmatic, like the BJP; for others it is more pragmatic, like the Congress. Thus Ashutosh Varshney finds that

> Gujarat 2002 was different from Delhi 1984, only in that the Delhi violence was strategic, whereas the Gujarat pogrom were (sic) primarily ideological. Hindu nationalism is ideologically anti-Muslim, but Congress ideology has never been anti-Sikh.
> (Varshney 2017)

Electoral appeals on the basis of religion and caste or disaffection and hatred against another community is forbidden by law. Recently, on 2 January 2017, a seven-judge bench of the Supreme Court clarified and reaffirmed section 123(3) of the People's Representation Act of 1951 that no candidate or his/her agent can appeal for votes on the grounds of religion, race, caste, community or language. It went further and widened its scope by adding:

> Religion has no role in electoral process which is a secular activity. . . . Mixing religion with State power is not permissible while freedom to practice profess and propagate religion of one's choice is guaranteed. The State being secular in character will not identify itself with any one of the religions or religious denominations.

Yet this became a model is being replicated across the country. After Godra, a strident new polarising politics has been launched, with its perpetrators threatening to replicate this Gujarat model of vote bank consolidation in other states.

Spearheaded by Bajrang Dal and the VHP, militant organisations of the Sangh Parivar, the BJP focused on the issue of religious conversions in tribal areas to displace the Congress from its dominant position there. In the Dangs, a tribal district in south Gujarat bordering Maharashtra, Christian tribals were subjected to unprovoked brutal atrocities and savage intimidation, beginning in 1997, carrying on through 1998 and peaking in 1999. Charge and counter-charge were traded in this melee of conversion and reconversion.

Ghanshyam Shah, a well-respected Gujarati social scientist, reviewing the events in the Dangs, came to this damning conclusion:

> Instead of solving their basic issues of survival, the present agitation focusing on Christian missionaries has been fostered from the outside, diverting the prevailing tension and dividing the Dangis on religious lines which are a non-issue for the Dangis.
> (Shah 1999: 118)

Following the burning of a train in Godhra on 27 February 2002 – first described as an accident but later constructed as deliberate act of terror – a pogrom against Muslims (described by some as a genocide) spread terror across almost all of Gujarat. The subsequent state elections witnessed an overt corrosive politics of hate and fear to polarise the electorate and consolidate the majority community 'vote bank' within a dangerous identity politics with overt and covert state government connivance.

Thus in Odisha communal tensions were raised by a self-appointed *gau rakshak* (cow protector), Rabindra Pal, locally known as 'Dara Singh', who turned his attention from cattle smugglers to Christian missionaries. What followed was the gruesome murder by a mob, instigated by him, who burnt Dr Graham Staines, an Australian missionary doctor, and his young sons alive in their jeep at night at Manoharpur, Odisha, on 21 June 1999. For the horrible murder, Dara Singh was finally sentenced to death, later commuted to life, and his twelve accomplices to life imprisonment, though later they were acquitted.

The investigative commission set up under Justice D.P. Wadha concluded that 'no authority, organisation or any other person played any role in or in connection with the killings' (Raju 1999: 280). He found the 'gruesome murder . . . a blot on the fair name of India known for its tolerance' (Raju 1999: 269). He was emphatic that 'the murder of Graham Staines clearly has the effect of subverting the secular foundations of the India polity' (ibid, 270), but blamed this on the frenzied perpetrators, not on those who inspired and motivated them.

The good judge confined himself to his legal brief and failed to indict those responsible for creating the social conditions of prejudice and hate that precipitated such atrocities. There were legal precedents for this with the Macpherson Report (Macpherson, William 1999), which indicted the institutional racism of the British police force. The Sri Krishna Commission Report of 16 February 1998 that inquired into the Mumbai riots of December 1992 and January 1993 did indict such players – but even with the change of government in Maharashtra, no action was taken against them.

In the aftermath of the Manoharpur tragedy, the simmering tensions in Odisha were ripe to be exploited by those using communal identity politics of hate for electoral gain. Eventually the communal cauldron did boil over in Khandamal. The riots at Christmas, 2007, when seven churches were burnt, were a dress rehearsal to up the ante. In fact the Odisha riots in Khandamal were modelled on the post-Godra ones.

Swami Lakshmanananda Saraswati's killing with four others at his ashram on 23 August 2008 provide the occasion. The executions were claimed by Maoist cadres, but it was blamed on Christians by the Hindutvawadis and used to launch a pogrom targeting Christians in a deliberate attempt to consolidate a Hindu vote bank. The violence against Christians was legitimised as a response against conversions. This is another version of Newton's law of motion (action and reaction as equal and opposite) infamously used by the then Gujarat Chief Minister to rationalise the post-Godra pogrom against Muslims that he presided over.

The pogrom against Christians in Khandamal which followed was a shocking replicate of Godra in Gujarat, in almost the same sinister detail. Inciting passions by taking the murdered swami's body in solemn procession through the villages for his funeral rites many miles away with stopover rallies with increasingly menacing mobs was a replay of a similar journey of the fifty-three burnt bodies proceeding from Godra to Ahmedabad. The inaction of the state governments in both instances allowed the mayhem to continue unabated for several days, until media exposure created outrage in the rest of the country.

But there was one very crucial difference: the genocide in Gujarat, which had the explicit if not implicit support of the state government, yielded rich electoral returns for the BJP, which has won a crushing majority in the state legislature since. The pogroms in Khandamal did not yield the same electoral dividend; the state government was not as forthcoming in its support, since the BJP was the junior partner in the coalition there. This has proved a real setback for the party there.

Post 2014, the saffron identity politics of hate and majoritarianism has upped the ante and becomes strident whenever there is a need to rescue the saffron agenda of the BJP when it flags or fails. Its communal agenda of violence follows the same pattern. Minority appeasement is still an explosive issue on which political mobilisation yields rewarding electoral returns without effectively addressing the underlying marginalisation and alienation of a community beleaguered from without by its opponents and from within by its extremist leaders.

In the aftermath communal tensions must be kept on a slow boil, for ready use in emergencies only, so that developmental growth can accelerate. Moreover, in a majority–minority conflict it is always the weaker side that suffers the most. Aggressive stances on either side only polarise a conflict-ridden situation. This only benefits extremist leaders while sacrificing the most vulnerable to violence and prejudice: the poor, especially the women and children.

However, once the dominance of a party is established it will not need to resort to the communal polarisation. It will then project its good governance and development agenda. However, communal antagonisms are kept simmering as a standby, just in case this flounders. If this neoliberal development succeeds it will be to the greatest advantage of the upper class, upper caste with the proper politically correct 'cultural nationalism'. Once the minorities are taught a lesson and shown their place, the majority is free to set and pursue their own agenda: saffron neoliberalism (Teltumbde 2014). The minorities and the marginalised will find themselves excluded and disempowered, generating other kinds of tensions and conflicts.

The Gujarat model

In the BJP campaign in Gujarat the poor and the marginalised are conspicuous by their absence. Neither was 'growth with equity' nor 'equality with 'development' prioritised. Yet the spin on the Gujarat model as the ideal for the whole country was a repeated theme of the BJP's election campaign. Caught between the rich who profit most from the economic growth, and the poor who benefit from the welfare measures, this free-market model of capitalist development may well benefit the neo-middle class in the short term. But the huge costs it inflicts on the environment and the poor and the gross inequality between the haves and the have-nots make for long-term instability, which will sooner rather than later betray the aspirations of the very classes that initially may have benefitted from it. Yet business leaders that were the first to promote Modi as the PM needed him to do for India what he had begun in Gujarat. But the obvious question was not raised: what kind of development and for whom?

The parameters of this Gujarat model of development were not elaborated in this campaign, nor was its performance there subject to critical public scrutiny in either the campaign or after. But the results speak louder than rhetoric. A serious critique exposes the Gujarat model as more myth than reality, more propaganda than performance, more top-down implementation than down-up consensus. The official statistics for growth and the HRD figures for Gujarat do not compare favourably at all with other high-performing states in the country. There is sure-fire evidence of uneven growth and skewed development. Thus with regard to capital inflows from abroad:

> Gujarat's share in the cumulative FDI inflows into India since 2000 is only 4%, which is exceeded or matched by many states (Maharashtra 31%, Delhi 19%, Karnataka 6%, Tamil Nadu 6%, Andhra Pradesh 4%).
>
> (Ghatak 2014: 39)

The failure of this neo-con developmental model will compel the BJP to return to the identity politics and polarise the electorate to enthuse their cadres and mobilise party support before it begins to fatally haemorrhage. We have seen this strategy before: polarising communities to mobilise them, and then using the politics of difference, even the politics of hate, to consolidate support. Already with the UPA 'the growth process is so biased, making the country look more and more like islands of California in a sea of sub-Saharan Africa' (Dreze and Sen 2013: ix). Now with growth being so uncritically and exclusively privileged, such contradictions are likely to increase by quantum leaps and bounds. Indeed,

> economic growth can certainly help to improve people's lives (not only by raising per capita income but also by generating public revenue that can be used for purposes of social advancement of the people) . . . a deeper analysis of the relation between economic growth and social progress is seriously overdue in India.
>
> (Dreze and Sen 2013: ix)

However, the social inequalities created by the neoliberal development model of growth without equity precipitates dangerous tensions and political unrest; unequal distribution further stymies growth. As the model begins to unravel, democratic institutions and procedures become the first casualty to an authoritarian response. This has happened elsewhere before. It did happen here with the Emergency of 1997. And then as now, the biggest losers are the weakest in society, the poor and the minorities on whom the greatest burden is inflicted. A rising tide of growth may lift all boats, but it does not bring a more equitable relationship between the big and small ones. Moreover, those with leaky boats and those with none are severely disadvantaged by such a tide.

Thus when tribals and Dalits protest to claim their due, their oppressors obfuscate facts, manipulate events, and muscle their way to impose their version of the 'truth'. As we well know, it is always the victors who write the history that prevails to rationalise their story. Their persistent agenda, hidden in the subtext of policy, is majoritarian and class interests disguised as concerns of the nation. These vested interests use this 'nationalism' as a hegemonic project to imbed their hidden agenda into the mainstream agenda, so that it goes unquestioned and unchallenged. The marginalised and the minorities become the flotsam and jetsam of society. When they revolt, they are called terrorists and secessionists, and are hunted down by agencies of the state; when they seek alternatives in another religious tradition, they are denigrated and persecuted by cadres of the Sangh Parivar and their *gharvpasi* programmes. They are treated as people who must know their place and be told keep to it.

If the poor and marginalised have much to fear from this Gujarat model of development projected to the national scene, and minorities have much to dread with the Gujarat model of communal polarisation re-enacted on the national stage. Now the saffron agenda is married to the neoliberal and this 'odd couple' is legitimised with the grab-all *shibboleth* of 'nationalism'. All dissenters of whatever hue are targeted as 'anti-nationals', thus identifying the party with the government and the government with the nation. This subverts any substantive democratic politics, which get hijacked by a corrosive identity politics of hate for short-term electoral returns. This is surely a gross perversion of the democratic republic as envisaged in the Constitution we gave ourselves, as sovereign, socialist, secular, and democratic for our quest for justice as liberty, equality, and fraternity so evocatively expressed in the Preamble.

Projecting possibilities

There is now a consensus among scholars working on communal conflict in India that communal violence is becoming endemic to our political system. Paul Brass (2003) characterises *The Production of Hindu-Muslim Violence* as institutional riot systems lying dormant until activated by politicians for their own benefit. Varshney (2002) emphasises the role intra- and inter-communal networks play in the background. Berenschot (2011) discusses how patronage politics makes people dependent on such politicians. By reducing people's dependence for this patronage the potential for violence can be reduced. But once a party gains power and dominance such violence is redundant, only to be reactivated as and when needed.

Communal divides are setting the political agenda and further reinforcing an already dangerous polarisation of communities, which encourages a chauvinist politics of identity. For all its short-term gains at the hustings, eventually this can only lead to national disaster. There is an inevitable point of diminishing returns for this politics of hate, and crossing that line opens the door to becoming a failed state. The traumatic experience of some other countries in the subcontinent could still presage our own future.

Certainly, we do not want communal violence and religious fanaticism to polarise us to a tipping-point where pogroms spill over into genocide and a 'final solution'. Are we careering into a *Clash of Civilisations* on this subcontinent, similar to what Samuel Huntington is predicating for the 'West versus the rest' (Huntington 1996)? Will this subcontinent, or rather Indic civilisation as we know it, survive this violence or will it lead to another partitioning of the subcontinent as almost happened on the Sri Lankan island?

Obviously a just and equitable resolution of such dangerous social tensions must be in terms of human rights for all and collective rights for each community. Certainly, minority rights for a community must be compatible with fundamental rights in the Constitution. This requires a negotiation between national representatives and community ones, but at the grassroots, neighbourhood (Mohalla) committees are a viable place to start. But when the representatives themselves become stridently extremist, they silence the very voices within their respective communities that might make for a sustainable social compact on the basis of both human and cultural rights. A viable context for this requires an understanding of 'human rights in popular consciousness' (Anderson, M. 1998: 5), as also a sensitivity to minority cultures and their vulnerabilities. Continuing violence against communities 'establishes collective fear. . . . When fear becomes a way of life . . . a culture of terror has emerged' (Sluka 2000: 22–23).

The divide between the religious majority and the minorities is the most politically exploited one today. A nation polarised thus by communal divides of various kinds cannot work for the common good and a common future. Even in a population of 1.2 billion, it is not possible to have a stable and prosperous national society if we alienate 172 million Muslims, who are 14.23 per cent of the population, as second-class citizens. It gets more complicated when we add to this Christians 2.30 per cent, Sikhs 1.72 per cent, and other religious minorities. It all adds up to a good one-fifth of the population. Identity politics reinforces divisions and strengthens the control of traditional, authoritarian, and conservative leaders who mobilise their people behind them. The consequent displacement of interest politics does not serve the real interests of the community, least of all the poor and marginalised among them.

There is an inherent contradiction between the exclusive particularism of Hindutva and the expansive pluralism of Hinduism. Sooner rather than later this must unravel. There are many other anomalies and contradictions. Blaming all uncomfortable difficulties as inherited from an earlier UPA will soon begin to wear thin. Our present predicament is one of 'intense politicisation and fierce contests for power together with violence, fragmentation and chaos, and a concomitant longing for authoritarian control' (Mishra 2014). Delivering on the BJP campaign promises, '*Ache din aane wale hain*' (Good times are coming!) will demand a very strong Prime Minster who will have to be projected as increasingly larger than life, who gets things done, and not one sensitive and concerned with the rights for the minorities and the marginalised.

This opens the door to decisionism (Hirst 1988), the political theory that Carl Schmitt (1888–1985) used to justify the Third Reich. Bold decisions were lauded as self-legitimating, drawing the validity from their form not their content as long as they are taken by the right political authority. The sudden decision on 'demonetising' is precisely an example of this. It projects a decisive leader, regardless of the decision and what is achieved and who pays the price.

For 'as far as most essential issues are concerned, making a decision is more important than how the decision is made' (Schmitt 1985: 55–56). Pandian and Roy elaborate on this:

> The Decisionist dream of the subalterns is that the leader is one like us, yet could decide/do what we cannot. . . . such perception leads the common people to identify with the idealised leader as the compensation for the lack in their lives.
>
> (Pandian and Roy 2014: 31)

Implied here is a messianism that bestows unquestioned authority in the leader to deliver on the utopian expectations of the followers. Inevitably, greater trust is placed in the leader than in the institutions of governance. It is possible for strong leaders to shore up democratic institutions, but they can undermine them as well, especially when checks and balances are not in place. Hence, the crucial role of a free and critical media, an impartial judiciary, and the supremacy of Parliament and a formally recognised and effective 'loyal opposition' there. Otherwise an authoritarian leader can readily lead to selective violence that scapegoats the minorities and marginalised.

At first the leader is projected as 'great little man', a person who embodies both the greatness the followers long for and the littleness with which he can identify with them. From office boy to president is the American legend. Ours now is 'Chaiwala to PM'. This affirms ordinariness of our everyday lives even as it opens them to extraordinary expectations with unreal promises. The neo-middle class is particularly prone to this kind of appeal.

However, in pursuit of this utopian goal the decisionist leader faces an intractable dilemma. As the promises come closer to fulfilment, the more does the felt need for, and the fascination with, such an authoritarian leader diminish. Delivering on the promises may render the leader redundant. But if the promise fails, the commitment and devotion of the followers very quickly turns to disenchantment and disillusionment. Celebrities once feted are brought down and forgotten as rapidly as they were earlier built up. Dictators who fall behind that curve in their pursuit of power meet the same fate.

Political leaders are not an exception to this. We have seen this with changes of governments. However, when such a fate overtakes these leaders, they may not go gently into that night. Retirement is the last option only when all others fail. Indeed, even as they begin to lose their pre-eminence, they fall back on even more stringent authoritarian means to shore themselves up, until there is an implosion with unpredictable consequences. With many authoritarian leaders, such a fall from grace is all too familiar. And once again it is the last and the least, the minorities and the marginalised, that pay the highest price when the unravelling begins.

If the mantra of development so successfully marketed in the election campaign becomes growth without equity, the consequent inequalities will become a nightmare of increasing oppressive poverty for those marginalised. Trickle-down economic theory precipitates relative inequalities and resentful injustices that it cannot address. It is rejected by sensible economists like Amartya Sen and good pastors like Pope

Francis. More recently even the World Bank and the IMF have questioned it. The consequent instabilities can bring extreme and violent responses and not only the poor, Dalits and tribals, and marginalised minorities will be the worst victims. If the Hindutva inspiration of the BJP becomes majoritarianism, it will alienate minorities, divide our people, and destroy India's rich diversity.

Brutal repression only drives the problem underground to fester there before erupting with even greater extremisms, whether of religious fundamentalisms or political violence. Repression only confirms the worst suspicions on both sides and provokes a bitter and excessive response, kicking off an escalating spiral of violence. This is a classic case of a self-fulfilling prophecy. On the contrary, reconciliation and harmony the necessary condition for political stability and economic growth must be premised on justice and equity, not on power and repression.

The present electoral system has worked to the advantage of the privileged, even as it has begun to reach out and include some subaltern groups, namely the backward classes and castes. However, it has failed the marginalised and other weaker sections, like religious and other minorities, tribals, and dalits. Such groups have felt manipulated and used. The exclusion of a large majority among the poor and underprivileged still leaves them without an effective democratic voice. We once had voted for a Fabian socialism with Gandhian characteristics. Today they have been displaced by big capitalism and middle-class consumerism.

Moreover, electoral politics has led to a vested political interest in elected representatives across the board. Once elected these have little to do with the people they are supposed to represent.

There is a need to hold such representatives accountable to their electors if the system is to be effective. Civic activism must be a continuing process and not sporadic attempts that emerge at the time of elections. The right to recall is one such instrument, but it is a difficult one to put into practice. Unfortunately political parties have developed vested interests in the present electoral processes and this puts the kind of advocacy needed to reform the system beyond their agenda.

Moreover, in India, majorities and minorities are constructed communities, and so what is constructed can be deconstructed and reconstructed with fluid boundaries that allow for open and inclusive and multiple and fluid identities. Singular and totalising identities make for hostile communal divisions which are readily politicised and spill over into conflict and violence (Sen 2006). We need to draw on our rich composite Indic culture and the pluralist traditions of this land to recapture the open spaces we have lost to communal polarisation and partisanship. This is the common ground we must first recover together, and then move together to higher ground.

This civic activism must transcend identity politics, whether of caste or religious, linguist or ethnic community, and reach beyond to other similarly disadvantaged groups. It must be a process that must begin at the grassroots, in our schools and local communities. But it must be scaled up with a top-down facilitation as much as it needs a bottom-up activation. Mohalla committees and student camps for communal harmony are examples of this. Small steps in a long journey to get back to the path we chartered for ourselves with our Constitution and then lost to the saffron wave.

An epic saga

Nation-building in the historical experience of the West, where the idea of a nation-state originated was premised on the imperative for political unity and brutal uniformity. As people constructed a common socio-cultural identity, they sought to give political and economic expression to it as a nation-state. Local languages and dialects, ethnicities, and subcultures were all subsumed in a uniformised national identity, 'imagined communities' (Anderson 1983) with the 'invented traditions' (Hobsbhawn and Ranger 1983) based on selective memory.

The temptation of the *Old Societies and New States* in their *The Quest for Modernity in Asia and Africa* (Geertz 1963) has been to enforce a brutal uniformity as imperative for political unity, thus replicating the process that carved out the nations-states of the West. Wars of national liberation and civil wars do precisely this. But this can hardly be viable, except at unacceptable costs, for India, which is a multicultural, pluri-religious society, and a multi-nation state.

In addressing this conundrum, our Constitution enshrined minority rights as the statutory expression of a minimum protection for vulnerable religious and linguistic groups, a baseline for a pluralism that will preserve our diversity. This defines the context in which identity politics must function. But the transition from old hierarchies and persistent hegemonies to egalitarian and celebratory pluralism does not go uncontested and is still incomplete. After the trauma of the Partition in 1947, a defining moment for India was the founding of the Republic. If we renege on this through political short-sightedness and opportunism, we risk falling back into the earlier chaos again.

Today our polity is hurtling into an authoritarian polity and a free-market economy. Electoral waves have seen a swing from Left to Right and back again. Moreover, there has been a continuing advance of an aggressive, majoritarian religious right, as also of a defensive, minority religious fundamentalism among both the majority and the minorities in this land. These are but mirror images of each other; they feed on each other and spill over into horrendous violence. Such religious fundamentalism is a 'militant piety' (Armstrong 2000: ix) that transforms anxiety and fear into anger and rage. It is a defensive reaction against a threat from the 'other' on the 'outside', whether these be religious extremists or secular ones. Unless we can understand where this negativity is rooted, we will not be able to contain its aggressive militancy.

Politicising the nation on the basis of majority and minorities, could easily lead to a majoritarianism that does not respect democratic rights or the civil liberties of minorities or other dissenters. This is the very antithesis of an inclusive, participatory democracy. Such a politicisation around negative ideologies and exclusive identities might in the end replace one dominant group with another, whether this be caste, class, or regional groups. Rather a politicisation of real issues and concerns based on an egalitarian ideology and a democratic praxis is necessary. Much of what is happening in the nation today does not augur well for the future of this saga of our 'nation in the making', or rather a multi-nation state in progress.

We began our democratic saga with a massively illiterate and a relentlessly poor people. Varshney does not exaggerate when he claims for India that universal franchise

> came to the West after the Industrial Revolution – that is, after incomes had reached a substantially high level. India was to practice it at a very low level of income . . . for the first time in human history, a poor nation has practiced universal franchise for so long.
> (Varshney 2013: 3–4)

Many thought it would be a failed experiment. Many other developing nations have fallen prey to authoritarianism. The sceptics at that time asked: will India survive? Today the question is will India be a great nation? Amartya Sen traces the

> historical roots of democracy. . . [to] a long tradition of public arguments, with toleration of intellectual heterodoxy. . . . when, more than half a century ago, independent India became the first country in the non-Western world to choose a resolutely democratic constitution, it not only used what it had learned from the institutional experiences in Europe and America (particularly

Great Britain), it also drew on its own tradition of public reasoning and argumentative heterodoxy.

(Sen 2005: 12–13)

And half a century and more later democratic India is still here. Our democratic odyssey since then has been truly epic. Yet what we achieved with exemplary success is an electoral democracy, where we have fallen grossly short is on substantive democracy. Ambedkar had warned us of the emptiness of political democracy without economic democracy, and, I would add, social and cultural democracy too: 'one man one value' (Ambedkar 1978: 47). This is the substance of democracy, whether the man be economically poor or rich, culturally different or similar. Elections are but a means to these ends. If we fail here, authoritarianism would be ever more attractive and eventually even irresistible to our people, whether of the political Right or of the Left, the religious chauvinists or the secular rationalists. Just now it seems the religious is on the ascendency.

So even as we celebrate the 'dance of democracy' with this the sixteenth general election of our Republic, we cannot be unaware that the very idea of India as projected by Constitutional vision in now under stress, and we must draw on the historical roots of our tradition of public reasoning to rescue our democracy. The only remedy for a failing democracy is more effective democracy, and for a multicultural, multilingual, pluri-religious civilisation like ours, there can be no other route to fulfilling our 'tryst with destiny' than in an egalitarian, pluralist, secular, democratic state. We now seem to be at the crossroads once again. We have been there before in 1975–1977. Will the saffron sweep at the hustings in UP begin a 'dance of death' for the 'idea of India' envisioned in our Constitutions as a socialist, secular democracy? The jury is still out on this.

Note

1 This is a modified version of the paper that appeared in *Social Action*, April–June, Vol. 65, No. 2 2015, "Election 2014: Implications for Dalits and Minorities in India", 107–127.

References

Ambedkar, Bhimrao Ramji. 1978. *States and Minorities*. Lucknow: Buddha Vihar.

Anderson, Benedict. 1983. *Imagined Communities: Reflections on the Origin and Spread of Nationalism*. Verso: London.

Anderson, Michael R. and Sumit Guha (eds.). 1998. *Changing Concepts of Rights and Justice in South Asia*. New Delhi: Oxford University Press. Introduction by ed.s pp. 1-5

Armstrong, Karen. 2000. *The Battle for God*. New York: Alfred A. Knopf.

Berenschot, Ward. 2011. *Riot Politics: Hindu Muslim Violence and the Indian State*. London: Hurst & Co.

Bhushan, Sandeep. 2014. 'How the Television News Industry Scripted the Indian Elections', *Caravan*. http://caravanmagazine.in/vantage/television-scripted (accessed on March 17, 2017)

Brass, Paul. 2003. *The Production of Hindu-Muslim Violence in Contemporary India*. Seattle: University of Washington Press.

Chatterji, Angana. 2009. *Violent Gods: Hindu Nationalism in India's Present, Narratives From Orissa*. Gurgaon: Three Essays.

Dreze, Jean and Amartya Sen. 2013. *An Uncertain Glory: India and Its Contradictions*. New Delhi: Penguin.

Geertz, Clifford (ed.). 1963. *Old Societies and New States, the Quest for Modernity in Asia and Africa*. London: The Free Press of Glencoe.

Ghatak, Maitreesh, Maitreesh Ghatak, Parikshit Ghosh, Ashok Kotwal. 2014. 'Growth in the Time of UPA: Myths and Reality', *Economic and Political Weekly*, 49(34): 34–43.

Hirst, Paul. 1988. 'Carl Schmitt – Decisionism and Politics', *Economy and Society*, 17(2), May: 272–282.

Hobshawn, Eric and Terence Ranger (eds.). 1983. *The Invention of Tradition*. Cambridge: Cambridge University Press.

Huntington, Samuel P. 1996. *The Clash of Civilizations and the Remaking of World Order*. New York: Simon and Schuster.

Macpherson, William, 1999. The Stephen Lawrence Inquiry, https://www.gov.uk/government/uploads/system/uploads/attachment_data/file/277111/4262.pdf (accessed on March 17, 2017)

Mishra, Pankaj. 2014. 'The New Face of India', *The Guardian*, May 16. www.theguardian.com/books/2014/may/16/what-next-india-pankaj-mishra (Acessed on March 17, 2017)

Nandy, Ashis. 1994. *The Illegitimacy of Nationalism*. New Delhi: Oxford University Press.

Palshikar, Suhas. 2013. 'With Modis at the Helm', *The Indian Express*, July 30. www.google.co.in/search?q=%22With+Modis+at+the+helm+Suhas+Palshikar%22+Indian+Express&oq=%22With+Modis+at+the+helm+Suhas+Palshikar%22+Indian+Express&aqs=chrome.69i57.13966j0j7&sourceid=chrome&es_sm=93&ie=UTF-8 (accessed on March 17, 2017)

Pandian, M. S. S. and Satyaki Roy. 2014. 'Decisionism' and the Cult of Narendra Modi' A Note', *Economic and Political Weekly*, 49(30), June 21: 25–31.

Raju, M. C. (ed.). 1999. *Wadhwa Commission Report: A Critique*. New Delhi: Media House.

Sampath, G. 2014. 'Mandate of 2014: The Triumph of Spin', *LiveMint*, May 20. www.livemint.com/Opinion/hNdjVFTqfkl0nEd690YsDK/Mandate-2014-Triumph-of-the-spin.html (acessed on March 17, 2017)

Savarkar, V. D. 1989. *Hindutva: Who Is a Hindu?* 6th ed. New Delhi: Bharati Sahitya Sadan (1st ed. 1923).

———. 1964. 'Hindu Rastra Darshan', in *Samagra Savarkar Wangmaya* (Vol. 6). Pune: Maharashtra Prantik Hindusabbha.

Schmitt, Carl. 1985. *Political Theology: Four Chapters on the Concept of Sovereignty*. Trans. George Schwab. Chicago: University of Chicago Press.

Sen, Amartya. 2005. *The Argumentative Indian: Writings on Indian History, Culture and Identity*. London: Allen Lane, an imprint of Penguin Books Ltd.

———. 2006. *Identity and Violence: The Illusion of Destiny*. New Delhi: Penguin Books India.

Shah, Ghanshyam, 1999, "Conversion, Reconversion and the State: Recent Events in the Dangs", Economic and Political Weekly, Vo. 34, No. 6, 6 Feb., pp. 312-318.

Sluka, Jeffery A. (ed.). 2000. *Death Squad, the Anthropology of State Terror*. Philadelphia: University of Pennsylvania.

Teltumbde, Ananda. 2014. 'Saffron_Neoliberalism', *Economic and Political Weekly*, 49(31), August 2: 10–11.

Varshney, Ashutosh. 2002. *Ethnic Conflict and Civic Life: Hindus and Muslims in India*. New Haven: Yale University Press.

———. 2017. 'When the State Looks Away', *Indian Express*, March 1. http://indianexpress.com/article/opinion/columns/when-the-state-looks-away-4548604/

———. 2013. *Battles Half Won – India's Improbable Democracy*. New Delhi: Penguin.

9 Aam Aadmi Party's electoral performance in Punjab

Implications for an all India political scenario

Pritam Singh

Introduction

The Aam Aadmi Party's (AAP) victory in four Lok Sabha seats out of a total of thirteen from Punjab in the 2014 General Election was of historic significance in breaking the duopolistic control of Shiromani Akali Dal (SAD) and Indian National Congress (henceforth Congress) over Punjab politics (see Appendix A).[1] This electoral performance of AAP in Punjab also assumed additional significance because it lost everywhere else in the country where it had put up candidates. The electoral humiliation of the party in the rest of the country can be assessed from the fact that 414 of its 434 candidates in the country forfeited their security deposits (*The Tribune* 2017). The party retrieved some of its honour in winning the Delhi Assembly Elections and inflicting a massive defeat on the BJP in February 2015.

The impressive performance of the party in Punjab, though humiliated in the rest of the country except during the February 2015 Delhi Assembly Election, is a puzzle that needs to be cracked. Before we discuss why it is a puzzle, let me quickly interject that solving this puzzle, though interesting for its own sake, is important from an all India political perspective. It would indicate to us the potentialities and limitations of the AAP challenge to the Hindu nationalist BJP and the semi-secular Indian nationalist Congress. It is a puzzle not only because it won four Lok Sabha seats in Punjab while it lost everywhere else; it is a puzzle also because none of the top leaders of the party either before or after the split came from Punjab and the party still managed to stage a stunning electoral victory. Further, it is not only that the top leaders of AAP did not come from Punjab but, in fact, that some of the top leaders in the pre-split party such as Arvind Kejriwal and Yogendra Yadav came from Haryana, a state with which

Punjab has been involved in many inter-state conflicts relating to borders, river waters, and the capital city of Chandigarh. This Haryana background of these top leaders, however, did not act as a powerful counter force to AAP's electoral success in Punjab as one would have normally expected.

I must quickly add two qualifications to this observation about Haryana-Punjab conflict and the Haryana background of a section of the AAP's top leadership. First, that Haryana and Punjab, despite the conflicts over borders, river waters, and the capital city, share many things in the realm of economy, characteristics of the population, and history. This shared history, geography, and culture between Punjab and Haryana does enable, other things being equal, a political activist from Haryana to understand better the political culture of Punjab than a political activist from another state in India can. Second, Yogendra Yadav, one of the top leaders of the pre-split party and a leading figure of a faction in the post-split period, have had some important associations with Punjab, including having studied in a Khalsa High School (though not in Punjab), having proficiency in Punjabi language, having studied and taught at Panjab University, Chandigarh, and having many close personal friendships with many Punjabis.[2] The bulk of the top leadership in the party not only did not come from Punjab; most of those leaders, especially those who came from regions of India other than Punjab and Haryana, did not seem to possess any reasonable knowledge of the history, dynamics, culture, and ethos of Punjab. This remains the picture even now as far as the top leadership of the AAP is concerned. And still, not only AAP did as well as it did during the 2014 general elections, it emerged as the main opposition party in the Punjab Assembly after the 2017 election and thus relegated the once mighty SAD to a third place in the Punjab Assembly. It cannot be ruled out, however, that the Haryana dimension of the top leadership of the AAP, or more generally the non-Punjabi character of this Delhi-based leadership, might become a hurdle in continuing its success in the future. After the 2017 election outcome, a section of the party leadership in the Punjab unit represented by Sukhpal Khaira is openly becoming critical of the role of Delhi-based leadership, though a substantial section still remains docile and submissive to the Delhi-based leadership in spite of having misgivings about that leadership. The outcome of this inner-party turmoil will shape the character of AAP in Punjab and its future potentialities and limitations at least in Punjab but perhaps even beyond. We will explore this later.

Coming back to the puzzle outlined previously, the key to resolving that puzzle lies in understanding the emergence and suppression of two movements in the contemporary history of Punjab and the consequences of the suppression of those two movements. These two movements are the Maoist Naxalite movement of the late 1960s and the Akali *morcha* (agitation) of the early 1980s. The latter was for the protection of Punjab's river water rights and for other economic, political, and religious demands, and the subsequent armed Sikh opposition movement against Delhi's attack on the Golden Temple in 1984, which is erroneously characterised by most journalistic-style academic writings as a secessionist Khalistan movement for carving a theocratic Sikh state out of India. This chapter will attempt to throw light on these two movements to highlight both the similarities in the political culture of Punjab with the political culture in other states in India as well as the huge differences in the political culture of Punjab from the rest of India. By using the term 'the rest of India', I do not intend to imply that there is one uniform political culture in India outside Punjab. On the contrary, I firmly believe that there are massive inter-state differences in India: I look upon the states as homelands of various nationalities at different levels of their nationality developments, and by using the term 'the rest of India', I merely aim to emphasise the specificity of Punjab's political culture in contrast with the political culture in other states in India.[3] By analysing the emergence and suppression of the two movements mentioned here, and the political and cultural fallout from the suppression of those two movements, I hope to crack the puzzle of the amazing electoral success of AAP in Punjab while it miserably failed in the other states of India.

The rest of the chapter discusses aspects of Punjab's specificity, the Naxalite movement in Punjab and its suppression, the Akali movement and the armed Sikh resistance movement and its suppression, and the implications of the suppression of these two movements for the emergence of AAP as a political force. We will also briefly discuss the prospects of AAP in Punjab in the light of its past successes and its vulnerability due to the Haryana and non-Punjabi dimensions of its top leadership and the Delhi-based, over-centralised organisational structure of the party. Finally, we will examine in the light of this analysis the potentialities and limitations of AAP challenge to Hindu nationalist BJP and semi-secular Indian nationalist Congress.

Specificity of Punjab

One aspect of Punjab, which distinguishes it from all the other states in India, is that it is the homeland of the Sikh people. Punjab is the only state in India where the Sikhs are in a majority. The Sikhs are only 1.7

per cent of India's population, but about 58 per cent of that of Punjab. About 77 per cent of India's total Sikh population is settled in Punjab in contrast with the marginal presence of the Sikh community in majority of the other states in India (see Appendix B). The majority status for the Sikhs in Punjab is a relatively recent phenomenon – they became the majority religious community only after the territorial reorganisation of Punjab on linguistic basis on 1 November 1966. This duality of the Sikh location – a minority in India but a majority in Punjab – is a continuing source of political conflict, tension, and accommodation between the Sikh majority Punjab and Hindu majority India. This duality of the Sikh location offers a primary insight into understanding the difference between electoral trends in Punjab and most other states in India. The absence of the Modi wave in Punjab during the 2014 General Election while this wave is considered to be the major influence in other states, especially in north and west India, is a telling illustration of this dialectic of a Sikh majority in Punjab and a Hindu majority in most other states in India. Even when there is convergence of electoral trends in Punjab and the rest of India, as for example during the emergence of electoral success of regional parties in the 1967 Assembly elections in many states or the anti-Congress vote in the General Election after the *Emergency*, this convergence manifests itself through the regional specificity of Punjab. Both during the 1967 Assembly elections and post-*Emergency* General Election in 1977, the regional specificity in Punjab manifested itself through the massive electoral victories of Shiromani Akali Dal, almost the sole articulator of Punjab's regional interests and the Sikh community's political aspirations.[4] This political monopoly of Akali Dal is being questioned in the wake of political change brought about by APP upsurge in Punjab. We discuss this potentially important political development in Punjab later.

The foundations of the Sikh faith were laid by Guru Nanak (1469–1539) who came from an upper caste Hindu Khatri background, but showed rebellion, in a precocious manner even as a child, against the practices of his parents' faith. He soon matured as a great spiritual teacher, poet, and communicator. He chose Punjabi, the language of the masses in Punjab, as his medium of communication in opposition to Sanskrit and Arabic chosen by the priestly class of the two dominant religions – Hindu and Islam – of that time in Punjab. He attracted a community of followers who came to be known as 'Sikh' – the meaning of the word 'Sikh' is disciple or follower (Singh 1994: 1). His denunciation of the caste system and gender inequalities attracted many lower caste men and women mainly from Hindu backgrounds but some from Muslim backgrounds too to his fold. He also denounced the atrocities committed by the Moghul King Babur through powerful poetry and had to face a brief period of imprisonment before Babur realised that Nanak was not an ordinary political rebel and that he was a person of great spiritual learning. This was a period of great social and political turmoil in India, especially in north India. Many other spiritual leaders such as Kabir, Ravi Das, and Namdev, to just mention a few, were also preaching similar teachings especially relating to caste as Nanak's in other regions of what we now call India. All of them were part of what came to be known as the Bhakti movement. Guru Nanak travelled to all corners of India and beyond to meet spiritual leaders of similar leanings and to also debate with and question the traditional religious figures. What distinguished Nanak from other saints of the Bhakti period is that he understood the importance of organisation for spreading his teachings. Therefore, before his death, he appointed his successor Guru Angad (1504–1552) as the second guru of his followers who had come to be called Nanakpanthis or more generally as Sikhs. The fifth Guru, Guru Arjan Dev (1563–1606), compiled the teachings of all the Sikh gurus, but also of other spiritual teachers such as Baba Farid, Kabir, and Ravi Das, into a major work that came to be called Adi Granth and subsequently Shri Guru Granth Sahib (SGGS) which became the holy Sikh scripture. It is clear from the teachings contained in SGGS that the Sikh gurus applauded the ancient Hindu scriptures but also criticised very sharply many Hindu religious practices and rituals.[5] The growing Sikh faith had to go through very severe persecution; the faith not only survived these persecutions but grew to such strength that one Sikh chieftain Ranjit Singh (1780–1839) became the sovereign ruler of the Punjab in 1799.[6] The independent sovereign state of Punjab that lasted for half a century was eventually annexed by the expanding British Empire in 1849 and made a part of the colonial India. A rich heritage of their own religious scripture (SGGS) and the memory of having been rulers of an independent empire impart a distinctive identity to the Sikhs and their homeland Punjab. This distinctive identity of the Sikhs and Punjab in India and especially in north India, which is heavily Hindu, is a central component of the distinctive political culture of Punjab. An understanding of this distinctive political culture is critical to grasping the background to the emergence and suppression of the two movements, and the consequences of that suppression for the response AAP has received in Punjab.

The rise of the Naxalite movement in Punjab and its suppression – consequences for AAP

Three socio-economic and cultural processes can be identified as contributing to the emergence of the Naxalite movement in Punjab especially in the form in which it emerged in Punjab. First, the split in the international communist movement between pro-Soviet Union and pro-China blocs leading to a split in India's communist movement was the overarching and visible factor in giving a flip to the emergence of the Naxalite tendency in Punjab's communist movement.[7] Second, the 1968 radical upsurge in youth and other radical movements all over the world contributed to radicalising the educated Punjabi youth and thus facilitated their attraction towards the Naxalite movement.[8] Third, a majority of the Punjabi youth that got attracted towards the Naxalite movement came from a Sikh religious and cultural background,[9] and the history of the evolution of the Sikh community over the last five centuries shows a clear armed struggle tendency coexisting with a non-violent one (Singh 2007). Right from the beginning of the twentieth century, a distinctive Leftwing tendency that has been politically active and at times very influential among the Punjabi Sikhs has drawn upon the armed struggle tradition among the Sikhs to attract them to its political perspective and practice. The Ghadar Party activists, Kartar Singh Sarabha and the very well-known Indian revolutionary Bhagat Singh, are examples of the continuing armed struggle Leftwing tendency among the Punjabi Sikhs. The emergence of the Naxalite movement in Punjab in the 1960s was not a sudden freak political development; it represented a strong historical bond with the militant tradition in Sikhism and the impact of this tradition on a militant Leftwing tradition in Punjab. This historical bond coupled with the split in the international communist movement and the radical upsurge among the youth in the 1960s created the conditions for the rise of the Naxalite movement in Punjab. Taking any of these three dimensions singly would distort the understanding of the movement in Punjab.

This movement was very brutally suppressed through state repression (Judge 1992; Singh 2010). Nearly 100 activists were physically liquidated by Punjab police and these liquidations were presented by the police as 'encounters' (Singh 2010). It is not commonly known that, in post-independent India, this method of liquidation – i.e. killing in police custody – was innovated by Punjab police and later transmitted to other regions of India.[10] Apart from these killings, there were thousands of sympathisers who were tortured in varying levels of brutality, and further many more thousands who were abused, harassed, and monetarily exploited. The suppression of this movement left thousands of families broken, discontented, helpless, and angry. This network of thousands of families had virtually no political home in the existing political parties. These families considered the Parliamentary communist parties as traitors and the non-communist parties (such as Akali Dal, Congress, Jana Sangh/BJP, Janata) as contemptible citadels of bourgeois economic and political power. In the rise of AAP in 2013/2014 suddenly emerged a platform of hope for this whole array of previous activists, new activists, and silent sympathisers. They felt fired with the prospect of strengthening a party which could challenge the existing political parties. Dr Gandhi who defeated the Congress candidate Parneet Kaur, the wife of Congress leader Amarinder Singh, from Patiala, is an example of thousands of such activists, former activists, and sympathisers of the Naxalite movement. He is a doctor by profession and has dedicated many years of his life providing good and, if necessary due to the circumstances of the economic conditions of his patients, free medical services. He is a product of the Naxalite movement, and the inspiration behind his siding with the poor and marginalised came from his association with the movement. He had, as a student, actively participated in building up the Punjab Students Union (PSU), the most powerful student organisation Punjab has ever seen. PSU was closely aligned with the Naxalite movement. After the brutal suppression of the Naxalite movement, thousands of students who had participated in the activities of PSU pursued a range of different activities in the post-Naxalite phase. Some took to their professional duties as doctors, school teachers, journalists, academic scholars, agriculture extension service providers, and theatre activists, etc. with zeal and sought the meaning of their lives in the post-Naxalite phase through their work that they imagined contributed to improving the living conditions of the oppressed. Some became active in farmers' organisations and the trade unions of government employees and industrial workers. Some became active in human rights and civil liberties organisations. Some took to fighting prejudice and ignorance by advancing the work of rational thinking through organisations such as Tarksheel Society (Rational Society). Some took to organic farming. No doubt, some were drowned into depression and alcoholism while many just became inactive and immersed themselves in the mundane routine of family life. Even those who became politically inactive and confined themselves to the domesticity of daily family life kept themselves informed in varying degrees about the social and political changes taking place in Punjab, India, and beyond.

The Naxalite movement in Punjab had especially attracted the students, youth, and young school teachers. Those who were attracted to the movement undoubtedly represented the most idealistic elements of Punjabi youth. When AAP came on the scene, it was like a breath of fresh air for these idealists and erstwhile idealists who had now entered the middle or late middle stage of their lives. There were certainly some from a new generation of young Naxalites or pro-Naxalites who in most cases were children of the old activists, and some from this new generation were active in student union activities, mostly in the Malwa belt of Punjab where the AAP acquired most influence. All these erstwhile activists, politically inactive sympathisers, and the new activists became the foot soldiers of AAP. Their dormant energies were unleashed and they provided a momentum to AAP's political work which no other established political party in Punjab had. They played a crucial part in the AAP's electoral victories in all the four seats the AAP won but particularly in the Faridkot and Sangrur constituencies, and to a lesser extent in the Patiala constituency. These constituencies formed areas where the Naxalite movement had had a substantial following, especially among the youth.

Now, let us move on to the other component of AAP's mass support, namely those individuals and groups who were, in one way or another, involved in the Sikh militant movement against the Indian state after 1984.

The Sikh militant movement, its suppression, and the consequences for AAP

The Sikh militant movement against the Indian state, which is mistakenly viewed as a Khalistan movement by shallow academic and journalistic commentators, has one similarity and one big dissimilarity with the 1960s and 1970s Naxalite movement. The similarity is that both inspired primarily the Sikh youth in Punjab and both were very brutally crushed by the power of the Indian state. The spread of the Sikh movement was far wider and its suppression was much deeper than the Naxalite movement (Singh 2008, 2010; Pettigrew 1995; Mahmood 1996). The one big dissimilarity was that the Sikh movement was indigenously inspired, unlike the Naxalite movement where one of the sources of its rise was the split in the international communist movement and its ramifications in India's communist movement.

While the suppression of the Naxalite movement affected thousands of families, the suppression of the Sikh militant movement affected hundreds of thousands of families whose members were liquidated by India's security forces or tortured, abused, humiliated, or subjected to extortion. Punjab has 12,581 villages (Government of Punjab 2013: 3) and every village has one or more families whose members were either liquidated or tortured. Some villages had many such families, e.g. Sur Singh Wala village in Amritsar district which had nearly 100 of its young men liquidated by the Indian state.[11] This large-scale suppression of a movement which was widely spread out through the state left a substantial section of the Sikh population disgruntled, angry, humiliated, and rebellious, but without a political home in any of the existing political parties. At one stage around 1989, these angry masses did find a political home in Simranjeet Singh Mann–led Akali Dal, and this resulted in massive election victories of this Akali Dal–supported candidates to the Lok Sabha during the 1989 elections in Punjab.[12] However, Mann was not able to organise this support in a sustainable manner, and literally millions who had voted his candidates to victories again became homeless politically. Some of those supporters were reintegrated into the mainstream Akali Dal led by Prakash Singh Badal, but a strong residue of discontentment against existing political parties remained. The emergence of AAP on the scene electrified this discontented mass. The mainstream Akali Dal's alliance with the BJP annoyed this discontented mass and the Mann-led Akali Dal did not inspire confidence among them except a small section who had built long-term personal ties with Mann. It is this discontented mass which migrated almost wholesale in its support to AAP and ensured its electoral victories.

More sources of support to AAP

Apart from the pro-Naxalite and pro-Sikh militancy sections of the Punjabi population which ensured AAP electoral victories, there were three other sources of support for AAP. One was the enthusiastic support of the Sikh diaspora, the second was the upper caste Hindu youth in Punjab, and the third was the Dalit voters. The reason behind diaspora's support to AAP can be traced to the support extended to AAP by pro-Naxalite and pro-Sikh militancy sections of Punjab's population. Many supporters and activists of the Naxalite and Sikh militant movements had moved abroad to escape state repression. They were dissatisfied with all existing mainstream political parties, and they became enthusiastic supporters of AAP. The diasporic support to AAP extended beyond sympathisers of the Naxalite and the Sikh militant movement. Many Punjabi migrants to the west had experienced life which was free from small-scale, day-to-day corruption. They longed for such a state of affairs in their homeland state of Punjab and AAP offered them hope of such a corruption-free future. The diaspora played an active part not only in generating generous financial resources for AAP but also in persuading their relatives and family members in Punjab to vote for AAP candidates.

There were two other sections of Punjabi society that became sympathetic to AAP. One section consisted of the upper caste Hindu youth, especially in the towns in the Malwa region of Punjab where AAP candidates won, and the other section consisted of Dalit voters especially in the Doaba belt where their number is substantial. The upper caste Hindu youth of the new generation was different in its political orientation than the previous and old generation which had seen partition and was much more sympathetic to either the open Hindu nationalism of the BJP or the veiled Hindu nationalism of the semi-secular Congress. This new generation was not particularly attracted to Akali Dal, although a few politically ambitious among the new generation did hitch themselves on to Akali Dal.[13] This new generation was not even attracted to Leftwing ideologies, partly because of their class location in the trading communities of Punjab, but felt fascinated with the AAP's rise to power in Delhi. Through the process of elimination, the AAP seemed like an attractive political home to semi-idealistic sections of the upper caste Punjabi Hindu youth.

The Dalit voters were disillusioned with the Congress, a party they had supported for many years, and also with the BSP for the opportunism of many BSP leaders. The AAP winning substantial support among the Dalits in Delhi touched the imagination of Dalit voters in Punjab too and this resulted in massive voting by Punjabi Dalit voters in favour of AAP. Though AAP did not win any seats in the Doaba belt where Dalit vote is substantial, its candidates, even the ones who were complete novices in politics, managed to get lakhs of votes. In the two Doaba constituencies of Jalandhar and Hoshiarpur, AAP scored 24.42 per cent and 22.19 per cent of the vote respectively while in Anandpur Sahib, which is a mixture of Doaba and Malwa areas, the AAP candidate got 28.14 per cent of the votes (see Appendix A).

The absence of Modi wave

BJP won only two seats: i.e. from Jalandhar and Hoshiarpur, which are Hindu majority constituencies. If there was any Modi wave of some sort, it was confined to just these two constituencies. In Amritsar, where Arun Jaitley was put up as the BJP candidate with great fanfare, he was trounced by a big margin of over one lakh votes by Congress's Amarinder Singh, who was strongly supported by the Sikh voters for his brave decision in resigning from the Congress party and Lok Sabha as a protest against Operation Blue Star. Here the Sikh voters chose Amarinder Singh over AAP's Dr Daljit Singh because he seemed to be a better bet in defeating BJP's Jaitley. In the Sikh majority constituencies in the Malwa (where AAP won four seats from Sangrur, Faridkot, Patiala, and Fatehgarh Sahib), there was complete absence of a Modi wave. If there was any wave, it was a AAP wave. Sikh voters, including those who were ideologically sympathetic to the Naxalite and other left currents, voted enthusiastically for AAP. Punjab stood politically different in a stark way from all the neighbouring north Indian states in having rejected Modi's Hindutva ideology and politics.

The current position of the AAP

AAP, due to various factors but primarily due to its internal organisational problems, has not managed to keep up the momentum it had gained in Punjab during the 2014 General Election. AAP's Punjab unit is currently in turmoil. The turmoil has various dimensions partly related to it being a victim of its own success. Its central leadership did not understand the Punjab specificity behind its success and made serious blunders. One of the most serious blunders it has made is in removing the Punjab convenor Sucha Singh Chhottepur from the convenorship on the basis of an allegation that he accepted Rupees two lakhs from a party supporter. The allegation seems frivolous and motivated more by the desire to strengthen the hold of Delhi-based leadership over the Punjab unit than to weed out corruption as proclaimed by the Delhi-based party leadership. Chhottepur had hit back saying that his entire political career was without any blemish, and that this ouster had been masterminded by Haryana- and UP-based political leaders to weaken the hold of Punjab-based leaders in the Punjab unit of the AAP.[14] This row threw into sharp relief the contradiction facing all political parties in Punjab, except Akali Dal, namely that they have to win the electoral preferences of Punjab's voters, but their politics and especially organisational set-up is controlled by Delhi-centred political parties which are not governed by the interests of Punjab but by how Punjab fits into their all India political strategy. This contradiction has especially acquired importance for AAP because Punjab is the only state in India from where it won Lok Sabha seats and from where, at one stage, it seemed it could win the election to the Punjab

State Assembly. The media coverage of the present turmoil has highlighted this glaring weakness of AAP's Punjab organisational set-up. Its Congress and Akali opponents are harping on this vulnerability of AAP, and the AAP leadership is not able to rebut this charge and has been thrown into a position of defensiveness on this issue. Chhottepur retaliated against his ouster by setting up a new political party called Apna Punjab Party (APP) with the sole purpose of drawing a sharp attention to the absence of Punjabi organisational control of AAP in Punjab. Of all AAP political leaders in Punjab, he is the most experienced and has a clear mass base in Gurdaspur district, his home district. The charge levelled by the Delhi-based leadership against him did not stick and his credibility, instead of being damaged, was enhanced because of this charge. He was seen as a victim of conspiracy hatched by Haryana- and UP-based political leaders who hold the top leadership positions in the party's central organisation based in Delhi. It is extraordinary that he has even drawn support from political leaders from the Congress party and Akali Dal as a man whose political career is clean.

The damage to AAP from its Punjab imbroglio has been further enhanced by corruption and moral turpitude charges against some AAP ministers in Delhi who had to be sacked from their Cabinet positions. Even the AAP mentor Anna Hazare has expressed deep disappointment with Kejriwal and AAP.

Though the AAP did win enough seats in the 2017 Assembly election in Punjab to become the main opposition party but not winning the majority, which it was hoping to do and form the government in Punjab, the credibility of AAP as a potential third national alternative to Congress and BJP has been severely undermined by the Assembly election results and the organisational and political blunders it made in Punjab (Singh 2017).

Conclusions

AAP staged stunning electoral victories from Punjab during the 2014 general election. This was in sharp contrast with AAP candidates losing every seat it contested in the rest of India. The explanation of AAP's unique electoral success in Punjab lies in the specificity of Punjab, namely that it is the only Sikh majority state in India. Two movements in Punjab which had substantial base amongst the Sikh population – the Maoist/Naxalite movement in the late 1960s and early 1970s, and the Sikh militant movement against the Indian state in the 1980s and 1990s – were crushed with brutal state terror. The suppression of these two movements left large sections of the Sikh population angry and humiliated and at the same time without a political home among any of the existing political parties. The emergence of the AAP on the political scene energised the sections of the Sikh population that had been left discontented because of the suppression of the two movements. The politically reactivated individuals and groups with backgrounds in the Naxalite movement and the Sikh militant movement provided the enthusiastic foot soldiers for AAP's election machine in Punjab. No other political party had been able to win such large number of activists especially from the younger generation to their party fold. These activists were the key to the electoral success of AAP in Punjab in 2014.

Between the 2014 General Election and the 2017 Punjab Assembly Election, a contradiction that already existed in the AAP's organisational set-up in terms of the conflict between the need for regionally responsive politics and centrally controlled organisational arrangement, became more acute with the emergence of open conflict between the Punjab-based leadership and the Delhi-based central leadership. In one sense, this contradiction is not unique to Punjab. All the major political parties in India are centrally controlled and that is one reason that state-based regional parties have been growing up in all the states, especially in the non-Hindi speaking ones. Akali Dal in Punjab represented this regionally oriented turn in politics in many states of India. However, Akali Dal's close alliance with the Hindu nationalist BJP deprived Akali Dal from legitimately claiming that it represented regional interests of Punjab in the same way regional parties in other states such as in Tamil Nadu, West Bengal, Orissa, Andhra Pradesh, and Telangana could do. This weakness of Akali Dal politics opened the avenue for AAP to claim representing Punjab's and especially Sikhs' interests. The recent turmoil in Punjab's AAP in the form of Punjab-based leadership being undermined by non-Punjabi leadership in the central organisational set-up in Delhi has taken away that critical claim of AAP as representing Punjab's interests. This claim gets further weakened by Haryana background leaders being in control of the central party machine in Delhi. Due to several inter-state conflicts between Haryana and Punjab, the claim of AAP to represent Punjab's interests gets further undermined.

The contradiction between Punjab-based leadership and its control by Delhi-based leadership was obscured during the 2014 general election. The coming out of this conflict in the open from 2016 onwards has harmed AAP in Punjab, though it still remains a substantial player as the main opposition party to the newly elected government in

Punjab. This new government is technically a Congress party one, but the victory of the Congress is primarily due to the popularity of Punjab Congress chief Amarinder Singh among the Sikhs because of his bold pro-Punjab stand in the past on Operation Blue Star and river water dispute. The Congress was also able to win the election because the urban upper caste Hindu voters were influenced by the media campaign, supported both by the Congress and the Akalis, against AAP that it (AAP) was close to Sikh militant factions. Ideologically, the upper caste urban Hindus have a long history right from the late nineteenth century onwards to being close to various variants of Hindutva but electorally, they constitute the most conscious section of Punjabi electorate in voting tactically almost en bloc to protect and advance what they consider as their strategic interests. This section of Punjabi voters is concentrated in a few urban constituencies and is internally a highly networked community. The tactical voting by this segment leads them to vote for Congress in one election, BJP in another, and even the Akali Dal in yet another one as for example they did in 1985 to defeat the Sikh militant factions who were in the post-1984 scenario challenging Akali Dal supremacy in Sikh politics. The upper caste Punjabi Hindu vote is concentrated in twenty to twenty-five urban constituencies where BJP had, once, made a clean sweep by winning nineteen seats. In the 2017 Assembly election, the BJP won only three because of the vote transfer this time to the Congress. There is also a rumour circulating very widely but difficult to substantiate that in the last phase of the election, the BJP's central leadership had concluded that Akali Dal was losing this election due to anti-incumbency and, therefore, there was a risk of AAP capturing power in Punjab, which the BJP leadership thought of as a bigger threat than the Congress and thus advised its core voters to vote for Congress. AAP did not win from a single Hindu majority constituency and Congress made a clean sweep from the Hindu majority constituencies as BJP had done in the past.

AAP, having been weakened in Punjab, makes it a weak political rival at an all India level to BJP and Congress. Had AAP remained strong in Punjab and its strength could be carried to other states, AAP might have replaced the Congress as the main rival of BJP and might have emerged as a stronger rival to BJP than the Congress has ever been. Its recent weakening in Punjab makes it unlikely that it will replace the Congress as the main all India rival to BJP, and in that sense, it is a setback to the emergence of a stronger all India rival to BJP. From the viewpoint of emergence of anti-BJP political forces in India, the weakening of AAP in Punjab is not only a loss to Punjab's anti-BJP front (or more specifically in Punjab to an anti–Akali Dal front) but also to anti-BJP politics at an all India level. This may lead to AAP reconsidering its over-ambitious political project which, in turn, might lead the party to think and plan about forging alliances with other non-BJP and non-Congress political tendencies in the country and thus to emerge as a part of a third alternative rather than it alone becoming the third alternative.

Notes

1. I wish to acknowledge the research assistance provided by Rajkamal Singh Mann and the information supplied by many others who chose to remain anonymous. I also thank an anonymous reviewer for highlighting the strengths of the chapter and providing the useful comments. The usual disclaimer applies.
2. I must mention here that Yogendra Yadav has been my friend for over three decades. Due to Yadav's falling out with the AAP, its leadership may now be reluctant to acknowledge that his association with Punjab and knowledge of Punjabi language and culture were crucial factors in building the first network of leading AAP activists, which includes Sumail Singh Sidhu, a very promising young man with excellent academic and political credentials, who was initially entrusted with the task of organising the party in Punjab. I can also share this information that Yadav's role was central in the selection of Sucha Singh Chhottepur, who remained the convenor of AAP until only a few months before the 2017 Punjab Assembly elections. We will discuss later the issue of Chhottepur being removed from this role and its implications for AAP in particular and Punjab politics in general.
3. For a further elaboration of this point, see Singh (1999, 2008).
4. See Singh (2014) for an analysis of the dynamics of Akali Dal politics in Punjab and India.
5. I am currently developing my thoughts on this dialectically contradictory relationship between Sikh thought (as enshrined in SGGS) and the Hindu tradition. My current thinking is that Sikhism is neither just one of the variants of Sanatani Hindu tradition as the Hindutva ideologists would want the Sikhs to believe, nor is it totally unrelated to that tradition as the proponents of complete Sikh sovereignty articulate, although there is more weight in the sovereignty view.
6. See Singh and Rai 2009.
7. See Brar (1994) for a helpful explanation of the communist splits worldwide and their impact on India's communist splits.
8. See Singh (2016) for the 1968 context of the emergence of the Naxalite movement.
9. See Singh (1985, 1997) for a further development of this aspect.
10. A senior Punjab police officer confided in me a conversation he had with Indira Gandhi, India's Prime Minister during the period of the upsurge of the Naxalite movement. He was escorting Mrs Gandhi at Chandigarh airport, and the worried Mrs Gandhi shared with the officer that the Naxalite movement in Bengal was a great headache for her. The officer

told Mrs Gandhi that the 'Punjab method' should be used to deal with the movement in Bengal. On Mrs Gandhi enquiring from him about the Punjab method, he replied: 'kill them after arresting them and declare that they were killed in encounter'. This officer claimed or rather boasted that, after this suggestion of his, the Punjab method was copied in other states in India.

11 This is based on the information supplied by Gurcharan Singh Chani in his documentary on state repression in Punjab, which covered the village in depth. Chani has clarified to me (in personal correspondence) that 'it was not a film and that it was raw footage which was unedited. It had no commentary and contained only the interviews of the villagers. It was shot in 1989 and shown to very selected friends'. I had the privilege of being one of those selected friends.

12 During that election, both the father and the widow of Beant Singh, the security guard of Mrs Indira Gandhi who had assassinated her because of her decision to send the army into the Golden Temple in the 1984 Blue Star Operation, were massively voted to electoral victories to the Lok Sabha by the Sikh voters as a collective retaliation against the Blue Star Operation decision by Mrs Gandhi.

13 I identified and analysed the dimension of Hindu entry into Akali Dal in Singh (2011) and in Chapter 2 of Singh (2008).

14 I have never met Sucha Singh Chhottepur, but I had two brief telephone conversations with him when he was thinking of joining AAP and had sought my advice. I made enquiries about him through family and friends. The overwhelming impressions I formed after the information I received was that he was an honest man and not a corrupt politician interested in only making money from a political career.

Bibliography

Brar, Bhupinder. 1994. *Explaining Communist Crises*. New Delhi: Ajanta Publications.

Government of Punjab. 2013. *Statistical Abstract of Punjab*. Chandigarh: Economic Advisor to Government of Punjab.

Judge, Paramjit Singh. 1992. *Insurrection to Agitation: The Naxalite Movement in Punjab*. Bombay: Popular Prakashan.

Mahmood, C.K. 1996. *Fighting for Faith and Nation: Dialogues With Sikh Militants*. Philadelphia: University of Pennsylvania Press.

Pettigrew, J. 1995. *The Sikhs of the Punjab: Unheard Voices of State and Guerrilla Violence*. London: Zed Books.

Singh, Harbans. 1994. *The Heritage of the Sikhs*, 2nd ed. New Delhi: Manohar.

Singh, Patwant and Jyoti Rai. 2009. *Empire of the Sikhs: The Life and Times of Maharaja Ranjit Singh*. New Delhi: Penguin Books.

Singh, Pritam. 1985. 'Marxism in Punjab', *Economic and Political Weekly*, March 30.

———. 1997. 'Marxism, Indian State and Punjab', *International Journal of Punjab Studies*, 4(2): 237–250.

———. 1999. 'Capital, State and Nation in India: Reflections With Reference to Punjab', *International Journal of Punjab Studies*, 6(1), January–June: 85–99.

———. 2007. 'Political Economy of the Cycles of Violence and Non-Violence in the Sikh Struggle for Identity and Political Power: Implications for Indian Federalism', *Third World Quarterly*, 28(3): 555–570.

———. 2008. *Federalism, Nationalism and Development: India and the Punjab Economy*. London, New York: Routledge. A paperback edition and also a Special Indian reprint was brought out in 2009.

———. 2010. *Economy, Culture and Human Rights: Turbulence in Punjab, India and Beyond*. New Delhi: Three Essays Collective.

———. 2011. 'Punjab's Electoral Competition', *Economic and Political Weekly*, February 10: 466–467.

———. 2014. 'Class, Nation and Religion: Changing Nature of Akali Politics in Punjab, India', *Commonwealth and Comparative Politics*, 52(1), February: 55–77.

———. 2016. 'The Origin, Influence, Suppression and Resilience of the Maoist/Naxalite Movement in India: 1967–Present', *Socialist History*, 50: 85–104.

———. 2017. 'Aam Aadmi Party as Third Player in Punjab Politics', *EPW Web Exclusive*, January 21. www.epw.in/node/148240/pdf.

The Tribune. 2017. 'Kejri Broom Eyes Clean Sweep: Stung by a String of Controversies, AAP Going All Out to Regain Lost Ground', January 9.

Appendix A

Table 9.A.1 Vote share and results of General Elections 2014 for Punjab state

Constituency	Party	Winner	Per cent of votes secured	
			Over total electors in constituency	Over total votes polled in constituency
Gurdaspur	INC		23.7	33.2
	BJP	**BJP**	**32.14**	**46.25**
	AAP		11.56	16.63
Amritsar	**INC**	**INC**	**32.69**	**47.94**
	BJP		25.73	37.74
	AAP		5.59	8.2
Khadoor Sahib	INC		23.46	35.24
	SAD	**SAD**	**29.89**	**44.91**
	AAP		9.24	13.89
Jalandhar	**INC**	**INC**	**24.52**	**36.56**
	SAD		19.95	29.74
	AAP		16.38	24.42
Hoshiarpur	INC		22.42	34.64
	BJP	**BJP**	**23.34**	**36.05**
	AAP		14.37	22.19
Anandpur Sahib	INC		20.69	29.77
	SAD	**SAD**	**22.2**	**31.94**
	AAP		19.56	28.14
Ludhiana	**INC**	**INC**	**19.25**	**27.27**
	SAD		16.44	23.28
	AAP		17.98	25.48
Fatehgarh Sahib	INC		22.42	30.37
	SAD		22.39	30.34
	AAP	**AAP**	**26.29**	**35.62**
Faridkot	INC		17.27	24.34

Constituency	Party	Winner	Per cent of votes secured	
			Over total electors in constituency	Over total votes polled in constituency
Firozpur	SAD		19.12	26.95
	AAP	AAP	30.98	43.66
	INC		29.99	41.29
	SAD	SAD	32.06	44.13
Bathinda	AAP		7.45	10.26
	INC		32.47	42.09
	SAD	SAD	33.75	43.73
Sangrur	AAP		5.76	7.47
	INC		12.73	16.49
	SAD		22.57	29.23
	AAP	AAP	37.43	48.47
Patiala	INC		21.81	30.75
	SAD		21.52	30.34
	AAP	AAP	23.14	32.62

Source: Election Commission of India

Appendix B

The Sikh share in the population of India, Punjab, and the other states of India

Table 9.B.1 Religious composition of India's population 2001 and 2011 (%)

Religion	2001	2011
Hindu	80.456	79.8
Muslim	13.4344597	14.225
Christian	2.34102413	2.298
Sikh	1.86812532	1.721

Adapted from:

Source of data: For 2001 http://censusindia.gov.in/Census_Data_2001/Census_data_finder/C_Series/Population_by_religious_communities.htm (Date accessed 24 April 2017)

Source of data: For 2011 www.censusindia.gov.in/2011census/C-01.html (Date accessed 24 April 2017)

Table 9.B.2 Religious composition of Punjab's population 2001 and 2011 (%)

Religion	2001	2011
Hindu	36.94	38.49
Muslim	1.57	1.93
Christian	1.20	1.26
Sikh	59.91	57.69

Adapted from:

Source of data: For 2001 http://censusindia.gov.in/Census_Data_2001/Census_data_finder/C_Series/Population_by_religious_communities.htm (Date accessed 24 April 2017)

Source of data: For 2011 www.censusindia.gov.in/2011census/C-01.html (Date accessed 24 April 2017)

Table 9.B.3 Punjab's religious communities as a share of their all India population 2001 and 2011

Religion	2001	2011
Hindu	1.09	1.11
Muslim	0.28	0.31
Christian	1.22	1.25
Sikh	75.94	76.82

Adapted from:

Source of data: For 2001 http://censusindia.gov.in/Census_Data_2001/Census_data_finder/C_Series/Population_by_religious_communities.htm (Date accessed 24 April 2017)

Source of data: For 2011 www.censusindia.gov.in/2011census/C-01.html (Date accessed 24 April 2017)

Table 9.B.4 Sikhs as a share of different Indian states' population 2011 (%)

State/UT	Percentage of Sikhs
India	1.72
Jammu & Kashmir	1.87
Himachal Pradesh	1.16
Punjab	57.69
Chandigarh	13.11
Uttarakhand	2.34
Haryana	4.91
NCT Of Delhi	3.40
Rajasthan	1.27
Uttar Pradesh	0.32
Bihar	0.02
Sikkim	0.31
Arunachal Pradesh	0.24
Nagaland	0.10
Manipur	0.05
Mizoram	0.03
Tripura	0.03
Meghalaya	0.10
Assam	0.07
West Bengal	0.07
Jharkhand	0.22
Odisha	0.05
Chhattisgarh	0.27
Madhya Pradesh	0.21
Gujarat	0.10
Daman & Diu	0.07
Dadra & Nagar Haveli	0.06

(*Continued*)

Table 9.B.4 (Continued)

State/UT	Percentage of Sikhs
Maharashtra	0.20
Andhra Pradesh	0.05
Karnataka	0.05
Goa	0.10
Lakshadweep	0.01
Kerala	0.01
Tamil Nadu	0.02
Puducherry	0.02
Andaman & Nicobar Islands	0.34

Adapted from:

Source of data: For 2011 www.censusindia.gov.in/2011census/C-01.html (Date accessed 24 April 2017)

10 The 'people' and the 'political'

Aam Aadmi and the changing contours of the anti-corruption movement

Nissim Mannathukkaren

Introduction

One of the most fascinating aspects of modern social science is, despite its claim to scientific status, its utter failure in predicting historic events (after all predictability is the cornerstone of science). Here the failures of political scientists and sociologists in predicting the collapse of the Soviet Union (see Hollis 1998), or the explosions of the Arab Spring, and that of the economists in predicting the global financial crisis of 2008, for example, are marked in the recent times. Thus, it is not surprising that the social scientists failed to foresee the emergence of something like the Aam Aadmi Party (AAP), one significant development in India's post-independence history. What was more surprising was that the position adopted by many scholars in assessing the movement, and the party which was born out of it: a dismissal of it as a force which is weakening democracy, and as one which is a part of the political right. This position was articulated by different poles of the ideological spectrum from Marxism to postcolonial theory.

In this chapter, I look at the way in which the anti-corruption movement has changed its character from its origins in anti-political civil society activism to the transformation into an electoral force, Aam Aadmi Party, which in the present is vying for political power in more than one state. In the short period of its existence, the party has seen some spectacular highs and lows. The highs were when the party came to power in Delhi in 2013, secured four Parliamentary seats out of the thirteen in Punjab (2014), and finally, recorded a historic victory in the Delhi in the Assembly Elections of 2015 when it won sixty-seven out of the seventy seats and 54 per cent of the votes. The lows were when the party saw a split in the leadership with the departure of intellectuals like Yogendra Yadav and Prashant Bhushan in 2015, and its failure both to win the Punjab Assembly Elections in 2017 (despite originally expected to do so) and to make a mark in the 2017 Goa Assembly Elections.[1] This has stalled its national ambitions.

I will argue that a one-sided dismissal of the anti-corruption movement and the AAP as a part of the economic and political right does not allow us to understand the conditions which have given rise to it, and its changing contours. An understanding of this would require going beyond seeing concepts of the 'people' and the 'political' in a reductionist fashion and also make sense of the contradictions. Understanding the Aam Aadmi phenomenon would also require attention to the possibilities that inhere in it in altering the structure as well as its limitations. The most significant transformation has been in the AAP positioning itself as a centrist formation with some Left characteristics and placed in opposition to the Rightwing Hindu nationalist party, the Bharatiya Janata Party (BJP). This is especially relevant in the context of the decline of the Congress Party, the main centrist formation since India's independence, and the surge of the Right. But the question is if the AAP can go beyond being a centrist formation and the contradictions which currently characterise it.

The origins

The Aam Aadmi phenomenon has its origins in the India Against Corruption (IAC) movement founded by Arvind Kejriwal and a few civil society activists. Soon the IAC found a mascot in Anna Hazare, a veteran Gandhian activist, to lead it with the hopes of converting it into a mass movement. Corruptions scandals, of behemoth proportions, that rocked the Government of India from 2010 provided the context for the emergence of the anti-corruption movement. It has to be also located in the larger context of the 'enormous void at the heart of India's democratic system' (Nandy 2011). Similarly, as Yogendra Yadav argued:

> While the third space in India's politics has expanded to include new issues and energies, the Third Force has shrunk in politics. This disruption of the party-movement dialectic led to a moral vacuum and the emptying of politics of real life substantive questions.
>
> (Yadav 2013)

This was not a movement like the anti-corruption movements from before where the demand was only for the resignation of the government

(Nigam 2013: 38). But here, Hazare went on a fast until death if the demands of the movement were not met: among which, the main ones were the establishment of a stronger and effective *Lokpal* (Ombudsman) than the one that the government proposed, and the participation of civil society in the formulation of the bill that would institute the Lokpal. The movement, which although was located in the Indian capital, New Delhi, caused some reverberations across urban centres of the country. Soon the social media in India, mainly used by the urban middle-class youth, went viral about India's very own revolution, its Tahrir Square. Yet, the movement lost steam in a few months, with the inability of the fasts and agitations conducted by it to really achieve anything substantial. This was the movement when Kejriwal broke away from Anna Hazare to form a political party despite the former's virulent distaste for party politics in the beginning.

Rightwing technocracy?

Both the anti-corruption movement and the political party drew sharp criticisms from the beginning. Prabhat Patnaik, for example, saw the Aam Aadmi movement as 'an avoidable trend in Indian politics' which if emulated in other parts of the country will lead 'to enfeeblement rather than invigoration of democracy' (2013). One of the major reasons why the Anna Hazare movement was also deemed to be an avoidable trend was because of its Rightwing character. This critique took two forms: religious and political-economic. First, there was the obvious critique of the movement as one, at least in the initial stages, which saw the display of Hindu nationalist motifs or that of people singing *vande mataram* (the national song of India, which is in fact a hymn to a Hindu goddess).[2] Thus one journalist called it 'The Jagran at Jantar Mantar' – the word *jagran* clearly marking it as a movement mainly informed by the Hindu idiom and lacking any wider appeal (Naqvi 2011a). Anna Hazare and his group of activists who were putting pressure on the government to bring about a Lokpal was also seen as an extra-constitutional, moral authority 'standing outside of, and with supervisory powers over, the legal-constitutional authorities' Chatterjee (2011). Chatterjee went on to argue, erroneously, in my view, that this is akin to the authority of the religious clerics over the government in post-revolution Iran. He also compares the populism of the movement to that of the Tea Party in the USA.

Despite the Rightwing character of a religious/moral kind ascribed by many, the other casting of the Rightwing character is in political-economic terms. This does not deny the masculine nationalism, and the hawkish and powerful state that is sought by the urban middle classes, but it did not see the movement as being appropriated by Hindu Rightwing elements. Instead, it argued that by the virtue of the fact that the focus was on corruption, the enemy that was posited is not an external one, but an internal one which fractured the notion of a united Hindu nation. Thus, what is Rightwing is the urge to whittle down democracy, social justice, and move to 'technocratic containment' of the masses through focus on 'clean governance', 'technocratic rule', and 'fast growth' keeping in line with neoliberal politics rather than a 'democratic containment' through reservation and other economic and social welfare programmes (Giri 2011a). Similarly, Gudavarthy argues that the Anna Hazare movement and the 'new politics' of the urban middle classes have also inaugurated the 'neoliberalisation of politics' in which the middle classes benefit disproportionately, leaving the lower classes to the trickle downs (Gudavarthy 2014: 16). Aam Aadmi Party too was cast in similar terms. It was argued that 'a substantial segment of its support base consists of people who make no secret of their wish to vote for Narendra Modi in the Parliamentary elections [as a mascot of neoliberal development], and the AAP has done little to counter Modi's "appeal"' (Patnaik 2014). And similar to Giri, Patnaik emphasises the technocratic aspect: 'democracy is not people acting as a collective subject but a group of messiahs, consisting of well-intentioned technocrats who alone have "expertise", acting permanently on their behalf' (2014).

Even when there are elements of truth in these assertions, there are some critical theoretical problems as well, and this has been borne out by the formation of the AAP and its actual trajectory since then. These assertions ignore the conditions that have given rise to the Aam Aadmi phenomenon. They seek to foster a myth as well, but this time the myth of a pure politics, which does not exist in reality. Yes, of course, Anna Hazare's history of dalliance with Hindu Rightwing motifs, his curious mixture of Gandhi with violent methods (the anti-alcohol campaign in his village involved the flogging of people who violated the code), and the messianic tendencies of the movement, in which the leaders have seemingly arrogated to themselves the moral high ground and the right to speak for the whole of society, were deeply problematic. Yet, the casting of the anti-corruption movement as a Rightwing one in religious terms missed the contradictory nature of movements such as these which allow different future possibilities.[3] People singing *vande mataram* are not necessarily Hindu fundamentalists and everybody that took up Hazare's call did not believe in his dictum of chopping off the hands of the corrupt. Moreover, the protestors belonged to a diverse range of ideological and political affiliations. To have reduced this to a Rightwing upsurge on the basis of some symbols at the protest is to fail in understanding why the movement struck a chord among such large numbers of people with contradictory economic and political interests. Such failure is seen in the example of the journalist who deridingly termed the protest as the 'jagran', and, writing within a few days afterwards, that 'from being an absolute sceptic, I now confess to a grudging admiration for anything that rattles so many people' (Naqvi 2011b), demonstrating the pitfalls of going only by a surface understanding of any social phenomenon. Similarly, the fact that some numbers of Aam Aadmi supporters were backers of Rightwing politics in the form of BJP and Narendra Modi either before, or now, in the national arena, in itself, does not conclusively establish the Rightwing nature of Aam Aadmi politics.[4] For that, the engendering conditions of the rise of the BJP and Narendra Modi as a phenomenon has to be analysed, and also the reasons for the latter being seen as the only viable option in national politics. Without this, a critique of Aam Aadmi support will be an empty one.

The critique in terms of political economy is on a stronger ground. This was especially true of the Anna Hazare movement which had a single-point agenda of corruption. In it there were many antidemocratic tendencies: the authoritarian implications of the proposed Lokpal (provisions like the combination of executive and judicial functions in the institution), and the middle classes' hypocrisy which would look down upon the political class but not the equally corrupt corporate class etc. But, even here, I argue that the trajectory that the Aam Aadmi movement is not just one of 'technocratic containment'. At the present, there are more contradictions on display.[5] Thus, while the committee constituted by the AAP to formulate the election manifesto for the 2014 Lok Sabha Elections was overly represented by business interests, the decision of the AAP government to disallow Foreign Direct Investment (FDI) in retail in Delhi caused great consternation among the outward-looking national bourgeoisie. The Delhi government was the first state to withdraw permission for FDI in retail (CNN-IBN 2014). This decision has not been reversed even after two years in power. Similarly, the latter also took on the corporate-government nexus by targeting big MNCs like Reliance Industries Limited (Nigam 2014a; Subramaniam 2015),[6] again to the surprise of many, for the main critique against the Anna Hazare/Aam Aadmi movement was that it was only opposing the political class (see Giri 2011b). Soon after AAP's victory in Delhi in 2015, a financial analyst wondered if similar victories elsewhere will not lead to a stalling of the neoliberal reform process (Chakravarty 2015).

At the same time, it is important to note that AAP is only against crony capitalism and not capitalism (Varshney 2013).

Crucially, there is a significant shift in the class composition of the movement from the Anna Hazare phase, when it was mainly the urban propertied and middle classes who were part of it, to later when it expanded to include the 'urban poor – drawn from the working classes in the informal sector, small traders, hawkers, migrants, etc.'.[7] The movement also moved away from a single-issue movement (anti-corruption) – one with an element of anti-politics, to a 'populist political organisation articulating real life issues of the ordinary citizens like inflated power bills and the inequitable distribution of water' (Ramani 2014). The 2013 Election Manifesto was full of proposals that veered to the Left: fighting privatisation of water, strengthening the public school system, demolishing monopoly capital in the electricity sector, getting permanent status for contract labour, and empowering unorganised sector workers (Crowley 2013).[8] Slums became the major areas of support for AAP. Thus, economically, the programme is more populist with some Left characteristics.

But the biggest challenge to the argument of a technocratic containment is the turning of the movement which was supposed to embody orderly, neoliberal rationality into one which was supposedly anarchic and chaotic, at least, for a brief time during the first forty-nine-day AAP government. The movement's protest politics in the form of street protests and agitations continued even after the party came to power in Delhi and was often led by Arvind Kejriwal, the Chief Minister himself, leading to an unprecedented situation not seen in India since the Communist Party–led governments in Kerala and W. Bengal in the 1960s, which practiced the policy of 'agitation and administration' together. This led to the big media, which was one of the main reasons for the rise of the Aam Aadmi, and a section of the urban middle classes turning their back on it, demonstrating the limits of the technocratic containment argument.

The discourse of corruption

The concept of corruption, which was the main tool of mobilisation for Anna Hazare and also for the Aam Aadmi Party in the initial stages, was another issue that was taken up by the radical critics. In their view this focus on corruption is the single most important way to obfuscate structural and systemic aspects of inequality and deprivation:

> [the] discourse on corruption is basically a dispute about the way in which socially generated surplus is distributed under the

conditions of the rule of property and capital. Wealth, or any asset, in this view, is legitimate when its owners can currently demonstrate their legal claim over such a resource, and is illegitimate, when they cannot. Access to an asset is legitimate when it has been acquired by the unsullied operation of the free market, without fear, favour or influence, or when it is yours by inheritance.

(Sengupta 2011)

In this discourse, bribes are seen as corruption, but not a low/non-living wage leading to a moral equivalence between the corruption of the rich, and the poor and desperate. It also ignores other forms of corruption in which, for example, the state would encourage practices like 'encounter killings' by the armed forces for cash and professional rewards (Sengupta 2011). Similarly, another critique is based on the argument that it is entirely hypocritical for the middle class to be part of the 'India Against Corruption' movement because, as Partha Chatterjee argues, 'the middle class, from top to bottom, is the biggest beneficiary of corruption in government because it is the middle class which populates the government, inhabits it, runs it on a daily basis' (2011). This hypocrisy arises from the fact that the middle classes, as Arjun Appadurai argues, inhabit two selves, one 'built on the fantasy of a Western self . . . which imagines itself as impersonal, apolitical and civic-minded to a fault' and the other which is, 'a living, local, biographic self embedded entirely in friends, family and ties of blood, marriage and caste' (Appadurai 2011). This contradictory self is perhaps what inhibits the middle classes, and the Aam Admi movement, to move to contending with the structural framework like that of the socio-economic structure (and categories like that of capitalism and feudalism), and other substantive concerns like universal rights to health, education, employment, food and so on (Patnaik 2013, 2014), or the rising inequality in India (Khilnani 2014).

While the critique of the discourse of a singular focus on corruption at the expense of larger structural questions in the Anna Hazare and Aam Aadmi movements is correct, what it misses is the potentiality of the issue of corruption to expand beyond that. Even a narrow understanding of corruption is not completely bereft of any significance. There are many kinds of corruption. Even simple acts of corruption in the public institutions can eat away people's livelihoods and dent the delivery of public services. And corruption that is associated with crony capitalism that leads to the private appropriation of vast public resources is another form of primitive accumulation which has severe consequences for communities and classes on the margins. The most important policy decision of the Narendra Modi–led BJP government was the initiation of the demonetisation of high-value currency notes in November 2016. Despite the critical negative consequences of the gigantic exercise, especially for the poor, demonetisation seemed to enjoy legitimacy (as seen in the election mandates for the BJP in UP Assembly Elections). It shows the importance of the discourse of corruption among the public and its acceptance of the government narrative that demonetisation is a war against the rich, even if it is not factually proven.

The radical critique mostly subscribes to a zero-sum view of political transformation in which either it is revolution or nothing. Reformist changes do not have a place. What are not delineated are the contours of the interim period or the paths until a revolutionary society is constituted. This ignores that even Marx was for reformist struggles like the ones for eight-hour working days, while laying the foundation for a revolution. Movements based on single-point agendas like corruption might not overthrow the ruling structure, but it does gnaw at it, forcing it to make concessions that it would not have otherwise made. That is why one cannot dismiss formal democracy even if it is not a social or participatory democracy (Huber, Rueschemeyer and Stephens 1997: 24). The virulent attempt by the then ruling party to vilify the Lokpal activists in the beginning showed that even moderate attempts to reform the system could be greatly threatening to the ruling elite. And it is relevant to note that the present ruling party has not appointed a Lokpal despite the coming into effect of the Lokpal and Lokayuktas Act 2013 as a consequence of the anti-corruption movement. The present central government has also not given assent to the Delhi Lokpal Bill passed by the Kejriwal. It is also important that both the Lokpals are much weaker than originally envisioned by the activists.

The people and the political

When a class-based critique of Aam Aadmi movement is made, simultaneously, the absolute disenchantment with what politics has become in the last few decades of postcolonial India has to be made sense of. The routinisation and mechanisation of politics in its clientilistic form, which has led to the evisceration of the democratic aspirations of the masses, is not something that should escape the lens of any analyst. This has been further compounded in the last two and half decades that neoliberal capitalism has become the dominant discourse and practice. One only needs to look at the trajectory of the mainstream Communist parties to understand how what were radical forces once have turned into political machines that have staked everything at the altar of electoral politics and state power (Mannathukkaren 2010a). When we turn a critical eye towards the emerging Aam Aadmi politics, it is equally important to read it in the context of the spectacular failures of the parties that claim to represent the working classes and the peasants and the transformations that they have undergone in the recent times.

In this scenario of a huge vacuum created by the degeneration of the Left parties, it is not surprising that AAP has got a groundswell of support. It is remarkable that a political formation has managed to break the gridlock of electoral machinery controlled by elites with both money and muscle power. And what is more significant is that this has been achieved without mobilising explicitly on the basis of pre-existing identities of caste, religion, and ethnicity.[9] The Delhi Assembly Elections of 2013 showed that mere appeals on the basis of identity alone were no longer tenable and issues of governance have come to the fore (Nigam 2013: 40). The same was the case with the Delhi Elections of 2015. Of course, in a society with vast inequalities between caste, religious, and ethnic groups as there are within them, it is inevitable that there is political mobilisation on the basis of ascriptive identities and there is nothing inherently regressive about that. But when the latter itself has fallen prey to the degenerative tendencies of formal and electoral politics, it is progressive that a new secular identity is envisaged even if it is not devoid of the majoritarian impulses of nationalism or domination by upper castes as we will see later.

The mistake that the radical critique of Anna Hazare and Aam Aadmi movements makes is in seeing the new political formations and the people who constitute them in a reductionist fashion. There is no scope for intervention, say by activists and intellectuals, as 'the people' are already made and cast in stone; there is no sense of politics as a terrain of becoming and transformation; and there is no concept of politics as an educative process. It does not see, as Ernesto Laclau does, 'the construction of the "people" is the political act *par excellence*' (Laclau 2005: 154). Laclau goes on to argue that:

> Strictly speaking, there is no 'people' prior the making of a demand. The very performative nature of making a demand creates a people out of nothing. This makes the particular demands of the people closely linked with democracy, which is not necessarily connected to a space (parliament, for example) but a form of political subjectification.
>
> (Laclau 2005: 171)

Instead, in the critique, people are reductively seen as the creatures of their base instincts and economic interests.

Partha Chatterjee, claiming to follow Laclau, saw the Hazare movement as a populist one where 'the people' identify as their enemy the entire political class and bureaucracy. This is contradictory, in Chatterjee and the others' accounts, as we have seen before, for the people themselves are blameless here. For Chatterjee, thus the 'principal moral and emotional force' of the Anna Hazare movement was 'antipolitical' and that is what he sees as dangerous in it (Chatterjee 2011). Gudavarthy argues in the same vein:

> while the 'new politics' has made a rhetorical use of available democratic protest forms, its substantive core seems to be nudging towards a new hegemonic frame that demands more law, more centralisation, more surveillance, more majoritarianism, less tolerance for deliberation, and in fact more contempt for the idea of democracy and vocation and politics itself.
>
> (Gudavarthy 2014: 14)

While, again, there are elements of truth in these arguments, it does not allow for contradictions or possibilities. It does not explain how the anti-politics of the Anna movement transformed into the electoral politics of AAP. As Faisal Devji points out, the social movements that brought about the Eastern European revolutions and the Arab Spring have been anti-statist and anti-political parties. Therefore, it is 'remarkable that "India Against Corruption" has produced the Aam Aadmi Party (AAP)' (Devji 2014). Chatterjee also misreads Laclau. Laclau does not call everything that simply speaks of 'the people' as populist. On the contrary, he argues that 'populism consists in the presentation of popular-democratic interpellations as a synthetic-antagonistic complex with respect to the dominant ideology'. Thus, there is a revolutionary/radical edge to populism although Laclau is quick to clarify that populism is not *'always* revolutionary' (Laclau 1977: 173; original emphasis). For Laclau, *'all* struggles are, by definition, *political'* (2005: 154; original emphasis).

What is missing in the critique is an understanding as to why such disenchantment with politics has arisen, and what politics is being shunned. India is a democracy in which the core institutions have significantly degenerated since the 1970s (even where there is evidence for increasing participation in the formal democratic process). It is one in which the last two decades have seen the corporate plunder of national resources and the destruction of the tribal homelands with complete collusion of state power (Mannathukkaren 2011). Thus, there is the emerging contradiction in India between democratic deepening in the form of welfare measures and the institutionalisation of rights in the form of NREGA, RTI, etc. on one hand, and on the other, agrarian crisis, farmers' suicides, rural-urban divide, land grab, and tribal displacement (Gudavarthy 2014: 2–3). And it is one in which the police, the most visible arm of the state, flaunt and misuse their unchecked power with impunity. An astounding thirty million cases are pending in the courts, and 250,000 undertrials are languishing in prisons (Mannathukkaren 2011). Thus, even representative democracy is marked by the structural condition of unaccounted and extra-judicial violence (Gudavarthy 2014: 7). Without understanding this context, it is difficult to be sceptical of the populist mobilisation as Chatterjee is when he argues that 'that not everything that moves the people is worthy of support' (Chatterjee 2011; see also Appadurai 2011).[10] The politics that had become the target of the movement is one that is a skeleton of what politics should be. In the present context, anti-politics and depoliticisation are not characteristics of just middle classes, but the poor classes as well (see Mannathukkaren 2015).

It is intriguing then that as a postcolonial theorist, Chatterjee would question the populist nature of the mobilisation considering that he is the proponent of the concept of 'political society' which was precisely coined to understand social mobilisations which fall outside the purview of 'civil society'. And political society for Chatterjee was the dominant mode of politics in much of the Third World (see Chatterjee 2004; for a critique, see Mannathukkaren 2010b).[11] While Chatterjee rightly argues that all populist movements cannot be supported simply because they mobilise large numbers of people, he discounts the possibility that the populist movements can themselves move away from populism to more radical, and structural issues. While this has not happened, the transition from an 'apolitical' anti-corruption movement, which had the political class as the enemy, to a political party contesting in the electoral arena itself negates this pre-determination of populism as apolitical. As Yadav put it:

> Moving from the Anna movement to AAP, those who hated politics of any kind left us anyway. Anti-politics used to bother me. I felt politics was part of the problem, but it should also be part of the solution. That sort of I-hate-politics strand left us anyway. Those who stayed back did have an unease. But people learn.
> (Yadav 2013)

And remarkably, this has happened in a very short time, questioning assessments such as these:

> No matter how earnest, India's middle class has yet to view the political class as legitimate, the party system as the main way to achieve programmatic changes. Until that happens, middle class activism will be consciously set up in opposition to electoral politics, rather than as a potent force within it.
>
> (Sitapati 2011: 41)

Thus, the transition to viewing politics as legitimate is the unexpected change that has characterised the movement. Of course, the fact that AAP in power for more than two years has also had made compromises in the electoral arena has dented the confidence in the party to rise above the 'muck' of politics.

The role of the middle classes

The critics' reductionist approach is seen in understanding the role of the middle classes as well. It ignores that historically there are cases when the middle classes have a played a progressive role in democratisation, either as allies of working classes or on their own (Rueschemeyer, Stephens and Stephens 1992).[12] This is where seeing the Aam Aadmi phenomenon as a mere continuation of ruling class politics or as one which perpetuates the hegemony of the upper and middle classes is simplistic. The contours of this politics are evolving. Thus, as a commentator notes: 'From leaning right as part of the Anna (Hazare) agitation to emerging as the natural leader of those on the margins – Muslims, Dalits and the economically poor – Kejriwal's transformation is truly one of a kind in politics' (Subramaniam 2015). People and their desires and actions in their myriad contradictions and complexities have to be made sense of and contended with (Srivastava 2014). They cannot be pre-emptively dismissed as not conforming to the blueprint of a progressive and revolutionary politics conceived theoretically.[13] Much of the radical critique is along these lines, which sees the middle classes as incapable of rising above their narrow economic interests. It does not ask, for example, why did the politically apathetic middle classes come out on the streets? It also does not examine the new kind of middle-class discontent and movements that have arisen in the last two and a half decades since liberalisation (Devji 2014).

Further, the critique ignores the varied and diverse nature of the 'middle classes' in terms of income, occupation, and values leading to a lumping together of the various strands within it.[14] Vinay Sitapati argues that the heterogeneity ensures that middle-class activisms themselves are different and '[w]hat was unique about the Anna Hazare movement was that diverse middle-class activisms were able to craft a campaign that appealed to all their interests' (2011: 40).[15] Thus, issues like corruption can act as an empty signifier. Ernesto Laclau sees empty signifiers as unifying a 'multiplicity of heterogeneous demands in equivalential chains' (2005: 154).

The critique misses the potential for a progressive transformation of at least some sections of the middle classes. The volunteer base of AAP is primarily middle-class youth (Ramani 2015). Economic and social structures only condition politics, they do not mechanically determine it. Class positions do not automatically produce class interests, but the latter are historically constructed (Rueschemeyer, Stephens and Stephens 1992). If initially during the Anna Hazare phase of the *Aam Aadmi* phenomenon, the radical critique was that the movement included only the middle classes, later, the critique, befuddled by the participation of substantial section of the poor and working classes, theorised it by seeing the latter as being taken in by the promises of the middle classes. Thus, it is merely a strategy on the part of the middle classes, a 'masterstroke' which converts a middle-class agenda into a multi-class one (Giri 2013). This is another version of the false consciousness thesis which sees the people as naively participating in their own exploitation and the poor as always being hegemonised by the upper classes.

What it misses is the contradictory nature of people's consciousness, the capacity and agency of people to question structures of domination whenever new pathways of hope have been cut. In the case of the Aam Aadmi phenomenon, Roy, based on field research, argues, 'it is the attraction of undertaking extraordinary action and performing preferred selves' that mobilised large numbers of common people. These performative aspects of citizenship which 'emphasise the ownership ties that bind citizen and state, and that invest the owner-citizen with the right to demand answers, accounts, and accountability from his government' (2014: 46, 52) are crucial and need to be studied. A one-sided and simplistic dismissal of the people is an elitism that refuses to engage with the real world and the scale of desperation that has spawned this new politics. This realisation dawned on at least a few of the trenchant critics of the initial phase of the Anna Hazare movement:

> The Hazare phenomenon has made it possible for a lot of ordinary men and women to actualize their desires of being in public

space, of articulating their discontent, of discovering solidarities. This is something for us to build on, not to dismiss, especially, and even if we are not comfortable with a lot of the content of the things that get said when people meet under the tricolour.

(Sengupta 2011)

This does not mean progressive social transformation is linear or easy by any means. After all, to convert the propertied members of the Resident Welfare Associations (RWAs) who see the world through the prism of their residential colonies[16] or the *khap panchayats* with their monstrous and dangerous prejudices to a progressive politics might seem an insurmountable endeavour. Besides, the idealistic middle-class youth tend to prefer solution-based public policy measures rather than well-defined ideological transformations (Ramani 2015). At the same time, as Antonio Gramsci asks, how can a new language emerge if we do not engage with the existing languages, however despicable they seem? Gramsci (1985: 102) had argued that it

> must work towards the elaboration of what already exists, whether polemically or in other ways does not matter. What matters is that it sinks its roots in the humus of popular culture as it is, with its tastes and tendencies and with its moral and intellectual world, even if it is backward and conventional.

The most interesting aspect of democratic politics is how egalitarian aspirations of the masses gain a dynamic of their own once they find an outlet. Thus, if the anti-corruption movement was initially accused of being a foreign-funded NGO activism which wanted to impose the World Bank agenda in the country, the concerns of the people which became a part of it escaped such limits and horizons. This is what has transformed what many critics termed as a movement which was merely a creation of the media and consisting of middle classes (the editor of a magazine called it the 'comical revolution of an obsolete man' consisting of 300 people [Joseph 2011]) to one which secured nearly 54 per cent of the votes.

The Aam Aadmi in power

The significant trends of the AAP in power have been the focus on public provision of health and education (Sebastian 2016; *Hindustan Times* 2017). The maximum share of the budget in the first year was allocated to education (Joshi 2016). And education allocation was increased by 100 per cent and health by 50 per cent (Lahariya 2016: 16). There is some significant transformation happening in at least some of the government schools (Bhatnagar 2017). The government has undertaken populist welfare measures like free or subsidised electricity and water for the economically poorer classes. *Mohalla* (community) clinics set up with the intention of taking free healthcare to the community has attracted international attention. But the implementation of the policy has lagged behind substantially. Only 110 clinics of the 1,000 planned have become functional (*Hindustan Times* 2017). Yet, as a public health specialist writes, the Mohalla 'concept could ultimately lead to universal health coverage at affordable cost' (Lahariya 2016: 17). The other important measure is with regard to strengthening the public school system and the regulation of the private school sector. One of the major problems with the latter was the exorbitant fees charged. The government passed a Bill (again, critically, yet to receive assent from the centre) which allows it to bring criminal charges against schools which charge exorbitant fees (Sebastian 2016). The promise of building 500 new government schools, though, again, has been largely incomplete (*Hindustan Times* 2017).

One of the structural issues facing Delhi is the five million people living in precarious conditions in 1,650 unauthorised colonies/slums. AAP had promised to provide secure property rights to these. It also envisaged a rehabilitation programme which involved the building of new houses in the colonies. But the government initiatives in implementing this has been stuck in bureaucratic wrangle with the central government (*Hindustan Times* 2017). Further, merely regularising the colonies without the provision of basic infrastructure and amenities is hardly an improvement of the living conditions to these underclasses. The movement on the latter is slow. Further, programmes like participatory budgeting towards which initial steps were taken are on the back-burner now. Yet, what this policy emphasis on public health and education shows is that technocratic neoliberal and technocratic rationality is not the only logic of the Aam Aadmi Party as the critics argued in the beginning.

At the crossroads

The Aam Aadmi phenomenon in the present is at a crossroads. A movement that claimed an astounding party membership of ten million crore as early as January 2014 cannot but be contradictory with various economic classes and social groups being represented. It attracted members as diverse as big capitalists, radical civil society activists opposed to the state, upper-class professionals, activists of the mainstream communist parties, and so on in the beginning. Thus, it would naturally display a contradictoriness in its ideology and programme leading to a vacillation when confronted with structural deprivations and inequities. Besides, as a party which is still largely Delhi-based, it is governed by the particular structural dynamics of a big city. But as it has evolved to a take a position on the centre-Left, and against the Right, it cannot continue on this path of vacillation. If it has to counter the Right, it has to move to a sustained critique of the most egregious forms of divisions that characterise Indian society. This cannot be realised without sustained struggles and a comprehensive ideology and theory. Patnaik had argued before that the AAP ideology 'apotheosises non-thought' (Patnaik 2014). Some can argue that there is merit in overcoming deadening and paralysing dualisms, and the search for ideological purity. It is a fact that there is no purity in the real world, but only contradictions and contaminations, and we can acknowledge with Laclau that populist movements are overdetermined by a multiplicity of meanings. At the same time, these dilemmas and heterogeneity cannot be stretched to the extent of being ideologically empty. For an empty ideology only aids the prevailing dominant structures of power. Here is where the limits of Laclau's empty signifier lie in that, as Žižek argues, it can become one without content, vague, and which ignores the economic structure of capitalism (Weber 2011: 11). Laclau has tendency to see capitalism as a discursive entity which is 'produced through metaphors and symbolization [which] does not exist *per se*' (Weber 2011: 14; see also Laclau and Mouffe 2001). Any radical transformation of existing social structures and relationships has to contend with the material and discursive reality of capitalism. As Zižek writes:

> The fate of whole strata of population and sometimes of whole countries can be decided by the solipsistic speculative dance of capital, which pursues its goal of profitability in a blessed indifference with regard to how its movement will affect social reality. Therein resides the fundamental systemic violence of capitalism, much more uncanny than direct precapitalist socioideological violence. This violence is no longer attributable to concrete individuals and their 'evil' intentions but is purely objective, systemic, anonymous.
>
> (Žižek 2006: 566)

There cannot be a radical political agenda which does not contend with this. The greatest threat to Indian society is now neoliberal capitalism conjoined with Hindu majoritarian nationalism, which is increasingly displaying authoritarian and fascist tendencies.[17] If the AAP fails to engage with and articulate the fundamental divisions in society, and articulate an alternative political and economic programme, it would not be in a position to confront Hindutva. AAP has not, so far, made an attempt to outline the structural inequalities that characterise society, say, in terms of class, caste, or gender. The biggest hindrance, despite it positioning itself as the primary opponent of the BJP, is the persistent endeavour to identify itself as a post-ideological phenomenon. It argues that the ideology discourse is obsolete and there is a need for 'transcending' the binary of Left and Right ideologies. This obviously leads to further claims that the party is 'solution focused rather than ideology driven' (Yadav 2013).[18] The party has not moved away from this position since then. Here the question is this: what kind of solutions are envisaged when there is a clear trend of the avoidance of identifying some of the fundamental problems in society? Then there is the issue of the seeming agreement of the party with some of the worst tendencies of 'the popular' like that of a hegemonic and violent nationalism, xenophobia and racism (see Mannathukkaren 2014), or religious conservatism. Here the popular itself is not interrogated.

As a party in its nascent stages, which seeks to challenge the dominant parties in society, it is to an extent understandable that AAP does not want to take positions on extremely divisive issues, lest it alienates people even before it has had a chance to establish itself. The vagueness of some of its central concepts like 'corruption', 'Aam Aadmi', and 'the people' is a logical outcome of this position (Nigam 2014a).[19] But if this ideological obfuscation is going to be a continuing tendency when the AAP grows its roots, then it could be convincingly argued that the Aam Aadmi movement/party will be a part of the status quo. Yadav, when he was a part of AAP, argued that the party wanted to model itself after the African National Congress (ANC), among other similar models, which have acted as an umbrella for people's movements (Yadav 2013). While this is not a problem, it very crucially ignores that the ANC took a neoliberal turn long ago after abandoning its original economic programme of nationalisation, leading to deleterious consequences for the majority of the Black African population.[20] India has got some of the most egregious forms of inequalities and deprivations in the world, which have not been eliminated even after more than two decades of market-led growth (in fact, they have been accentuated by market-left growth).[21] Is it really the case that the problem is in the inability to find a solution because of an excessive focus on ideologies as the AAP thinks, or is it that there has not been ideologies which spoke for the most exploited sections of the population? When the whole world has come under the hegemony of a predatory and speculative capitalism, the effects of which are starkly evident across nations, is it the case that the Left needs to be rejected because it does not have an intelligent economics as Yadav argues or is it that the Left is more relevant than before? Thus, it should be obvious that what the AAP is ushering in is not necessarily a revolution of the popular by any means.[22] And there should not be any illusions regarding this.

The question therefore is whether the potential of what Ernesto Laclau and Chantal Mouffe outline as radical democracy in which struggles against different forms of injustice come together and, according to them, 'symbolic overdetermination as a concrete mechanism for the unification of these struggles' (Laclau and Mouffe 2001: 11) will realise itself. This can be possible only if the poor and working classes part of Aam Aadmi politics can transform the party beyond its present concerns and if the party can go back to the initial steps made in aligning with some important civil society groups interested in a radical democracy. Punjab, unlike Delhi, has more concrete possibilities regarding this as AAP there is a formation which has attracted a significant number of Dalits, and people with a history of radical Left and militant Sikh activism (Pritam Singh, this volume). In the initial stages of the anti-corruption movement, Sengupta pointed out, 'despite everything, I see in the present circumstances, an opening, the bare outline of a possibility' (Sengupta 2011). Nigam argued later after the 2013 Delhi Assembly Elections that 'the most important part of this experiment is the fact that rank outsiders who speak the language of ordinary people have now taken charge, however temporarily. The beginnings of a new political culture are already becoming visible' (Nigam 2014b). The biggest contribution of the Aam Aadmi politics is ushering in a new class of people who have no prior political experience and in generating interest in politics among ordinary people (Palshikar 2015). This scope for extraordinary agency among 'political novices' is significant in an Indian party system characterised by dynastic politics (Roy 2014: 52).

But the structural limitations in a radical transformation of Aam Aadmi politics are still immense. The main limitation being the positioning of the AAP as a post-ideological formation as discussed previously. It does not have any programme to counter neoliberal capitalism and democratise economic production. Even as it seeks to ameliorate the condition of the economically poor, the working classes are not the agents of transformation.[23] And this is critical since, empirically, the single most important variable in the construction of the welfare state is trade union strength, or rule by working class/social democratic parties (Huber, Rueschemeyer and Stephens 1997: 327). In fact, movements like the Aam Aadmi are made possible by the fact that the labour and the trade union movement in India have been decimated, and the Left as a social movement and electoral force has declined. Equally critical is the domination of Aam Aadmi politics by upper castes with Other Backward Castes, Scheduled Castes, and Muslims who are the overwhelming majority of the Delhi population in a minority among the AAP MLAs. Women are similarly severely underrepresented (Ramachandran 2016). The new secular politics, like the old secular politics, still passes off as progressive by invisibilising caste. Further, the emergence of AAP as a moral alternative was constructed on the image of a completely transparent and democratic party.[24] But that itself has taken a beating with the emergence of a 'high-command culture' in AAP which was demonstrated in the run-up to the Punjab Assembly Elections (Bhushan 2016).[25] AAP's initial success was in providing an antidote to the routinisation of democracy (Palshikar 2015), but itself is now being threatened by routinisation.[26] This is not surprising considering that a formation like AAP will be forced to play by the rules set by the established national parties leading to a severe denting of its initial transformative potential.[27]

Despite this, and the fact that the Aam Aadmi Party's programme is hardly revolutionary, it is still immensely threatening to the Rightwing government and, also, the establishment. The big media, despite its initial promotion of the anti-corruption movement, is virulently against AAP. As a media scholar puts it: 'It is difficult to think of another instance in which a large section of the electronic media has so determinedly closed ranks against one political formation and in favour of the ruling party' (Bhushan 2016). There is a huge vacuum in the Left of the centre of the Indian political spectrum and in the sphere of the party-social movement dialectic. AAP has aspects of social movement in it (Devji 2014), but it is a long way from being a genuine Left alternative despite the fact the anti-corruption movement itself having changed its contours quite drastically to culminate in the electoral politics of AAP which has positioned as a Left-of-centre populism. It is a formation focused on the lower classes, but, as Palshikar argues, for it, class matters but 'without being the focal point of contestation' (2015). Yet, it would not be correct to argue as the radical critique has that AAP is an avoidable trend in Indian politics. It might be that the Aam Aadmi phenomenon will turn out to be an utter failure; but, its failures will not be more catastrophic than the ones that have already given birth to the Indian postcolonial misery.

Notes

1. It also lost the Municipal Corporation of Delhi elections in April 2017 and secured only 26 per cent of the votes.
2. There was also the participation of religious figures like Baba Ramdev in the Anna Movement. Besides, Rashtriya Swayamsevak (RSS) leaders supported the movement (see Subrahmaniam 2015).
3. I am not making this argument post the transformation of the anti-corruption movement into a political party, but had contended the same during the height of the former (see Mannathukkaren 2011).
4. The critique is also not able to explain how the Aam Aadmi Party moved on to seeing Narendra Modi as the main target in the 2014 Lok Sabha elections. At the same time, I am not discounting that many supporters of the Aam Aadmi movement would have Rightwing nationalist views on issues like Kashmir and that they would be the bearers of racist and xenophobic worldviews as demonstrated in New Delhi. Yet, it is, electorally, seeking to be the main opposition to the BJP.
5. The tussle between multiple class interests in the AAP is clearly visible again in Punjab (see Yamunan 2016).
6. This, as Nigam points out, is unprecedented, for even the Communist parties have rarely challenged the corporate classes. Because of this, the AAP government was subjected to a media blackout (Nigam 2015).
7. Even during the later stages of the Anna Hazare movement, it had become what even critics called it as a 'genuinely cross-class phenomenon' (Sengupta 2011).
8. This is not surprising because Delhi, as a teeming metropolis, has huge inequalities and deprivations. Nearly 25 per cent of population does not get piped water, and the per capita water availability is 3.82 litres against the WHO minimum of 40 litres (Saha 2015).
9. Only the Left parties have achieved this in any significant measure.
10. Similarly, Appadurai argues that the Anna Hazare movement exemplified fascist tendencies in that it tried to 'take politics out of the polity' (Appadurai 2011).
11. Aditya Nigam rightly argues that with such a position, Chatterjee's 'idea of "political society" lies in ruins, that it collapsed at the precise moment of its encounter with the popular' (2011).
12. This has to be done by accounting also for the ambivalent as well as regressive role played by the middle classes both in a contemporary and historical perspective (see Krishna 2015).
13. It was felt that the Yogendra Yadav/Prashant Bhushan camp's dissension in the AAP had the resonance of intellectuals/ideologues without a mass base trying to capture a party/movement built by Kejriwal and other activists (Ashraf 2015a; Nigam 2015).

The 'people' and the 'political' 257

14 In case of Aam Aadmi politics, there is also the significant participation by affluent Non-Resident Indians (NRIs).
15 The way in which the Anna Hazare Movement used Gandhian motifs to popularise middle-class concerns (Sitapati 201: 43) is an obvious reflection of the melding of different strands of thought. AAP's politics is also influenced by different strands like the legacies of the JP Movement and Lohiate socialism (Roy 2014: 53).
16 Structurally, of the middle classes, 56–62 per cent are privately employed (Sitapati 2011: 41). Moreover, the new middle class in India is marked by a 'politics of reaction [which blends] market liberalism and political and social illiberalism' (Fernandes and Heller 2006: 495). Many RWAs have been openly flouting laws and indulging in activities like the appropriation of public lands for residential colonies. As Sinha points out, RWAs have an antagonistic relationship with, and are fearful of, domestic workers and other marginalised working groups (Sinha 2015).
17 Neoliberalism across the world has led to the strengthening of capital and the weakening of labour. This has huge, negative consequences for the political participation of the subordinate classes (Huber, Rueschemeyer and Stephens 1997: 338).
18 It is interesting that Yogendra Yadav, who made this formulation before he was removed from the party, is considered to be on the Left.
19 Aditya Nigam argues that such a vagueness, in fact, is needed. According to him, any movement/party that wishes to play a transformative role should be able to 'take the people along'. Taking a definite position on crucial, structural issues at this stage would be ineffective as the people that are being drawn towards it are 'doing so precisely because its appeal is limited to "corruption"' and would be divided otherwise even before the movement is built.
20 An OECD Report from 2011 states that inequality levels have grown sharply since the end of apartheid in South Africa, despite a growing economy. Black Africans were the worst placed in terms of income distribution (OECD 2011: 51, 54).
21 Inequality has grown steeply in India as well since early the 1990s despite the fact that the economy has expanded strongly (OECD 2011: 49). India has the highest headcount poverty among the seven Emerging Economies, and it has seen only modest reductions in poverty in the last two decades (OECD 2011: 48).
22 Kejriwal's twitter bio reads: 'Political revolution in India has begun'.
23 Despite attracting the poor and ordinary classes and volunteers from them, the leaders of AAP come mainly from the economically secure sections (Palshikar 2015) leading to a class divide. This also translates into a construction of a party elite of 'expert problems-solvers' and 'educated people' (Roy 2014: 53).
24 This was seen in the radically new practice of openness about the sources of party funding and the intense consultations undertaken with the people about candidate selection, pressing problems at the local level through initiatives like Delhi Dialogue and *Jan Sabhas* (Ashraf 2015b).
25 Delhi government advertisements have featured Arvind Kejriwal alone without mentioning the party (*The Wire* 2015).

26 This is clear in the party's changing attitude to civil society groups under compulsions of party politics; ironically, these are the groups with which some of the top leaders of the party have worked with before (Delhi-based senior civil society activist, personal communication, 2 April 2017).
27 Parties like Viduthalai Chiruthaigal Katchi (VCK) in Tamil Nadu with a radical Dalit agenda painfully realised this as it entered the political mainstream (see Nilakantan 2017).

Bibliography

Appadurai, Arjun. 2011. 'Our Corruption, Our Selves', *Kafila*, August 30. http://kafila.org/2011/08/30/our-corruption-our-selves-arjun-appadurai/ (accessed on November 10, 2017).

Ashraf, Aijaz. 2015a. 'Meet the Dynamic Dozen Who Helped AAP's Ragtag Band Defeat the Mighty BJP Army', *Scroll*, February 9. https://scroll.in/article/705316/meet-the-dynamic-dozen-who-helped-aaps-ragtag-band-defeat-the-mighty-bjp-army (accessed on November 10, 2017).

———. 2015b. 'Yogendra Yadav's Rebellion Is an Example of Intellectual Arrogance', *Scroll*, March 29. https://scroll.in/article/716885/yogendra-yadavs-rebellion-is-an-example-of-intellectual-arrogance (accessed on November 10, 2017).

Bhatnagar, Gaurav Vivek. 2017. 'How Delhi Government Schools Are Revamping Their Approach to Education', *The Wire*, June 10. https://thewire.in/145618/how-government-schools-in-delhi-are-revamping-their-education-syste/ (accessed on November 12, 2017).

Bhushan, Sandeep. 2016. 'The AAP's Tussles With Big Media and Big Parties Reflect the State of TV News Today', *Caravan*, October 17. www.caravanmagazine.in/vantage/aap-tussles-big-media-big-parties-state-tv-news-today (accessed on November 10, 2017).

Chakravarty, Manas. 2015. 'Could a Potential AAP Win Derail Policy Reforms?' *Live Mint*, February 8. www.livemint.com/Opinion/J3yuoD1EQSXELs0sziE4lN/Class-conflict-the-tail-risk-of-an-AAP-win.html (accessed on November 11, 2017).

Chatterjee, Partha. 2004. *The Politics of the Governed: Reflections on Popular Politics in Most of the World*. New York: Columbia University Press.

———. 2011. 'Against Corruption = Against Politics', *Kafila*, August 28. http://kafila.online/2011/08/28/against-corruption-against-politics-partha-chatterjee/ (accessed on November 11, 2017).

CNN-IBN. 2014. 'India Inc. Flays Kejriwal's Decision to Withdraw Retail FDI From Delhi', January 14. www.news18.com/videos/politics/aap-fdi-delhi-ftp-sanyal-chunk-661671.html (accessed on November 11, 2017).

Crowley, Thomas. 2013. 'India's Post-Ideological Politician', *Jacobin*, December 11. www.jacobinmag.com/2013/12/indias-post-ideological-politician (accessed on November 12, 2017).

Devji, Faisal. 2014. 'The Centre Cannot Hold', *The Hindu*, January 7. www.thehindu.com/todays-paper/tp-opinion/the-centre-cannot-hold/article5547467.ece (accessed November 10, 2017).

Fernandes, Leela and Patrick Heller. 2006. 'Hegemonic Aspirations: New Middle Class Politics and India's Democracy in Comparative Perspective', *Critical Asian Studies*, 38(4): 495–522.

Giri, Saroj. 2011a. 'What Is Right-Wing About the Anti-Corruption Movement?', *Kafila*, August 26. http://kafila.online/2011/08/26/what-is-right-wing-about-the-anti-corruption-movement-saroj-giri/ (accessed on November 12, 2017).

———. 2011b. 'Which Populism?' *Kafila*, September 10. http://kafila.online/2011/09/10/which-populism-saroj-giri/ (accessed on November 12, 2017).

———. 2013. 'Pehele AAP, Pehele AAP, Phir Modi', *Sanhati*, December 10. http://sanhati.com/excerpted/8713/ (accessed on November 11, 2017).

Gramsci, Antonio. 1985. *Selections From Cultural Writings*. Eds. D. Forgacs and G. Nowell-Smith. London: Lawrence and Wishart.

Gudavarthy, Ajay. 2014. *Maoism, Democracy and Globalisation: Cross-Currents in Indian Democracy and Globalisation*. New Delhi: SAGE Publications.

Hindustan Times. 2017. 'Two Years of AAP Government in Delhi: A Complete Report Card', February 14. www.hindustantimes.com/delhi/two-years-of-aap-government-in-delhi-a-complete-report-card/story-4QC7wJiSYuIbbt-e2DEoLPL.html (accessed on November 12, 2017).

Hollis, Martin. 1998. *The Philosophy of Social Science*. Cambridge: Cambridge University Press.

Huber, Evelyne, Dietrich Rueschemeyer and John D. Stephens. 1997. 'The Paradoxes of Contemporary Democracy: Formal, Participatory, and Social Dimensions', *Comparative Politics*, 29(3), April: 323–342.

Joseph, Manu. 2011. 'The Anna Hazare Show', *Open Magazine*, April 9. www.openthemagazine.com/article/voices/the-anna-hazare-show (accessed on November 11, 2017).

Joshi, Mallica. 2016. 'One Year of AAP in Delhi: Kejriwal Takes Baby Steps, Has Miles to Go', *Hindustan Times*, February 14. www.hindustantimes.com/delhi/one-year-of-aap-in-delhi-kejriwal-takes-baby-steps-has-miles-to-go/story-72hTkOcf3A1ucguhzaKrTL.html (accessed on November 11, 2017).

Khilnani, Sunil. 2014. 'Rahul, Modi, Kejriwal All Underplay How Rising Inequality Threatens India's Future', *The Times of India*, January 31. http://timesofindia.indiatimes.com/edit-page/Rahul-Modi-Kejriwal-all-underplay-how-rising-inequality-threatens-Indias-future/articleshow/29619292.cms (accessed on November 11, 2017).

Krishna, Sankaran. 2015. 'Notes on the Dramatic Career of a Concept: The Middle Class, Democracy, and the Anthropocene', *Alternatives*, 40(1): 3–14.

Laclau, Ernesto. 1977. *Politics and Ideology in Marxist Theory*. London: New Left Books.

———. 2005. *On Populist Reason*. London: Verso.

Laclau, Ernesto and Chantal Mouffe. 2001 (1985). *Hegemony and Socialist Strategy: Towards a Radical Democratic Politics*, 2nd ed. New York: Verso.

Lahariya, Chandrakant. 2016. 'Delhi's Mohalla Clinics: Maximising Potential', *Economic and Political Weekly*, January 23: 15–17.
Mannathukkaren, Nissim. 2010a. 'The Conjuncture of Late Socialism in Kerala: A Critique of the Narrative of Social Democracy', in K. Ravi Raman (ed.), *Development, Democracy and the State: Critiquing Kerala Model of Development*, pp. 155–171. London and New York: Routledge.
———. 2010b. 'The "Poverty" of Political Society: Partha Chatterjee and the People's Plan Campaign in Kerala, India', *Third World Quarterly*, 31(2): 295–314.
———. 2011. 'Promises of India's "Two Minute Revolution"', *Countercurrents*, May 25. www.countercurrents.org/nissim250511.htm (accessed on November 12, 2017).
———. 2014. 'Who Is the Aam Adami?', *The Hindu*, January 26. www.thehindu.com/features/magazine/who-is-the-aam-aadmi/article5614055.ece (accessed on November 12, 2017).
———. 2015. 'Development as Disenchantment: Mapping the Ambivalences of the Kerala "Model"', Unpublished Manuscript.
Nandy, Ashis. 2011. 'Push Comes to Shove', *The Hindustan Times*, August 24. www.hindustantimes.com/india/push-comes-to-shove/story-y0D0LdJBaS8M70Qkq9bcBK.html (accessed November 12, 2017).
Naqvi, Saba. 2011a. 'The Jagran at Jantar Mantar', *Outlook*, April 10. www.outlookindia.com/article/-The-Jagran-At-Jantar-Mantar/271279 (accessed on November 12, 2017).
———. 2011b. 'As Red as Herrings Get', *Outlook*, May 2. www.outlookindia.com/article/As-Red-As-Herrings-Get/271492 (accessed on November 11, 2017).
Nigam, Aditya. 2013. 'Winds of Change Rise of the BJP and Challenge of an Alternative', *Economic and Political Weekly*, December 28: 37–40.
———. 2014a. 'AAP and the Ideology Warriors', *Kafila*, January 11. http://kafila.online/2014/01/11/aap-and-the-ideology-warriors/ (accessed on November 11, 2017).
———. 2014b. 'No Time for Parties', *Outlook*, January 15. www.outlookindia.com/website/story/no-time-for-parties/289182 (accessed on November 11, 2017).
———. 2014c. 'Xenophobia, Racism and Vigilantism – Danger Signals for AAP', *Kafila*, January 17. http://kafila.online/2014/01/17/xenophobia-racism-and-vigilantism-danger-signals-for-aap/ (accessed on November 11, 2017).
———. 2015. 'Reading the Power Struggle in AAP', *Kafila*, March 7. https://kafila.online/2015/03/07/reading-the-power-struggle-in-aap/ (accessed on November 11, 2017).
Nilakantan, R.S. 2017. '"Panthers in Parliament" Chronicles TN Dalit Movement's Transformation Into Political Party', *The Wire*, March 30. https://thewire.in/119922/panthers-in-parliament-chronicles-the-dalit-movements-transformation-into-political-party/ (accessed on November 11, 2017).

OECD. 2011. 'Divided We Stand: Why Inequality Keeps Rising', December. www.oecd.org/els/soc/dividedwestandwhyinequalitykeepsrising.htm (accessed on November 12, 2017).

Palshikar, Suhas. 2015. 'Gatecrasher's Gig', *Outlook*, February 23. www.outlookindia.com/magazine/comments/gatecrashers-gig/293406 (accessed on November 12, 2017).

Patnaik, Prabhat. 2013. 'Time for Change: India Needs a Rights-Based Redistributive Programme', *The Telegraph*, December 11. www.telegraphindia.com/1131211/jsp/opinion/story_17667428.jsp (accessed on November 11, 2017).

———. 2014. 'Rule by Messiahs', *Indian Express*, January 8. http://indianexpress.com/article/opinion/columns/rule-by-messiahs/ (accessed on November 11, 2017).

Ramachandran, Rajesh. 2016. 'Why Is There No Adequate Representation by Common Men & Women in the AAP Cabinet in Delhi?' *Economic Times*, February 14. http://economictimes.indiatimes.com/news/politics-and-nation/why-is-there-no-adequate-representation-by-common-men-women-in-the-aap-cabinet-in-delhi/articleshow/50977916.cms (accessed on November 11, 2017).

Ramani, Srinivasan. 2014. 'A Multi-Class Urban Party', *The Hindu*, January 3. www.thehindu.com/opinion/lead/a-multiclass-urban-party/article5530823.ece (accessed on November 12, 2017).

———. 2015. 'Managers vs. Ideologues in AAP', *The Hindu*, March 21. www.thehindu.com/opinion/lead/managers-vs-ideologues-in-aap/article7016170.ece (accessed on November 11, 2017).

Roy, Srirupa. 2014. 'Being the Change: The Aam Aadmi Party and the Politics of the Extraordinary in Indian Democracy', *Economic and Political Weekly*, April 12: 45–54.

Rueschemeyer, Dietrich, Evelyne Stephens and John Stephens. 1992. *Capitalist Development and Democracy*. Cambridge: Cambridge University Press.

Saha, Devanik. 2015. 'Through AAP, Delhi's Vast Underclass Speaks Up', *India Spend*, February 4. www.indiaspend.com/cover-story/through-aap-delhis-vast-underclass-speaks-up-84915 (accessed on November 12, 2017).

Sebastian, Kritika Sharma. 2016. 'AAP Gets Its Homework Right', *The Hindu*, February 12. www.thehindu.com/news/cities/Delhi/AAP-gets-its-homework-right/article15618149.ece (accessed on November 12, 2017).

Sengupta, Shuddabrata. 2011. 'Hazare, Khwahishein Aisi: Desiring a New Politics, After Anna Hazare and Beyond Corruption', *Kafila*, August 27. http://kafila.online/2011/08/27/hazare-khwahishein-aur-bhi-hain-hazare-there-are-things-still-left-wanting-what-is-to-the-left-of-anna-hazare-and-india-against-corruption/ (accessed on November 12, 2017).

Sinha, Subir. 2015. 'On the Edge of Civil Society in Contemporary India', in Alf Nilsen and Srila Roy (eds.), *New Subaltern Politics: Reconceptualizing Hegemony and Resistance in Contemporary India*, pp. 225–254. Oxford: Oxford University Press.

Sitapati, Vinay. 2011. 'What Anna Hazare's Movement and India's New Middle Classes Say About Each Other', *Economic and Political Weekly*, July 23: 39–44.
Srivastava, Sanjay. 2014. 'One Set of People vs. Another Set of People', *Hindustan Times*, January 15.
Subrahmaniam, Vidya. 2015. 'Reaching for the Stars: The Incredible Rise of Arvind Kejriwal', *The Hindu Centre for Politics and Public Policy*, February 25. www.thehinducentre.com/the-arena/article6929534.ece (accessed on November 11, 2017).
Varshney, Ashutosh. 2013. 'Politics as Unusual', *Indian Express*, December 23. http://indianexpress.com/article/opinion/columns/punjab-elections-amarinder-singh-sidhu-aap-parkash-singh-badal-akali-dal-4497982/ (accessed on November 11, 2017).
The Wire. 2015. '11 Mentions of Kejriwal, None of AAP in 2-Minute Delhi Government Ad', June 18. https://thewire.in/4210/11-mentions-of-kejriwal-none-of-aap-in-2-minute-delhi-government-ad/ (accessed on November 11, 2017).
Weber, Barret. 2011. 'Laclau and Žižek on Democracy and Populist Reason', *International Jorunal of Zizek Studies*, 5(1), 1–17.
Yadav, Yogendra. 2013. 'We Were Never a Force of the City-State of Delhi: For Us, Delhi Was a Deliberate Choice', *Indian Express*, December 30. http://indianexpress.com/article/opinion/columns/we-were-never-a-force-of-the-citystate-of-delhi-for-us-delhi-was-a-deliberate-choice/ (accessed on November 12, 2017).
Yamunan, Sruthisagar. 2016. 'Riding the Anti-Incumbency Wave, the Aam Aadmi Party Is Gaining Ground in Punjab', *Scroll*, September 19. https://scroll.in/article/816393/riding-the-anti-incumbency-wave-what-explains-aam-aadmi-party-gaining-ground-in-punjab (accessed on November 12, 2017).
Žižek, Slavoj. 2006. 'Against the Populist Temptation', *Critical Inquiry*, 32(3): 551–574.

11 The 2014 national elections from the margins of modern India

Uday Chandra

On 16 May 2014, Narendra Damodardas Modi was voted in by 31 per cent of the Indian electorate as India's new Prime Minister (*FP Politics* 2014). The BJP currently enjoys a clear majority in the Lok Sabha, a remarkable result that overturns a quarter century of multi-party coalition governments in New Delhi. In fact, with its allies, the BJP is within striking distance of an absolute or two-thirds majority needed to amend the constitution as they deem fit. After winning power in the states of Maharashtra, Haryana, Jharkhand, Jammu and Kashmir, Goa, Assam, Bihar, Himachal Pradesh, and Uttar Pradesh, the BJP aims to secure a dominant position in the Rajya Sabha too.

Now, with the advantage of hindsight, we may probe into the wider socio-political implications of the BJP's rise to power in the 2014 national elections. Drawing on my own research over nearly a decade in rural eastern and central India, I analyse the election results and their implications from these 'tribal' margins of the country. My argument, briefly, is that the 2014 elections signify the coalescence of political developments from above and below that have given rise to a new social contract based on the twin logics of governance and representation. This new social contract ought to be seen as a departure from both the 'Nehruvian consensus' during the heyday of the 'Congress system' (Kothari 1964) as well as the 'second democratic upsurge' following the *Emergency* (Yadav 2000). The Nehruvian consensus, which existed during an era of one-party rule in the early decades after independence, rested on the unstated assumption of power concentrated in the hands of a benevolent upper caste Hindu elite. The democratic upsurge after the turbulent years of the *Emergency*, however, challenged the domination of an elite minority and broadened the social bases of power to include leaders from OBC, SC, and ST communities across India. The current phase in India's democratic history draws on both these earlier phases but also departs from them. It consolidates the power of the Centre in order to undertake a welfarist agenda of 'good governance', yet it also seeks to deepen democratic representation amongst the myriad insurgent fragments that make up the Indian nation today.

Although the United Progressive Alliance (UPA), too, attempted to combine the twin logics of governance and representation over the last decade, the new BJP-led government consolidates and repackages recent trends in Indian politics and society. A new consensus has emerged in the country in the early twenty-first century, and I refer to it as 'Hindu fascism'. This political consensus is Hindu because it explicitly understands the nation to be so. It is, furthermore, fascist because it melds together an emphasis on organic social unity, political stability, and a powerful state. The new Hindu fascist consensus, however, is arguably more fragile than the Nehruvian consensus of the 1950s and 1960s. This is not only because the Nehruvian Congress lacked a serious political rival in the early postcolonial decades, but it is also because the Modi government must enter into complex negotiations with the multiple margins that it seeks to represent within its organic Hindu nationalist vision of Indian society. Hindu fascism in contemporary India, I argue, must be seen as an uncertain social formation subject to centrifugal forces that threaten to hollow out the political centre. What some recent commentators have called the 'Bahujanisation' of Hindutva (Gudavarthy and Suthar 2014) ought to be seen as an open-ended process. Its precise contours will depend, ultimately, on the manner in which Dalit, Bahujan, and Adivasi groups are able to assert their own political agendas within the broad umbrella of Hindu fascism.

The nation and its margins

In a perceptive essay written after the 2009 national elections, Yogendra Yadav (2009) argued that political parties that had emerged during the second democratic upsurge as advocates of 'social justice' had reached a 'dead end'. These parties, Yadav claimed, had defined social justice too narrowly in terms of reservations in the public sector and educational institutions, and identified political success exclusively with electoral wins for leaders of marginalised communities. For these reasons, the social bases of power had certainly broadened since the 1980s, but advocates of social justice had failed to attend adequately to pressing problems such as poverty, inequality, and gender discrimination in the country. The Third Front had thus failed to capture the public imagination, and, over time, it had ceded ground to a Congress-led coalition at the national level. In response, Yadav recommended rethinking the politics of social justice by amending and widening the scope of affirmative action policies to target the poorest and most marginalised sections of Indian society. Such a change would not only overcome the roadblock posed by reservations being captured by a few within historically discriminated groups, but also bring women and Muslims within the ambit of affirmative action policies.

The UPA government led by Manmohan Singh did, in fact, arrive at a similar conclusion to Yogendra Yadav's. Its flagship programmes such as the National Rural Employment Guarantee Act (NREGA), for instance, targeted rural unemployment and poverty without using caste as the sole criterion for targeting welfare beneficiaries (Khera 2011). Other UPA initiatives in rural livelihoods – promotion, skills development, universal education, and mid-day meals for schoolchildren – did not distinguish between beneficiaries on the basis of caste. Socioeconomic deprivation, conceptualised in multidimensional terms, came to be identified as the principal criterion for policy interventions. Of course, it is true that administrative corruption and systemic leakages in delivering public goods hampered the effectiveness of state welfare programmes such as NREGA (Shankar and Gaiha 2013). The effectiveness of welfare programmes was, moreover, uneven: whereas they were successfully implemented in states such as Bihar and West Bengal, that was certainly not the case in, say, Jharkhand or Uttar Pradesh. A similar problem beset the public distribution system for essential commodities, which worked well in Chhattisgarh, for instance, but not in adjoining Madhya Pradesh. In sum, the UPA government's new welfare agenda, which supplemented reservations for marginalised groups, inaugurated a new phase of 'good governance' in Indian politics that ventured beyond the caste-centred politics of social justice in the two previous decades. However, insofar as the UPA's welfarism fell short on implementation, islands of misery and discontent remained, and the BJP would target these islands strategically during Narendra Modi's 2014 election campaign.

States such as Jharkhand and Chhattisgarh with large Adivasi and Dalit populations had, in particular, missed out on the 'silent revolution' (Jaffrelot 2003) that swept through north India in the previous generation. They also had divergent experiences with the UPA's new welfarism over the past decade, Jharkhand being one of the poorest performers in the country and Chhattisgarh making big strides towards poverty alleviation. Both states grew out of movements for statehood and autonomy, though the BJP-led government of Atal Bihari Vajpayee played a decisive role in eventually carving these small states out of Bihar and Madhya Pradesh (Tillin 2013). In Chhattisgarh, the Congress, in fact, formed the first government under Ajit Jogi's leadership. Thereafter, the BJP has held power for three consecutive terms in a state in which 31.8 per cent of the population are Adivasis and 11.6 per cent are Dalits (Thachil 2011). Moreover, the RSS and its affiliate organisations have worked extensively in the fields of education, healthcare, and development there. In Jharkhand, the formation of the new 'tribal' state in 2000 mocked aspirations for Adivasi autonomy over the past century. The new state excluded the Adivasi-majority districts in neighbouring Chhattisgarh, Odisha, and West Bengal, and included districts of Bihar in which non-Adivasis were overwhelming in the majority. As a consequence, the 2001 census recorded only 26.3 per cent of Jharkhand as Adivasi, and the 2011 census shows the corresponding proportion to be 26.2 per cent of the state's population (Ojhal 2013). The BJP has clearly benefited from the demographics of the new state and vied for power with the Jharkhandi parties over the past fifteen years. Let us now consider each state in turn to analyse why the BJP, which midwifed their birth, has continued to enjoy electoral success there.

In Chhattisgarh, the BJP under the leadership of Dr Raman Singh has been in power since 2003. The successful re-election of the BJP in subsequent state elections in 2008 and 2013 was arguably built on two foundations: public goods delivery and cultural outreach activities. To understand the BJP's politics of 'good governance' through effective public goods delivery, it is important to appreciate how it had to be presented as 'apolitical' to rural communities that distrusted them (Thachil 2011: 436). Jean Drèze and Reetikha Khera (2010) explain that, soon after coming to power, the Raman Singh government sought to dismantle networks of traders who ran ration shops, which were then placed under the direct control of local bodies such as village panchayats and self-help groups. Additionally, the BJP government delivered foodgrains directly to these locally-run ration shops, and eliminated middlemen who typically profited from siphoning off a proportion of the grains to sell at higher prices in the open market. Over 85 per cent of households with ration cards, Drèze and Khera (2010) found in September–November 2009, received their full quota of 35 kilogrammes of grains at the stipulated subsidised prices; the rest received at least 25 kilogrammes. Only 17 per cent of households below the poverty line missed a meal in the quarter preceding their survey as opposed to 70 per cent in Bihar, though their poverty headcount ratio stood at 56 and 55 per cent respectively in 2009–2010. Drèze and Khera (2013) thus calculated an implicit reduction of poverty by at least 39 per cent on account of Chhattisgarh's well-functioning public distribution system. To the extent that 'political will' matters in delivering 'good governance', it is obvious that the BJP government in Chhattisgarh had strategically targeted its poorest and most marginalised citizens through its welfare agenda.

Good governance was accompanied by cultural outreach activities aimed at poor voters, especially Adivasis who are not traditionally BJP voters. Vanvasi Kalyan Ashrams (VKAs) sought to fill a vast gap in the state's social infrastructure where teacher absenteeism in state-run schools ranked among the highest in the country and a primary health centre is usually over ten kilometres away (Thachil 2011: 443–447). While social scientists such as Tariq Thachil, Jean Drèze, and Reetikha Khera have focused narrowly on the instrumental logic of public goods delivery over multiple election cycles, the BJP's good governance agenda rests crucially on the cultural politics of the RSS and its affiliates who run schools and mobile health centres. The anthropologist Peggy Froerer (2007) has examined the rise and growth of VKAs run by the Sangh Parivar as part of its wider campaign against Christian missionaries and their wards in rural Chhattisgarh and nearby Odisha. The VKAs actually seek to emulate Christian missionary activity by focusing on existential concerns over illness via everyday practices of healing. Amit Desai (2007) found a similar focus on the politics of the body during his fieldwork in eastern Maharashtra, along the border with Chhattisgarh, where both disease and witchcraft threaten rural Adivasi communities and draw them closer to their benefactors from the Sangh. The VKA's commitment to social service in the realms of educational and healthcare far exceeds the instrumental quid pro quo logic of elections. Much like the Christian missionaries whom they seek to emulate as well as supplant, VKA volunteers consciously embody an ethos of selflessness and austerity, which draws ordinary villagers to them in circumstances where state-sponsored welfare activities are sorely lacking. For the Sangh, furthermore, Adivasis practice a '*jangli* Hinduism', which differs from 'mainstream Hinduism', and education is more about their civilising mission than secular considerations such as investing in human capital or winning votes locally (Froerer 2007: 41). Remaking Adivasis as 'proper' Hindus is a goal that exceeds the bounds of secular politics even as it has clear implications for the BJP in elections. By the time of the 2009 national elections, for the first time in the region's history, more Adivasi voters preferred the BJP (43 per cent) over the Congress (40 per cent) (Saxena and Rai 2009). Tariq

Thachil's (2011: 460) surveys conducted around this time found that that Adivasis (and Dalits) who participated in the VKA's activities were 55.82 per cent more likely to vote for the BJP than those who did not participate in these activities. Good governance and cultural outreach undoubtedly complement each other, but their logics and goals are distinctive.

Adivasis in Jharkhand, by contrast, have been far less attracted to either the cultural politics of the Sangh Parivar or unfulfilled promises of good governance by the BJP. On its own, the BJP has never won a simple majority in the Vidhan Sabha over four electoral cycles, but it has to come to power in each cycle so far. On every occasion, the BJP has allied with a Jharkhandi party to form an uneasy coalition government, thrice with the Jharkhand Mukti Morcha (JMM) and, most recently, with a JMM splinter group, the All India Jharkhand Students Union (AJSU). As a measure of political instability in Jharkhand, consider that, in the past fifteen years, the state has been ruled by six Chief Ministers, two of whom – Shibu Soren and Arjun Munda – have enjoyed three truncated terms in power, and it has further experienced three uncertain periods under President's rule. It is not surprising then that 'many of the poorest adivasis . . . in rural Jharkhand . . . did not really know, and moreover did not care, much' about who exactly ruled in Ranchi at a given point in time (Shah 2010: 7). Indeed, as one of the anthropologist Alpa Shah's informants puts it, '[W]hat does it matter? What will it bring?' (ibid: 5). If Chhattisgarh is the BJP's model of good governance, therefore, Jharkhand is apparently the very opposite: a model of mis-governance.

Amidst such apathy as one discovers during fieldwork, it is easy to forget that elections are routinely held in Jharkhand and that the BJP has won power each time. It has done so by adopting a two-pronged strategy. On the one hand, it has appealed to the non-Adivasi majority in the state, seeking to consolidate the Hindu vote across caste lines. By doing so, it has taken advantage of the demographics of the state that it had helped create in 2000. There is, after all, no viable political rival for the BJP as it appeals to voters in unreserved constituencies. In undivided Bihar, the Janata Dal and its fragments would have contested these seats, but the politics of creating a new state have ensured that the likes of Laloo Yadav and Nitish Kumar concentrate their energies farther north. Additionally, the Congress, which once enjoyed popular support in the Jharkhand region after independence, has long ceased to be a political force there. Furthermore, the JMM, which earlier enjoyed a critical mass of non-Adivasi support during the movement for Jharkhand, especially from so-called backward caste groups, has been more or less confined to the reserved constituencies. For the BJP, mercantile and landed castes have been at the heart of their electoral consolidation of the Hindu vote in the state. Equally important to the rise of the BJP, however, albeit often neglected, is the upward mobility of traditional service castes in Jharkhand's villages such as *telis* and *lohras* and their identification with the BJP. The recent ascension of Raghubar Das, who belongs to the oil-pressing *teli* caste, to the Chief Minister's chair, makes it amply clear how much these new bases of support matter to the BJP.

On the other hand, the quarter or so of Jharkhand's population that is officially classified as 'scheduled tribe' (ST) has posed a trickier challenge for the BJP. A Maoist insurgency has engulfed the scheduled areas in Jharkhand over the past decade. Although splintered into numerous outfits, the CPI (Maoist) and their breakaway factions have enjoyed considerable popular support in the countryside. While this support has not led to the formation of 'liberated zones' in rural Jharkhand, it has rendered rebel leaders from various Maoist groups as legitimate electoral candidates in the eyes of the poor Adivasis. Above all, the JMM has benefited from current or former Maoists who have used their bullets to win ballots in rural Jharkhand. As Deepu Sebastian Edmond (2014) reports, of the twenty-two such candidates in the 2013 state election in Jharkhand, the JMM fielded eight. The BJP, unused to such intimacy with the extreme left, fielded two such candidates, though one of them was eventually dropped because the Maoist splinter group to which he belonged complained of the police cases against him (Edmond 2014). What is noteworthy, however, is the BJP's willingness to grapple with the messiness of Maoist politics in pursuit of power.

In a similar vein, the cultural politics of indigeneity that dominates Adivasi lifeworlds (Chandra 2013) has been harder to penetrate for the BJP. Popular discourses of indigeneity have, since colonial times, pitted the Munda, Santal, Oraon, and Ho against the *diku*, a resident alien who is a caste Hindu from the plains of Bihar or Bengal. To reconcile these opposites today in a unified whole is easier said than done. Additionally, the historical depth and strength of Jharkhand's churches, especially its Catholic and Lutheran churches, has made it harder for the BJP and allies to replicate their success in Chhattisgarh among Adivasis in Jharkhand. Yet, as a proselytising RSS ideologue in the state explained to me, the logics of Hindutva and indigeneity are not incompatible. Whatever their antagonisms in the past, Hindutva as the ideology of a Hindu nation-in-the-making can potentially accommodate Adivasi claims to a distinctive and prior sociological formation in particular places. Claims to indigeneity, in other words, do not unsettle the overarching order of the Hindu nation. As such, we should not be surprised by the BJP's stunning recent victory in the JMM's stronghold in the Santal Parganas, where Louis Marandi defeated Hemant Soren in the state election after losing to him narrowly in 2009. Marandi is a Santali Christian woman whose victory after a Modi-backed campaign in the Dumka constituency, held for long by the Shibu Soren and his son, suggests that neither indigeneity nor even Christianity pose an insurmountable challenge to the BJP in Jharkhand.

Despite the differences between Chhattisgarh and Jharkhand outlined so far, what is striking is how similarly fared during the so-called Modi wave last year. In the 2014 Lok Sabha elections, the BJP won ten out of eleven seats in Chhattisgarh and ten out of twelve seats in Jharkhand. Notably, the party won all five reserved constituencies in Chhattisgarh, including all four ST constituencies, and four out of six reserved constituencies in Jharkhand, including three out of five ST constituencies. If we aver that a combination of 'good governance' and cultural outreach explains the BJP's performance in Chhattisgarh, then we can say with an equal conviction that neither holds the key to understanding the results in Jharkhand. If the former teaches us about what Hindutva under Modi offers to the margins of the nation today, then the latter shows how both Adivasi and non-Adivasi voters can repose their faith in the BJP without any deep ideological commitment to the Sangh's ideology. Governance and representation emerge, accordingly, as key elements of a pragmatic new social contract in the 'tribal' margins of India today. The new welfarism inaugurated by the UPA is thus amalgamated with a deepening process of democratisation by which the nation and its myriad margins interpenetrate each other. For the Hindu nation-in-the-making, top-down social engineering and developmentalism are as vital as negotiation with social forces from below.

The making of Hindu fascism

Standard leftist commentaries on fascism, as Jairus Banaji (2002) has pointed out, often suffer from two basic flaws. They assume that fascism is simply 'the dictatorship of the most reactionary elements of finance capital' that is imposed on the masses. Furthermore, these leftist accounts of fascism tend to imagine it as an aberration from 'normal' politics, a cataclysmic event that unsettles everyday life. Banaji draws on the writings of the communist historian Arthur

Rosenberg and the psychoanalyst Wilhelm Reich to argue that fascism must be seen as a mass phenomenon within its social-psychological and cultural-historical contexts. Fascism ought not to be seen as a top-down imposition on the masses. What distinguishes it from other forms of reactionary politics is that 'it is supported and championed by masses of people' (ibid: ix). As Reich (1946: xi) put it,

> Fascist mentality is the mentality of the subjugated 'little man' who craves authority and rebels against it at the same time. It is not by accident that all fascist dictators stem from the milieu of the little reactionary man. The captains of industry and the feudal militarist make use of this social fact for their own purposes.

Reich, as a psychoanalyst, overstates the role of 'mentality' in explaining mass support for fascism. This leads him to ignore the contingent and strategic nature of subaltern agency in fascist movements. Nonetheless, we may safely conclude that social forces from both below and above interact to produce fascism in modern times. Whereas reactionary forces may reap the rewards of fascism, it would be impossible without the active participation of ordinary men and women with their own aspirations (Browning 1992). Moreover, fascism is not an 'event' isolated from the dynamics of the 'everyday' (Das 2006), but a phenomenon borne out of the fabric of everyday life. The rise of Hitler – or, indeed, Modi – did not occur in a day, but arose out of the peculiar historical circumstances of their societies. It must also be noted that fascist leaders came to power through democratic elections rather than the usual coups d'état that bring military dictatorships to power across the Third World.

But, a sceptical reader may ask at this point: is it fair to characterise Modi and the BJP as 'fascists'? Might we not see them simply as conservatives or Hindu nationalists? In response, let us ask ourselves what we mean by 'fascism' in the first place. Fascism is a social revolution, whether violent or silent, by which a significant majority of the democratically empowered masses come to regard the rise of a charismatic, authoritarian leader as a symbol of their unity and emancipation (Gregor 2001; Paxton 2005). The state under fascism is both omnipotent and non-existent: the people are the state and the state stands for the people. The fascist state represents the sum total of social forces sans their antagonisms and contradictions, that is, it conjures an organic social unity (*fasces* in Latin literally means 'a bundle'). Such unity rests on the fear and hatred of the Other, whether in the form of ethnic, religious, and sexual minorities or political rivals. The fascist state promises social stability, national solidarity, and popular rule. It relies on the active participation and, indeed, sacrifices of ordinary people who identify with the organicist ideology propounded by the Great Leader. Whereas many commentators treat mass participation in fascist politics to be a mark of irrationality, it is far more useful to take actions of ordinary men and women to be meaningful and contingent. Social scientists can legitimately seek to understand why and how they come to identify with the organic unity of the new revolutionary collective conjured by a distinctive leader. A fascist consensus in any society is thus a negotiated outcome, not one that is produced mystically *sui generis*.

To understand fascism in this manner is to admit the possibility that it is not merely a political phenomenon confined temporally to interwar Europe. Indeed, as A. James Gregor (2001), one of the leading scholars of fascism today, notes, it is likely that fascism will not remain a twentieth-century affair because it will reappear in our own times in new forms. In the case of the BJP under Narendra Modi, the authoritarian cult of personality is tied to a new national unity in which religious minorities, leftists, and environmentalists are, for instance, treated as social deviants. Support for Modi from the 'tribal' margins of the nation as well as a critical mass of Dalit and Bahujan populations is, moreover, undeniable. In the infamous anti-Muslim pogrom in Gujarat under Modi's leadership in 2002, for instance, the participation of marginalised Adivasi groups such as Dharalas was especially conspicuous (Lobo 2002; Devy 2002). The BJP is no longer simply a conservative upper caste party dominated by Brahmins and Banias. It is a party that seeks to appeal to anyone who is willing to see his/her own self-advancement and that of his/her community with national progress. Modi's victory is not merely a personal achievement for him, but a symbol of popular sovereignty. Modi's repeated assertion that he grew up poor and understands the needs of the poor better than other politicians, including those he displaced within the BJP, must be seen in this light (see, e.g. *Outlook* 2017). The state under Modi's leadership promises to be strong and decisive, unencumbered by the humdrum modalities of coalition politics. Yet strength and decisiveness are as much the Prime Minister's qualities as they are of the populace that exercises its sovereignty through democratic elections. If the personalisation of power under Modi is evident in the way his Cabinet colleagues are rarely seen or heard of nowadays, popular identification with him may be seen among trolls in cyberspace as well as in middle-class homes and slums. To mock or criticise Modi in the public sphere, therefore, may be an invitation to be punished by the state or the demos at large. Fascism, in this sense, is alive and well in contemporary India.

Contemporary Indian fascism, of course, takes a distinctive Hindu majoritarian form. Much like its German predecessor, Hindu fascism in India traces its roots to nineteenth-century Indo-European notions of Aryan supremacy. As Dorothy Figueira (2002) has shown, the mythology of Aryan pasts co-evolved in Europe and South Asia, generating frenetic calls for reform and purity on the one hand and demonisation of the Other on the other hand. In India, the efforts of upper caste elites, alongside colonial officials and Christian missionaries, to construct 'Hinduism' as a world religion on par with the Abrahamic faiths may be seen as a decisive break from the past. Figures such as Dayanand Saraswati and Vivekananda were pioneers in Hindu nationalist thought. They abhorred caste and saw the territorial limits of Victorian India as a sacred space, violated by Muslim and Christian invaders over the centuries, which necessitated a return to a mythical golden age when all Indians qua Hindus apparently enjoyed peace and prosperity. In their own characteristic ways, Bal Gangadhar Tilak, Mohandas Gandhi, and Vinayak Savarkar took on the mantle of their nineteenth-century predecessors and gave practical form to notions of Hindu majoritarianism. Gandhi, who emerged as the leader of the Congress in its campaign for decolonisation and bid for power, showered fulsome praise on his friend Benito Mussolini when he visited him at the height of his popularity in Rome (Gandhi 1931; Hayes 2011: 8). It was Gandhi who remade Hinduism as a viable form of mass politics, effacing the traditional marks of caste that threatened to render asunder the Indian nation-in-the-making. It was also Gandhi who explicitly discouraged cow slaughter by Muslims Lelyveld (2011) and forbade conversion to Islam or Christianity (Roberts 2016: 111–151). Each of these aspects of Gandhian politics would become key planks of Hindutva over the twentieth century. By comparison, Savarkar's mass following was negligible, and Tilak's political activities were confined to the Bombay Presidency. Long before Modi, therefore, the seeds of Hindu fascism were sown by his predecessors, perhaps most notably by M.K. Gandhi.

Accordingly, the BJP under Modi today owes much to its proto-fascist ancestors. If Gandhi was fascinated by Mussolini's fascist experiment in Italy, the RSS has been equally fascinated with the Nazis in Germany. *Mein Kampf* is widely available and read in contemporary India, and it is easy enough for Hindu fascists to replace Jews with Muslims in their ideological fantasies. Narendra Modi, like most BJP leaders, entered politics after a lengthy training in Hindu fascism in the ranks of the RSS. Modi represents the apogee of this religious ideology, replacing the covert violence of earlier Hindu violence against Dalits and religious minorities with an overt belligerence towards the non-Hindu Other. Within four months of taking over as Chief Minister of Gujarat, Modi masterminded anti-Muslim pogroms in the cities of central and south Gujarat, especially in areas where electoral competition, underemployment, and Muslim in-migration were high (Dhattiwala and Biggs 2012). Once Lebensraum had been created, and Muslims killed or forced into ghettoes, a model Hindu society was hailed as a new golden age of peace and prosperity. Caste divisions were neatly subsumed within the organicist ideology of Hindu fascism (Shani 2007). Furthermore, the selective participation of Dalits and Adivasis in these pogroms (Lobo 2002; Devy 2002) pushes us to consider the calculations that individuals and groups make in the course of their negotiations with Hindu fascism. After three terms as Chief Minister of the state of Gujarat, Modi now promises to take his brand of Hindu fascism to an all-India level. The Nehruvian catchphrase 'unity in diversity' has thus acquired a far more sinister connotation today.

Beneath the bluster and bombast of the BJP under Modi, however, cracks do exist. In a country where over four-fifths of the population is nominally 'Hindu', the fact that only 31 per cent voted for the BJP in the 2014 national elections suggests that there is a long, arduous road ahead for the Hindu fascists. Even among those who did vote for the BJP in the 2014 elections, we cannot assume that all of them are committed *a priori* to the core ideology of Hindu fascism. Nor can we assert that Hindu fascism exercises a kind of hegemony over the subaltern classes *in toto*. The 'Bahujanisation' of Hindutva is an open-ended process by which Dalit, Bahujan, and Adivasi groups assert and negotiate their own political agendas within the broad umbrella of Hindu fascism. These negotiations are context-specific, and the calculations that underpin them ought to be understood in their strategic contexts in each region. A good example is the decision of Ram Vilas Paswan's LJP to ally with the BJP in Bihar in the 2014 elections. Upper caste commentators often infer from this strategic marriage of interests that *all* Dalit communities in Bihar are turning to Hindutva today. Such an inference is as misleading as it is false. It fails to capture the partial, contingent, and, ultimately, reversible nature of cross-caste political alliances that propel Hindu fascism today. Mere lip service to the organicist ideology of Hindutva suffices for now, and instances of deeper social change in the form of, say, 'Sanskritisation' are rare. All we can say is that, in the present historical conjuncture, a range of social forces from above and below have coalesced to bring Narendra Modi's BJP to power.

Insofar as we may speak of fascism in contemporary India, it is an uncertain socio-political formation. Hindu fascists may have won handsomely for now, but their success remains uncertain in the long run. Only one in seven Indians and one among five eligible voters endorsed the BJP in its greatest moment of triumph. The BJP knows that the first-past-the-post system worked to its advantage in the 2014 elections, but it could easily work against the party in future as it did in 2004 and 2009. The social forces from above and below that drive Hindu fascism today do not work in happy unison because their claims compete and even undercut each other at times. The federal structure of Indian democracy, within which Hindu fascism has emerged, also encourages fissiparous tendencies in different regions and localities of the country. Lastly, Hindu fascism faces a conundrum as far as the economy is concerned. On the one hand, private corporations supporting the Modi campaign, most notably Reliance and the Adani Group, have already seen their profits rise appreciably (Ismail and Thakur 2014), and the prospect of quick environmental clearances and sweetheart land deals excite them now. Yet, on the other hand, it is not at all clear how the Modi government will balance the divergent interests of the country's half a billion poor men and women, the urban salaried classes, and big business. If the new government fails to deliver populist economic policies, it will undoubtedly be punished by future voters. But if the Modi government fails to attend to the interests of big business, it will end up where the UPA did. There is much confusion and little certainty in the corridors of power. The tried-and-tested ways of balancing economic growth and welfarism seem inadequate, but the alternatives are not so easy to find either. In sum, it is fair to say that an uncertain fascism has assumed power in India today. It is here to stay and will assume protean forms as it seeks to remake Indian society in its own image. But it will not go unchallenged either.

Conclusion

This chapter has argued that a Hindu fascist consensus dominates Indian politics today, consolidating the gains of the second democratic upsurge of the previous generation and consciously seeking to emulate the Nehruvian consensus of the early postcolonial era. Narendra Modi's victory in the 2014 national elections promises organic social unity, political stability, economic growth, and a powerful state. Yet this victory rests on a complex coalition of social groups and interests, which gives Hindu fascism today its vitality even as it threatens to fragment its carefully crafted ideological consensus. In the margins of modern India, negotiations with Hindu fascism take myriad forms in states such as Jharkhand and Chhattisgarh, and a measure of the mass support for the BJP there cannot be understood without acknowledging the pragmatic compromises and calculations that undergird these cross-caste alliances. If the term 'fascist' seems too strong to describe the BJP today, it is because popular common sense tends to isolate the term spatially and temporally to interwar Europe. Rethinking the nature of fascism in the light of global experiences over the past century, however, pushes us to consider that our own times are pregnant with fascist possibilities. In fact, even new socio-political formations such as the Aam Aadmi Party (AAP) have tended to mimic the BJP's outreach tactics and authoritarian personality cult with some success. We need to appreciate that fascist formations such as the BJP or even AAP are quite content to work within democratic structures to produce and sustain majoritarian rule. Subordinated castes and 'tribal' groups are now increasingly seen as valued members of the Hindu nation-in-the-making. Even religious minorities may, in theory, be accommodated under a Hindu majoritarian order as long as they acquiesce in their second-class status, or better still, indigenise or renounce their 'foreign' religions. Pogroms are unnecessary when violence can assume subtler forms. In a world where dictators for life pretend to rule by popular consent, Hindu fascists are unlikely to let go off the tag of the 'world's largest democracy'.

Bibliography

Banaji, Jairus. 2002. 'The Political Culture of Fascism', *South Asia Citizens Web*. www.sacw.net/2002/BanajiSept02.html.

Browning, Christopher. 1992. *Ordinary Men: Reserve Police Battalion 101 and the Final Solution in Poland*. New York: Harper Collins Publishers.

Chandra, Uday. 2013. 'Negotiating Leviathan: Statemaking and Resistance in the Margins of Modern India', Unpublished Ph.D. dissertation, Yale University.

Das, Veena. 2006. *Life and Words: Violence and the Descent Into the Ordinary*. Berkeley: University of California Press.

Desai, Amit. 2007. 'Witchcraft, Religious Transformation, and Hindu Nationalism in Rural Central India', Unpublished Ph.D. dissertation, London School of Economics and Political Science.

Devy, Ganesh N. 2002. 'Tribal Voice and Violence', *Seminar*, 513: 39–48.

Dhattiwala, Raheel and Michael Biggs. 2012. 'The Political Logic of Ethnic Violence: The Anti-Muslim Pogrom in Gujarat, 2002', *Politics & Society*, 40(4): 483–516.

Drèze, Jean P. and Reetika Khera. 2010. 'Chhattisgarh Shows the Way', *The Hindu*, November 13.

———. 2013. 'Rural Poverty and the Public Distribution System', Centre for Development Economics Working Paper No. 235. www.cdedse.org/pdf/work235.pdf.

Edmond, Deepu Sebastian. 2014. 'Maoists in Jharkhand Eye New Future Through Electoral Democracy', *Indian Express*, December 23.

Figueira, Dorothy M. 2002. *Aryans, Jews, Brahmins: Theorizing Authority Through Myths of Identity*. Albany: SUNY Press.

FP Politics. 2014. 'BJP's 31 Percent Vote Share: Here's Who Didn't Vote for Narendra Modi', *FirstPost*, May 19. www.firstpost.com/politics/bjps-31-percent-vote-share-heres-who-didnt-vote-for-narendra-modi-1531813.html.

Froerer, Peggy. 2007. *Religious Division and Social Conflict: The Emergence of Hindu Nationalism in Rural India*. New Delhi: Social Science Press.

Gandhi, M.K. 1931. *Letter to Romain Rolland*, December 20. www.gandhi-manibhavan.org/gandhicomesalive/comesalive_letter18.htm.

Gregor, A. James. 2001. *Phoenix: Facism in Our Time*. New Brunswick: Transaction Publishers.

Gudavarthy, Ajay and Sudhir Kumar Suthar. 2014. 'Politics Without Opposition', *The Hindu*, October 9.

Hayes, Romain. 2011. *Subhas Chandra Bose In Nazi Germany: Politics, Intelligence, and Propaganda 1941–1943*. New York: Columbia University Press.

Ismail, Netty and Pooja Thakur. 2014. 'India's Ambani, Adani Gain $1.3 Billion in a Day on Modi Win', *Bloomberg News*. www.bloomberg.com/news/articles/2014-05-16/india-s-ambani-adani-gain-1-5-billion-in-a-day-on-modi-victory (accessed on November 14, 2017).

Jaffrelot, Christophe. 2003. *India's Silent Revolution: The Rise of the Lower Castes in North India*. New York: Columbia University Press.

Khera, Reetika (ed.). 2011. *The Battle for Employment Guarantee*. New Delhi: Oxford University Press.

Kothari, Rajni. 1964. 'The Congress "System" in India', *Asian Survey*, 4(12): 1161–1173.

Lelyveld, Joseph. 2011. *Great Soul: Mahatma Gandhi and His Struggle With India*. New York: Knopf Publishers.

Lobo, Lancy. 2002. 'Adivasis, Hindutva and Post-Godhra Riots in Gujarat', *Economic & Political Weekly*, 37(48): 4844–4849.

Ojhal, Sanjay. 2013. 'Marginal Fall in Tribal Population in Jharkhand', *Times of India*, June 1. https://timesofindia.indiatimes.com/city/ranchi/Marginal-fall-in-tribal-population-in-Jharkhand/articleshow/20374392.cms.

Outlook. 2017. 'I Sold Tea But I Did Not Sell the Nation, Congress Dislikes Me Because of My Poor Origins: Modi', November 27. www.outlookindia.com/website/story/i-sold-tea-but-i-did-not-sell-the-nation-congress-dislikes-me-because-of-my-poor/304859.

Paxton, Robert O. 2005. *The Anatomy of Fascism*. New York: Vintage Books.

Reich, Wilhelm. 1946. *The Mass Psychology of Fascism*. Trans. Theodore P. Wolfe. New York: Orgone Institute Press.

Roberts, Nathaniel. 2016. *To Be Cared For: The Power of Conversion and Foreignness of Belonging in an Indian Slum*. Berkeley: University of California Press.

Saxena, Anupama and Praveen Rai. 2009. 'Chhattisgarh: An Emphatic Win for the BJP', *Economic & Political Weekly*, 44(39): 125–127.

Shah, Alpa. 2010. *In the Shadows of the State: Indigenous Politics, Environmentalism, and Insurgency in Jharkhand, India*. Durham: Duke University Press.

Shani, Ornit. 2007. *Communalism, Caste and Hindu Nationalism: The Violence in Gujarat*. Cambridge: Cambridge University Press.

Shankar, Shylashri and Raghav Gaiha (eds.). 2013. *Battling Corruption: Has NREGA Reached India's Rural Poor?* New Delhi: Oxford University Press.

Thachil, Tariq. 2011. 'Embedded Mobilization: Nonstate Service Provision as Electoral Strategy in India', *World Politics*, 63(3): 434–469.

———. 2014. *Elite Parties, Poor Voters: How Social Services Win Votes in India*. Cambridge: Cambridge University Press.

Tillin, Louise. 2013. *Remapping India: New States and Their Political Origins*. London: Hurst & Co.

Yadav, Yogendra. 2000. 'Understanding the Second Democratic Upsurge: Trends of Bahujan Participation in Electoral Politics in the 1990s', in Francine R. Frankel et al. (eds.), *Transforming India: Social and Political Dynamics of Democracy*. New Delhi: Oxford University Press.

———. 2009. 'Rethinking Social Justice', *Seminar* 601.

12 Big national parties in West Bengal

An exceptional outcast?

Maidul Islam

In 1967, the decline of the 'Congress system' (Kothari 1964: 1161–1173; Kothari 1970) was noticed in both India and in the state of West Bengal. West Bengal was among the nine states where Congress lost power (Chatterjee 1997: 15). For a decade, from the late 1960s to the late 1970s, the state witnessed a transitional period from an unstable and chaotic political system to a long-term political stability (Kohli 1997: 336–366). Such a stability was not provided by the big national parties like the Indian National Congress and the Bharatiya Janata Party (BJP), but instead by the small national parties and regional players, first by the Communist Parties (1977–2011) and later by the Trinamool Congress (2011 onwards).[1] From 1977, in the last four decades, the big national parties (the Congress and the BJP) have been unable to gain political power in West Bengal. In fact, from the late 1990s, the big national parties have been largely trapped in selected zones of the state. From the 1998 Lok Sabha election onwards, in all subsequent Parliamentary and Assembly elections, the big national parties have been always relegated to third and fourth places in terms of vote shares. From the late 1990s onwards, the main political battle has been between the CPI(M)-led Left Front and the Trinamool Congress. In this respect, West Bengal is very similar to Tamil Nadu politics where the big national parties have been unable to capture political power in the state for almost five decades. The story of political stability in West Bengal anchored by small national parties has effectively led to a different electoral system that has been largely immune to the political appeal of big national parties. From the 2014 Lok Sabha election onwards, the BJP has emerged as a dominant party in the national political scene with the continuous decline of the Congress. After the 2014 Lok Sabha election, the BJP is trying to grow in West Bengal when compared to its fringe status in the last three and a half decades in the state. In this context, this chapter looks at whether there is any possibility of increasing the influence of big national parties among the electorate of West Bengal especially after 2014 Parliament and 2016 Assembly elections in the state. In order to do such an exercise, one must tell the story of the limited presence of the Congress, the continuing decline of the Left, the consolidation of the Trinamool, and the attempts of the BJP to become the main opposition player in the state.

Limited presence of the Congress

The continuous decline of the Congress in West Bengal can be noticed in the last four decades. Barring the 1984 Lok Sabha election, in which the party got sympathy votes for the assassination of the then Prime Minister, Indira Gandhi, it has never reached a two-digit tally in Lok Sabha out of forty-two seats in the state of West Bengal. The 1977 Lok Sabha and Vidhan Sabha elections in West Bengal were wave elections against the Congress while the 1984 Lok Sabha election was a wave election in favour of the Congress. Barring these two election years, the Congress was able to manage a vote share of 35 per cent to 42 per cent in all Parliament and Assembly elections in West Bengal from 1980 to 1996. From 1998, the vote share of the Congress got significantly reduced and the party's influence got restricted in three Muslim majority districts of Malda, Murshidabad, and North Dinajpur in North Bengal. From the 2001 Assembly election onwards, most of the Congress members of the state legislature have been elected from these three districts. On the other hand, from 1998 onwards, all its members of the Lok Sabha have been elected from these three districts except in 2004 Lok Sabha election.[2] This was because, in late 1997, there was a split in the Congress and on 1 January 1998, the Trinamool Congress emerged as a new regional political party in West Bengal under the leadership of its founder and current Chief Minister of West Bengal, Mamata Banerjee.[3] From 1998 to 2011, the Congress was relegated to third place in the state politics and the Trinamool became the main opposition party in the state. The Congress could now float in West Bengal only as an alliance partner with either Trinamool or the CPI(M) led Left Front. Thus, it made pre-poll political alliances with the Trinamool Congress in the 2001 Assembly election, the 2009 Parliament election, and the 2011 Assembly election and with the CPI(M)-led Left Front in the 2016 Assembly election.

In the 2016 Assembly election, the Congress has been able to become the major opposition party in the West Bengal Assembly after two decades with the support of the Left. In fact, the Left-Congress alliance in 2016 Assembly election has actually helped the Congress more than the Left (Chatterjee and Solomon 2016). In terms of seats, the Congress became the second largest party, even in the 2011 Assembly election with the support of the Trinamool. Thus, it is basically dependent on either Trinamool or the Left in order to hold on to its limited support base. Even as an opposition party in the state, the Congress is ineffective and it is grappling to hold on to its organisational erosion with the recent intrusion of Trinamool in the Congress bastions of Malda, Murshidabad, and North Dinajpur. In this context, it is very unlikely for the Congress to revive in the near future from its currently marginal status in the political field of West Bengal.

The decline of the left

The limited presence of the Congress in contemporary West Bengal is coupled with the decline of the CPI(M)-led Left Front from the 2008 panchayat election. After enjoying three decades of unchallenged power in West Bengal, the Left was first severely challenged in the 2008 panchayat election, particularly at the lowest two levels of panchayat system (the Gram Sabhas and the Panchayat Samitis). In the May 2008 panchayat election in West Bengal (when the Left was still supporting the Congress-led first United Progressive Alliance government from outside), it somehow managed to win thirteen Zilla Parishads out of seventeen, but it lost a significant number of Panchayat Samitis and Gram panchayats. The two results of the 2006 Assembly election sweep by the Left and the starting point of erosion of the Left in 2008 were at a time when there was a political understanding between the Left and the Congress at the national level. Subsequently, the Left got 43.3 per cent votes in the 2009 Lok Sabha election, 41.1 per cent in the 2011 Assembly election, 29.95 per cent in the 2014 Lok Sabha election, and, finally, it was reduced to 25.69 per cent votes in the 2016 Assembly election while contesting a little over 200 seats. In 2016 Assembly election, the Left had a pre-poll seat-sharing arrangement with the Congress. The Congress got 12.25 per cent of the votes by contesting ninety-two seats. With one NCP candidate and another Left-Congress backed independent, the alliance got a little over 38 per cent of the votes, which was not very different from the 2014 Lok Sabha election when the combined vote share of Left and Congress was 39.29 per cent. The issue is that the independent strength of the Left in West Bengal is continuously dwindling irrespective of whether there is any alliance among the non-Left forces or not. In 2001, there was an alliance between the Congress and the Trinamool, but the Left still managed to get 199 seats (two-third majority) and over 48 per cent of the votes (5 per cent more than the 2009 Lok Sabha election and 7 per cent more than the 2011 election when Trinamool and Congress had an electoral alliance).

The interesting fact is that in the last decade, while the Congress is able to hold on to its restricted territory by either aligning with Trinamool or the Left, the sharp decline of the Left Front during the same period can be easily noticed. In 2004 Lok Sabha and 2006 Vidhan Sabha elections, the Left Front got 50.8 per cent and 50.2 per cent of the votes respectively. In contrast, the Left got only 29.95 per cent of the votes in the 2014 Lok Sabha election, a loss of nearly 20 per cent of the votes in one decade. Moreover, in terms of seats in the Assembly, the Left has been relegated to the third position behind the Congress. In this respect, as an opposition in West Bengal politics, the Left is facing a severe crisis than the Congress in the 1980s and 1990s. Barring the 1984 Lok Sabha election wave, the Congress maintained a vote share between 35 and 42 per cent in all Parliament and Assembly election from 1980 to 1996 after the rout of 1977; this is far more than what the Left has performed in the 2014 Parliament and 2016 Assembly elections after their defeat in 2011 Assembly election. In the recent by-elections of the Parliamentary constituencies of Tamluk and Coochbehar, and Monteswar Assembly constituency in November 2016 and Kanthi South Assembly constituency in April 2017, the Left further eroded.

In one decade between 2006 and 2016, the poor has actually dumped the Left for Trinamool (Sardesai and Basu 2016). In 2006, the Left managed to get 55 per cent of the votes among the poor (a comfortable majority). However, among the poor voters, the Left got 43 per cent in 2011, 36 per cent in 2014, and only 23 per cent in 2016. If one analyses the electoral results from 2006 to 2016 then it is clear that the major reason for the continuous debacle of the Left in West Bengal from the 2008 panchayat election is because of its desertion of Left politics, i.e. to serve the class interests of the poor, workers, and peasants, along with its inability to invent any alternative Leftwing populist mobilisation instead of following a liberal or neoliberal path. It has little to do with the seat adjustment with the Congress, which is nothing but a result of its debunking of the core left politics after 2006.

The current crisis of the Left had started after the 2006 Assembly election. Such a crisis was fundamentally linked with its inability to provide a counter-hegemonic politics of alternative to neoliberal developmentalism. In fact, neoliberal hegemony has partly influenced the policies and political thinking of the Bengal Left, which was trying to mimic the Chinese model of corporate-led industrial development, which has been called 'neoliberalism with Chinese characteristics' (Harvey 2005: 120–151). The Left forgot to acknowledge that in a country where multiparty democracy is the order of the day, unlike the Chinese and the Vietnamese case, the modernist logic of transition from agriculture to industry has to be negotiated at many levels and in a democratic manner instead of a centralised imposition from above. Moreover, the Left was also unable to understand the complexities of such a forced transition from agriculture to industry, under conditions of 'postcolonial capitalism' that is driven by the dual logic of 'primitive accumulation' on the one hand and 'governmentality' on the other (Sanyal 2007).

Significant sections of urban Bengali middle class, which was traditionally the Left's support base right from the 1940s till the late 1980s, turned against the Left in the decade of 1990s with neoliberal reforms and the rise of corporate sector offering better opportunities for this class. After almost fifteen years, the Left was able to significantly mobilise this class, particularly in the 2006 Bengal Assembly election on the plank of corporate industrialisation. On the other hand, the peasantry and landless agricultural labourers have historically constituted the solid rural base of the Left, which has remained consistently loyal till the 2006 Assembly election despite the fact that some studies show that the Left had a decline of 5 per cent of rural poor votes while an increase of 16 per cent votes and 18 per cent votes among the urban middle classes and urban rich respectively when compared with the 2001 Assembly election (Yadav and Kumar 2006). In the 2006 Assembly election, out of forty-eight seats in Greater Kolkata – once the non-Left bastion throughout the 1990s and the residence of a big pool of urban middle classes – the Left won thirty-four seats while the non-Left parties won only fourteen seats. So, apart from traditional rural constituencies, an urban middle-class support base for the Left has developed in the recent past. The big capital and urban middle classes in West Bengal, like elsewhere in the country, has been mostly benefited than other strata from neoliberal economic policies and is assertively demanding the fulfilment of its class aspirations. Now, there is a certain tension between the peasant and urban middle-class support base, which the Left faced on the issues of industrialisation and Special Economic Zones (SEZ).[4] Thus, the class orientation and the class support behind the 2006 verdict in favour of the Left was different from any major election between 1977 and 2001.

In 2006, the Left gave the slogan, 'agriculture is our base and industry is our future'. This was an attempt to effectively reconfigure the political field, along with an actual process of depoliticisation and desperation of the Left Front, which had lost its class perspective in its drive for corporate-led industrialisation. This depoliticisation was represented in its consensual practice within the Left parties, which avoided asking pertinent questions like what kind of industry and for whom? Thus, building 'consensus' on corporate-led industrialisation was an outcome of a lack of ideological struggle inside the largest communist party in Bengal, effectively speaking the rhetoric of TINA (there is no alternative). In such a context, the people were faced with a historic irony that it was the same Left Front which expropriated their land, livelihood, and peasant economy for a corporate model of industrial development in the last decade of the Left regime, once implemented Operation Barga, and redistributed land among the people in the first decade of the Left Front government. This expropriation of land by the Left Front government from the people created a sense of disrespect towards the Left among the people. A feeling of humiliation by the people became particularly strong after coercive tactics were employed by the Left Front government, as evident in tragic episodes of Singur and Nandigram. Thus, the Left made a great mistake by taking refuge to violence rather than earning consent from the people by politically convincing them for land acquisition. The success and viability of a long-term political project would depend on the nature of people's active participation and consultations rather than eradicating the space of political dissent with violent methods. For a successful hegemony over the people, a consensus is always better than coercion because the limits of repression can be exposed sooner or later with a resistance to the power bloc – the repressive agency. From an ethical viewpoint, a Left Front government cannot justify coercive methods even if it believed that a particular project of development is *good* and *just* for a collective entity called the 'people'. In other words, for a successful hegemony, it has to earn *legitimacy* from the people.

But why the people in Bengal turn against the Left Front on a series of elections between 2008 and 2011 after the massive drive for corporate-led industrial development despite the fact that the same people gave a thumping verdict for the Left in 2006 Assembly election? Basically, this popular verdict against the Left was not overnight. It was a result of sedimented discourses of a sense of victimhood and neglect of several democratic demands comprising of socio-economic issues and questions of political empowerment, connected with caste and community issues that the Left has traditionally overlooked. In the 2011 Census, West Bengal was below the national average in access to electricity, access to tapped drinking water, access to banking services, and access to television. Moreover, in health and education, it was still a moderately performing state even after such a long regime of the Left Front. Those unfulfilled democratic demands of education, health, and infrastructure development got a nodal point in the land acquisition agitation of Singur and Nandigram to implode the Left. This is not to say that the Left has not delivered on certain structural changes that had benefited the rural economy. Indeed, the Left has tried to uplift the basic material living conditions of working classes and peasantry. The Left implemented land reforms and effective institutionalisation of decentralised democracy via Panchayati Raj, which ensured the empowerment of traditionally marginalised sections of the rural population. The distributive policies of agrarian reforms and local representation in the first decade of the Left Front government were later overshadowed by the dominance of the strong machinery of 'party society' and the agency of school teachers in the countryside that the Left Front regime was thoroughly dependent on (Bhattacharyya 2016).

From 2008, the Left started losing its traditional support among the scheduled castes, scheduled tribes, and Muslims, which constituted of an overwhelming section of the rural poor. The inability to address socio-economic and political questions of weaker sections is due to the *lack* of Left's creative imagination in understanding the dynamics and constitutive character of the 'people'. Since the category of 'people' has always been articulated in *class terms* within Leftwing political discourses, the Left simply could not understand deeply in prioritising its agenda to fulfill the democratic demands of socio-economic development and political empowerment of marginalised identity groups. This was reciprocated by an overrepresentation of the upper caste *Bhadrolok* (Brahmins, Kayasthas, and Baidyas) from a middle-class background in the political leadership in most tiers of party, legislative, and Cabinet members in the government within the Left Front in Bengal (Lama-Rewal 2009: 370–373, 388–390). This *Bhadrolok* Left leadership has often been culturally alien to the working class and the peasantry. In the past, this cultural non-identification of the Left's basic classes with the leadership had thus always opened up the conditions for an emerging crisis in the future. During the phase of 2006–2011, one could indeed witness such a crisis of the Left, where cultural alienation of the people with an arrogant Left leadership only widened in the context of a governmental push for corporate industrialisation.

The current crisis of the continuous decline of the Left after the 2011 Assembly election is a result of three processes. First, the denial syndrome of the Left leadership in accepting several mistakes during the Left Front regime. The present Left leadership has not been able to honestly and frankly articulate to the people about their strengths and shortcomings along with a lack of clarity for what the Left stands for in the twenty-first century. Second, there are (a) the lack of experience of the current Left leadership in doing opposition politics even if there are conditions to mobilise anti-Trinamool voters on issues like agrarian crisis in rural Bengal, (b) the attempts to recapture land from the beneficiaries of land reforms by rural elites and land mafia in the countryside, (c) the extortion rackets in the state, and (d) the corruption (chit funds and primary school teacher recruitment scams) during the Trinamool regime. The present crop of Left Front leaders in Bengal has enjoyed power in the government for an uninterrupted thirty-four years. As a result, the inertia of staying in power for so long has been a deterrent for the existing Left leadership to quickly equip themselves into militant anti-government politics. Third, the Left has been unable to reach out to large sections of the young population with a fresh vision of an alternative path of hope and opportunity, complemented with an absence of a new generation of young leaders. These weaknesses of the Left have created conditions for the consolidation of the Trinamool in the state even if the party has no strategic vision for the future of Bengal, but only thrives on short-term tactical considerations of creating dole-centric beneficiaries.

The consolidation of the Trinamool Congress

In the 2014 Lok Sabha election in West Bengal, for the first time, all four major political formations – the Left Front, Trinamool Congress, Indian National Congress, and the BJP – fought separately in all forty-two Lok Sabha seats. In this election, the Trinamool Congress secured 39.79 per cent of the votes, the Left Front got 29.95 per cent of the votes, the BJP got 17.02 per cent of the votes, and the Congress got 9.69 per cent of the votes. Evidently, the Left Front in West Bengal was routed. Clearly, the only gainers in terms of vote share in the 2014 election in Bengal are the Trinamool and the BJP when compared with the previous 2009 Lok Sabha and 2011 West Bengal Vidhan Sabha elections. Trinamool became successful with a regionalist agenda and without being part of any major political alliance (Kailash 2014: 64–71). In Bengal, the Trinamool emerged as a viable alternative to BJP by consolidating the anti-BJP votes comprising of minorities and liberal-secular sections of the electorate. The minorities relied more on Congress in North Bengal, helping it to win four minority-concentrated seats (Malda North, Malda South, Behrampore, and

Jangipur) out of the original six minority-dominated Lok Sabha constituencies in the state. The two Left MPs are Muslims and won from minority-dominated seats of Raiganj and Murshidabad with a slim majority, both of which were previously held by the Congress. On the other hand, a section of the middle-class support base of Left Front that wanted an aggressive industrialisation and urbanisation by displacing the peasantry shifted towards the BJP in Bengal. The Left leadership in Bengal was already rejected in the Assembly election in 2011. The 2014 election only reinforced the fact that the people do not want a tired and unimaginative Left leadership, detached from the people and people's movements.

The post-poll survey data of National Election Study of Lokniti shows that the Trinamool Congress was supported by all major sections of the population. Even where the Trinamool is politically weak on the question of women's security, 42 per cent of women still voted for the party. The vote share of the Left, on the other hand, had significantly dwindled among the marginalised groups, especially among the Dalits, Adivasis, and Muslims. These three communities along with the poor have voted in large numbers for the Trinamool Congress. Chief Minister Mamata Banerjee's aggressive campaign against the BJP's prime ministerial candidate Narendra Modi actually attracted the Muslim voters towards Trinamool in South Bengal. The political commentators suggest that 'the aggressive manner in which Mamata Banerjee countered Narendra Modi in her electoral speeches, could be one of the key factors behind the AITC's success among the minority community' (Chatterjee and Basu 2014: 220–221). In an overall analysis, it can be argued that the poor and the weaker sections are almost losing their confidence in the Left. The trend of increasing support of the poor and the Muslims for the Trinamool can be also noticed in the 2016 Assembly election. According to the CSDS post-poll survey data, the Trinamool Congress has been able to increase its support base among the poor from 21 per cent in 2006 to 52 per cent in 2016. Similarly, among Muslims, it enhanced its support from merely 22 per cent in 2006, 35 per cent in 2011, 40 per cent in 2014 and 51 per cent in 2016. In contrast, 38 per cent of the Muslims supported the Left and the Congress alliance while 6 per cent voted for the BJP in the 2016 Assembly election (Sardesai and Basu 2016). The Trinamool-led West Bengal government has also started giving various kinds of assistance to the poor among which four welfare schemes have ensured enormous popular support: Khadyasathi (rice and wheat at Rs 2 per kg), Sabooj Sathi (free bicycles for schoolchildren), Kanyashree (cash incentives to girls for continuing school education), and

Yubashree (financial assistance to unemployed youth). In the context of an impending agrarian crisis in rural Bengal and farmer indebtedness, these welfare schemes have actually ensured a solid rural support base of Trinamool. In a state where 82 per cent of family households exist with less than Rs 5,000 as the monthly income of highest earning member,[5] the welfare schemes are a huge bonus for the people. Simultaneously, the Trinamool has been able to manage considerable sections of the non-corporate capital and the informal sector labour force.

Moreover, the post-poll survey of the Centre for the Study of Developing Societies (CSDS) suggests that the voters think that the performance of the Trinamool-led government has been much better than the Left Front on three aspects – condition of roads, electricity supply, and supply of drinking water (Sardesai and Basu 2016). Even if the perception of some voters is that the Trinamool-led government has been relatively corrupt than the Left Front regime, a large number of voters have actually supported the Trinamool on the development plank (Banerjee and Attri 2016). The popularity of Chief Minister Mamata Banerjee among significant sections of the electorate and the increasing support of women voters (as high as 48 per cent in the 2016 Assembly election) has been important factors for the consolidation of the Trinamool (Aasaavari and Mishra 2016).

Today, Trinamool as a leader-centric party has actually transformed itself from articulating a Centre-Right political agenda during its proximity with BJP during the phase of 1998–2006 to a Centre-Left populist politics from the Singur agitation after the 2006 Assembly election. Trinamool's hands-off policy on SEZ and land acquisition, its opposition to foreign direct investment in retail and its opposition to demonetisation clearly indicates that the party has been more focused on the prime constituency of the informal sector. Simultaneously, its anti-Centre politics like opposition to the Centre's decision of interest rate cuts in bank savings schemes, its opposition to the delay of funds disbursement by the central government in NREGA and several welfare schemes have a traction among the Bengalis.

Trinamool has been able to win away substantial sections of the erstwhile Left Front voters and potential Left supporters in the state for three prime reasons. First, primarily as a regional player, the Trinamool has been more Bengal-centric than the Left. In contrast, the Left has to weigh its various political options and key decisions on the political-tactical line while keeping a balance between its other strong bases in Kerala and Tripura. Second, the visibility of a subaltern image of the Trinamool party organisation has been relatively more than the

Left. The Left had an educated middle-class leadership. In contrast, the visibility of several Trinamool functionaries, including some in the top party leadership hailing from the lower-middle class background, has been instrumental for mobilising the poor. Finally, it has been able to manage the vast sections of the informal sector, the domain of 'political society'[6] in contrast to the Left, which has still some hold over the workers in the organised sector through trade unions. In a situation where the Trinamool is getting further consolidated and the Left and Congress are on the decline, the opposition space is open, which the BJP is eyeing to capture. Can it actually rally significant sections of the Bengal electorate in the coming years? That is the question that I shall now try to answer.

The game of the BJP

One significant trend in West Bengal is the growth of the Bharatiya Janata Party (BJP), inspired by the *Hindutva* ideology of Rashtriya Swayamsevak Sangh (RSS) in the state. In the 2009 Lok Sabha election, the BJP contested forty-two seats in West Bengal and polled just 6.14 per cent of the votes while in 2011 Vidhan Sabha election, it polled only 4.06 per cent of the votes and did not have a single Member of Legislative Assembly (MLA). Within three years, the BJP's vote share increased more than four times as it polled 17.02 per cent in the 2014 Lok Sabha election. Not only has it won two Lok Sabha seats (Darjeeling in North Bengal and Asansol in South Bengal), it has also come second in three Lok Sabha seats (Kolkata North, Kolkata South, and Malda South). In thirteen Lok Sabha seats, the BJP has polled more than 20 per cent of the votes.[7] The post-poll survey of CSDS suggests that in the 2014 Lok Sabha election, the BJP has been relatively popular among the upper castes and urban educated middle class than among other sections of the population (Chatterjee and Basu 2014: 216–220).

The recent rise of vote share of the BJP in Bengal was also a result of the increase in low scale communal conflicts. In fact, police records and newspaper reports suggest that low-scale communal clashes have increased in rural Bengal. Such incidents of communal violence generally occurred in Bengal, annually, between twelve and forty from 2007–2012 and it suddenly peaked at 106 in 2013 (Das 2014). After 2014 Lok Sabha election, a noted social scientist has pointed out in an interview to a Bengali newspaper that the two states where the BJP has performed beyond anyone's expectations are Assam and West Bengal and the BJP might try to make communal polarisation in these states in order to grow further (Chattopadhyay 2014). In 2014 Lok Sabha election, the degree of polarisation was greater in states with a higher Muslim population and West Bengal was no exception (Sardesai, Gupta and Sayal 2014: 28–44).

After the 2014 Lok Sabha election, an interesting phenomenon was noticed in terms of an unprecedented growth of BJP's Muslim membership in some pockets of Birbhum and North 24 Parganas (Bagchi 2014). In fact, most of them were erstwhile supporters of the Left Front who have joined the BJP, as the Left leaders were failing to guarantee security against the political violence of the Trinamool in several districts of Bengal. However, the BJP lost momentum in the 2015 civic election by becoming a distant fourth without winning any municipality corporation in the state. In the 2016 Assembly election, the party lost nearly 7 per cent of the votes from the 2014 Lok Sabha election and just polled 10.16 per cent, even lower than its electoral performance in the 1991 Lok Sabha and Vidhan Sabha elections of over 11.5 per cent of the votes in the state during the Ramjanmabhoomi movement. In the 2016 Assembly election, the BJP contested 291 seats but forfeited the deposit in 263 seats and won only three seats. But in the by-polls after the 2016 Assembly elections, while the Trinamool has further consolidated and has increased its vote share, the BJP has significantly gained at the cost of the Left.

Thus, there is no denying the fact that the BJP is growing in Bengal particularly from the 2014 election onwards. This growth of the BJP is also linked with the recent growth of the RSS after the 2011 Assembly election. According to an organisational report of the RSS, while there were just 580 shakhas in West Bengal in 2011, the number rose to 1,280 in 2014 and 1,492 in December 2016 (Chanda 2017). There are three principal reasons for the growth of the BJP in the state. First, the continuous decline of the Left as an alternative political-ideological force from the local neighbourhoods. The retreat of the Left has also created conditions for competitive political articulation grounded upon religious identitarian politics between the BJP and the Trinamool. The possibility of identitarian politics in the wake of the collapse of the organised mainstream Left in West Bengal was already predicted by a noted political analyst (Bhattacharyya 2010: 51–59). Second, significant sections of the Hindi-speaking population from northern and western India in some cities, like Kolkata, Howrah, Asansol, and Siliguri, are now seeing the BJP as their natural choice.[8] Third, in a highly competitive world, there is the anxiety of a section of educated middle-class youth and upper caste students under the age of twenty-five who are uncertain about their future in a state with lack of employment opportunities due to limited expansion of the private formal sector on the one hand and nearly 50 per cent reservation in education and jobs in the government sector on the other. The post-poll survey of CSDS has shown how these sections have voted for the BJP in the 2014 Lok Sabha election in Bengal. This is also the same young population who have not seen the demolition of Babri mosque, the post-Babri riots, the Gujarat genocide, and the attacks against the Christian minorities in the 1990s and early 2000s.

After the massive victory in the 2017 Uttar Pradesh Assembly election, the Sangh Parivar organised the Ram Navami celebrations in some parts of the state with unprecedented fervour. People were surprised to see armed processions of Hindutva activists carrying swords, machetes, and tridents. Young students and children were also mobilised to take part in this procession.[9] However, it would be wrong to see this Hindutva assertion during the Ram Navami celebrations as a spontaneous reaction of the Hindus. This is because an overwhelming majority of Hindus in West Bengal and in several parts of India do not rally behind the BJP-RSS just like Muslims in Bengal and India do not vote for Muslim parties like the Muslim League, MIM, Jamaat-e-Islamibacked WPI, etc.[10] The Ram Navami processions were well organised by the RSS-BJP leadership after the UP election results. The jubilation and show of strength were the most important motives, along with a counter to Muharram celebrations in some parts of Bengal. The campaign in social media by the RSS-BJP along with the visibility of those processions in the electronic media although created a spectacle.

The major strength of the BJP in the state is that it is still an untested party. In fact, apart from a section of urban upper caste and middle-class voters, the BJP has been already able to gain some support among few Tribal pockets of North Bengal, neighbouring Assam, and one Tribal pocket, neighbouring Odisha. It is also interesting to note that in the 2016 Assembly election, the BJP had fielded sixteen scheduled caste and one schedule tribe candidate from unreserved constituencies, far more than the Left and the Trinamool. In doing so, the BJP is clearly sending a message of reaching out to significant sections of non-upper caste voters, who are still alienated from the party. But, the absence of a dominant, intermediate landed caste across rural Bengal, which might be comparable to the Lingayats and Vokkaligas of Karnataka, the Vellalas of Tamil Nadu, the Reddys and Kammas of Andhra, the Yadavs, Jats, and Rajputs of North India, or the Marathas in Maharashtra, is an impediment for an anti-upper caste politics (Chattopadhyay 2013: 99–101). However, after the 2014 Lok

Sabha elections, scores of central leaders of the BJP are often coming to the state in order to motivate the local organisation, which shows that the party is seriously looking for some inroads in Bengal. Being in the central government, the BJP has some influence over a section of voters where the state BJP unit is able to highlight any policy of the central government as an advertisement for the party as well.

In contrast to the strengths of the BJP, the party has major weaknesses in Bengal. First, it lacks a mass leader, which could match up to the popularity of Mamata Banerjee. West Bengal has witnessed the rise of Jyoti Basu as an opposition leader during the Congress period while the emergence of Mamata Banerjee during the Left Front regime. BJP is yet to score on that front. Second, West Bengal has a history of long stable regimes if a government is voted back to power with a comfortable majority (Bhattacharyya 2009b: 326–345). Barring the period of instability during 1967–1977 when no decisive mandate was in favour of any single political formation, the logic of long years of stability has been the case during the Congress system, the Left Front regime, and has been continuing at present during the Trinamool regime. Third, the large presence of Muslim minorities constituting 27 per cent of the population, with the potential to influence the electoral outcome without a prominent minority party, unlike Assam, could deter the polarising tactics of the RSS-BJP. Fourth, a new educated middle class is slowly growing among the OBCs and Dalits under the Trinamool regime because, in government jobs and education, the reservation policy is now strictly getting implemented. Fifth, the popularity of the incumbent Trinamool government among both urban and rural poor has created conditions in which the BJP is finding it difficult to make a viable social coalition for larger political mobilisation. Sixth, factional fights in the BJP at various levels have been a reality in Bengal along with a lack of discipline among its new entrants due to the absence of a popular leader. Finally, West Bengal is an extremely politicised state, which has been largely a 'party society' (Bhattacharyya 2009a: 59–69) with everyday politics in many local institutions including that of educational institutions, local clubs, and citizen's platforms. The strong presence of the Left and the Trinamool in the existing local institutions is a counter to the RSS at the social sphere.

Given the multipolar nature of the contest, the division of votes among the opposition parties, the dole giving strategy of the West Bengal government, and the consolidation of the poor, significant sections of the Scheduled Caste groups, Other Backward Classes, and Muslim minorities behind the ruling party, it will be difficult to dislodge the Trinamool from power in the near future. At this moment, the BJP is fighting for the second place in the state in order to become the prime opposition party. In the 2019 Lok Sabha election, if the BJP becomes second in the state in terms of vote share then it would be a morale booster for the party for the 2021 Assembly election. If the BJP is able to become the primary opposition party in the 2021 Assembly election, then the political discourse of West Bengal might significantly change from discussing basic issues of health, education, and employment to religious identitarian issues and dietary habits. The current political discourse in the state is already pointing out towards such an ominous trend. The phenomena of using religious symbolism in political mobilisation in contemporary West Bengal is certainly a regressive turn of events after all the gains made by the largely secular democratic and progressive political culture of the state in the last six decades.

If the Left continues to decay in the state, then it is not impossible for the BJP to become the main opposition party in West Bengal. The point, however, is that both the big national parties, the Congress and the BJP, are still unable to make a significant dent in Bengal in order to capture political power. In other words, the big national parties are an exceptional outcast in Bengal in the last four decades when compared with most states in the country. All evidence and political dynamics of the state shows that there is no reason to believe that this trend will soon change in favour of the big national parties.

Notes

1 The Trinamool Congress was originally a state party from 1998 to 2016. From September 2016, it was recognised as the seventh national party by the Election Commission of India along with BJP, BSP, CPI(M), CPI, INC, and NCP.
2 All calculations are made from the Election Commission of India data. In 2004 Lok Sabha election, the Congress managed to win the Darjeeling Lok Sabha seat in North Bengal with the support of local Gorkha parties in the hills.
3 Information gathered from All India Trinamool Congress website. All India Trinamool Congress, About the Party. http://aitcofficial.org/the-party/ (accessed 15 April 2017).
4 Prabhat Patnaik predicted the tensions and emerging contradictions out of these contesting social forces just after the 2006 West Bengal Assembly elections (Patnaik 2006: 23–25).
5 *Socio-Economic Caste Census*, 2011, http://secc.gov.in/stateSummaryReport (accessed 24 April 2017).
6 The concept of 'political society' has been innovatively formulated by Partha Chatterjee (Chatterjee 2004, 2011).
7 All calculations for 2009, 2011, and 2014 elections are based on the Election Commission of India data.

8 According to the Linguistic Survey of India (2011), the Hindi-speaking population is over 7 per cent in the state.
9 'Sangh Parivar organise unprecedented Ram Navami celebration across Bengal', *Hindustan Times*, 5 April 2017, www.hindustantimes.com/kolkata/sangh-parivar-organise-unprecedented-ram-navami-celebration-across-bengal/story-eEuaCHGT1N3RdU6Vo7pHwN.html (accessed 2 May).
10 In 2014 Lok Sabha elections, the Muslim parties like Badruddin Ajmal and Siddiqullah Chowdhury-led AIUDF (All India United Democratic Front), WPI (Welfare Party of India), and SDPI (Social Democratic Party of India) together got less than the NOTA vote of 1.1 per cent. In the 2016 Assembly elections, the Muslim parties like IUML, SDPI, and WPI together contested forty seats, forfeited deposits in all those seats and got a mere 0.12 per cent of the votes, much less than the NOTA vote of 1.52 per cent.

Acknowledgement: An earlier version of this paper was presented in September 2014 at a conference on Election 2014 at the Jamia Millia Islamia, New Delhi. A final version of this paper was presented at a workshop at the Centre for Studies in Social Sciences, Calcutta (CSSSC) on 12 January 2018. I have benefited from the discussions by the participants of the Jamia conference and the CSSSC workshop. Also, I am grateful to Dwaipayan Bhattacharyya and Partha Chatterjee for comments and suggestions while writing this paper. The essay represents the views and analysis of the author alone.

Bibliography

Aasaavari, Asmita and Jyoti Mishra. 2016. 'Historic Sweep Powered by Mamata', *Indian Express*, May 22. http://indianexpress.com/article/elections-2016/explained/mamata-banerjee-tmc-west-bengal-historic-win-analysis-2812918/ (accessed on April 24, 2017).
Bagchi, Suvojit. 2014. 'Lotus Bloom in West Bengal', *The Hindu*, August 6.
Banerjee, Souradeep and Vibha Attri. 2016. 'Corruption an Issue in West Bengal, But Development No. 1', *Indian Express*, May 22. http://indianexpress.com/article/elections-2016/explained/west-bengal-tmc-mamata-banerjee-corruption-development-2812946/ (accessed on April 24, 2017).
Bhattacharyya, Dwaipayan. 2009a. 'Of Control and Factions: The Changing "Party Society" in Rural Bengal', *Economic & Political Weekly*, 44(9): 59–69.
———. 2009b. 'West Bengal: Permanent Incumbency and Political Stability', in Sandeep Shastri, K. C. Suri and Yogendra Yadav (eds.), *Electoral Politics in Indian States: Lok Sabha Elections in 2004 and Beyond*, pp. 326–345. New Delhi: Oxford University Press.
———. 2010. 'Left in the Lurch: The Demise of the World's Longest Elected Regime?', *Economic & Political Weekly*, 45(3): 51–59.
———. 2016. *Government as Practice: Democratic Left in a Transforming India*. New Delhi: Cambridge University Press.

Chanda, Aishik. 2017. 'RSS in Bengal Has Grown Threefold in Five Years, Says Report', *The New Indian Express*, March 27. www.newindianexpress.com/nation/2017/mar/27/rss-in-bengal-has-grown-threefold-in-five-years-says-report-1586535.html (accessed on April 26, 2017).
Chatterjee, Jyotiprasad and Suprio Basu. 2014. 'Bipolarity to Multipolarity: Emerging Political Geometry in West Bengal', *Panjab University Research Journal: Social Sciences* (Special Issue in collaboration with Lokniti, CSDS, Delhi), 22(2): 211–223.
Chatterjee, Jyoti Prasad and Sam Solomon. 2016. 'West Bengal: Left-Congress Alliance Weak in Arithmetic and Chemistry', *Indian Express*, May 22. http://indianexpress.com/article/elections-2016/india/india-news-india/west bengal-left-congress-alliance-weak-in-arithmetic-and-chemistry-2813058/ (accessed on April 24, 2017).
Chatterjee, Partha. 1997. 'Introduction: A Political History of Independent India', in Partha Chatterjee (ed.), *State and Politics in India*, pp. 1–39. New Delhi: Oxford University Press.
———. 2004. *Politics of the Governed: Reflections on Popular Politics in Most of the World*. New York: Columbia University Press.
———. 2011. *Lineages of Political Society: Studies in Postcolonial Democracy*. New York: Columbia University Press.
Chattopadhyay, Partha. 2013. *Janopratinidhi* (in Bengali). Kolkata: Anustup.
———. 2014. 'Kingkartabya?' (in Bengali) Interview by Subhoranjan Dasgupta, *Ei Samay*, August 19.
Das, Madhuparna. 2014. 'Communal Clashes Soar in Bengal', *Indian Express*, March 14. http://indianexpress.com/article/india/politics/communal-clashes-soar-in-bengal/99/ (accessed on September 1, 2014).
Harvey, David. 2005. *A Brief History of Neoliberalism*. Oxford: Oxford University Press.
Kailash, K.K. 2014. 'Regional Parties in the 16th Lok Sabha Elections: Who Survived and Why?', *Economic & Political Weekly*, 49(39): 64–71.
Kohli, Atul. 1997. 'From Breakdown to Order: West Bengal', in Partha Chatterjee (ed.), *State and Politics in India*, pp. 336–366. New Delhi: Oxford University Press.
Kothari, Rajni. 1964. 'The Congress "System" in India', *Asian Survey*, 4(12): 1161–1173.
———. 1970. *Politics in India*. Hyderabad: Orient Longman.
Lama-Rewal, Stephanie Tawa. 2009. 'The Resilient *Bhadrolok*: A Profile of the West Bengal MLAs', in Christophe Jaffrelot and Sanjay Kumar (eds.), *Rise of the Plebeians? The Changing Face of Indian Legislative Assemblies*, pp. 361–392. New Delhi: Routledge.
Patnaik, Prabhat. 2006. 'Left in Government', *Frontline*, May 20–June 2, pp. 23–25.
Sanyal, Kalyan. 2007. *Rethinking Capitalist Development: Primitive Accumulation, Governmentality and Post-Colonial Capitalism*. New Delhi: Routledge.

Sardesai, Shreyas and Suprio Basu. 2016. 'Poor Dump Left for Trinamool, Muslims Solidly Behind Didi', *Indian Express*, May 22. http://indianexpress.com/article/elections-2016/explained/west-bengal-muslims-mamata-banerjee-tmc-left-2812930/ (accessed on April 23, 2017).

Sardesai, Shreyas, Pranav Gupta and Reetika Sayal. 2014. 'The Religious Fault Line in the 2014 Election', *Panjab University Research Journal: Social Sciences* (Special Issue in collaboration with Lokniti, CSDS, Delhi), 22(2): 28–44.

Yadav, Yogendra and Sanjay Kumar. 2006. 'Why the Left Will Win Once Again', *The Hindu*, April 16.

13 National elections in a tribal state

The 2014 Lok Sabha elections in Meghalaya

Cornelia Guenauer

Introduction

The northeastern states of India – Assam, Arunachal Pradesh, Manipur, Meghalaya, Mizoram, Nagaland, and Tripura – are not only geographically located at the verge of the Indian state but also on the brink of the political landscape of the Indian nation. Ahead of the 2014 Lok Sabha election, the murder of a college student from Arunachal Pradesh in New Delhi called to mind the uneasy relationship between the northeastern states and the rest of India, which is characterised by discrimination against people from the northeast and a general lack of knowledge of the political and social realities in the states. In electoral terms, parties and political observers have long neglected the states, which only send 24 representatives to the 542-seat strong national Parliament and, thus, have only a limited influence in terms of government formation. Ahead of the 2014 national elections, however, the region emerged as an important battleground as the assumed fractured verdict turned every seat into a potential decisive factor (Haokip 2014). Accordingly, campaign activity in the states increased, with the BJP launching an aggressive campaign, challenging the status quo of regional politics, which had been dominated by the Indian National Congress (INC) and various regional parties.

The northeastern states not only differ in many aspects from the rest of India but they also differ tremendously from each other in terms of social, religious, linguistic, political, and overall demographic set-up.[1] However, a common trait can be found in a shared sense of estrangement from the Indian state. Different groups across the states – reaching from civil society organisations over militant insurgency groups to recognised political parties – have employed this sense of estrangement 'as a politico-cultural capital for bargaining with the Indian state' (Dev 2007: 241), turning ethnically based regionalism into a central factor of local politics. Accordingly, elections in most of the states have traditionally been fought between the various regional parties and the Congress, while the BJP had only a very limited support base in the region. Ahead of the 2014 election, the Congress had been dominating the political landscape in the region, ruling in five of seven states and having thirteen sitting Members of Parliament from the region. However, during the run-up for the 2014 election, a newly founded coalition of ten regional parties, the North-East Regional Political Front (NERPF), as well as an aggressively campaigning BJP challenged the Congress's hold in the region, heralding potential change in the political landscapes.

The chapter focuses on how the Lok Sabha elections unfolded in Meghalaya and provides insights into the political dynamics of the state. Similar to other northeastern states, the political discourse in Meghalaya is dominated by a feeling of estrangement from the Indian state and by an anxiety over the influx of outsiders into the state. Accordingly, during national elections, campaigners in Meghalaya have to manoeuvre in a blurred space between national and regional politics. They have to respond to the national notion of unity as well as to regional ideas of difference and autonomy. To analyse the specific conditions and dynamics of electoral politics in the predominantly tribal state of Meghalaya, the chapter approaches first the historic factors and processes shaping the political landscape of the state and, secondly, discusses the 2014 Lok Sabha elections by paying attention to the commonalities and differences in the two constituencies of Meghalaya. In the conclusion, the chapter widens its focus by relating the political trends to the national development and by providing a short overview of the electoral trends in the other northeastern states.

Conditions and dynamics of competitive politics in Meghalaya

Similar to Indian politics in general, the political landscape of Meghalaya has been characterised by the rise of regional parties, a diversification of the party system, and fragmented election results, leading to coalition governments and even to problems of governance. While major cleavages connected to regional politics in many parts of India are drawn along lines of religion, caste or class, 'Meghalaya represents a typical case wherein social cleavages at a primary level are based mainly on ethnic considerations of "tribe" and "non-tribe"' (Dev 1999: 2482).[2] To a certain extent, this could be attributed to Meghalaya's status as a tribal state, dominated by the Garo (or Achik, the preferred self-description, 30 per cent), and the Khasi and Jaintia people (together 49 per cent), which are all recognised as Scheduled Tribes.[3] To explain the dominance of tribal identity as a key determinant for social, political, and economic cleavages, it is essential to comprehend the continuing effects of colonial and subsequent postcolonial political practices in the area.

In the late nineteenth century, the British had brought most of the area of today's Northeast India under their control. To administer the area more effectively, the British authorities introduced an Inner Line separating the plains of Assam, where they had established large tea estates from the densely forested hills, which were hard to access and appeared not to be very profitable for investments. While the plains became part of the colonial economy and infrastructure, the new regulation restricted the access to the hills, simultaneously exempting the area beyond the line from the colonial laws applicable to the rest of British India. The population living beyond the line was left alone to manage their own affairs provided that they did not interfere with British interests in the plains. Drawing on colonial writings, Patricia Mukhim emphasises that the Inner Line was primarily meant to protect colonial economic interests and used as 'an instrument to fence what the British called the savage tribes within their territories so that they do not harass or ambush the plains people who work for the British in their tea gardens' (Mukhim 2012). Accordingly, colonial narratives justified the line by depicting the hill areas, especially the Naga Hills, as inhabited by savages, wild warriors, and primitive tribes constituting a threat to the British subjects in Assamese villages and tea plantations. In the following decades, this narrative changed, becoming increasingly dominated by a more romantic and paternalistic story-line depicting the line as 'protecting these primitive peoples [beyond the line] from the onslaught of more advanced groups in the plains' (Karlsson 2011: 33).[4] As the British established a hill-station at Shillong, today's capital of Meghalaya, the surrounding Khasi Hills did not become as isolated as the rest of the hills area. Due to its mild climate the town served as summer capital and military cantonment, leading to a large-scale migration of clerks, merchants, labourers, soldiers, and plantation owners from Nepal, Assam, Bihar, and Rajasthan and increasing the population of the erstwhile small settlement.

After independence in 1947, the Garo, Khasi, and Jaintia Hills, making up today's Meghalaya, became part of the much larger state of Assam. The new international border between India and East Pakistan turned the region into an area connected to the rest of the India solely through a narrow strip of land and, simultaneously, into a strategic border region of the young Indian state. In addition, the post-independence strategies of integration continued the former segregation of certain areas. Following a protectionist approach, the new government, advised by the British anthropologist Verrier Elwin, introduced different measures to empower and protect minorities. To define who was to be recognised as a minority, the new government adopted the system of categorising the heterogonous population of the northeast in a set of tribes, which colonial administrators and ethnographers once had codified as part of a larger administrative project to classify and ultimately control the subjects of the British empire in a more effective way (McDuie-Ra 2007: 75–77). As one of these protectionist measures, the Sixth Schedule of the Indian Constitution was drafted to protect the rights of tribal minorities from being subsumed within the rights framework of a dominant non-tribal population and 'to enable them to maintain their distinctiveness, rather than encourage their assimilation with the rest of society' (Deshpande 2013: 65–66). The establishment of Autonomous District Councils (ADC) in the areas covered by the schedule provided a certain degree of autonomy to the concerned tribal population, e.g. regarding land rights, customary laws, education, and health administration. As McDuie-Ra describes, the persistence of these colonial categories in conjunction with provisions such as the Sixth Schedule created not only new dilemmas but also turned colonial categories into the key concepts for social, political, and economic claims:

> Not all tribal areas were included in the Sixth Schedule and those communities that were granted special privileges and rights have consistently attempted to exclude all 'others' from accessing these advantages. The Sixth Schedule, district councils, and the formalising of traditional institutions has created a complex over-lapping of formal and semi-formal institutions, spreading a concept of autonomy that has been used to justify ethnically exclusive 'homelands' to be fought for and preserved through political and also violent means. The constitutional provisions in the Sixth Schedule have served as a form of affirmative action and have benefited many of the tribal communities in the region. However they have also embedded the category of 'hill tribe' into the political and economic institutions of the Northeast, and made tribal identity the key determinant of social, political, and economic status.
> (McDuie-Ra 2007: 93)

This observation is central for understanding political conditions and dynamics of Meghalaya, which was founded based on demands for a separate state for the hill tribes. The Garo Hills, Khasi Hills, and Jaintia Hills have been among the areas included in the Sixth Schedule, thus having their own Autonomous District Councils to safeguard the rights and interests of the ST population. Yet, the Assamese Language Act of 1960, which made Assamese the official language in the whole state, boosted political movements claiming that the Indian and Assamese governments neglected the hill areas and tried to assimilate their tribal population. Based on these calls, the All-Party Hill Leaders' Conference (APHLC) led a struggle for a separate state for the hill tribes. This movement finally resulted in the formation of Meghalaya as a full-fledged state in 1972 (McDuie-Ra 2007: 97–98).

While the motion for a separate Hill State was mainly based on broader categories distinguishing between hill and plains people, the mode of political mobilisation in Meghalaya changed soon, invoking more differentiated and narrowly defined dichotomous categories, such as tribal vs. non-tribal, indigenous tribal vs. non-indigenous tribal, or even Garo vs. Khasi. Since the formation of the state, the resistance against the influx of outsiders into Meghalaya and the alleged danger of being outnumbered by them has become a dominant discourse within the state. In this context, influx in contrast to migration also subsumes people from other parts of India, often denoted as non-tribals or non-indigenous people, allegedly endangering local culture and tradition as well as taking the jobs of the locals.[5] Against the background of a diffuse feeling of threat and insecurity, different civil society actors such as the Khasi Student Union (KSU) have opposed migration, often by resorting to violence and intimidation directed at non-tribal residents – even if some of them belonged to families who have lived in Meghalaya for generations. Anti-outsider riots, which repeatedly took place in 1979, 1987, 1992, 1997, and 1998 as well as the recent agitations for an Inner Line Permit (ILP) preceding the 2014 Lok Sabha elections illustrate the lingering anxiety over demographics and its repeated use to mobilise political support (McDuie-Ra 2007: 99). During the ILP agitations of 2013, different pressure groups voiced the need to regulate the influx of people coming to Meghalaya. Their aim was to safeguard indigenous culture and tradition by making it obligatory for every non-Indian as well as for every Indian citizen from outside of Meghalaya to obtain a special permit to enter the state. The months of agitation involved day-long strikes, *bandhs* (curfews), road blockades, as well as violent attacks on paramilitary patrols. Vehicles and shops were set on fire and three people, all shop owners not belonging to an ST community, were burned alive. Interestingly, the same groups arguing against outside interference referred to the colonial Inner Line, established by the British in 1873, and the protectionist discourse connected with it to legitimise their demand.

Census data from the last twenty years show however that, with 86.1 per cent, the STs are far from becoming a minority in the state and that the ST communities are also growing faster than the general population in Meghalaya (Census 2011). Nevertheless, since the early 1990s, the number of regional parties claiming to feel the need to protect the identity and rights of the tribal population against the threat of non-tribal domination has increased especially in the Khasi-Jaintia Hills (Election Commission of India 1991–1999).[6] Yet, the Indian National Congress (INC), who grew strong after a fraction of the APHLC led by Williamson Sangma joined the local Meghalaya Congress Committee (MPCC) in 1976, remained powerful, holding the Shillong Lok Sabha seat since 1999 and forming the current state government. In contrast, the other big national party, the Bharatiya Janata Party (BJP), could not make any significant inroads into the political landscape of the state. This can be attributed to the religious set-up of Meghalaya with a Christian majority where the Hindu nationalist agenda does not find many takers but rather evokes fears over forced conversions.

To sum it up, tribal identity has become crucial factor in social, political, and economic matters in Meghalaya, due to (a) administrative decisions made by the British, (b) political strategies of integration in the post-independence, and (c) modes of political mobilisation in the recent past. Thus, despite of official numbers pointing into a different direction, a feeling of threat to be outnumbered has widely spread in the state. While non-dominant groups are at the margins of political decision-making, parties with ethno-regional agendas have emerged. Although they have not been able to establish themselves as an alternative to the national parties, they shape the context of political communication and, thus, the backdrop of the 2014 Lok Sabha elections in Meghalaya.

The 2014 elections

Meghalaya is represented in the Lok Sabha through two seats: the Tura constituency covering the Garo Hills with roughly half a million voters and the Shillong constituency comprising the Khasi and Jaintia Hills with approximately one million voters. Although Meghalaya is one of the smallest in India, the elections in the two constituencies are fought against very different backgrounds. The aspect of development is one distinguishing the two constituencies, with the 'Garos often express[ing] the view that the Garo hills is the most neglected segment of Meghalaya' (Dev 2007: 259). Due to Shillong's status as a hill-station and its later role as capital of Assam, the Khasi Hills had been administered differently from the Garo Hills. Shillong became a centre for education and administration while the Garo Hills until today remain insufficiently connected to the state capital. The perceived negligence can also be seen as a factor in the rise of insurgency groups in the Garo Hills, demanding a separate state as homeland for the Garo people. In contrast, the conditions in Shillong and the surrounding Khasi Hills benefitted the rise of a local tribal elite and an urban middle-class. Thus, while political leadership in Garo Hills was kept confined to few families, the Khasi Hills produced a larger pool of potential leaders and subsequently a more intensified competition for political leadership (interview with Mukhim 2014).

Common to election campaigns in both constituencies was the absence of professional advertisement strategies, large-scale media campaigns, and the use of social media for campaigning. Campaigning mainly took place at the grassroots level, where the individual candidates and their aides organised their campaigns by following strategies of localisation. Thus, the potential of individuals to mobilise people through their local networks and through using locally adjusted campaign strategies was more important than a uniform, centrally planned campaign structure. Consequently, the candidate as well as his/her networks of supporters played a major role during campaigning, often outshining party ideologies.

The Shillong seat: rise of the BJP in a Congress bastion

The ILP issue had been a major topic during the campaigns for the Autonomous District Council (ADC) elections in the Khasi and Jaintia Hills which took place only six weeks prior to the Lok Sabha elections. The ADC elections were interpreted as semi-finals to the 2014 Lok Sabha elections and media interpreted their outcome as indicating the trend for the general elections (Mohrem 2014). Regional parties, especially the Hill State People's Democratic Party (HSPDP) and the Khun Hyinniewtrep National Awakening Movement (KHNAM), used the ILP issue as their main campaign turf. While the Congress won fourteen seats in the Jaintia Hills and formed the executive committee of the Jaintia Hills District Autonomous Council (JHDAC) through an alliance with independent candidates, they failed to secure the required amount of seats in the Khasi Hills. Instead, the regional parties (United Democratic Party [UDP], KHNAM, and HSPDP) together with an independent candidate formed an eighteen-seat strong coalition as All Regional Parties' Alliance (ARPA) constituting the executive committee. After this result, newspaper reports and observers agreed in their analysis that the regional parties had grown stronger due to the successful adaption of the ILP issue and assumed that regional forces could actually win the Shillong seat, if they were able to stand united behind one candidate.

The elections in the Shillong Lok Sabha constituency were a multi-corner contest as, all in all, eight candidates competed for the Shillong seat.[7] The announcement of the candidates not only marked the beginning of the election process in Meghalaya but also revealed deep discrepancies, splitting the regional parties as well as the local Congress Committee. The ARPA did not transform into a pre-poll alliance for the Lok Sabha elections as the three parties could not settle on a common candidate. While the UDP went ahead with fielding its own working president Paul Lyngdoh as candidate, the KHNAM and the HSPD supported the independent candidate PBM Basaiawmoit, a former Presbyterian reverend, who had contested elections as the HSPD candidate in the 2009 Lok Sabha elections. His opponent Paul Lyngdoh was known as former leader of the KSU and founder of the KHNAM, which he later left to join the UDP. Thus, two strong regional figures competed against each other, possibly splitting the vote share for the regional parties.

At the same time, fights within the Meghalaya Pradesh Congress Committee (MPCC) – the regional subdivision of the Congress party – preceded the final announcement of the renewed candidature of sitting MP Vincent Pala, a business tycoon and one of the richest candidates in the entire northeast (*The Northeast Today* 20 April 2014). The All India Congress Committee (AICC) had taken the decision to nominate Pala against the protest of the Meghalayan Chief Minister Mukul Sangma, who together with other leaders of the MPCC accused Pala of backing several independent candidates during the 2013 Assembly elections. The fight over Pala's candidacy exposed a deep division within the MPCC, dividing the party into a Pala fraction, supported by MPCC president DD Lapang, and an anti-Pala fraction, led by Mukul Sangma. Reports and local rumours indicated that some Congress Members of Legislative Assembly (MLA), especially those who had previously felt betrayed by Pala, even backed PBM Basaiawmoit during the Lok Sabha elections. This influenced public discourse as people talked about these issues along the campaign trail, altering the context of campaigning. The split within the MPCC stood as a blatant contradiction to the invocation of unity in diversity used by the party to distinguish itself from the regional parties and the BJP. Thus Congress campaigners were busy underlining the unity of the party and the unity of the Congress became a common mantra during campaigning. Nevertheless, the division within the party took its toll not only because opposition candidates used it as a platform to attack the party and its candidate but also because the MPCC spent a considerable amount of their campaign time with internal meetings or – as a senior party leader put it – with 'smoking the peace pipe'.

Apart from the struggle over the announcement of candidates, central issues highlighted during campaigning centred on the development of the region. While the Congress referred to flagship programmes and implemented projects, the opposing candidates alleged the sitting candidate and ruling Congress government of corruption and non-performance resulting in price rise, slowdown of economic growth, continuing influx of migrants into the state, and the persistence of the inter-state border dispute with Assam. Campaigners also addressed the existing anxiety over changing demographics, playing along the same rhetorical lines which had been used during the ILP agitation to mobilise political support by highlighting outside threat, outside influence, and domination. They broached the issue from different angles varying from locality to locality. In the coal areas of the Jaintia Hills, this got articulated though the issue of Foreign Direct Investments (FDI). The opposition alleged that by allowing FDI, the Congress was responsible for the import of coal from outside the country which directly affected the coal trade in Meghalaya. This was connected to the larger discourse on the need to protect the local population from outside threat and influx, here in the form of coal import, and simultaneously linked to a discussion on the right of self-determination as well as outside interference, here in form of the central government which allowed the FDI. In the Khasi Hills, these issues were invoked by talking about the need to safeguard tribal interests. The Congress campaigner argued for the strengthening of traditional institutions as a means to increase self-governance and to become more independent from the political system of India. Similarly, Basaiawmoit and Paul Lyngdoh invoked the need to protect the 'genuine' or indigenous tribals of Meghalaya. As Karlsson points out, this new category of indigenous tribals brings together two different concepts, (a) the international circulating concept of the Rights of Indigenous People and (b) the affirmative action programmes of the Indian state, e.g. in form of the Sixth Schedule. Thus, this political assertion invoked during campaigning works within the framework of Indian nation-state but also evades its supremacy (Karlsson 2013: 37). In addition, it is connected to the local narrative concerned with outside threat. Thus, the category provides three different frameworks which campaigners can invoke while contesting elections and navigating between the national and regional levels of politics.

Another factor during the elections for the Shillong seat can be seen in religion. In fact, campaigners hardly addressed religious issues directly. It rather played a more subtle role, which can be summed up in four ways: (a) religious rituals were integrated at specific stages of campaigning, e.g. Pala started his election campaign with a prayer meeting attended by his family, supporters, and elders of the Catholic Church at his house in Shillong; (b) the respective church network also worked as mobilising structure. While church elders did not directly ask their community to vote for a specific candidate, Basaiawmoit had lot of supporters in Jaintia Hills who knew him from his association. This made up for the lacking grassroots presence of the KHNAM and the HSPDP in the Jaintia Hills. (c) Religion figured in the form of biblical references and metaphors which especially Basaiawmoit frequently integrated in his addresses to the voters, e.g. speaking of the wolf in sheep's clothing or when referring to his symbol, the candle (Basaiawmoit 2014). (d) Religion played a role in public discourse on elections and denomination was often depicted as influencing voter's decision. As already mentioned, Basaiawmoit had earlier been a Presbyterian priest. Pala, on the other hand, was a Catholic and as such was perceived by the voters as the Catholic candidate. In everyday conversations these were known facts and the basis for positioning both candidates at opposing ends of a spectrum regardless of their party affiliation. Paul Lyngdoh, from a Presbyterian background, seemed to lose out in this spectrum to the authority of Basaiawmoit, the former reverend. While Basaiawmoit linked his connection to the church closely to his engagement for indigenous people, Lyngdoh drew on tribal identity to counter the assumed influence of religion on elections. Urging voters not to be swayed by misuse of religion, he put tribal identity as factor for voting-decision before religious identity, stating that 'I come from the Presbyterian Church and my grandfather was a Catholic by religion, but if people question my identity, I will tell them I am a Khasi, son of the Hynniewtrep land' (Paul Lyngdoh as cited in the *Shillong Times* 8 April 2014).

In the end, it became clear that it had been a close run between Basaiawmoit and Pala, leaving Paul Lyngdoh far off. Pala managed to win the Shillong seat but was left with a much smaller margin than in 2009. As predicted, the division among the regional parties had been crucial for Pala's win. At the first sight, the decrease of Pala's winning margin could have been seen as indicating an increasing dominance of regional parties. Looking closer at the votes' share revealed that this could rather be ascribed to the performance of the BJP, who did not compete in the 2009 elections but secured over 15 per cent of the votes in 2014. Comparing the combined percentage of votes of the two strong regional candidates of 2009 and 2014, it becomes obvious that these parties also lost shares of their votes (2009: combined 46.22 per cent; 2014: 44.48 per cent; Election Commission of India 2009; Election Commission of India 2014). The strong performance of the BJP, who did not succeed to secure a single seat in the 2013 Assembly elections, came as surprise to the other parties. The BJP swept votes especially in the urban areas of Shillong, former Congress strongholds with a large non-tribal population. This can be attributed to the demographic context, in which the anti-outsider rhetoric of regional parties did not work well and to the national 'Modi Wave', which through TV, social media, and newspapers reached especially the urban areas of Shillong. Overall, the outcome indicated a further fragmentation of votes, mirroring the disunity within the parties while the strengthening of the BJP referred to changing constellations at the national level.

The Tura seat: David vs. Goliath

The Lok Sabha elections in the insurgency affected Garo Hills were preceded by a deteriorating law and order situation. Due to ongoing negotiations between the government and the Achik National Volunteer Council (ANVC) – a militant group aiming at carving a homeland for the Garo people out of Meghalaya and Assam – the elections for the Garo Hills Autonomous District Councils had been postponed and the Lok Sabha elections were held amidst tight security measures. Insurgency is nothing new to the region, where the influence and violence of the ANVC culminated between 1995 and 2003, but it had calmed down after a peace treaty was initiated in 2004. In frustration over the slow pace of the peace process, a fraction broke away from the ANVC, calling itself the Garo National Liberation Army (GNLA). In 2012, the GNLA was declared a terrorist organisation and subsequently banned. In retribution, GNLA militants started to attack security forces and turned the Garo Hills into a battlefield. Over the last five years, more and more armed groups have broken away from the ANVC, making the situation even more complex. Extortion, kidnapping, intimidation, and random killings have increased over the last years, leaving the population, who not only have to fear insurgency groups but also endure massive counterinsurgency operations, under the impression that militants are the actual rulers in the Garo Hills. The situation raised questions regarding the power of the Congress government in the state and led to allegations of a strong militant-politician nexus as the root of the problem (Choudhury and Khan 2014). Therefore the 2014 elections took place at a sensitive point in time in the Garo Hills.

The elections for the Tura seat were a head-on fight between only two candidates, P.A. Sangma (NPP) and Daryl William Cheran Momin (INC). The contest between the two candidates soon got termed as a fight between David and Goliath, as the twenty-seven-year-old Momin, who had just entered politics, had to compete against the veteran political leader P.A. Sangma (Mukhim 2014). Although the former Lok Sabha speaker Sangma had won the Tura seat eight times before and was famous for his personal appeal, grassroots connectivity, and the ability to draw support, his candidature came as a surprise. He had announced earlier that he would not contest for the seat held by his daughter Agatha Sangma and observers had assumed the sixty-seven year old would withdraw from active national politics. Agatha Sangma explained the decision of her father to contest the Tura seat by referring to the law and order situation and the lack of governance, which required a seasoned and strong leader. She also claimed that the BJP, a coalition partner of the NPP at the national level, wanted P.A. Sangma back in active politics due to his status as a big leader from the northeast (Ghosh 2014; Loiwal and Laitphlang 2014). In contrast, Momin, who had just returned from Australia, where he had completed his Master of Business Administration, had only quite recently joined politics and was relatively unknown in the region. He had been handpicked by Congress Vice President Rahul Gandhi, to whom he appealed due to his status as youth and as a newcomer to politics. In addition, Momin was not only said to be close to the family of the present Chief Minister Mukul Sangma but could also invoke the legacy of his grandfather Williamson Sangma, Meghalaya's first Chief Minister and leading Figure of the APHLC.

Despite P.A. Sangmas's strong status, observers expected a tough fight – mostly because they considered the fight to be actually between P.A. Sangma and his former apprentice Mukul Sangma. The Chief Minister acted as a political mentor to Momin and spent most of the campaign time in the Tura constituency.[8] His absence from any campaigns in the Shillong constituency was interpreted by some as sign of his open conflict with Pala and as evidence for the split within the MPCC. Mukul Sangma on his side referred to his status as Garo and his influence in the Garo Hills, where a large part of his family and clan is based, to explain his focus on the Garo Hills during campaigning. The importance of his status as a leader from the Garo Hills for the campaign is noteworthy. As previously mentioned, political leadership in the Garo Hills is restricted to a few families and there have been not as many leaders competing for power as in the Khasi Hills (interview with Mukhim 13 March 2014). The rise of Mukul Sangma to an established leader from the Garo Hills was a substantial threat to the former dominance of P.A. Sangma, who had to accept a poll debacle with his newly founded NPP in the 2013 Legislative Assembly elections. Against this background, the challenges for both candidates appeared to be even and there were no clear predictions regarding the election outcome for the Tura constituency.

Since Tura appeared to be a swinging seat, the campaigns started with much more noise and attention than in the Shillong constituency. Rahul Gandhi launched the campaign for Momin in Resubelpara, the headquarter of the newly created North Garo Hills District which had been an election promise by the Congress nine years ago. He spoke about past achievements of the UPA government and various flagship programmes, highlighted the need for unity, and referred to the legacy of Momin's grandfather as well as his youth and potential to initiate change. Basically, this set the tone for the Congress's campaign in the Garo Hills. P.A. Sangma also started his campaign in the new North Garo Hills District but focused on the bad law and order situation and the failure of the government to deal with the insurgency. Opposing Momin, the NPP emphasised the experience and leadership qualities of P.A. Sangma, which would be necessary to lead the Garo Hills out of the existing chaos. In addition, P.A. Sangma attacked the Congress and especially Mukul Sangma for recent scams and alleged nexus with militant outfits, making him responsible for the current law and order situation.

Notably, both campaigns underscored the need to protect tribal identity, although they argued in very different ways. P.A. Sangma supported the notion for a separate Garoland state, stating that 'I understand the inner feelings of my tribesmen (Garo) for a separate Garoland state and, therefore, I accepted to make Garoland my main election plank apart from other critical issues in terms of infrastructure and social development' (IANS 2014). Simultaneously, he projected the creation of a separate state as the only solution for the ongoing conflict. As the NPP was in an alliance with the BJP, P.A. Sangma stated that a new BJP government at the centre would appoint a second state reorganisation committee in view of various groups demanding smaller states (One India 2014). Subsequently, movements such as the Garo Hills State Movement Committee (GHSMC), a conglomeration of several Garo organisations demanding Garoland, supported P.A. Sangma by asking the electorate to cast their vote in favour of the candidate with the Garoland demand as part of his manifesto. In contrast, Congress campaigners depicted the topic of Garoland as 'just an election issue to woo voters' (IANS 2014). To emphasise the pro-tribal politics of the Congress, Mukul Sangma referred to past achievements benefitting tribals, especially highlighting the Sixth Schedule of the constitution as a means for protecting tribal identity: 'You own the land, government has no ownership. You have rights over forest and natural resources. This was guaranteed by the visionary leaders of the Congress' (Mukul Sangma as cited in the *Shillong Times* 28 March 2014). Nevertheless, the constant focus on past achievements by the Congress as well as the NPP rhetoric on Garoland could not cover the lack of issues during campaigning.

With only two aspirants, Tura was the constituency with the least number of candidates in the 2014 elections. Combined with an absence of issues, the campaign for the Tura seat had become a battle of personalities (Sarma 2014). These may be the reasons for the fact that the constituency had the highest share of voters opting for the 'None of the Above Option' (NOTA) in the whole of India (Simha 2014; *The Economic Times* May 16, 2014).[9] Nevertheless, P.A. Sangma managed to win with 52 per cent of the votes against Momin who secured 44 per cent (Election Commission of India 2014). The NPP performed well in the Garo strongholds. In addition they also managed to secure a large share of votes in the constituencies with a large concentration of non-Garos such as Phulbari where, accordingly to Rajesh Dev, voters look 'upon Mukul Sangma as a person with multiple ethnic identity and, possibly, loyalty' (Dev 2007: 259). After the election, Mukul Sangma attributed the loss of the Congress to the absence of a third candidate who could have split the votes just as in the Shillong constituency (interview with Mukul Sangma, 2014). Since the Tura constituency differs from the Shillong constituency especially in the regard of the role and importance of individual personalities, the question whether a third candidate would have broken into P.A. Sangma's dominance instead of taking away further votes from the INC is debatable. P.A. Sangma interpreted the outcome as a confirmation of his status as a leader in the region, respectively explaining the loss in the 2013 Legislative Assembly elections with voters' confusion over the new party symbol (interview in 2015).[10]

Conclusion: status quo or change ahead?

The specific dynamics of competitive politics in Meghalaya can be traced to colonial policies introduced for administration purposes, post-independence Affirmative Action programmes and modes of political mobilisation of the last decades. The interlinkage of these processes turned tribal identity into a key category of the socio-political discourse in the state and created the current political conditions distinguishing Meghalaya from other Indian states. In addition, the 2014 Lok Sabha elections were preceded by unrests in the state, concerned with protecting the rights of the Khasi-Jaintias and respectively of the Garos against outside domination and interference. This figured during election campaigns, as the rhetoric around safeguarding indigenous tribals became a common platform for campaigning for all parties in the two constituencies. The focus on the category of indigenous tribals during campaigning can be seen as an approach of candidates to tackle the problem of having to manoeuvre in a blurred space between national and regional politics. By using this concept, they not only invoked the regional narrative characterised by an anxiety of demographics but also operated within the larger affirmative action framework of the Indian state as well as transgressing it by drawing on the international circulating discourse on indigenous rights. In the Shillong constituency this was accompanied by religion as another important but subtle factor for campaigning. Although it is hard to assess as to which degree religion had an impact on the election outcome, it influenced the public discourse and provided a counterweight to the focus on ethno-regional issues. In contrast, elections in the Tura constituency can be best understood as a fight of personalities, drawing on their capacities as Garo leaders, in which the candidate with the stronger track record as an experienced leader defeated the younger candidate drawing on his youth appeal. Although, the status quo was retained – with Congress keeping the Shillong seat and the Tura seat remaining within the family of P.A. Sangma – Meghalayan politics with all its peculiarities also followed some of the national trends of the 2014 elections: the split within the MPCC reflected the general condition of the grand old party, just as AAP remained insignificant, and, although it would be too early to speak of a Modi wave, the BJP performed surprisingly strong.

Overall, the Congress lost several seats in the northeastern states, while the BJP made some major inroads. The Congress could keep his hold in Manipur and Mizoram but lost one seat in Arunachal Pradesh and several seats in Assam to the BJP. Modi had campaigned extensively in Assam, mainly targeting the local, conservative Hindu community. He attracted huge gatherings, talking about the government's neglect towards the region. However, just as Rahul Gandhi and other visiting national leaders, he remained auspiciously silent on critical issues like the Armed Forces (Special Powers) Act (AFSPA) or human rights violations. Nevertheless, Modi's efforts paid off and the BJP, who formerly held only three seats, could secure seven seats in Assam, doubling its tally from four to eight seats in all northeastern states taken together. Thus, the BJP, who also benefitted from regional parties splitting up minority votes, secured the same amount of seats in the region as the Congress, who held three seats in Assam, two in Manipur, and one each in Arunachal Pradesh, Mizoram, and Meghalaya. In Tripura and Nagaland the status quo was retained, with the two seats of Tripura remaining in the firm grip of the Communist Party of India Marxist (CPI[M]) and the lone seat in Nagaland remaining with the Naga People's Front (NPF). After the election, however, the NPF, who is just like the NPP part of the North-East Regional Political Front (NERPF), extended its support to the NDA coalition (PTI 2014).

Summing it up, the BJP managed to make inroads into some of the northeastern strongholds of the Congress, gaining not only from a weakening Congress but also from the vote splitting between regional parties. In addition, the BJP could secure the support of the regional party front NERPF, whose members the NPP and NPF each secured one seat. Considering that the Congress managed to keep some of its strongholds, it would be an exaggeration to describe the BJP's 2014 success in the region as a saffron wave hitting the northeast. Nevertheless, the BJP performed unexpectedly well in some states and the verdict of the elections heralded changes ahead: due to organisational weakness and leadership problems, the Congress has been increasingly losing its ground in the northeastern states since 2014, while the BJP has been expanding its influence in the region substantially by winning Legislative Assembly elections in Assam and in Tripura and by forming the government together with a coalition of regional parties in Manipur, Arunachal Pradesh, Nagaland, and Meghalaya.

Notes

1 Various scholars have pointed out that, given the extreme local diversity and different historical trajectories, it is problematic to club together this mosaic of communities and local dynamics into one single analytical unit. Using the idea of an alleged uniform northeast as analytical category, thus, bears the risk to overlook the complex nature of local problems (for a more detailed discussion, see Haokip 2011).

2 Regarding the definition of the Scheduled Tribes (STs) the Indian Ministry of Tribal Affairs states: 'According to Article 342 of the Constitution, the Scheduled Tribes are the tribes or tribal communities or part of or groups within these tribes and tribal communities which have been declared as such by the President through a public notification. [. . .] The essential characteristics of these communities are: primitive traits, geographical isolation, distinct culture, shy of contact with community at large, economically backward' (Ministry of Tribal Affairs 2009). Emic usage of the term 'tribe' often echoes the essentialist approach of a bureaucratic category implied in this definition, used to legitimise claims to power and resources (Dev 2004: 4751). In this chapter, the term 'tribal/non-tribal' is understood from a constructive perspective and as such considered as a political resource (compare Lentz 1995; Büschges and Pfaff-Czarnecka 2007).

3 While the Khasi and Jaintia are closely linked by religion, language, and social and political habits and therefore often described as one group, the Hynniewtrep people, the Garo, differ in most aspects. A common trait of all three communities is the matrilineal kinship system. This feature is often emphasised to mark their cultural difference to other groups and especially to north and south India. Apart from these groups there are a number of other tribal groups (5 per cent), such as the Rabha, Koch, Hajong, and Karbi, as well as non-tribal minorities, like the Bengali, Assamese, Nepali, Bihari, and a so-termed Muslim community (Karlsson 2011: 27; Census 2001).

4 This was easier to communicate to the public back home, where evolutionist theory, world fairs, human zoos, and a romantic imagination of the noble savage influenced public discourse.

5 Speaking on Assam and Tripura, Sanjoy Hazarika describes how 'the movement of people for economic and environmental reasons [has been] reshaping and transforming the demographic, ethnic, linguistic and religious profile of large parts of the population [and] stirred a potent brew of hatred, suspicion and fear' (Hazarika 2000: 7). Similar trends can be found in Meghalaya. Simultaneously, it can be argued that different affirmative action programmes – such as the reservation of fifty-five out of sixty seats in the Legislative Assembly for ST members or the reservation quota regarding government jobs (40 per cent Garos, 40 per cent Khasis and Jaintias, 5 per cent other STs and SCs) – have even strengthened the tendency to draw differences along tribal lines as they provide incentives for invoking a specific tribal identity.

6 In this chapter, the term 'regional party' is used to describe parties which mostly participate in elections only in one state and, simultaneously, are based on a state or region-specific agenda, e.g. the National People's Party (NPP), which was launched as explicit tribal-centric party just prior to the 2013 LA elections, claiming to protect the rights of the indigenous people of Meghalaya. In Meghalaya, regional parties started to make inroads into politics first through participating in local politics. Consequently, the boundaries between local pressure groups such as the Khasi Student Union and certain regional political parties, e.g. Khun Hyinniewtrep National Awakening Movement (KHNAM), are often blurred (McDuie-Ra 2007: 118).

7 Public discourse focused on mainly three candidates: PBM Basaiawmoit (IND), Paul Lyngdoh (UDP), and Vincent Pala (INC). Apart from this there was one candidate from the Indian Communist Party as well as one candidate from the newly founded Meghalayan wing of the Aam Admi Party, and two independent candidates. As the BJP has played a negligible role in Meghalayan politics, their candidate Shibun Lyngdoh was mentioned during discussions but rarely depicted as a serious threat to the other candidates.
8 Though both have the same surname, their families are not related as Sangma is a common name in the Garo Hills.
9 Four per cent voted NOTA in the Tura constituency. The NOTA option allows voters to express their disapproval of all candidates. Nevertheless, the NOTA option has no impact on the election results, as the candidate getting the most of the remaining votes will be declared winner even if the maximum number of votes are cast for NOTA.
10 Since writing this chapter, P.A. Sangma passed away on 4 March 2016. He was succeeded by his son Conrad Sangma, who won the by-election to the Tura constituency in 2016 and has become Chief Minister of Meghalaya in 2018.

Bibliography

Basaiawmoit, P. B. M. 2014. Election appeal and songs published by candidate himself.

Büschges, Christian and Johanna Pfaff-Czarnecka. 2007. 'Einleitung: Ethnizität als politische Ressource', in Christian Büschges and Joanna Pfaff-Czarnecka (eds.), *Die Ethnisierung des Politischen: Identitätspolitiken in Lateinamerika, Asien und den USA*, pp. 9–18. Frankfurt a. M.: Campus.

Census of India. *Meghalaya. Data Highlights: The Scheduled Tribes.* 2001. http://censusindia.gov.in/Tables_Published/SCST/dh_st_meghalaya.pdf (accessed on September 10, 2012).

Choudhury, Ratnadip and Said Khan. 2014. 'Nightmare in Garo hills', *Tehelka Magazine*, 11(36). www.tehelka.com/meghalaya-garo-hills-indias-new-terror-capital/ (accessed on April 2, 2015).

Deshpande, Ashwini. 2013. *Affirmative Action in India*. New Delhi: Oxford University Press.

Dev, Rajesh. 1999. 'General Elections 1996, 1998: Community Loyalties and Regional Outlook', *Economic and Political Weekly*, 34(34/35): 2481–2485.

———. 2007. 'Ethno-Regional Identity and Political Mobilization in Meghalaya: Democratic Discourse in a Tribal State', in Ramashray Roy and Paul Wallace (eds.), *India's 2004 Elections: Grass-Roots and National Perspective*, pp. 240–266. New Delhi, Thousand Oaks, London: SAGE Publications.

Election Commission of India. 1991–1999. *Election Results – Full Statistical Reports*. http://eci.nic.in/eci_main1/ElectionStatistics.aspx (accessed on September 10, 2012).

———. 2009. *Constituency Wise Detailed Results*. General Elections, 2009 (15th Lok Sabha). http://eci.nic.in/eci_main/archiveofge2009/Stats/VOLI/25_ConstituencyWiseDetailedResult.pdf (accessed on September 10, 2012).

———. 2014. *Constituency Wise Detailed Results*. Election Commission of India, General Elections, 2014 (16th Lok Sabha). http://eci.nic.in/eci_main/archiveofge2014/33%20-%20Constituency%20wise%20detailed%20result.pdf (accessed on September 10, 2012).

'The Game of Throne: The War in Every 5 Years, the Lok Sabha Elections'. 2014. *The Northeast Today*, April 20, pp. 24–30.

Ghosh, Shubham. 2014. 'PA Sangma Back in Action, to Contest From Tura', *Oneindia*, March 11. www.oneindia.com/india/pa-sangma-back-action-contest-from-tura-1410132-lse.html (accessed on May 5, 2015).

Haokip, Thongkholal. 2011. 'Conceptualising Northeast India: A Discursive Analysis on Diversity', *Bangladesh e-journal of Sociology*, 8(2): 109–120. www.bangladeshsociology.org/BEJS%208.2%20Conceptualising%20Northeast%20India.pdf (accessed on January 29, 2013).

———. 2014. 'Northeast to the Centre', *Indian Express*, April 7, p. 10.

Hazarika, Sanjoy. 2000. *Rites of Passage: Border Crossings, Imagined Homelands, India's East and Bangladesh*. New Delhi, New York: Penguin Books.

IANS. 2014. 'PA Sangma Bats for Smaller State', *OneIndia*, April 4. http://wwaw.oneindia.com/india/tura-candidate-pa-sangma-bats-for-smaller-states-lse-1424397.html (accessed on May 5, 2015).

Karlsson, Bengt. 2011. *Unruly Hills: Nature and Nation in India's Northeast*. New Delhi: Orient Blackswan.

———. 2013. 'The Social Life of Categories: Affirmative Actions and the Trajectories of the Indigenous', *Focaal-Journal of Global and Historical Anthropology*, 65: 33–41.

Lentz, Carola. 1995. '"Tribalism" and Ethnicity in Africa: A Review of Four Decades of Anglophone Research', *Cahiers des Sciences humaines*, 31(2): 303–328.

Loiwal, Manogya and David Laitphlang. 2014. 'Former Lok Sabha Speaker P. A. Sangma to Contest From Tura', *Indiatoday*, March 11. http://indiatoday.intoday.in/story/former-lok-sabha-speaker-p-a-sangma-to-contest-polls-from-tura/1/347888.html (accessed on May 5, 2015).

'Lok Sabha Polls 2014: Meghalaya Has the Highest Percentage of Voters Pushing NOTA', *The Economic Times*, May 16. http://articles.economictimes.indiatimes.com/2014-05-16/news/49898617_1_nota-button-nota-option-election-official (accessed on May 5, 2015).

McDuie-Ra, Duncan. 2007. 'Civil Society and Human Security in Meghalaya: Identity, Power and Inequalities', Ph.D. dissertation, University of New South and Wales, School of Social Scienes and International Studies.

Mohrem, H.H. 2014. 'The Year of Two Elections', *The Shillong Times*, Janurary 6. www.theshillongtimes.com/2014/01/06/2014-the-year-of-two-elections/ (accessed on May 5, 2015).

Mukhim, Patricia. 2012. 'Other Side of the Inner Line Permit', *The Shillong Times*, October 5. www.theshillongtimes.com/2012/10/05/other-side-of-the-inner-line-permit/ (accessed on May 5, 2015).

———. 2014. 'In Tura It Is David vs Goliath', *The Shillong Times*, March 5. www.theshillongtimes.com/2014/03/21/in-tura-its-david-versus-goliath/ (accessed on May 5, 2015).

'Mukul Espouses Secularism; Purno "Promises" Garoland'. 2014. *The Shillong Times*, March 28. www.theshillongtimes.com/2014/03/28/mukul-espouses-secularism-purno-promises-garoland/ (accessed on May 5, 2015).

PTI. 2014. 'North East Regional Political Front Extends Support to NDA', *The Hindu*, May 15. www.thehindu.com/news/national/north-east-regional-political-front-extends-support-to-nda/article6011966.ece (accessed on May 5, 2015).

Sarma, Dhiraj Kumar. 2014. 'LS Elections in 2014: Predictions for the NE', *Eclectic Northeast*, April, pp. 26–33.

Simha, Vijay. 2014. '15 Small Facts That Say Big Things About the Election Modi Won', *Sify.com*, November 26. www.sify.com/mobile/news/15-small-facts-that-say-big-things-about-the-election-modi-won-news-columns-ol0kkvdidgegj.html (accessed on May 5, 2015).

'UDP Candidate Takes a Dig at BJP Bashers'. 2014. *Shillong Times*, April 8. www.theshillongtimes.com/2014/04/08/udp-candidate-takes-a-dig-at-bjp-bashers/.

14 Electoral politics in Jammu and Kashmir (J&K) and the problem of communal polarisation

Aijaz Ashraf Wani

Introduction

The Jammu and Kashmir (J&K) state, it may be mentioned, is in the words of Karan Singh ' a wholly artificial creation' (Nehru 1997:589). It is a 'created state,'[1] in that it came into existence by a deliberate act on the part of British imperialism. For their colonial interests, the British clubbed three diverse regions – Jammu, Kashmir, and Ladakh – with no commonality in geography, history, ethnicity, culture, and economy together and handed it over to their favourite, Gulab Singh – a Jammu Dogra supporter of the Raj and the male heirs of his body (Pannikar1989). This arrangement was honoured by the successive governments of Independent India for larger national interests. However, the 'created' rather than natural or evolved nature of the state created its own problems expressed in the competing agitational politics of sub-nationalism – regional and sub-regional autonomy, separate statehood for regions, complete merger with India, right to self-determination, etc. – problems with which the Indian state and the governments of J&K have remained confronted with ever since the abolition of princely order.

Since the J&K state is a colonial construct bringing together areas with distinct history, culture, geography, ethnicity, and so on, plurality of politics has remained the hallmark of the J&K state, and this plurality is essentially the result of cultural diversities that crisscross the geographical and cultural landscape of Kashmir. The state of J&K lies on the northern fringes of the Indian subcontinent. In 1947, before 45 per cent of its territory became the northernmost state of the Indian Union, the area of this largest princely state of British India was 222,797 sq. km. The three main administrative entities within the princely state of J&K included the province of Jammu, with the Siwaliks and Outer

Hills, which has been the heartland of Dogra control in the Punjab; the province of Kashmir, a structural basin that lies between the Pir Panjal and the Himadri, purchased by Dogras from the British in 1846; and the provinces of Ladakh and Baltistan, region of greater Himalayas, the former conquered by the Dogras in 1834 and the latter in 1840. Similarly, there were other distinct political entities which, as a result of their geographical location, had to formulate some type of political relationship with the princely state, like the Gilgit Agency, which the British attached to J&K for political convenience in 1889, and which the Dogra state leased back to them in 1935. Similarly, Poonch was brought under the formal control of J&K in 1936 (Rai:2004).

The J&K state is not only a conglomerate of three distinct regions – Jammu, Kashmir, and Ladakh – but there are regions within regions marked off from one another by geography, culture, and history. Though these regions were integrated into one single political entity in 1846, the politics of regional and sub-regionalism continues to be stubbornly informed by their respective histories and cultures – thus the resistance against hegemony and the demand for sub-regional autonomies and Hill Councils. The state represents a diversity based on region, religion, caste, and ethnicity. The dynamics of regional and sub-regional assertions lies in the overlapping, multiple, and layered identities, which determine the nature of politics in the state as well.

J&K is not only religiously diverse, with three major religions of South Asia having their followers in the state, but there are regional, cultural, tribal, caste-based, and linguistic diversities as well. The three major regions of the state are not only culturally and socially diverse, but they are also diverse in terms of their geographical terrains and their historical roots. Region is an important marker of the identity in the state and cuts across the religious continuity. Muslims as well as Hindus of one region not only perceive themselves as different from their co-religionists of the other regions but also emphasise their regional identity.

These diversities in the state are so placed that a complex social and political environment is generated. There is no clear-cut context of 'majority' and 'minority'(Chowdhary 2010:5). Majority in one context becomes minority in another. For example, despite being part of the largest religious group of the state, the Kashmiri Muslims perceive themselves as a minority in the context of the larger reality of India. Similarly, the Hindus of Jammu and the Buddhists of Ladakh, although constitute majority in their respective regions, when viewed in the context of the Muslim majority character of the state, they perceive themselves as a minority. This minority sentiment of the two regions is also viewed strongly in the context of Kashmir-centric political and economic power context of the state (ibid).

While Kashmir made a transition from autocratic system to democracy in 1947, the manner in which electoral politics unfolded in the state undermined, for most period, the very basic features of a democratic polity. For a long time, the state remained under one-party dominance of either the National Conference or the Congress. What is more important to is the fact that this dominance was ensured by the continuous rigging of elections and depriving any space to oppositional politics. Furthermore, communalisation of politics around religious lines remained a feature of the state politics, which got the state divided on religious and regional lines. However, the communal divide that the state witnessed during the Parliamentary and Assembly elections of 2014 is unprecedented. This chapter attempts to analyse the rise of communal forces in the politics of Jammu and Kashmir (J&K). Making an analysis of the 2014 Lok Sabha election and the 2014 State Assembly elections, this chapter attempts to highlight how this communalisation of politics played out in the state right from its inception and how it reached its climax during the 2014 elections.

Historical background

Before analysing the 2014 Parliamentary and State Assembly elections, a bit of electoral history, especially since 1987, when the state started getting into the grip of insurgency, will be helpful in understanding the issues of the changing nature of electoral politics, separatism, and communalism in the state. In 1951 the NC government began preparations to convene a Constituent Assembly in Srinagar despite the pressures from the UN against the decision.[2] A seventy-five-member Constituent Assembly was elected, theoretically on the basis of universal adult franchise. NC 'won' all seventy-five seats uncontested, 'the first instance of Indian-administered Kashmir's sorry history of utterly farcical elections' (Bose 2003: 55). There was no question of anyone opposing NC in the Valley, where Abdullah was running a virtual party-state. But no contest was permitted even in Jammu where the Praja Parishad, a 'Hindu nationalist' group, was arbitrarily prevented from participating in the polls. The manner in which this election was conducted made a mockery of any pretence of a democratic process and set a grim precedent for future 'free and fair elections' in J&K (Bose 2003: 55). This process of denying democracy continued with full backing of the centre, leading to the turning of semi-loyal opposition within the Valley into a completely disloyal opposition and, in Jammu and Ladakh, mobilisation on communal lines leading to demands of a complete merger with the Indian by the hindus of Jammu Union by Jammu and Union Territory states by Buddhists of Ladakh. (Korbel:226–37; Bazaz 2009:487–502; Puri:96 96–98; Beek 2004)

In 1987 Jammu and Kashmir witnessed the highly rigged election jointly fought by the NC–Congress combine against the Muslim United Front (MUF) an eleven-party alliance including Jamiat-e-Islami (Gauhar: 119; Jagmohan 1991: 163). The NC–Congress won thirty-eight and twenty-four respectively; BJP, two, while MUF won four seats despite credible expectations of doing better. The flawed election became the immediate cause of the insurgency against the Indian state that engulfed Kashmir valley but spread to the Jammu region also. Rebels, who were drawing mass support in Kashmir, were also getting active support from Pakistan (this gave the insurgency movement a pro-Pakistan Muslim movement character). The insurgency was at its peak during 1990–1999, with Pakistan pumping in better-trained militants in large numbers. The Armed Forces Special Powers Act and Disturbed Areas Act, giving enormous powers to the army, were extended to the state. Democracy remained in suspension and the state was put under governor's rule for the six years. The insurgency was not communal in the sense that it was not directed against the non-Muslims of the state but against the Indian state. However, with the killing of some Kashmiri Pandits, the insurgency got communalised. The killing were finally exploited by the then Governor Jagmohan, who faciltiated the mass migration of Kashmiri Pandits from the Valley in 1990.

In 1996 after having crushed insurgency with full military might the electoral process was restored, and Parliamentary elections were held in the state in May 1996 and State Assembly elections in September–October 1996. The National Conference returned to power with a thumping majority, winning fifty-seven out of seventy-five seats, while BJP also increased its tally from two in 1987 to eight seats in the 1996 Assembly elections. However, there were reports of malpractices and coercion during elections by security forces, especially in rural areas. The NC formed the government and Farooq Abdullah became the Chief Minister, thus ended the seven years of governor's rule. In 1999 the BJP-led National Democratic Alliance (NDA) formed a government at the centre, and NC became NDA's ally at the centre. This further weakened Farooq Abdullah and his party's position within the state because BJP is the frontrunner in its opposition to the special status enshrined in Article 370 of the Indian Constitution for the state of Jammu and Kashmir. The National Conference government completed its term in 2002 and fresh elections were held. NC performed badly as its seats declined from fifty-seven in 1996 to twenty-eight in 2002. The newly formed People's Democratic Party (PDP) established in 1999 who came with a new vocabulary of 'healing touch' and 'peace with diginity' won sixteen seats, Congress won twenty, and BJP also reduced to one from eight in 1996. Finally NC was kept out of power and a PDP-Congress coalition government was formed with PDP patron Mufti Mohammad Sayeed as Chief Minister for the first three years. During the coalition era the mainstream politics got expanded considerably, and state society relationships were restored as there was fall in the militancy related incidents. The main focus of the coalition was to restore dignity and ensure peace and development of the people. However, in 2008, the PDP–Congress coalition led by Ghulam Nabi Azad transferred forest land to the Shri Amaranth Shrine Board (SASB) (charged with the responsibility of ensuring a smooth *yatra* of Hindus to the holy cave) at the Baltal Area of Sonmarg to erect a pre-fabricated temporary structure for pilgrims during the yatra. The Chief Executive Officer of the Board asserted that the land has been permanently transferred to SASB. This raised the apprehensions that the move was aimed at changing the 'demography character' of the state. To resist the order, the separatists (Geelani faction, PDP was also accused of fuelling the protests and labelled as the party preaching 'soft separatism') urged people to hold protests and demonstrations till the order was revoked, this led to the unprecedented civil protests and pro-independence uprising against the controversial order. The order was revoked by the Chief Minister Ghulam Nabi Azad before PDP withdrew its support to him. However, the move led to the counter protests in Jammu, as the BJP and other like-minded parties perceived it as an insult on 'Hindu sentiments' and mobilised people for the restoration of the original order. The situation got communalised to the extent that there was a boycott of trade between the two regions. Rekha Chowdhary writes:

> In both the regions, the agitation brought in focus the radical elements who sought to mobilize people around the emotive issues. In Kashmir, people were mobilized by the Geelani-led Hurriyat conference (as well as by PDP) around the fear of demographic change (the fear that by systematic efforts the Muslim-majority character of the state will be changed) and in Jammu the mobilization took place around the religious sentiments of Hindus (supposedly hurt by the revocation of the Land order).
>
> (Chowdhary 2008: 6)

In 2008 the elections for the state Legislative Assembly were due and subsequently were held in seven phases from 17 November 2008 to 24 December 2008. The elections, like in 2002, produced a fractured mandate. NC emerged as the single largest party with twenty-eight seats; PDP increased its tally to twenty-one from sixteen in 2002. However, BJP gained as it won eleven seats compared to just one in 2002. Congress won seventeen against twenty-one in 2002, and others got eleven seats. Since no political party was in a position to form the government of its own and, in the light of recent conflict between PDP and Congress, the stage was set for yet another coalition government, however, this time between National Conference and Congress. Accordingly, serious debates started between the NC and Congress leaders to work out the modalities of the coalition: the two parties reached to a consensus on 2 January 2009. Unlike the previous coalition that was based on rotational policy of the Chief Minister, the new coalition decided that there will be no rotational Chief Minister and NC President Omar Abdullah was given the charge of the top post for a full six years. (Accordingly Omar Abdullah was sworn-in as the CM of Jammu and Kashmir on 5 Jan 2009.) It is pertinent to mention that in the 2009 Parliamentary elections BJP failed to win any seat even in the Jammu region, forget Kashmir.

The 2014 Parliamentary election in Jammu and Kashmir (J&K)

The Parliament election in 2014 took place in Jammu and Kashmir (J&K) after the 2010 mass uprising. Seen a a semi-final before the upcoming Assembly elections, all political parties nominated their big guns to contest the elections.[3] The pre-poll alliance between the National Conference (hereafter NC) and Congress made the contest directly between Congress and BJP in Jammu and Ladakh and also between the NC and the Peoples Democratic Party (hereafter PDP) in Kashmir. The six Parliamentary constituencies – three of Kashmir valley (Anantnag, Baramulla, and Srinagar), two of Jammu (Jammu and Udhampur), and one of Ladakh (Ladakh) – went to polls in five phases, with all the sitting MPs losing their seats and National Conference and Congress getting replaced by the Bhartiya Janata Party (hereafter BJP) and People's Democratic Party (PDP). The National Conference earlier represented the three Parliamentary constituencies of the Kashmir valley, while the Congress represented two seats of the Jammu, and the one of Ladakh was represented by an independent. Congress and National Conference went in this election under a pre-poll alliance.

Under this seat-sharing arrangement the Congress got Jammu-Poonch and Kathua-Udhampur-Doda and Ladakh Parliamentary constituencies, the other coalition partner National Conference (NC) contested from Srinagar, Anantnag, and Baramulla Parliamentary constituencies, respectively.

Analysis of issues in Parliamentary elections 2014 and mobilization strategies

The central issues over which the political parties tried to woo voters in their favour were varied in nature – ranging from regional issues to general issues. Ruling coalition partners (Congress–National Conference) mobilisation strategy revolved around attacking BJP's prime ministerial candidate Narendra Modi and his party's agenda, which they described as 'communal and divisive'. At the same time, they also sought votes from the people on the basis of the 'good work done during their term'. Chief Minister Omar Abdullah while addressing election rallies in various parts of the Poonch and Rajouri districts said, 'There is no Modi wave in the country particularly in the Jammu and Kashmir state. All assertions in this regard circulated by the BJP were a mere hoax'. While hitting out at Narendra Modi, BJP's prime ministerial candidate Omar Abdullah said 'a person (Modi) who had equated death of Muslims in 2002 Gujarat riots with the killing of canines cannot deliver justice. He lacks traits to head a pluralistic society like India' (*The Hindustan Times* 1 April 2014). He urged people to vote for the coalition candidate as the 'all round development, massive economic upliftment and peace that has taken place in the state during the last five years owes a lot to UPA government' (ibid). Congress candidate for the Udhampur-Doda Parliamentary constituency Ghulam Nabi Azad accused BJP for propagating the policy of divide and rule. While addressing election rallies in the Kathua district he said, 'Congress party is connected to people at the grassroots which is evident after the incorporation of 73rd amendment in J&K Panchayati Raj Act, 1989. UPA introduced Food Security Bill which ensures two meals to every citizen of the country'. Taking a dig at BJP and other parties he stated 'BJP and other parties only know "divide and rule" provoking people on the basis of religion' (*The Hindustan Times* 7 April 2014).

However, a majority of the opposition political parties raised the issue of corruption and mis-governance of the UPA government at the centre and that of the NC–Congress coalition in the state. Among the key issues that the BJP raised were the failure of the NC–Congress coalition to create development council for Jammu, to provide a one-time rehabilitation package to three lakh refugees, and to grant citizenship rights to West Pakistan refugees in Jammu. In addition, the BJP also promised the removal of regional disparity in the state as its top priority once the BJP-led National Democratic Alliance (NDA) assumed power in New Delhi. The party also promised to generate a positive debate in the country on the issue of Article 370 regarding whether it has done harm or favour to the state.

In the Kashmir region, the electoral contest was between the NC and the PDP. Banking on the anti-incumbency factor, the PDP chose to raise the issues like the civilian killings in 2009 and 2011, uprisings, and the hanging of Parliament attack convict Afzal Guru, as well as the mis-governance of NC–Congress government. Furthermore, it also targeted the coalition government for having failed in addressing the concerns of the people. During his address in the election rallies in various parts of the Baramulla constituency, Mufti Mohammad Sayeed, the then PDP President, advocated for Indo-Pak peace and argued that the security and stability was dependent upon the regional peace. Taking a dig at the National Conference he said, 'NC has contributed to the worsening of the situation through mis-governance and denial of justice, the party has not learnt any lesson from the tragedies of 2010 unrest' (ibid). In contrast, the coalition government leaders mobilised people around the containment of Modi, or what they call communal or divisive forces, and the people-oriented policies of the Manmohan Singh–led United Progressive Alliance (UPA) government at the centre, of which the NC was an alliance partner. Addressing the joint election rallies in various areas of the Anantnag constituency, both the NC and the Congress leaders targeted BJP's prime ministerial candidate Narendra Modi. For instance, Saifuddin Soz, President of the J&K unit of the Congress party, said, 'Modi represents Nazi mindset, and his vision of India is suffocating; he represents a mindset prevalent in Germany where Jews were massacred and where only Christians were safe' (*The Hindustan Times* 3 April 2014). Addressing the same rally, Dr Farooq Abdullah told the gathering that 'the common goal of coalition is to keep Modi out of power; he accused Modi of having massacred Muslims in Gujarat' (ibid).

Analysis of the overall verdict in J&K election

The six Parliamentary constituencies – three in Kashmir valley (Anantnag, Baramulla, and Srinagar), two in Jammu (Jammu and Udhampur), and one of Ladakh – went to polls in five phases with all the sitting MPs losing their seats and the National Conference (NC) and the Congress party being replaced by the BJP and the PDP. The National Conference earlier represented the three Parliamentary constituencies of the Kashmir valley, whereas the two seats of the Jammu were represented by the Congress, and the Ladakh seat was represented by an independent. As compared to the 2009 Parliamentary elections, there was a clear increase of voting percentage in 2014 elections (see Figure 14.1).

The increase in voter turnout as compared to 2009 was due to the increase of voter turnout in Jammu and Udhampur constituencies where votes were consolidated in favour of the BJP and the Modi factor played an important role. Whereas the Kashmir region voter turnout in different districts was almost same as it was in 2009 elections, voter turnout slightly increased in the Anantnag constituency and decreased in Baramulla Parliamentary segment, while it remained almost same as in 2009 election in Srinagar constituency. However, Jammu and Udhampur showed a significant increase in voter turnout as compared to the 2009 elections. Ladakh Parliamentary segments saw a slightly lower voter turnout as compared to the 2009 elections (Table 14.1).

The alliance partners not only suffered defeat, but their vote share also witnessed a considerable decline as compared to the 2009 Parliamentary elections, particularly that of the NC. The party's vote share dipped to 11.1 per cent from 19.1 per cent while the Congress ended up securing 22.9 per cent of the votes as against 24.7 in 2009. The PDP's vote share remained intact at 20.5 per cent while

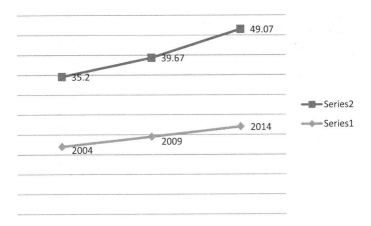

Figure 14.1 Overall voter turnout in J&K in 2004, 2009, and 2014
Note: Figures are in percentages.
Source: Centre for the Study of Developing Societies (CSDS) Data Unit

the BJP's vote share went up from 18.6 per cent in 2009 to 32.4 per cent (Table 14.2). The huge rise in the BJP's vote is largely due to the party's big victories over the Congress in the Jammu region. The party won the Jammu seat by a margin of over two and half lakh votes. The post-poll survey conducted by CSDS indicates a consolidation of Hindu voters behind the BJP in the Jammu region that raised issues like the abrogation of Article 370 and proper representation of aspirations of Jammu region.

Table 14.1 Constituency-wise voter turnout in 2009 and 2014

	Voter turnout (in %)	
	Parliamentary elections 2009	Parliamentary elections 2014
Srinagar	25.85	25.86
Baramulla	41.84	39.14
Anantnag	27.09	28.84
Udhampur	44.88	70.95
Jammu	43.09	67.99
Ladakh	71.86	71.40

Source: Election Commission of India (ECI) data compiled by Centre for the Study of Developing Societies Data Unit

Table 14.2 Jammu and Kashmir Lok Sabha result 2014: change in seat and voter share of parties

Party	Seats contested	Seats won	Seats change from 2009	Vote (%)	Vote change from 2009 (percentage points)
UPA	6	0	−5	33.98	−9.80
Congress	3	0	−2	22.86	−1.80
JKNC	3	0	−3	11.12	−7.99
BJP	6	3	3	32.36	13.75
JKPDP	5	3	3	20.54	0.49
JKNPP	5	0	0	1.22	−1.59
NOTA	6	0	0	0.88	0.88
Other Parties	6	0	−1	11.02	−3.73

Source: Election Commission of India (ECI)

Analysis of the verdict in the Jammu region

The Jammu-Poonch Parliamentary constituency comprises of four districts – namely Jammu, Poonch, Samba, and Rajouri – and twenty Assembly constituencies. The NC–Congress coalition together had thirteen MLAs including four sitting ministers, namely Tara Chand, Raman Bhalla, Sham Lal Sharma, and Shabir Ahmad Khan, in the region. The Congress party was trying to counter the Modi wave through its 'good work' during last twelve years (since 2002). The Kathua-Udhampur-Doda Parliamentary constituency was considered the stronghold of the Congress party as out of seventeen Assembly Constituencies the party had eleven MLAs, while its coalition partner NC was having one MLA from this Parliamentary constituency. In addition to this, the party was banking upon its candidate for the constituency Ghulam Nabi Azad – a very popular figure held in very high esteem owing to the unprecedented development that this area witnessed during his tenure as the state's Chief Minister (2006–2008). Thus, the two factors – Azad's persona and his development work – were believed to help him win. But the Modi wave and anti-incumbency factors appeared too strong to be defeated by these two factors, which is why his BJP rival Dr Jitender Singh was able to win the seat.

The two Parliamentary constituencies of the Jammu region witnessed brisk polling. Jammu-Poonch Parliamentary constituency saw 70.6 per cent turnout, 21 per cent more in comparison to the 2009 Parliamentary election, which had recorded 49.03 per cent voting. The Assembly segment-wise percentage remained as Samba (73.99), Vijaypur (76.21), Nagrota (74.92), Gandhi Nagar (66.30), Jammu East (64.35), Jammu West (64.23), Bishnah (74.92), RS Pura (76.10), Suchetgarh (75.92), Marh (80), Raipur Domana (75.11), Akhnoor (79.62,), and Chhamb (77.21), all in the Samba and Jammu districts; Nowshera (73.15), Darhal (62.12), Rajouri (60.75), and Kalakote (61.65), all in the Rajouri district; and Surankote (59.99), Mendhar (65.49), and Poonch Haveli (70.08), all in the Poonch district (*Daily Excelsior*, 10 April 2014). The Kathua-Udhampur constituency witnessed a high turnout of 72 per cent, an increase of 27.12 from the 2009 Parliamentary elections when only 44.82 per cent of the electorate had exercised their franchise. The constituency-wise voting percentage remained as in Kishtwar, 65.34; in Inderwal, 69.25; in Doda, 71.48; in Bhaderwah, 69.31; in Ramban, 67.26; in Banihal 61.48; in Gulabgarh, 81.53; in Reasi, 79.25; in Gool Arnas, 76.72;

in Udhampur, 75.19; in Chenani, 70.51; in Ramnagar, 66.72; in Bani, 65.79; in Basohli, 65.69; in Kathua 78.28; in Billawar, 71.20; and in Hiranagar, 76.63, respectively (*Daily Excelsior* 18 April 2014).

However, the results proved contrary to the expectations of coalition partners. In the Jammu region the BJP candidates in both the Parliamentary constituencies decimated the Congress. In Jammu-Poonch Parliamentary constituency, BJP's Jugal Kishore defeated his Congress Party rival by a huge margin of 257,282 votes. While Kishore polled 619,995 votes, accounting for 45 per cent of the total votes polled, Madan Lal Sharma of Congress got 362,715 votes, whereas PDP's Yashpal Sharma got 168,554 votes and secured the third position. This Parliamentary constituency comprises of twenty Assembly segments; BJP took lead in fifteen, including all those held by the Congress Ministers. The Congress led in just two segments.

In the Udhampur-Doda Parliamentary constituency, Congress stalwart and Union Minister for Health and Family Welfare Ghulam Nabi Azad failed to enter the Lok Sabha from his home state in his maiden bid. He lost to BJP's first timer, but formidable, political rival, Dr Jitendera Singh by 60,976 votes. Dr. Singh polled 487,369 votes while Azad secured 426,393 votes. The Congress, as expected, got a major chunk of votes from Chenab valley and overall it won eight out of seventeen Assembly segments, falling in this Parliamentary constituency. The Congress secured the lead in Kishtwar, Inderwal, Doda, Bhaderwah, Ramban, Banihal, Gool Arnas, Gulabgarh (Muslim majority populated constituencies). However, votes polled in these eight seats were far less as compared to the nine constituencies falling in the Kathua and Udhampur districts (predominantly Hindu-populated constituencies) of Hiranagar, Billawar, Basholi, Bani, Ramnagar, Chenani, and Reasi, where BJP secured a heavy lead over Congress and Panthers Party.

The BJP's win in Jammu and Ladakh was widely attributed to the Modi wave as Congress fared badly in the Assembly segments held by prominent Congress Ministers, including Deputy Chief Minister Tara Chand (Chhamb), Minister for PHE, Irrigation and Flood Control Sham Lal Sharma (Akhnoor), Housing Minister Raman Bhalla (Gandhi Nagar), Urban Development Minister RigzinJora (Leh), and Cooperatives Minister Dr Manohar Lal Sharma (Billawar). In the Marh constituency also, which is represented by the BJP, but from where Planning and Development Minister Ajay Sadhotra of the NC hailed, the Congress was defeated with a huge margin. Out of thirty-seven Assembly segments in the Jammu region, which comprised two Lok Sabha seats of Jammu-Poonch and Udhampur-Doda Lok Sabha seats, the BJP had leads in twenty-four segments (fifteen in Jammu and nine in Udhampur) while Congress could gain leads only in eleven segments, eight in Udhampur (mostly in the Ramban, Kishtwar, and Reasi districts) and three in the Jammu constituency.

Analysis of the verdict in Kashmir Valley

Since the emergence of the PDP on the state's political scene, the electoral politics, especially in the Valley, has become more intense and competitive. PDP was able to form a government in coalition with Congress after winning sixteen seats in the 2002 Assembly elections and, since then, has been a real competitor and a dominant player in Kashmir. However, in the previous two Parliamentary elections that the PDP fought it was able to win just one seat. National Conference, on the other hand, has historically dominated Kashmir valley when it came to Parliamentary elections. The 2014 Parliamentary election saw the debacle of the incumbent coalition government (NC–Congress) and the NC was routed in the Kashmir region by the PDP and its alliance partner, the Congress party, met the same fate at the hands of the Bharatiya Janata Party (BJP) in the Jammu and Ladakh regions (Table 14.3). National Conference lost the Srinagar Parliamentary seat after three decades. In Srinagar the PDP received 50.6 per cent of the vote share whereas the NC could manage only 37 per cent. This is significant taking into account the fact that Srinagar has historically been the bastion of the National Conference. Also in Anantnag, the PDP got a decisive vote share of 53.4 per cent as against 36 per cent received by the NC.

Table 14.3 Jammu and Kashmir Parliamentary constituency-wise Lok Sabha result in 2014

Parliamentary constituency	Region	Winning party	Winner vote (%)	Runner-up party	Runner-up vote (%)	Victory margin (votes)
Baramulla	Kashmir	JKPDP	37.6	JKNC	31.3	29,219
Srinagar	Kashmir	JKPDP	50.6	JKNC	37.0	42,280
Anantnag	Kashmir	JKPDP	53.4	JKNC	36.0	65,417
Ladakh	Ladakh	BJP	26.4	IND	26.3	36
Udhampur	Jammu	BJP	46.8	Cong	40.9	60,976
Jammu	Jammu	BJP	49.5	Cong	28.9	257,280

Source: Election Commission of India data compiled by Centre for the Study of Developing Societies Data Unit

In Kashmir valley, the PDP won thirty-eight Assembly segments out of forty-six. In Anantnag Constituency PDP won all the sixteen Assembly segments where PDP's Mehbooba Mufti defeated the sitting MP Mehboob Beg of NC by a margin of 65,417 votes. Also in Baramulla the party had the lead in eleven out of fifteen segments of the constituency.

It is important to mention that the alliance partners not only suffered defeat, but their vote share also witnessed considerable decline as compared to the 2009 Parliamentary elections, particularly the NC. The party's vote share dipped to 11.1 per cent from 19.1 per cent. What should be worrying factor for the state's historic party is the fact that its vote share has been consistently declining since 1998 Parliamentary election (Figure 14.2). It has gone down from 36.4 per cent in 1998 to 11.1 per cent in 2014. This is the indication of the fact that the electoral competition in the state has intensified.

One important lesson that this election had for political parties was that they could no longer take voters for granted. With the intensification of electoral competition, voters are also becoming conscious and with more options available to them, the survival of non-performing parties and candidates has become tough. They are evaluating political parties and leaders on the basis of their contribution and performance, which is why the NC–Congress coalition performed very badly. The pre- and post-poll National Election Survey (NES) 2014 in Kashmir conducted by the Centre for the Study of Developing Societies (CSDS) clearly showed

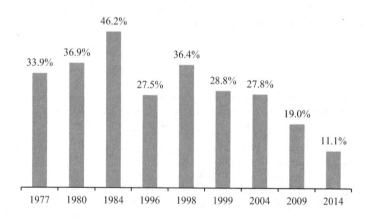

Figure 14.2 Vote share of National Conference in Parliamentary elections from 1977–2014

Source: Centre for the Study of Developing Societies Data Unit

voters' discontent against the coalition on account of the failure of the government to check corruption, inflation, together with poor healthcare, pathetic condition of roads, and so on. When voters were asked to compare the performance of the NC–Congress government with the previous PDP–Congress government, 40 per cent of the respondents opted for the latter and only 18 per cent for the former. Along with these issues of governance, the Afzal Guru's hanging and the killings of more than 100 youth in the 2010 protests were the other important reasons for the debacle of the National Conference in Kashmir as pointed out by Chief Minister Omar Abdullah himself. In fact, Omar Abdullah went online seeking feedback from people as to why they rejected the NC in the Parliamentary Elections[4] (*Greater Kashmir* 24 May 2014).

The results of the election in the Kashmir valley also dismantled the concept of 'traditional vote bank'. One of the biggest shocks that this election gave to the National Conference was the breakdown of its traditional vote bank in the Kangan Assembly constituency of district Ganderbal and in the Chrar-e-Sharif Assembly constituency of district Budgam. The NC candidates always represented these two constituencies since 1957, the year the first Assembly election in the state was held. The NC's own pre-poll analysis predicting that it was going to win the Srinagar seat was based on the assumption that it would receive decisive leads in Kangan and Chrar-e-Sharif (represented by two most prominent leaders of NC). However, it did not happen. The precise reason for this is voters of these areas, especially youth, no longer would cast their vote in favour of the NC since their forefathers were doing so. Now the political socialisation of the people (especially youth) in these areas is witnessing a shift as they no longer honour the party affiliations of their ancestors. For instance, the Gujjars were historically strong loyalists of Mian Altaf. However, over a period of time the PDP has made serious inroads in the Gujjar vote bank of the National Conference. In the 2008 Assembly elections, the PDP candidate Bashir Ahmad Mir gave a tough competition to Mian Altaf. The problem that the NC is facing is that their traditional vote bank seems to be drifting from them. Table 14.3 shows some of the areas, represented by key members of the NC and Congress, where the coalition unexpectedly lost ground in Kashmir.

Analysis of electoral trends in Ladakh

The Ladakh seat was won by the BJP by a very narrow margin. The country's area-wise largest Parliamentary segment – Ladakh – recorded one of the country's lowest victory margins in the Lok Sabha elections with BJP candidate Thupstan Chhewang defeating his nearest rival Ghulam Raza, a Congress rebel, who was fighting the elections as an Independent candidate with a narrow margin of thirty-six votes. Chhewang, who had won Ladakh Parliamentary seat as an Independent candidate in 2004, polled 31,111 votes while his nearest rival, Ghulam Raza, a Congress rebel, who was in the fray as Independent candidate, polled 31,075 votes. Another Independent candidate Syed Mohammad Kazim Sabri finished third with 28,234 votes while the Congress candidate Tsering Samphel finished at the bottom polling 26,402 votes. Raza was backed by powerful Imam Khomeini Memorial Trust (IKMT) while Sabri had the support of another major religious organisation Islamiya School Kargil (ISK).

This was for the first time in the history of Jammu and Kashmir that the BJP won the Ladakh Parliamentary seat. The victory of the BJP could be attributed to strong ideological differences between Buddhists and Shia Muslims in the Ladakh region, the Modi wave, BJP's commitment to give Ladakh the status of Union Territory and deep factionalism within the Congress. The failure of NC–Congress pre-poll alliance on the ground was evident in Ladakh. As per pre-poll alliance between the NC and Congress, Ladakh Parliamentary seat was given to Congress and NC was expected to back its alliance partner candidate. However, in reality not only the NC workers but even some prominent NC leaders from Ladakh region openly supported the candidature of one Aga Syed Kazim Sabri, an Independent candidate. The friction among the coalition partners was clearly evident by the support openly provided by the prominent NC leaders including the then Chief Minister's Advisor Qamar Ali Akhoon, MLA Kargil, and Minister for Science and Technology, MLA Zanskar, to the candidature of Sabri while former Minister Haji Nissar Ali and Chief Executive Councilor (CEC) LAHDC Kargil, Asgar Ali Karblaie were supporting Raza (*Daily Excelsior*, 17 May 2014).

Analysis of the 2014 Assembly election in Jammu and Kashmir (J&K)

Having performed exceptionally well in the 2014 Parliamentary elections winning both seats of Jammu and the only seat of Ladakh and having lead on twenty-four out of thirty-seven Assembly segments in the Jammu region in the 2014 Parliamentary elections, BJP was expecting a good show in the Assembly elections. The election was held in five phases from 25 November to 17 December 2015 in the wake of massive floods of September 2014 that brought unprecedented devastation to Kashmir. There were apprehensions regarding the holding of elections because the atmosphere was not seen conducive for such exercise in the aftermath of deluge. However, except the National Conference all major political parties including the Congress (coalition partner of National Conference), pleaded for the holding of elections on time. However, putting all speculations to rest and ignoring the objections of the NC, the Election Commission made two official visits to the state. On 7 October 2014 a team of Election Commission of India headed by the deputy election Commissioner Vinod Zutshi visited the state. This was followed by another full team visit of election commission of India on 18 October 2014, where they held detailed discussion with representatives of all the political parties and civil and police administration. After holding elaborate discussions with civil and police administration regarding the poll preparedness, the Commission announced that elections would be conducted on time. Major political parties welcomed the decision and, after initial reluctance, NC also decided to participate in the elections.

The separatist politics vis-à-vis elections has always revolved around call for boycott. Even after the restoration of political process, especially after 2002 elections, the separatist politics as well as their influence remained intact. Almost all the major separatist leaders have always took elections as a farcical exercise undertaken by the Indian state to divert the attention from the core issue of Kashmir and have always maintained that elections could be no substitute to right of self-determination for which they are fighting.

The mainstream politics got expanded during the period between 2002 up to 2014 from the earlier situation when the mainstream political parties were not in a position to organise the election rallies and reach to the electorate due to the threats and killing of the party leaders by the militants. From 2002, the Assembly elections voter turnout in the state increased with every passing election and the electorate of the state, especially in the Valley, has shown some amount of trust in the electoral process. However, the expansion of the electoral space has not taken place at the cost of the separatist sentiment and politics and in fact separatist space remains intact in Kashmir. The two are seen as reflecting two different spheres of politics – one dealing with issues of governance and other with conflict situations and its resolution (Chowdhary 2008: 5). Separatist politics remain reality despite the fact that mainstream politics has expanded and regained its lost ground after 2002 elections. The separatism remains relevant because of the long-standing and unresolved Kashmir issue, alienation, and mistrust on one hand and manipulation of electoral process through fraudulent means on the other hand. The fundamental reason for separatist ideology of poll boycott is that elections can't be portrayed as a substitute for plebiscite and self-determination as is used by the government of India. Even during the 2014 Parliamentary elections the separatists announced complete poll boycott. Jammu and Kashmir Liberation Front Chairman Muhammad Yasin Malik even called upon people to stay away from polls to safeguard the sacrifices (*Greater Kashmir* 5 March 2014). Even Hurriyat Conference (G) led by Syed Ali Shah Geelani said that by boycotting the elections, 'we want to make it clear that right to self-determination is the only solution of the Kashmir dispute and no other election or selection process is any alternative to that' (*Rising Kashmir* 1 May 2014).

With regard to 2014 Assembly elections the separatist position remained the same. Chairman Hurriyat Conference (G) Syed Ali Shah Geelani termed the eagerness to hold elections in Kashmir as unkind thinking of policy makers of India and the self-centred thinking of Kashmiri mainstream politicians. He said, 'At the time when destructive floods have snatched every thing from Kashmiri people and when they are living a miserable life, even talking about of elections is sorrowful and it proves governments in New Delhi and the Srinagar has nothing to do with the miseries of the people and they are only concerned with their benefits' (*Greater Kashmir*, 26 October, 2014; Wani Aijaz Ashraf,'Election: Finally the announcement is made', *Greater Kashmir*, 1 November 2014).

Chairman Hurriyat (M), Mirwaiz Umar Farooq said, 'at a time when Kashmiri people are in dire need of relief and rehabilitation, the mainstream political parties have agreed to elections. It is a deliberate attempt to showcase the return superficial normalcy in Kashmir'. He further said, that 'elections are not an alternative to the resolution to the long-pending dispute of Kashmir. Unless the issue is resolved as per the aspirations of its people, no elections have any in relevance in the valley' (ibid.).

The elections were fought by all political parties on all alone and there was no pre-poll alliance between any political parties, the BJP had some understanding with the separatist turned mainstream politician Sajad Gani Lone, the chairman of People's conference (the party enjoys strong base in North Kashmir's Kupwara district). Mr Lone met the Prime Minister Narendra Modi on 10 November 2014 and extended his support to him. The two discussed the possibility of his

(Sajad) forming an alliance with BJP after the Assembly elections in Jammu and Kashmir (*Rising Kashmir* 10 November 2014). Showering praise on PM, Lone said, 'Modi was so large hearted that it was tough to say whether I was meeting PM of India or my elder brother' (ibid).

Analysis of the key issues in Assembly elections

Soon after the announcement of the election was made, all the major political parties came up with their election manifestoes. All the parties had made relief and rehabilitation as the primary concern. The NC manifesto talked about the restoration of autonomy and Article 370, PDP's manifesto named 'Aspirational Agenda' promised pursuit of self-rule as the guiding framework for the resolution of the Kashmir issue. In addition, PDP will also use the Article 370 itself to restore the original special status of the state. The Congress party manifesto proposed two empowered regional councils, decentralisation of power, more cross-LoC confidence building measures and revival of the cases of detainees not involved in grave offences. However, there were sharp divergent lines in the BJP's manifesto named 'Vision Document for Jammu and Kashmir'. The party was salient on the Article 370 but said that if voted to power the party would give a complete identity to the state by renaming it as Jammu, Kashmir, and Ladakh. The party manifesto reads, 'Naming the state as Jammu-Kashmir and Ladakh will give the state its complete identity, and if voted to power, the party will rename it on priority'. The party promised to reserve three seats in the state Assembly for displaced Kashmiris (Kashmiri Pundits who left valley at the outbreak of militancy in 1989–1990) out of the forty-six Assembly seats meant for Kashmir valley. It also promised to reserve five seats for refugees from the twenty-four seats kept vacant for Pakistan Administered Kashmir (PAK).[5] The party has made development as the main plank for the elections terming it as its 'TIME' model. The acronym 'TIME' stands for Tourism, Infrastructure, Modernisation, and Empowerment.

Reflections on the BJP's electoral strategy

The BJP appeared desperate in its attempt to open its maiden account in Kashmir valley in the Assembly elections, and it tried to carefully craft a strategy. First, the party relied on what can be described as 'sectarian divide' or polarisation strategy. The party poll plan focused on wooing the Hindu vote bank in Jammu, the Kashmiri Pundits, Sikhs, Paharis, Gujjars, Buddhists in Leh, and Shia voters of the state. The

Party's state election committee president Nirmal Singh explained the party strategy in the following words, 'As per our information the Kashmiri Pandits (KPs)[6] can play a decisive role in at least six seats in the valley especially in its peripheries and therefore, to take this process forward a committee will be constituted within days to establish contact with each KP family'. Apart from KPs the party is also working on a strategy to get support of the Pahari-speaking people of the valley, Shias, Sikh community, and Gujjars. We are already getting a good response from these communities. To achieve its goal the core team of the party led by the Prime Minster Narendra Modi, party president Amit Shah deployed a team of 150 IT professionals, poll strategists, and organisational members of different wings of the party and other experts with a successful track record in all the three regions of the state, to do the ground work on each and every constituency and grey areas therein, in order to help the party in accomplishing the mission of forming its government (*Greater Kashmir* 11 November 2014).

BJP focused on issues like abrogation of Article 370, settlement of west-Pakistan refugees and giving better deal to Jammu & Ladakh in order to mobilize its voters. The election witnessed an intense campaigning by political parties. The ruling NC–Congress coalition having been wiped out in recently concluded Parliamentary elections chose not to enter into pre-poll alliance, whereas the BJP and the PDP were expecting to repeat their good performance. The BJP had maintained leads on twenty-four out of thirty-seven Assembly segments of the Jammu region in the recently concluded Parliament elections, whereas the PDP had lead on forty-two segments out of forty-six Assembly segments in the Kashmir region. However, BJP was desperate to reach out to people in Kashmir (especially Kashmiri Pandits who were in good numbers in some constituencies in Srinagar and, if the boycott prevailed, they were the deciders). It left no stone unturned to do that. For example, in the recently concluded Parliamentary elections, while the BJP was riding on the 'Modi wave', it set for itself the target of a 'Mission 44+' plan, the numbers required for a party in order to be able to form a government on its own. To achieve its 'Mission 44+' – BJP's national leaders, including Prime Minister Narendra Modi, party president Amit Shah, and Home Minister Rajnath Singh, addressed the election rallies Kashmir to wow voters in their favour. Addressing a public rally in Vijapur Jammu, Prime Minister Modi said:

> Since 1947, successive governments of the state have discriminated with Jammu and never cared for the people of this region. Congress party has cleverly been changing sides with NC and

PDP for the sake of power in Jammu and Kashmir. He further said that over the years the state has seen father-son-and father-daughter rule. They have made the state most corrupt and promoted nepotism.

(*Greater Kashmir* 9 December 2014)

On the same day the Prime Minister also addressed the election rally at Sheri Kashmir Cricket Stadium Srinagar and said:

In the past 30 years many people chose different paths (referring to armed insurgency) but could not achieve anything, nothing helped I want to tell them to shun those paths and join the path of *vikas* (development) my mission and slogan is *sab kasaath, sab kavikaas* (everybody's development, everybody's support). Development is the only solution. This is the only thing that can pull the people of Kashmir out of all troubles. He further said three families-Congress, father -son party (National Conference) and father-daughter (Peoples Democratic Party) have ruined J&K. They ensured everything for themselves, but let people to suffer. I urge you to throw all these three families out of the state and allow me to serve you. I will utilize my entire government to take JK to new heights of development.

(ibid)

Fearing rise of a Modi-led BJP in the Kashmir region, the mainstream parties NC, PDP, and Congress launched an aggressive campaign against Modi and BJP on the one hand and on the other hand urged the separatists to reconsider their boycott call as it was going to help the BJP. In fact the separatists themselves urged people to be aware of BJP and its designs. Syed Ali Shah Geelani, the hard-core separatist, appealed to the people and said:

I make a passionate appeal to all religious leaders and clerics to appraise people about the evil designs of BJP and their anti-Islam ideology. With all their power, money, and material they are trying hard to make an entry into the state and for this they with the help of some stooges from Kashmir and outside state are carrying their election campaign. We warn our people against their evil designs and ask them to be cautious and beware of BJP, which is using religion as a tool and is hell-bent to exploit religious sentiments while depicting their false sympathy with Muslim majority.

(*Greater Kashmir* 22 November 2014)

Since the statement did not evoke any negative reaction from other separatist leaders, it was taken as a semblance to softness in their call for an election boycott, and gave rise to the widely prevalent idea that the BJP must be kept at bay, which in turn meant that people should vote. PDP patron Mufti Mohammad Sayeed, urging people to be aware of the communal designs of BJP, while addressing a rally in Pulwama said:

> People of Jammu and Kashmir will give a befitting reply to any attempts at communalizing the situation, eroding the state's authority or diluting the constitutional position. PDP with the support of the people will defeat the designs aimed at diluting the distinct identity of the state.
>
> (*Greater Kashmir* 22 November 2014)

UPA chairperson and Congress president Sonia Gandhi, while addressing an election rally in district Bandipora of Kashmir, said:

> Save the secular and united cultural ethos of the state vote for the congress to defeat the communal elements who are out to dilute its social and cultural identity.
>
> (Ibid)

Analysis of the verdict

The elections produced a hung Assembly. The PDP emerged as the single largest party, securing twenty-eight seats, the BJP finished at twenty-five seats, the NC with fifteen, and the Congress with twelve. It is important to note that while BJP gained at the cost of Congress in Jammu, the PDP won many seats previously held by the NC. Out of the twenty-five seats that the BJP won, all are from the Jammu region and nineteen seats came from the Hindu-dominated areas of Jammu. The outcome reflected consolidation of the Hindu vote and the working of the Modi magic in the region. Singnificant gains for the BJP was winning of six out of thirteen seats in Chenab valley and Pir-Panchal regions, where Muslim votes were divided between the NC, the PDP, and the Congress party, while the Hindu vote consolidated in favour of the BJP. However it received a severe political setback by not winning a single seat in the Kashmir Valley. Taj Mohi-ud Din, senior minister in NC–Congress coalition government said:

> For the whitewash of the Congress in Jammu region, it was the wave of Modi which was responsible for it. . . . . . call it Modi

wave, wave of Hindutva or polarization this was the main factor for the drubbing of Congress in Jammu. In Valley, there was anti-incumbency factor which proved detrimental for the loss of both big and small guns in J&K politics.

With no political party in a position to form a government on its own, hectic parleys began for government formation. To keep the BJP at bay, both the NC and Congress offered unconditional support to PDP. Omar Abdullah, the working President of the National Conference, while expressing his desire to support PDP, said, 'I do not rule out or rule in anything but it was for PDP to approach him' (*Greater Kashmir* 24 December 2014). Ghulam Nabi Azad, former Chief Minister of the state from the Congress party, put forward the idea of a 'Grand Alliance' of PDP, NC, and Congress. Initially, the PDP hinted that 'grand alliance' is an option but later declined it on the grounds that the mandate was against both parties. The PDP also made it clear that party respects the mandate of the people of Jammu region. Union Finance Minister Arun Jaitley, while asserting that the BJP has bagged the highest vote share in the Assembly elections, said that (BJP) has the first right to form the government in J&K (*Greater Kashmir* 26 December 2014). At the same time BJP made it publicly clear that keeping BJP out of power will amount to disrespect of the mandate of Jammu. It also made clear that it is willing to do business with both NC and PDP and is in touch with the parties. BJP President Amit Shah said 'his party has been holding talks with both PDP and NC over government formation in Jammu and Kashmir' (*Greater Kashmir* 3 January 2014).

It needs mentioning that forging a coalition with the BJP whose ideology is diametrically opposed to both NC and PDP was not an easy affair. However, NC's internal rift over going with BJP forced it to abandon the idea, thereby paving the way for PDP. However, it took two months for PDP–BJP alliance to materialise as both parties were engaged in dialogue to iron out their differences over contentious issues. Finally a compromise formula was reached and Common Minimum Programme (CPM) – also called 'Agenda of the Alliance' – was worked out. It focuses on inclusive governance and development of the state, keeping out the controversial issues. While BJP softened its stand on rotational Chief Minister (agreeing to have Mufti Mohammed Sayeed as full-term Chief Minister), abrogation of Article 370, and settlement of West Pakistan Refugees, PDP on its part also softened its stand on revocation of AFSPA. Finally on 1 March 2015, PDP patron Mufti Mohammad Sayeed took over as the Chief Minister of the state for a full six years.

What has been apparent since the inception of this government is the fact that the hard-core Hindutva politics of BJP was trying to communalise each and every issue. From the day of oath-taking, the BJP, rather than acting as a responsible coalition partner, acted as an opponent. The first controversial line that brought the differences to forefront was on the issue of revocation of the AFSPA. In March militants carried out two *fidayeen* (suicide) attacks on security forces in Jammu. After some time another attack on police took place in the Shopian district of Kashmir. The attacks took place at a time when the issue of revocation of AFSPA was being raised. After these attacks, Chief Minister Mufti Mohammad Sayeed reiterated his commitment to revoke the controversial law from some areas of the state. However, the very next day the BJP legislators from Jammu protested against the statement of CM in the Assembly. They stormed into the well of the House amid anti-Pakistani slogans and weaving placards displaying No to AFSPA revocation.

Another contentious issue that brought coalition partners on loggerheads with each other is the return and resettlement of Kashmiri Pandits (who migrated en mass in the 1990s following the insurgency). BJP is demanding a separate homeland; the centre government asked the CM to expedite the process of identifying the land for the separate townships of KPs. The state government as per the media reports had agreed to it. However, the plan has been widely criticised not only by both the mainstream as well as separatist parties, but also by some Kashmir Pandit organisations (especially those who did not migrate out of Kashmir) and was termed as a conspiracy.

Fearing trouble in Kashmir Chief Minister Mufti Mohammad Sayeed, while rejecting any Israel-type settlement for Pandits, stated on the floor of state Assembly:

> I want to clarify that there is no plan for separate homeland (for Kashmiri Pandits). There should be no noise and rumors that separate colonies are being established for the migrant community. We are not going to take any decision in haste. We will take all stakeholders on board on return of KPs.
> (*Greater Kashmir*, 10 April, 2015)

Taking exception to the statements, the BJP responded by saying that the party officially supports separate homeland and proper security for KPs. Union Home Minister Rajnath Singh (who held meeting with the CM on the issue) stated that the centre is not going back on separate settlement of KPs (ibid). The chief spokesperson of the BJP, Mr Sunil Sethi, stated:

> For a temporary period, clusters are necessary in the valley because you cannot send KPs to their homes to get them killed.
>
> (ibid)

The third issue that led to serious trouble in Kashmir and loss of innocent lives is the release and re-arrest of separatist leader Masrat Alam. Masrat was imprisoned in 2010 on the charges of fuelling the 2010 anti-government demonstrations and organising pro-freedom agitation that resulted in 110 civilian deaths. His release led to a very strong tussle between coalition partners – PDP and BJP – with the PDP defending the release on the grounds that Supreme Court had challenged his continued detention. The BJP viewed it as softness towards anti-nationals. Its Party president Amit Shah even threatened the pull-out from the coalition if national security is compromised. Given that he was released on the Supreme Court's direction and the orders for his release were issued during the governor's rule, it was absolutely bizarre on the part of the BJP to target PDP and not to support the decision.

What is, however, more ironic is to see how the BJP very meticulously becomes the part of the jingoistic national media to ridicule the PDP by putting all the blame on it and save its (communal) image in the rest of India. It is troubling to see how the PDP spokespersons are being made testify their loyalty towards India, and the party being referred to as a separatist party and Mufti Mohammad Sayeed as pro-Pakistan and pro-separatist Chief Minister. On the top of this, the BJP leaders were siding with rabble rousers and categorically oppose the decisions of the government of which they are part and even pose questions to their PDP counterparts to test their loyalty.

Although it is too early to predict the future of this alliance, however, it is high time for the PDP to return to their drawing boards and rethink their strategy. It seems that the 'soft separatism' is finding it too difficult to withstand pressures of 'hardline Hindutva'. At present there seem to be too much mistrust and ideological difference among the coalition partners on issues concerning the state. With the death of Mufti Mohammad Sayed the crisis between the two coalition partners has deepened and carrying this coalition for six years is going to be a herculean task.

Soon after the death of Mufti Sayed, there was a renewed dialogue both at the inter-party as well as intra-party levels. Given the serious crisis that the coalition faced and the fact that no progress could be made on the 'agenda of alliance' during Mufti Sayed's time, therefore, soon after his death, PDP went into a hurdle to chalk out the future strategy. While review of the agenda of alliance did not yield much, the power politics prevailed and PDP under Mehbooba Mufti decided to continue the alliance. BJP state leadership and its cadre have become more assertive during this period. This was more visible during the 2016 summer uprising, when despite the widespread protests, killings, blinding, and months of lockdown, the BJP was not ready to hold talks with Hurriyat and even distanced and ridiculed PDP and Mehbooba Mufti for sending an invitation to Hurriyat leaders, though not as Chief Minister but party president of PDP, during the visit of Parliamentary delegation led by the home minister to break the deadlock. The differences between the coalition partners, and the desire of BJP to impose its agenda on the state, reached its zenith during the Assembly session in January 2017. In the backdrop of various BJP leaders constantly calling for abrogation of Article 370, Chief Minister Mehbooba Mufti on 30 January 2017 stated on the floor of Assembly that those working towards the weakening of Article 370, which grants special status to the state, are doing the 'biggest antinational act'. She further stated that a 'conspiracy is being hatched against our culture and state' in this regard (*The Indian Express* 31 January 2017).

BJP leaders like Ravinder Raina created an uproar in the Assembly on CM's state argument, claiming that Article 370 is defrauding the people of Jammu and Kashmir and its abrogation is the core ideology of BJP and even called for expunging the statement from Assembly records (ibid). The BJP is trying hard to impose its communal agenda on the state politics and PDP at present is finding it too difficult to resist it. It is creating a deep divide and atmosphere of suspension in the state. In fact many commentators have attributed the rise in militancy as well as popular uprisings to the communal agenda that BJP is trying to impose on the state.

Conclusion

Communalism or communal politics is not something new to Jammu and Kashmir. It was going side by side along with the secular progressive discourse of Kashmir even before independence. The roots of this can be traced to the pre-1947 politics of the state when Jammu and

Kashmir was under the autocratic and sectarian Dogra rule.[7] As stated previously, Jammu and Kashmir is not a 'natural' state but a 'constructed' one where identities of regions and sub-regions have always been contradictory to each other. Therefore, the dominant politics of three regions has always reflected the sharp divergence from each other. With religion as one of the primary determinant of the mobilisation, the politics of the state came to acquire a communal character at an early stage. The post-1947 developments, especially the way electoral politics was conducted, further intensified this divide. Post insurgency period has seen this communal divide reaching its climax.

The electoral politics of the state has always carried the imprints of communalisation with it, however, what the 2014 Parliamentary and State Assembly elections have done is to bring the communal forces at the centre stage of Jammu and Kashmir politics. As stated by BJP general secretary Ram Madhav, 'BJP has broken the J&K Jinx'. They hope to play the same role in J&K politics as had been played by Congress historically. Although the coalition, due to its ideological difference on serious issues related to the state, is finding it difficult to function smoothly, but for the sake of being in power they are somehow managing it. As stated by Mani Shankar Aiyer, 'The worst of a coalition of opposites, such as we have in Jammu & Kashmir, is that to keep the alliance going, the partners indulge in what can only be described as "competitive communalism"' (Aiyer 2015). While BJP may find it difficult to have its imprints on the Valley, however, it has certainly consolidated its position in mainland Jammu and Leh district of Ladakh. This communal politics is having an adverse impact on the political atmospheres of the state and has badly impacted the peace process both within the state as well as between India and Pakistan.

Notes

1 For details see, Aijaz Ashraf Wani, 'Ethnic Identities and the Dynamics of Regional and Sub-Regional Assertions in Jammu and Kashmir', *Asian Ethnicity*, Routledge Group, Vol. 14, No. 3 (2013).
2 On being approached by Pakistan, the United Nations Security Council passed a resolution in late March 1951, 'reminding the government and authorities concerned of the principles embodied in the Security Council resolutions of 21 April 1948, 3 June 1948 and 14 March 1950 and the United Nations Commission for India and Pakistan resolutions of 13 August 1948 and 5 January 1949, that the final disposition of the state of J&K will be made in accordance with the will of the people, expressed through the democratic method of a free and impartial plebiscite conducted under the auspices of the United Nations'. The resolution further warned that, 'the convening of a Constituent Assembly as recommended by the

General Council of the All Jammu and Kashmir National Conference and any action that Assembly might attempt to take to determine the future shape and affiliation of the entire state, or any part thereof, would not constitute a disposition of the state in accordance with the above principle'. (Dasgupta 1968: 406–07).

3 In Udhampur, the Congress fielded former Chief Minister of the state and then union health minister Ghulam Nabi Azad. BJP fielded its party heavyweights Jughal Kishor, State Party President, and Dr Jitendar Singh, member of the national executive and party spokesman. PDP also fielded its two candidates, Yash Pal Sharma and Arshid Malik, for the Jammu-Poonch and Udhampur-Doda Parliamentary constituencies, respectively. The move was criticised by the coalition partners as a policy to divide the votes (both of Muslims and Hindus) which for the coalition amounted in helping the BJP. In the Kashmir region in Anantnag Parliamentary constituency, the contest was between People's Democratic Party (PDP) president Mehbooba Mufti and NC Member of Parliament Mehboob Begh. In Srinagar, the electoral fight was between former CM and NC party patron Farooq Abdullah and former finance minister Tariq Hamid Qarra of PDP. In the Baramulla constituency, it was a four-way contest between two-time MP Sharif ud din Shariq of NC, former Deputy Chief Minister Muzaffar Hussain Baig of PDP, Awami Ittehad Party President Er Rashid and Salamudin Bajad of the People's Conference.

4 To know the reasons responsible for party's debacle in Parliamentary elections, the Chief Minister created an e-mail gupkar@gmail.com for receiving the online feedback from people, while launching the e-mail the CM said 'gupkar@gmail.com is my email id. I'd like to hear from you as to the reasons for the enormous setback the NC has faced in these elections'. See *Greater Kashmir*, 19 May 2014, 1. *Kashmir Reader*, 19 May 2014, 1. *Rising Kashmir*, 19 May 2014, 1.

5 Pakistan Administered Kashmir or Azad Jammu and Kashmir abbreviated as AJK or Azad Kashmir ('free Kashmir') is a self-governing administrative division of Pakistan. The territory lies west of the Indian-administered state of Jammu and Kashmir, and was previously part of the former princely state of Jammu and Kashmir, which ceased to exist as a result of the first Kashmir war fought between India and Pakistan in 1947. The Indian government and Indian sources refer to Azad Kashmir as 'Pakistan-occupied Kashmir' ('PoK') or 'Pakistan-held Kashmir' (PHK).

6 The Kashmiri Pandits (KPs) (also known as Kashmiri Brahmins) are a Brahmin community from the Kashmir Valley. They are the only remaining Hindu community native to the Kashmir Valley. Following the eruption of insurgency in late 1980s they migrated en mass from the Kashmir and settled in different parts of the India.

7 The people of Kashmir raised their voice against the discriminatory Dogra rule in 1931 when a major uprising broke out in Srinagar, which in terms of casualties and property damage, 'was possibly the most serious communal outbreak in India between the Moplah rebellion of 1921 and the Calcutta riots of 1946' (Snneden 2013: 13). This uprising forced Maharaja to undertake some reforms in his administration and give his subjects some political representation, which till then (1931) was banned in the state. It was on the recommendations of the Glancy Commission (appointed in the aftermath

of the 1931 Uprising) that the oppressed masses of Kashmir were allowed to form political parties in the state. In 1932 the modern educated youth of Kashmir who had returned from different universities outside the state formed the first political party in the state, called All Jammu and Kashmir Muslim Conference (MC), in October 1932 under the leadership of Sheikh Mohammad Abdullah, who by then had emerged as the undisputed leader of the oppressed masses (Wani 2007: 246). After the formation of MC the freedom struggle in Kashmir started in an organised manner against the Dogra rule. However, the beneficiaries of Dogra rule, Hindus of Jammu and Kashmir (called in Kashmir as Kashmiri Pandits), favouring the status quo, frustrated the efforts of Kashmiri leaders and like-minded people of their community to form a secular progressive platform which was conceived by Sheikh Abdullah and Prem Nath Bazaz in 1932, leading to the formation of All Jammu and Kashmir Muslim Conference (J&K MC). However, in no way did formation of MC meant that it was a communal party representing the interests of Muslims alone at the cost of Non-Muslims (Hindus and Sikhs). Rather it was a movement representing all those (without any consideration of caste, creed, religion, and region) who were worst sufferers under Dogra rule.

Bibliography

Aiyer, Manishankar. 2015. *Modi More of an Event Manager Than a PM*. New Delhi: India Today 2015. *India Today*, June 7. http://indiatoday.intoday.in/story/modi-event-manager-pm-congress-mani-shankar-aiyar-achhe-din-ha-ha-rahul-gandhi/1/442778.html (accessed on November 18, 2017)

Akbar, M.J. 1991. *Kashmir Behind the Vale*. New Delhi: Vikas Publications.

Austin, Granville. 1999. *The Indian Constitution, Cornerstone of the Nation*. New Delhi: Oxford University Press.

Bahera, Navnita. 2007. *Demystifying Kashmir*. New Delhi: Pearson Publishers.

Bazaz, P.N. 1967. *Kashmir in Crucibles*. New Delhi: Pamposh Publishers.

———. 1978. *Democracy Through Intimidation and Terror the Untold Story of Kashmir Politics*. New Delhi: Heritage Publishers.

———. 2003. *The History of Struggle for Freedom in Kashmir*. Srinagar: Gulshan Books.

Bhattacharjea, Ajit. 1994. *Kashmir: The Wounded Valley*. New Delhi: UBSPD Publishers.

Bose, Sumantara. 1997. *The Challenges in Kashmir*. New Delhi: Sage Publications.

———. 2003. *Roots to Conflict, Paths to Peace*. New Delhi: Vistaar Publications.

Chowdhary, Rekha. 2004. 'National Conference of Jammu and Kashmir: From Hegemonic to Competitive Politics', *Economic & Political Weekly*, 39(14).

———. 2008. 'Electioneering in Kashmir: Overlap Between Separatist and Mainstream Political Space', *Economic & Political Weekly*, 43(28).

———. 2010. 'Multiple Identity Poitics in Jammu and Kashmir', in Chowdhary Rekha et al. (eds), *Identity Politics in Jammu and Kashmir*. New Delhi: Vistaar Publishing Pvt. Ltd.
———. 2017. *Kashmir Politics of Identity and Separatism*. New Delhi: Manohar.
Dasgupta, Jyoti Bhushan. 1968. Jammu and Kashmir. The Hague: Martinus Nijhoff.
Gangly, Smith. 1998. *The Crisis in Kashmir: Potents of War, Hopes of Peace*. Washington, DC: Cambridge.
Gauhar, G.N. 2002. *Elections in Jammu and Kashmir*. New Delhi: Manas Publications.
Jha, Prem Shankar. 1996. *Kashmir, 1947*. Bombay: Oxford University Press.
Korbel, Josef. 2008. *Danger in Kashmir*. Srinagar: City Book Centre.
Lamb, Alastair. 1994. *Birth of a Tragedy*. Hertfordshire: Roxford Books.
———. 1997. *Incomplete Partition, the Genesis of the Kashmir Dispute 1947–1948*. Hertfordshire: Roxford Books.
Puri, Balraj. 1995. *Kashmir Towards Insurgency*. New Delhi: Orient Longman.
———. 2007. *Hindu Rulers, Muslim Subjects*. New Delhi: Permanent Black.
Snedden, Christopher. 2013. *Kashmir the Unwritten History*. India: Harper Collins.
Singh, Balbir. 1982. *State Politics in India: Explorations in Political Process in J&K*. New Delhi: Macmillan Publishers.
Verma, P.S. 1994. *Jammu and Kashmir at Political Crossroads*. New Delhi: Vikas Publishing House.
Wani, Aijaz Ashraf. 2007. The Popular Voice: Secular-Progressive Discourse in Kashmir(1932-47) The Indian Historic Review, ICHR/ Sage, Vol. XXIV,No.1, New Delhi. 2007.

15 Lok Sabha elections in (un)divided Andhra Pradesh

Issues and implications in Telangana and Seemandhra

Ritu Khosla

A new dimension has been augmented in the domain of state politics in India with the endowment of statehood status to Telangana on 2 June 2014. More captivating had been the transfer of power in the newly formed state and the upshot of the 16th Lok Sabha elections in the state. Elections were held prior to the configuration of the state. Andhra Pradesh went for polls as an integrated state and in effect the voters elected two governments, i.e. one for Andhra Pradesh and the second for the forthcoming state of Telangana. The calendar, however, for both the elections varied. The Lok Sabha elections were conducted in two phases in Andhra Pradesh: on 30 April 2014 the first phase of election elected MPs for seventeen Lok Sabha seats in Telangana region, while the second phase held on 7 May 2014 elected members for the twenty-five seats in Seemandhra. It had become imperative to form two governments as the new state of Telangana was to be constituted few weeks after the avowal of election results. In the elections both the regions witnessed the highest ever voter turnout in the state's election history – with 78.66 per cent in Seemandhra and 72.31 per cent in Telangana.

Studying the past elections

The Communist party of India, along with the people of Hyderabad, had pursued a battle against Nizam's domineering rule. But after the state of Andhra Pradesh got constructed, Indian National Congress wielded authority in the state by seizing the key issue of the Left, i.e. agrarian reforms, and ruled the state till 1983. Telangana Praja Samiti (TPS), formed by Madan Mohan in February 1969, contested in the general elections of 1971 and won ten out of fifteen seats in the Lok

Sabha in Telangana region and secured a high 47.5 per cent of the votes polled (Nag 2011: 61–62). But regardless of being victorious, Indira Gandhi did not give any weightage to the TPS that in turn had to opt for compromise in September 1971 and conflated with Congress. The bargain involved a continuation of Mulki rules, separate budget, accounts, and separate Pradesh Congress Committee for Telangana. Replacing Brhamananda Reddy, P.V. Narsimha Rao, hailing from Telangana region, became the new Chief Minister of state in 1971 (Haragopal 2010: 53) and thus Congress was able to maintain its position.

The party, however, lost its credibility in the state later as it failed to accommodate the divergent interests along the caste and class lines (Srinivasulu and Sarangi 1999: 2450). In addition, numerous changes of the Chief Ministers by the Congress High Command fabricated dissatisfaction amongst people. Captivating this popular discontent, N.T. Rama Rao (NTR), a leading film celebrity, formed a regional party called 'Telugu Desam Party' (TDP) in 1982 and the party was not even ten months old when it competed for general elections to the Andhra Pradesh legislative Assembly held in 1983. His party became victorious by winning 202 out of 296 seats and N.T. Rama Rao was sworn in as the tenth Chief Minister of the state. The Congress(I) that anticipated coming out as the single largest party gained only sixty seats (Tummala 1986: 379). In January 1983, a poll for Peddapalli Lok Sabha seat that comprised of two of the most backward districts of Telangana, Adilabad and Karimnagar, was conducted in which TDP secured three seats, Sanjay Vichar Manch got two, and Congress two. This was due to the shift of the harijan vote in favour of TDP (Shatrughna 1983: 1123). In 1988 during Zilla Parishad and Mandal Parishad elections in Ranga Reddy district, TDP won and this made NTR emerge as a strong leader in the Telangana rural belt. Reasons for the success of TDP included the support of backward classes to NTR, well-knit party functioning of TDP members while Congress was driven by factionalism, grassroot electioneering by party cadre, and the good rapport of party candidates with the electorates (Shatrughna 1988: 571). Over the period of time, Telugu people became unhappy with some of the policies of the Telugu Desam government and, taking advantage of this, Congress tried to re-strengthen its position and levied charges against Chief Minister N.T. Rama Rao that included violation of Income Tax and Wealth Tax laws, Urban Land Ceiling Regulations, corruption, misuse of power, casteism, nepotism, favouritism, atrocities against harijans, and disrespect towards courts and so on. Playing on the caste factor, Congress tried to make people of the Reddy community realise that TDP was dominated by Kammas and Reddy community was thus marginalised (Balagopal 1987: 1736). All this bolstered Congress in the 1989 general elections to the state legislature: as an outcome, Congress had a triumph with a commendable majority of 182 seats out of 294 (Shatrughna 1990: 201). During the following five years, three Chief Ministers, Dr M. Channa Reddy, N. Janardhana Reddy, and K. Vijaya Bhaskara Reddy held the reins of power. There was infighting of the Congress leaders too. Senior Congress leaders wanted to get candidates of their choice to be nominated, but when they failed in doing so they got their own candidates fielded against the official nominees (Balagopal 1995). The malaise of the Telugu public was reflected in pushing the Congress out and handing over the power again to the TDP in 1994. Other reason that added to its success include the cheap rice scheme promised by TDP that wooed the voters. NTR was later succeeded by N. Chandrababu Naidu after the demise of the former in 1995. It seemed that the bipolar contest had come to stand still in the state. Even the Bharatiya Janata Party (BJP) was not strong enough to face the challenge. So BJP came in alliance with TDP in 1999 even though TDP was not the part of National Democratic Alliance (NDA). TDP, being one of the major coalition partners at the federal level, bagged twenty-nine seats. In an NDA-led coalition government by Atal Behari Vajpayee, TDP was able to have at least four ministers and other key positions in different ministries. TDP's GMC Balayogi was also made speaker of Lok Sabha as a part of deal negotiated between the two parties to support NDA on the confidence motion in the Lok Sabha (Editorial 1998b: 805). The alliance with NDA was assumed as beneficiary by TDP as it thought to gain substantial power along with projects and good financial support from the union government. Furthermore, both the parties were in search for partners to prevent Congress from coming to power at the centre. While TDP and BJP became allies, the Left parties supported the Congress as they were not in favour of BJP coming to power. Formation of these alliances created a friction between TDP and Left parties that had been serving together under the umbrella of United Front. While the Left had warned Chandrababu Naidu to break the alliance if the latter support BJP, TDP found it difficult to go along with the Left as TDP made a marked shift in its policies by advocating economic reforms (Suri 2004: 1488). Thus increasing conflicts between the two resulted in the scrapping of their alliance.

Alliance with TDP proved to be helpful for BJP too as it managed to extend its influence beyond Hyderabad and adjoining districts in

Telangana (Editorial 1998a: 373). The party though had an influence in the regions of coastal Andhra and Telangana, but it was not strong enough to come out as the ruling party.

The alliance, however, over the period of time became weak as TDP tried to isolate itself from the adverse impact of policies followed by the BJP government. The policies created unrest among the public and, as a consequence, Chandrababu Naidu decided to keep BJP at an arm's distance. In fact he criticised Vajpayee's government for the price rise of essential commodities (Kumar 1999). Naidu thought that alliance with BJP would harm TDP's interests at the state level and thus denied any alliance or seat adjustment with the former in the state Assembly elections. BJP's success was in doldrums as it began to lose state after state. TDP also calculated that the close ties between the two triggered a fear of losing the Muslim votes that was quite crucial to win over few Parliamentary and Assembly constituencies.

The 2004 Assembly elections saw a resurfacing of the Congress party. TDP lost the elections with a difference of mere 5 per cent vote. The reasons for the loss of TDP as stated and analysed by Chandrababu Naidu in the official website of TDP included the alliance with BJP, the anti-incumbency factor against Naidu, the opposition by Naxalites, the promises of freebies by Congress, and too many forces joined together in the name of Telangana against the TDP. The TDP, after breaking its alliance with the BJP, adopted for populist policies by promising free electricity for farmers, Indiramma Housing Scheme for homeless, and so on. The TRS and the CPI came into alliance and announced the formation of the Telangana state if they came to power in the 2009 elections.

Election verdict 2014

The elections to the 16th Lok Sabha in the state of Andhra Pradesh once again reflected the upper hand of the regional parties in the state that veered around the local issues and agendas rather than on the national agendas. Telangana Rashtriya Samiti (TRS) emerged as the prominent contender in the region of Telangana, which saw the surfacing of new state leader K. Chandrashekhar Rao (KCR). Table 15.1 illustrates the electoral outcome in Telangana which clearly indicates the whooping victory of TRS with the party bagging eleven out of seventeen Lok Sabha seats, followed by the Congress securing two seats, the BJP and the Telugu Desam Party (TDP) each winning one seat, and, in combination, their pre-electoral alliance won two seats. The YSR (Yuvajana, Shramika, Rythu) Congress and the AIMIM (All India Majlis-e-Ittehad-ul Muslimeen) also fetched one seat each. The residual Andhra Pradesh (Seemandhra) saw an alliance between the TDP and the BJP, but the key holder in this deal remained that the TDP that registered remarkable victory after more than a decade. Table 15.2 indicates the electoral report card of the state of Andhra Pradesh. While the TDP came out in flying colours by winning fifteen out of twenty-one contested seats and its alliance partner gaining two seats, Congress party didn't even manage to open its account in the state where it had been in power since 2004. The YRS Congress emerged as the main opposition party in the state by winning eight seats.

The politics in the bifurcated states witnessed opportunism, defections, and policies of populism. The political developments at the time of elections indicated the struggle between major national parties to grab a share in political power of the two states that led to politics of opportunism. Before the construction of Telangana as a separate state, TRS president KCR committed to merge the TRS with the Congress once the bifurcation process was over. In an interview with a newspaper, KCR's daughter Kavitha said:

> Our stand is absolutely clear: If Congress carves out a separate state of Telangana, with Hyderabad as the capital city, we are ready for a merger. My father has said it earlier too, that we are not in this agitation for position or power. Once Telangana attains statehood, our job is done.
>
> (Sharma 2012)

Table 15.1 National Election Study 2014: Telangana

Parties	Seats contested 2014	Seats won 2014	Seat change from 2009
Congress	16	2	−10
BJP	8	1	1
TDP	9	1	−1
TRS	17	11	9
YRS Congress	13	1	1
AIMIM	4	1	0
Other parties	215	0	−2

Source: 2014. 'Statistics: National Election Study 2014': 134

Table 15.2 National Election Study 2014: Residual Andhra Pradesh

Parties	Seats contested 2014	Seats won 2014	Seat change from 2009
Congress	25	0	−21
BJP	4	2	2
TDP	21	15	11
YRS Congress	25	8	8
Other parties	283	0	0

Source: 2014. 'Statistics: National Election Study 2014': 132

KCR, however, didn't abide by his promise made before the poll. He even refused to have an alliance with the Congress when the latter came up with such a proposal. This evidently signifies that after spearheading the Telangana movement, the TRS was expecting to reap an electoral dividend in the region of Telangana. The coalescence of the Congress and the TRS would have not been a sagacious choice on the part of KCR as it would have made the TRS relinquish its seats to Congress. In the newly created state, Congress needed the TRS more than the latter needed the former. KCR, however, didn't entirely neglect Congress as the national election follow up was still awaited. KCR pointed that his party was ready to hand out support to Congress if the latter was able to grab the power at the centre. This came as a jolt for the Congress leadership as it felt betrayed by KCR. In the new predicament, Congress couldn't qualify to get a role of junior partner in the state and it also became a toilsome task for it to challenge Modi's leverage. Had Congress been able to manage an alliance with TRS, it arguably could have procured more Lok Sabha seats to counter the pressure generated by the Modi wave. Congress in order to counter the Modi wave and fetch more seats devised its Plan B by profiting from the goodwill produced by the creation of new state. It invited the Telangana Joint Action Committee leaders to join the party and contest the polls on Congress tickets for Parliament and the new Assembly (Ramachandran 2014). Unfortunately, even the Plan B was not able to meet the high aspirations of Congress leaders. Finally, Congress satisfied itself by finding a partner in the Communist Party of India. In the negotiations Congress demanded two Lok Sabha seats and twelve Assembly seats, but it had to settle down with a Khammam Parliament seat and nine Assembly seats.

Stamped with the mark of perfidy, KCR came up with a number of arguments in his justification for not amalgamating with Congress. He expressed his acrimony with Congress for not taking TRS in confidence while preparing the Telangana Bill; for tempting TRS legislators and members of Parliament to join the Congress; for delaying the scheduled day of the formation of the Telangana state to 2 June; for his disappointment on the behalf of central government for not preparing people of Seemandhra for bifurcation; and for opting for a post-election date for genesis of Telangana (Venkateshwarlu 2014a).

The chief loser in the electoral contest was the Congress party that suffered setbacks in both the regions. Though the central government's pronouncement to award statehood status to Telangana fetched Congress two Lok Sabha seats in the new state, the Congress leaders in the state were not proficient enough to seize the credit of party's initiative and the entire credit was successfully claimed by KCR. The Congress party's fancy to have strong influence in Telangana not only wrecked the party but also witnessed a complete knockout in truncated Andhra Pradesh consisting of the regions of Seemandhra and Rayalaseema, where a very strong simulation was generated against the party's resolution for bifurcation. It was for the first time in the record of Andhra Pradesh that Congress had no representation in Andhra Pradesh Assembly. As Tables 15.1 and 15.2 show, Congress lost twenty-one seats in the 2014 elections in comparison with the 2009 Lok Sabha elections. Congress had thirty-three members from Andhra Pradesh in 2009. The grudge of people of Seemandhra and Rayalaseema could be acknowledged from the reality that low attendance welcomed the Congress President Sonia Gandhi at the Andhra Muslim College grounds when she turned up to address an election meeting and the mob remained apathetic: it did not cheer once during her thirty-minute address ('Low turn-out at Sonia's 1st rally in Seemandhra post-division', 2014). It is ironic that mainly Congress felt the brunt of bifurcation of Andhra Pradesh. The reality is that this bifurcation was also supported by the BJP with the backing of the TDP and the YRS Congress.

TDP, which had previously objected to the division of Andhra Pradesh by emphasising the Naxal threat and its pledge to development (Editorial 2004: 1184), took a U-turn and supported a separate Telangana state in 2008 (Balakrishnan 2011). Such a move by Chandrababu Naidu grabbed his party electoral presence in both the states. The TDP–BJP alliance also kept both the parties in the limelight as it raised anxiety about the allotment of seats between the two parties. In the past, both the parties had a merger, but when Chandrababu Naidu lost the 2004 elections in the state he charged 'communal' BJP for the electoral debacle. Once again, the two parties merged to have success in Lok Sabha elections. Naidu and BJP leader Prakah Javadekar announced the alliance on 6 April with BJP contesting 47 out of 119 Assembly seats and eight out of seventeen Lok Sabha seats in Telangana, and 15 out of 175 Assembly seats and five out of twenty-five Lok Sabha seats in Andhra Pradesh. Chandrababu Naidu rationalised this fusion in the interest of the nation and to set free it from the crooked and incompetent rule of Congress (Venkateshwarlu 2014b). The merger proved not only advantageous in improving the electoral score of both political parties, it also opened the doors for the BJP in south India. The BJP that had always been a minor player in Coastal Andhra bagged two seats in the region. Even Naidu expected that this alliance will consolidate his stand in Seemandhra and would also get an opportunity to play key role in national politics if the BJP comes to power. The TDP, however, could have functioned even better if it had created a separate unit of party in Telangana as advised by some MLAs and leaders of region a few years back. Naidu dragged his feet back from the creation of such a unit as he feared repercussion in Seemandhra. The TDP even failed to capitalise on the organisational weakness of TRS as it did in 2009 Assembly elections where the TRS managed to get only thirty-nine seats.

The other political parties in the region were not able to perform up to the mark in the Lok Sabha elections. It was anticipated that the young and zealous leader Jaganmohan Reddy of YRS Congress would be able to do well, keeping in consideration his past track record. In the past he had defeated Congress and TDP candidates in by-elections.[1] By this time his magic could not work as people were not ready to elect such a candidate whose name was tangled in corruption charges. Albeit the party asserted to have a strong rural support because of the populist schemes administered by his father, the late Y.S. Rajasekhara Reddy. The memory of populist policies of YSR led the YSR Congress in bagging the second position in the state and emerged as the main opposition party. Even the social base of YRS Congress was not intact. With the proclamation of Chandrababu Naidu to appoint two leaders from Kapu and backward classes to the post of Deputy Chief Minister in both Telangana and Seemandhra if the party came to power, a large segment of these two communities switched their loyalty to TDP. Even the first-time voters and middle-class voters showed their inclination to TDP over YRS Congress (Venkateshwarlu 2014d). The YSR Congress demonstrated its influence in northern Andhra Pradesh,

Rayalaseema, and Palnadu, but could not gain adequate seats to form a government.

The formation of Telangana and TDP–BJP alliance also created insecurity amidst the Muslim community of the state that account for 12 per cent of the population in the undivided state of Andhra Pradesh. Political parties were reluctant to give party tickets to Muslim candidates as they were sceptical about their victory prospects. The 2009 Assembly elections in the undivided Andhra Pradesh had marked a sharp polarisation of votes against Muslims in the state. Hence the parties were wary of putting up Muslim candidates. In these elections four Muslims contested from the Congress party, out of which three won; from the TDP, one out of four Muslim contestants won; and none from the fourteen Muslim aspirants from the Praja Rajyam Party won the elections. Doubting the success of Muslim candidates, TRS president KCR made a declaration of not giving his party ticket to any Muslim candidate. He also stepped back from his earlier declaration of making a Muslim Deputy Chief Minister of the new state. (Gugavarthy 2014). In the 2014 elections, TDP and Congress had put up only one Muslim candidate each in Seemandhra for twenty-five seats. While TDP put up N.M. Farook in Nandyal, Congress handed a ticket to Abdul Waheed Shaik in Guntur. Minorities across Seemandhra have been traditionally Congress supporters (Vijayawada 2014a). But this time a considerable number of Muslim voters rendered their support to YSR Congress, primarily due to their anger with Congress over the decision of separate Telangana. But their expectations were not fulfilled by the YSR Congress either as it did not field any minority community contestant in the Lok Sabha constituencies in Seemandhra. So the politics of communal polarisation was not only played by Hindutva BJP but also by other political parties in the state except the AIMIM and the CPI (M) that opposed formation of Telangana state as they had an apprehension that it could strengthen Sangh Parivar in the state. Such a position by the two parties and subsequent growth of anti-Muslim sentiments led the AIMIM to win only one out of four contested seats in the 2014 Lok Sabha elections in Telangana. The party had no signs of a presence in Seemandhra either. Leaving aside the Muslim factor, the major reason that led to the failure of the party in Telangana was its firm stand against the creation of Telangana state.

Election issues

The prime issue that made an impact on the 2014 elections in the state was the Telangana movement and the bifurcation of Andhra

Pradesh. It also remained a prospect of worry for all the major political parties in the state. Though the parties like TDP and BJP claimed that the formation of Telangana would not have much influence on the upcoming elections as the resolution for the construction of the state had already been passed, but the reality was that the genesis of a new state made many parties modify their attitude towards the issue. They had realised that holding only a positive attitude to the demand could bag them confidence of the masses and secure their vote banks in Telangana region. Jagan Mohan Reddy, Congress MP, had earlier opposed the Telangana state formation but later his party adopted a neutral stand. Parties that favoured the demand were TRS, BJP, CPI, Lok Satta, and TDP, and those who opposed it included AIMIM and CPI (M). MIM even turned down the offer of KCR to join his Cabinet (Ifthekhar 2014). AIMIM, though it did not support the bifurcation of the state, in its report to Srikrishna Committee, Asaduddin Owaisi said that Rayalaseema should be merged with Telangana to create 'Greater Telangana' if the centre decides to bifurcate the state ('MIM Seeks Merger of Telangana, Seema' 2010). There were apprehensions in the minds of Muslims in the state that if Telangana was created, it would benefit the BJP. The merger of Rayalaseema with Telangana would have provided for the consolidation of the considerable Muslim population in the state. As far as the Congress was concerned, within Congress there were two conflicting views – party leaders at centre supported the demand and Congress leadership in the state protested against the move.

As per the post-poll survey carried out by the Centre for the Study of Developing Societies (CSDS) for CNN-IBN and *The Hindu*, the voting demeanour in Telangana was by and large patterned by the centre's last verdict on the controversial statehood issue (FP Staff 2013). Two parallel waves were witnessed in the two regions of Andhra Pradesh. While pro-Telangana sentiment was dominant in Telangana region, Seemandhra witnessed stiff opposition to the demand of a separate Telangana state. More interestingly, within the region the intensity of Telangana sentiment varied. The twin cities of Hyderabad-Secunderabad and Ranga Reddy districts in central Telangana were seen as 'medium intensity areas' where the Congress and AIMIM had larger manifestations and a better grasp than the TRS. In the southern districts of Nalgoanda and Mehaboobnagar, TRS also appeared to be overshadowed by the Congress and the TDP (Manoj 2014).

Apart from the state bifurcation, the issue of development in both the regions remained the major focus of the elections throughout the campaign. The development agenda itself was the main contentious issue that remained on the forefront. It was argued by the pro-Telangana parties that the region's contribution in state revenue was 76 per cent but it just received one-third of the total Andhra Pradesh budget. In the educational field, they received only 9.86 per cent aid in government primary schools and 37.85 per cent aid in government degree colleges (Jayashankar 2009).

Even so, the government of India selected nine districts belonging to the Telangana region out of thirteen in Andhra Pradesh under the BRGF scheme. It underlined the backwardness and underdevelopment in the region of Telangana. But if one studies the per capita income in state, the picture is quite different. The coastal Andhra region records a per capita income of Rs 36,496 followed by Telangana (including Hyderabad) with a per capita income of Rs 36,082, Rs 33,771 excluding Hyderabad city, and Rs 33,056 in Rayalaseema at 2007–2008 current prices (GOI 2010: 65). As per this data, Rayalaseema had better ground to accuse the union and the state government for neglect of the region.

Election manifestoes

With the acceptance of the demand of creating a separate Telangana state, the parties in contention kept the issue of development in mind while preparing their election manifestoes. During the election campaign, KCR promised the people of Telangana to redress the injustice done to the region in the past and assured them a 'Golden Telangana' in the future. He focused on the agriculture sector as 80 per cent of people resided in rural areas. Instead of removing hurdles in the path of economic development, KCR opted for following the policies of populism which currently don't appear to be a good idea for a state in its infancy. TRC, in its poll manifesto, spoke of the reconstruction of Telangana, the transformation of Hyderabad into a global software and hardware hub like Silicon Valley and Shanghai, building ten thermal power projects to overcome the power shortage, two-bedroom houses for the weaker sections, three acres of cultivable land to each scheduled caste family, and a 12 per cent job quota for the scheduled castes and minorities (Venkateshwarlu 2014c). The other promises made in the manifesto included Rs 1,500 pension for the physically handicapped, Rs 1,000 pension for widows, contract employees will be made permanent, restoration of lakes to their original form, Satellite Township around Hyderabad, special increments for Telangana employees, and free education from KG to PG. So KCR was all set with its goody bags ready for the people of region if they voted him into power.

Speaking regarding TDP, antagonists had continuously hit the TDP chief for vacillation on the tender issue of state bifurcation. In an endeavour to resume the lost reliability, Naidu went on *Padyatra*, like late YSR before the 2009 elections, around the state travelling over 8,000 km (ET Bureau 2014). Naidu attempted to infuse faith amid population of Seemandhra on their future by projecting the achieved progress in the state during his reign between 1995 and 2004 as Chief Minister. Naidu committed to turn Seemandhra into *Swarnandhra*. TDP seemed to be successful in persuading Seemandhra voters that the state would develop better under the leadership of Chandrababu Naidu, as he already had had a successful and noteworthy experience as Chief Minister for two terms in comparison with the inexperienced and stained leadership of Y.S. Jaganmohan Reddy. While TRS twirled around a one-point agenda, i.e. the creation of Telangana as a separate state and confined itself within the boundaries of Telangana, Chandrababu Naidu of TDP came up with 'Two Eyes Policy' that conversed about seeking fair justice to both the regions. TDP chief also promised the people of Telangana to provide them more job opportunities if the electorates brought his party to power ('Naidu pledges job creation' 2014). Naidu, who declined to create a separate Telangana unit of TDP, came up with two different manifestoes, one for Telangana and the other for residuary Andhra Pradesh. Unlike the past, Naidu-led TDP showed its inclination towards benefit to all sectors that included agriculture, employment, women safety, and so on. But regardless of all efforts, TDP couldn't become successful in Telangana since its top leadership hailed from Andhra Pradesh regions of Coastal Andhra.

In order to regain lost glory of Congress in Seemandhra, Sonia Gandhi justified its decision to bifurcate the state by asserting that the state reorganisation was done in a manner that protected the interests of Seemandhra. A special development package was announced for Seemandhra that included the setting up of special boards for distribution of Krishna and Godavari river waters. Polavaram multi-purpose irrigation project was granted national status that would receive 90 per cent funding from the centre and the balance of 10 per cent as a loan under the Special Category State status for Seemandhra ('Sonia slams TDP, BJP over poll pact; low turnout at rally' 2014)

Congress party's President Sonia Gandhi accused the BJP–TDP bond as a menace that could harm the secular fabric of India and presented her own party as the one that had always worked to preserve the secular tenets and ideology. During her election tour of Telangana she claimed TRS of having similar communal orientation like the BJP. She came up with the comprehensible idea and plan for Telangana's progress by spending an amount of Rs 40,000 crore to make Telangana green and prosperous. Talking about the previous works done by Congress in the region that included Rs 6,000 crore outer ring road in Ranga Reddy district and development of Rajiv Gandhi international airport, she committed that 1 of 100 satellite cities planned across the country would come up in Vikarabad in Ranga Reddy district ('TRS is Opportunistic, says Sonia' 2014). Thus all the political parties made tremendous efforts to have a strong foot in the newly created state.

Election campaign

Elections in the state witnessed an intense campaign. Thirteen Seemandhra districts witnessed a zealous contest among three major players: TDP–BJP, the YSR Congress, and the Congress. Each of the party came forward with their star campaigners to coax voters. Parties held marathon road shows in the day and addressed immense public gatherings at night. Each of the party tried to mark its visibility in the region and made efforts to gain attention to have a strong foothold in the residuary Andhra Pradesh that was to be inculcated on 2 June. The star campaigners for the BJP-led NDA were its Prime Minister nominee Narendra Modi and the former party president M. Venkaiah Naidu. BJP's prime ministerial candidate Narendra Modi addressed five meetings in a single day. He shared the dais with Naidu and Pawan Kalyan and made an attack at YSR Congress by asking the public to opt between '*swarnandhra*' and 'scam Andhra' ('YSR Congress, TDP clash for power in Seemandhra' 2014).

TDP brought forward its chief Chandrababu Naidu, Nara Lokesh, and Jana Sena leader Pawan Kalyan as its luminary campaigners. Narendra Modi participated in BJP's election meetings that were held at Karimnagar and Nizamabad and also shared the dais with Chandrababu Naidu at Mahbubnagar and Hyderabad.

Campaigning duties of YSR Congress were shouldered by Jaganmohan Reddy, his mother Vijayamma, and sister Sharmila. Calling himself the '*messiah*' of the underprivileged, Jaganmohan Reddy followed on the footsteps of his late father who died in a helicopter crash in 2009. Jaganmohan Reddy attracted the masses by promising to do a complete makeover of Andhra Pradesh if he came to power. YRS Congress promised to give Rs 1,000 per month for education for every child, waiver of loans for women self-help groups and building of 50 lakh houses for the underprivileged ('YSR Congress, TDP clash for power in Seemandhra' 2014). But the promotion by YRS was not up to the mark. Its chief Y.S. Jaganmohan Reddy campaigned only in

Hyderabad city on the final day of campaigning. Also his younger sister Sharmila paid a visit to only few districts. Congress, on the other hand, banked heavily on its celebrity K. Chiranjivi who was made campaign head in the region. Congress also brought in Prime Minister Manmohan Singh, Sonia Gandhi, and Rahul Gandhi to address public gatherings at Bhuvanagiri, Karimnagar, Chevella, Medak, Mahbubnagar, Nizamabad, Warangal, and Hyderabad to gain public attention and boost the drooping spirit of party cadre. Former Chief Minister N. Kiran Kumar Reddy, recently formed his own party 'Jai Samaikhyandhra Party' (JSP) also drew large crowds in north coastal Andhra and Rayalaseema areas by organising road shows (Umanadh 2014). Telangana Rashtra Samiti supremo KCR alone spearheaded the party's crusade all over the region ('Star campaigners descend on poll-bound Telangana' 2014).

The election campaign also saw personal attacks among leaders in the state. The attacks became most spiteful with TDP leader Chandrababu's accusing the Congress as a party of thieves and cheats. He also called YSR Congress as a party of robbers and KCR as a betrayer of Telangana ('Telangana's spiteful campaign is finally over' 2014). Even KCR criticised leaders of rival parties like Chandrababu Naidu and Ponnala Lakshmaiah (Congress) and specifically targeted people from coastal Andhra and Rayalaseema who have been living in various parts of Telangana for decades now ('Statehood issue, personal attacks mark Telangana poll campaign' 2014). Such statements by KCR against the people of Seemandhra forced TDP and other parties to launch a complaint against him with the Election Commission, but no action was taken against him. Even BJP's prime ministerial candidate Narendra Modi, while addressing series of public meetings as part of his 'Bharat Vijay Yatraa' in Telangana, attacked the UPA for being steeped in corruption and claimed that it will not be able to bring development to the newly carved out Telangana state. He pointed that Telangana became a reality because of the people who sacrificed their lives and not because of the Congress. Criticising the Congress rule he said, 'You gave power to Congress, it gave you naxalism, but I will give Telangana youth a bhagya rekha, not a line dividing two states. In Congress rule, there is no Jai Jawan Jai Kisan, but only Mar Jawan Mar Kisan' ('UPA unfit to rule Telangana: Modi' 2014).

Another poll issue that remained in talks in the region of Seemandhra was the search of a new capital for the state in the wake of the bifurcation of Andhra Pradesh. Interestingly, candidates cutting across party lines were divided over the location of the capital city and the demand ranged from Visakhapatnam, Vijayawada, Ongole to Guntur in coastal Andhra to Kurnool of Rayalaseema region. Congress leader and Union Tribal Affairs Minister Kishore Chandra Deo stressed the need to make Visakhapatnam the capital of Seemandhra as it would spur development in the six districts surrounding the coastal city. But his Cabinet colleague from Kurnool constituency, Kotla Jaya Surya Prakash Reddy, demanded capital status for Kurnool as it had plenty of water and other infrastructure required for a capital. The TDP candidate from Vijayawada Lok Sabha constituency assures voters that he would strive hard to secure the status of state capital for Vijayawada as Vijayawada is centrally located and it is equidistant from Visakhapatnam, Anantapur, Bangalore, and Chennai ('Permanent capital for Seemandhra a poll issue' 2014).

Politics in Andhra Pradesh is dominated by major castes like the Reddys, the Kammas, and the Kapus. Political parties in Andhra Pradesh have their affiliation to particular castes. The Congress is recognised with the Reddys, the TDP with the Kammas, and the TRS with the Velamas. Also the history has shown that the post of Chief Minister, apart from for few years, has always been taken by either of the two dominant castes, Reddys and Kammas, which jointly account for hardly 10 per cent of the population. The caste factor had been so strong in the state that during 1980s when Congress lost from TDP it filed a petition in High Court to issue a writ of Quo Warranto to the Chief Minister N.T. Rama Rao. In this petition it charged that TDP's rule has mainly benefited the Kamma community as most of the nominees of boards, committees, corporations, councils, and trusts have been nominated from Kamma community and Reddy community has been ignored (Balagopal 1987: 17360). As far as the Kapu community is concerned, it has a strong hold in the coastal Andhra region, especially in Vizianagaram, Anakapalle, Araku, Amalapuram, Rajahmundry, Kakinada, Narasapur, Machilipatnam, and Eluru, but ironically, no Kapu leader could ever become the Chief Minister of the state.

Caste politics again played a significant role in these elections. Having lost its ground in the Seemandhra region due to the bifurcation of Andhra Pradesh, the Congress party tried to revive itself in the residuary state of Andhra Pradesh through a Kapu–BC combination. It named Dr N. Raghuveera Reddy Yadav, a Backward Classes leader, as its new president for the Andhra Pradesh Congress Committee. While the party substituted Botsa Satyanarayana, a Kapu, but it gave the charge of party's campaigning to Chiranjeevi by pitching him as a luminary campaigner. Anam Ramnarayana Reddy was also made an important part of the party to balance the Reddy factor.

In an undivided Andhra Pradesh, the higher castes comprised 22 per cent of the state population. But after bifurcation, their population got shrunk to 10.7 per cent in Telangana, 11.8 per cent, and 24.2 per cent in coastal Andhra. As far as OBC is concerned, their presence became stronger in Telangana with a little loss in Seemandhra. They comprised 44.5 per cent in united AP, but after division of state they have witnessed a rise of 50.7 per cent in Telangana. However, the population decreased to 43 per cent in Rayalaseema and 39 per cent in coastal Andhra. Thus more changes in the caste equations were evident in Telangana politics. Before the division of state, KCR promised to make a Dalit as the first Chief Minister of Telangana, but once the state got formed, he took a U-turn. Later, Chandrababu Naidu pledged to give the chair of Chief Minister to a backward class's representative that comprised 56 per cent of the population in the Telangana region. Naidu was clever enough to make such a declaration. He had realised that he does not have a very strong hold in this region. He knew his strength in Seemandhra and wanted to be its Chief Minister. Thus, he did not declare a backward class Chief Minister from Seemandhra. The irony is that all major political parties in Andhra Pradesh have so far been identified with the upper castes (Sudhir 2014).

Summing up

As mentioned earlier the BJP entered into an alliance with the Telugu Desam in both Telangana and Seemandhra regions, contested 45 of the 117 Assembly and eight of the seventeen Lok Sabha seats in Telangana, and 12 of the 175 Assembly and four of the twenty-five Lok Sabha seats in Seemandhra. While the whole country witnessed a landslide victory of the Modi-led BJP party, the party managed to win just five Assembly seats and one Lok Sabha constituency in Telangana region. Telangana BJP president G. Kishan Reddy won from Amberpet constituency with a margin of more than 62,000 votes over his nearest rival. But in Seemandhra region the party managed to mark its presence. BJP won two of the Lok Sabha seats with K. Haribabu winning from Visakhapatnam constituency and industrialist Gokaraju Gangaraju romping the Narasapuram seat. While the former Union Minister D. Purandeswari and K. Jayaram lost Rajampet and Tirupati (SC) seats respectively.

Thus BJP helped in strengthening the hold of TDP in Seemandhra. Even Jaganmohan Reddy admitted that the wave in favour of Narendra Modi played a big role in his party's defeat in the Seemandhra region ('Modi wave played a part in our defeat, says Jaganmohan Reddy' 2014).

In the Telangana region, as mentioned earlier, the issue of state division took precedence over others and the 'Modi factor' did not work in rural areas as the BJP won mainly in Hyderabad city and surrounding areas. Prior to elections, Narendra Modi was very hopeful of its victory in Telangana. Describing Telangana and Seemandhra as two motherless new-borns, Modi during his campaign said he was ready to take responsibility of nurturing them with care.

The TRS generated a wave of its own. The victory of the TRS is not just a whirlwind campaign of one month, but of years of sweat and toil, which helped the TRS win the confidence of the electorate and the chance to form the first government of Telangana. People reposed faith in a party that they know took birth just to serve them. And with this emerged a new state leader KCR in Telangana who was sworn as its new Chief Minister.

In the wake of bifurcation of Andhra Pradesh there had been a steady shift of Congress MLAs, and other senior leaders to TDP in Seemandhra region. With Congress facing a certain rout in the region in the simultaneous elections to Assembly and Lok Sabha due to the public anger over division of the state, many senior leaders of Congress looked upon TDP to secure their political future. Congress failure in both Lok Sabha and Assembly elections was also due to the absence of strong leadership to match the persona of KCR or Chandrababu Naidu.

KCR coming to power in Telangana also led to defections among various political parties like the Congress. Many members of TDP left their party for TRS to have better electoral prospects. Defectionists that include Kadiam Srihari, A. Chandulal, T.N. Rao, and others were rewarded by TRS by including them in the state Cabinet. The TRS leadership was reported to be exerting pressure more on TDP leaders in the region as they saw TDP as a serious threat in Telangana. Accordingly, the TRS leaders played mind games through their continuous attempts to project TDP as anti-Telangana (Sukumar 2014). The rank and file of Congress collapsed with several union ministers from the region resigning, while some like D Purandeswari switched over to BJP. Moreover, the party also suffered a setback following the launch of JSP headed by former Congress Chief Minister N. Kiran Kumar Reddy (Vijayawada 2014b). In a shock to YSRCP chief Y.S. Jaganmohan Reddy, his party's newly elected MP from the Nandyal constituency joined the Telugu Desam Party and another rebel MP has reportedly been testing waters to cross over to the TDP. The defectionists justified their move on the grounds of bringing all-round development in their regions ('MP Deserts YSRCP, Joins Rival TDP' 2014).

The Telangana experience showed the increasing importance of leadership as one of the most important determining factors in the state-level elections. It is evident from the fact that state-level leadership had led to the victory of BJP in Gujarat, Madhya Pradesh, and Chhattisgarh. Even in residual Andhra Pradesh, BJP could come in power due the alliance with the TDP.

The TRS victory also receives attention because of the simple fact that TRS has been the only state-level party leading the movement for a separate state that has come to power after the creation of the intended state. This had been unlike Jharkhand Mukti Morcha (JMM), Uttarakhand Kranti Dal (UKD), and Chhattisgarh Mukti Morcha (CMM) that led the similar movement but could not come in power after the formation of their respective states. Even the Communist party of India that pursued a battle against Nizam's domineering rule in Hyderabad during the 1950s could not gain electoral victory after the state of Andhra Pradesh got constructed and power was captured by the Congress.

Note

1 Jaganmohan Reddy's YSR Congress party won by-polls in Andhra Pradesh by winning fifteen out of eighteen Assembly seats, including one Nellore Lok Sabha seat.

Bibliography

Balagopal, K. 1987. 'Congress(I) vs Telugu Desam Party: At Last a Lawful Means for Overthrowing a Lawfully Constituted Government', *Economic and Political Weekly*, 22(41): 1736–1738.

———. 1995. 'Andhra Elections: What Happened and What Did Not Happen', *EPW*, 30(3): 136–139.

Balakrishnan, Bhaskar. 2011. 'Telangana Demand Should Be Accepted', *The Hindu: Businessline*, November 8.

Editorial. 1998a. 'Changed Scenario', *Economic and Political Weekly*, 33(8): 373.

———. 1998b. 'Promises Not to Keep?', *Economic and Political Weekly*, 33(15): 805.

———. 2004. 'Telangana Factor', *Economic and Political Weekly*, 39(12): 1184.

———. 2014. 'Statistics: National Election Study 2014', *Economic and Political Weekly*, 49(39): 130–134.

ET Bureau. 2014. 'Chandrababu Naidu's TDP Sweeps Andhra With 102 Seats Out of 175; K. Chandrashekhar Rao Set to Be Telangana CM', *Economic Times*, May 17.

FP Staff. 2013. 'Telangana and Jagan Key to 2014 Polls in Andhra Pradesh: Survey'. www.firstpost.com/politics/andhra-pradesh-in-crossroads-of-telangana-potboiler-jaganmohan-avatar-979723.html (accessed on April 15, 2015).

GOI. 2010. *Report of the Committee for Consultations on the Situations in Andhra Pradesh*. New Delhi: GOI.

Gugavarthy, Ajay. 2014. 'Muslims of Telangana: A Ground Report', *Economic and Political Weekly*, 49(17).

Haragopal, G. 2010. 'The Telangana People's Movement: The Unfolding Political Culture', *Economic and Political Weekly*, 45(42): 51–60.

Ifthekhar, J.S. 2014. 'MIM Declines TRS Offer to Join Cabinet', *The Hindu*, May 23.

Jayashankar, K. 2009. 'Telangana Movement: The Demand for a Separate State'. http://im.rediff.com/news/2009/dec/Telangana.pdf (accessed on April 24, 2015).

Kumar, S. Nagesh. 1999. 'Second Thoughts in Andhra Pradesh', *Frontline*, 15(26), December 19–January 1.

'Low Turn-Out at Sonia's 1st Rally in Seemandhra Post-Division'. 2014. *Deccan Herald*, May 2. www.deccanherald.com/election/content/403816/low-turn-sonias-1st-rally.html (accessed on April 15, 2015).

Manoj, C.L. 2014. 'New TRS, Stable Congress in Close Fight in the New State Telengana', *Economic Times*, March 20.

'MIM Seeks Merger of Telangana, Seema'. 2010. *Times of India*, April 19.

'Modi Wave Played a Part in Our Defeat, Says Jaganmohan Reddy'. 2014. *The Hindu*, May 16.

'MP Deserts YSRCP, Joins Rival TDP'. 2014. *Deccan Herald*, May 25. www.deccanherald.com/election/content/409627/mp-deserts-ysrcp-joins-rival.html (accessed on April 15, 2015).

Nag, Kingsshuk. 2011. *Battleground Telangana: Chronicle of an Agitation*. New Delhi: Harpercollins.

'Naidu Pledges Job Creation'. 2014. *Deccan Herald*, April 12. www.deccanherald.com/election/content/398762/naidu-pledges-job-creation.html (accessed on April 15, 2015).

'Permanent Capital for Seemandhra a Poll Issue'. 2014. *Deccan Herald*, April 26. www.deccanherald.com/election/content/402215/permanent-capital-seemandhra-poll-issue.html (accessed on April 15, 2015).

Ramachandran, Rajesj. 2014. 'Election 2014: Congress' Plan B for Telangana Ensures Large Share of Votes and Seats for the Party', *Economic Times*, February 27.

Sharma, Nidhi. 2012. 'Telangana Rashtra Samithi Willing to Merge With Congress for Telangana', *Economics Times*, September 13.

Shatrughna, M. 1983. 'Anti-Congress Wave Unabated', *Economic and Political Weekly*, 18(26): 1122–1123.

———. 1988. 'TDP Consolidates Rural Vote', *Economic and Political Weekly*, 23(12): 571–572.

———. 1990. 'Andhra Assembly Elections: Congress and TDP', *Economic and Political Weekly*, 25(4): 201–202.

'Sonia Slams TDP, BJP Over Poll Pact; Low Turnout at Rally'. 2014. *Deccan Herald*, May 2. www.deccanherald.com/election/content/403826/sonia-slams-tdp-bjp-over.html (accessed on April 15, 2015).

Srinivasulu, K. and Prakash Sarangi. 1999. 'Political Realignments in Post-NTR Andhra Pradesh', *Economic and Political Weekly*, 34(34/35): 34–35.

'Star Campaigners Descend on Poll-Bound Telangana'. 2014. *Deccan Herald*, April 25. www.deccanherald.com/election/content/402132/star-campaigners-descend-poll-bound.html (accessed on April 15, 2015).

'Statehood Issue, Personal Attacks Mark Telangana Poll Campaign'. 2014. *Deccan Herald*, April 28. www.deccanherald.com/election/content/402725/statehood-issue-personal-attacks-mark.html (accessed on April 15, 2015).

Sudhir, Uma. 2014. 'India Matters: A "Casteing" Couch in Andhra Pradesh', April 5. www.ndtv.com/elections-news/india-matters-a-caste-ing-couch-in-andhra-pradesh-556334 (accessed on April 23, 2015).

Sukumar, C.R. 2014. 'Telangana Rashtra Samithi Goes Poaching for More Telugu Desam Party MLAs', *Economic Times*, October 29.

Suri, K.C. 2004. 'Telugu Desam Party: Rise and Prospects for Future', *Economic and Political Weekly*, 39(14/15): 1481–1490.

'Telangana's Spiteful Campaign Is Finally Over'. 2014. *Deccan Herald*, April 28. www.deccanherald.com/election/content/402837/telanganas-spiteful-campaign-finally-over.html (accessed on April 15, 2015).

'TRS Is Opportunistic, Says Sonia'. 2014. *Deccan Herald*, April 27. www.deccanherald.com/election/content/402488/trs-opportunistic-says-sonia.html (accessed on April 15, 2015).

Tummala, Krishna K. 1986. 'Democracy Triumphant in India: The Case of Andhra Pradesh', *Asian Survey*, 26(3): 378–395.

Umanadh, J.B.S. 2014. 'Curtains on Canvassing in Seemandhra', *Deccan Herald*, May 5. www.deccanherald.com/election/content/404611/curtains-canvassing-seemandhra.html (accessed on April 15, 2015).

'UPA Unfit to Rule Telangana: Modi'. 2014. *Deccan Herald*, April 22. www.deccanherald.com/election/content/401346/upa-unfit-rule-telangana-modi.html (accessed on April 15, 2015).

Venkateshwarlu, K. 2014a. 'Absolute Loser', *Frontline*, April 4.

———. 2014b. 'TDP: Telugu Modi', *Frontline*, May 2.

———. 2014c. 'Telangana Divided', *Frontline*, May 2.

———. 2014d. 'Dividends of Division', *Frontline*, June 13.
Vijayawada. 2014a. 'TDP-BJP Tie Up: Hard Choice for Minority Voters', *Deccan Herald*, May 2. www.deccanherald.com/election/content/403745/tdp-bjp-tie-up-hard.html (accessed on April 15, 2015).
———. 2014b. 'Congress in a Bind as Regional Parties Play Andhra Split Card', *Deccan Herald*, May 5. www.deccanherald.com/election/content/404425/congress-bind-regional-parties-play.html (accessed on April 15, 2015).
'YSR Congress, TDP Clash for Power in Seemandhra'. 2014. *Deccan Herald*, May 5. www.deccanherald.com/election/content/404437/ysr-congress-tdplash-power.html (accessed on April 15, 2015).

16 An inquiry into the causes and consequences of the saffron whirlwind that swept Uttar Pradesh in the 2017 Assembly election

Mujibur Rehman

Scholars and commentators following Uttar Pradesh's (UP) Assembly elections (held between 11 February and 8 March 2017) were stunned to hear the results that the Bhartiya Janata Party (BJP) won 312 seats out of 384 seats it contested in a 403 seat Assembly – and the massive nature of this mandate even amazed many of the BJP supporters. Seen as another Modi victory, some argue that this has ensured Modi's re-election in 2019, and he is destined to be India's Prime Minister for a second term. A tweet from Omar Abdullah, former Jammu and Kashmir (J&K) Chief Minister, "At this rate we might as well forget 2019 & start planning/hoping for 2024" (10 March 2017), reflected on how opposition leaders reacted to the outcome.[1] At least, three prominent factors could be attributed for considerable scepticism about the BJP's victory in the Uttar Pradesh's (UP) Assembly election among many observers of UP politics. The first one was the assumption that the whimsical decision to announce demonetisation policy on 8 November 2016 by Prime Minister Modi had generated enormous anger and frustration among voters across the caste and class; the second one was the presumed loss of the Prime Minister Modi's credibility among the voters owing to his failure to meet the electoral promises that he had made during the 2014 campaign. And the third factor was various anti-Muslim/anti-minority programmes like 'love jihad', *ghar wapsi* had unmasked the BJP's aggressive Hindutva face.[2] By doing so, the BJP had alienated Muslims in Uttar Pradesh, which lead to vote consolidation against the BJP, and given that Muslim voters are decisive in a significant number of Assembly constituencies in Uttar Pradesh, it could have led to its defeat.

Seen in this background, the outcome of the Uttar Pradesh election was a huge surprise. What are the reasons? What are the possible consequences for Muslim community and Muslim politics? In this chapter, I intend to share some of my thoughts on these two specific questions.

The argument:

> My main argument in this essay has three inter-related components. First, the Uttar Pradesh voters realised, I would argue, *that the political space created owing to the Akhilesh Yadav government's (2012–2017) colossal loss of credibility, the Modi–Shah led BJP was the best among the worst available choices.* Second, I would further argue that *Uttar Pradesh has not become abruptly fertile for the Hindu right politics, either in the months leading to the 2014 election or in 2017; instead it needs to be seen in continuity of a social base that the Hindu right already had since the 1930s or so, and nurtured over the years.* Third, *the rise of saffron power,* I would further argue, *is going to have deep ramifications for Muslim politics and Muslim community. It would systematically create political conditions for denying Muslims equal space to negotiate with political power, undermining the present democratic power structure; perpetuate Muslim backwardness through discriminatory policies like ban on cow slaughter; and pursue a deliberate policy of polarisation, leading to violence more often.*

To illustrate it further, the Congress party led by Rahul Gandhi, among others, was not seen as a serious contender on its own in the 2017 election. Its future was dependent on an alliance it could stitch together mainly with two other parties: the Samajwadi Party led by Akhilesh Yadav and the Bahujan Samaj Party (BSP) led by Mayawati. The last-minute decision by the Congress party to forge the alliance with the Samajwadi party barely diluted the anger that voters had for the ruling Samajwadi party; therefore, in the end, the intensity of anti-incumbency ran really deep; hence the voters were willing to give the Modi–Shah BJP a chance. On the issue of the Hindu right's social base, the BJP's social base was substantially harnessed during the Ayodhya movement in the 1980s. Though this base was not electorally rewarding for the BJP, the arguments and narratives of the Hindu right had percolated down to its last member clearly and the interregenum period did not see any counter-narrative, which is why the base was so receptive to the Modi campaign and embraced Modi wave uncritically. Therefore, the current electoral success needs to be seen in continuity of several decades, going back to pre-Partition days, than any abrupt explosion of the Hindu Right ideology in Uttar Pradesh purely owing to Modi–Shah leadership in recent years.

> While this is the general outline of the argument, the details are more complex.
> I will attempt to unravel some of the details in the following narrative.[3]

Explaining the BJP's landslide victory

The humiliating results for most of the prominent opposition parties – particularly the Congress(I) (forty-four seats with vote share of 19.31 per cent), the Bahujan Samaj Party (BSP) (no seats with vote share of 4.14 per cent), and the Samajwadi Party (SP) (five seats with vote share of 12.96 per cent) – in the 2014 Parliamentary election should have encouraged these parties to put together some sort of credible coalition to fight the BJP in the 2017 Assembly election in Uttar Pradesh. The underlying motive for these political parties could have been their own existence at least, if not for any grand ideological cause for secular and multicultural India.[4] Between May 2014 to March 2017, these parties had more than two and half years to work on their strategy to revive their political bases and fight the fast-rising BJP and Modi wave that had threatened their political existence. Far from that, what dominated the political discussion in the immediate months prior to the 2017 election was not any serious deliberation of alliance making, but the Yadav family feud, and the ensuing power struggle between the Chief Minister Akhilesh Yadav and his uncle, Ram Gopal Yadav, on the one side; and Mulayam Singh Yadav and his other brother, Shivpal Singh Yadav, on the other side. The feud was finally settled with Akhilesh Yadav managing to steal the Samajwadi Party's party presidentship from his father.[5] Sudha Pai has argued that this feud weakened the party, but her take on this is more of an exception compared to lot more commentators (Pai 2016). This Machiavellian move to outmanoeuvre his father was seen as some kind of a coup by many of Akhilesh supporters and even observers. An illusory hope spread afterwards that the Akhilesh Yadav–led Samajwadi Party would be able to return to power by winning the election, no matter how narrowly.

Only few weeks prior to the election in later part of January 2017, the Samajwadi Party (SP) stitched together a pre-electoral alliance with the Congress party,[6] and the Mayawati-led Bahujan Samaj Party (BSP) chose to go alone, making the Assembly Election a three-cornered election between the BJP and its allies, SP and the Congress, and the BSP. There were more than 312 recognised and unrecognised parties in the 2017 electoral fray. In an interview that was published on 18 February 2017 in *India Today*, Mulayam Yadav expressed his displeasure with the Congress alliance and argued it was only the Congress party that would benefit out of the alliance with Samajwadi party.[7]

Prime Minister Narendra Modi, however, chose to take the campaign seriously and addressed twenty-three meetings and two road shows himself. During the campaign he constantly reminded the gathered public/the spectators about the worsening economic condition of Uttar Pradesh and its deteriorating law and order. He even took a jibe at the Yadav family itself by asking this question: if Akhilesh could betray his own father, how trustworthy could he be?

At a campaign rally in Hardoi ahead of the third phase of elections, Modi said,

> Uttar Pradesh is my mai-baap (parents). I am not the son who would betray his mai-baap. You have adopted me, and it is my duty to work for you. Vote for full majority BJP government. I promise to show you all the ways of all the problems you are facing with in five years.[8]

As expected, the BJP campaign mainly employed a two-pronged strategy in Uttar Pradesh in 2017. First was a strategy of polarisation, and other was the strategy of development or *vikas*. The speeches delivered by Modi–Shah worked on these two aspects of the strategy, which simultaneously deepened the anti-incumbency feelings among the voters on the one hand and consolidated the Hindu votes. To elaborate on the strategy of polarisation, it is crucial to recall the context of two incidents: (a) Muzaffarnagar violence and (b) Dadri lynching. While both these incidents created conditions for the politics of polarisation that the BJP leadership sought to exploit, they also have significant implications for Muslim politics and Muslim attitudes, which I discuss later in this chapter. What is further important to underline is that the Union Home Ministry during the Manmohan Singh government said in Parliament that there were 247 incidents in UP in 2013 and 118 incidents in 2012, and there was an increase of up to 30 per cent at an all India level in 2013.[9] In a research paper by Gareth Nellis, Michael Weaver, and Steven Rosenzweig, political scientists at Yale University titled, '*Do Parties Matter in Ethnic Violence: Evidence from India*' have argued that BJP profits from riot electorally. In other words, polarisation creates rewarding conditions for the BJP in India.[10]

Mayawati, on the other hand, was not able to pull up her old strategy of social engineering of the 2007 Assembly elections, in which upper castes and Dalits could come together for the BSP. Satish Mishra, Mayawati's key advisor though remained with her, but his efficacy in creating the 2007 campaign magic was clearly missing.[11] She took her Dalit votes for granted and presumed that the best way to attract Muslim votes was by fielding as many Muslim candidates as possible regardless of their credibility. As a result, she ended up fielding for some of the history sheeters, like Muktar Ansari. She fielded ninety-seven Muslim candidates: the highest ever, twelve more than 2012; she also fielded 113 upper caste candidates (though the number of Brahmin candidates was down to sixty-six in 2017 from seventy-four in 2012); 106 Backward candidates, and 87 Dalit candidates. With this she declared that her party was inclusive, but she did recognise that a split in Muslim votes would only benefit the BJP, on which she was almost prophetic.[12]

During the 2017 campaign, the BJP chose not to nominate any Chief Ministerial candidate for Uttar Pradesh. Many saw it as a blunder by the BJP. It was argued that opposition parties might take a clue from Bihar elections in 2015 against Lalu-Nitish *mahagathabandhan*, in which *Bihari versus Bahari* became a major talking point in the campaign to resist Modi–Shah leadership. In the New Delhi Assembly election in 2015, the BJP fielded decorated police officer Kiran Bedi as its Chief Ministerial face, a former comrade in arms of Arvind Kejriwal during the Anna movement. Based on the Delhi experience, there is little to argue that the mere naming of a Chief Ministerial candidate would make a party invincible. In the background of the Modi wave, the BJP perhaps realised that by not naming a Chief Minister, it would keep the factional conflict within Uttar Pradesh's BJP under control and marshal its troops for a campaign with greater unity and dedication. Retrospectively, the BJP's thinking on this issue worked out well for its victory.

On 18 March 2017, the BJP, however, surprised everyone – including many of its sympathisers all over India and the rest of the world – by declaring controversial Gorakhpur MP, Yogi Adityanath (b. 1972) to lead Uttar Pradesh as its Chief Minister. Could the BJP have won the election with the same landslide had it named Yogi Adityanath as its CM candidate during the 2017 campaign? It remains an open question even today. No doubt, Adityanath's presence as a Chief Ministerial candidate could have polarised the election further. The political profile of Mr Yogi Adityanath is more than just being a Hindu hardliner. As the founder and patron of Hindu Yuva Vahini,[13] an anti-minority front set up in 2002, Mr Adityanath does have a political profile to be concerned about. That a politician with such a profile could be recommended and endorsed by Prime Minster Modi did provoke reactions even from his own supporters. Reacting to this appointment, political scientist Devesh Kapur, based at the University of Pennsylvania, USA, wrote in an op-ed in the *New York Times* on 27 May 2017:[14]

> The appointment of Adityanath thus seems to indicate that the BJP will employ anti-Muslim animus in its effort to consolidate Hindu votes in the 2019 national elections. But that strategy is clearly at odds with Modi's rhetorical focus on economic development. In fact, one of the likely consequences of Adityanath's promotion – and the negative signal it sends to India's largest religious minority – is that economic development will suffer.

As expected, the Uttar Pradesh Chief Minister Yogi Adityanath reiterated his commitment for development for all; though one of the first things he did was to shut down slaughter houses and stop the smuggling of cows for which he passed an order on 22 March 2017. It meant stopping the cow slaughter. This decision has been an anti-Muslim one since beef eating is primarily a Muslim food habit in India. Moreover, banning cow slaughter has been a favourite political agenda of the Hindu right for many years. This contentious issue was one of the major factor for the Bhartiya Jana Sangh (BJS) doing electorally well during the 1960s in Uttar Pradesh. Prior to this, one of the Congress Chief Ministers, Dr Sarvsri Sampurnanda who served as Chief Minister of Uttar Pradesh (UP) from 1954 to 1960, had banned cow slaughter in 1955, defying Nehru. Apparently, Nehru had even threatened to resign from Prime Ministership on this issue.[15]

Hindu conservatives of all hue and cry have been supporters of the cow protection movement that can be traced to colonial times. Historically, Mahatma Gandhi and Vinobha Bhave are some of the prominent names who supported the cow protection movement, but their strategies for protection have varied. As early as 1909, Gandhiji wrote:

> But, just as I respect the cow, so do I respect my fellow-men. A man is just as useful as a cow no matter whether he be a Mahomedan or a Hindu. Am I, then, to fight with or kill a Mahomedan in order to save a cow? In doing so, I would become an enemy of the Mahomedan as well as of the cow. Therefore, the only method I know of protecting the cow is that I should approach

my Mahomedan brother and urge him for the sake of the country to join me in protecting her.

(*Hind Swaraj* 1909, Chapter 10).

Had Gandhi been alive today, he would have protested the Dadri lynching with a fast onto death. Like Nayantara Saghal, Gandhi would have wanted a ban on man slaughter. But Gandhians like Anna Hazare are silent. While Gandhiji urged for the persuasive approach, the Hindu right believes in creating a climate of fear and intimidation.

Research suggests that the beef ban or the ban on cow slaughter impacted the livelihood of thousands of people of all faiths including Hindus, and yet the Bhartiya Janata Party (BJP) barely considered it necessary to explore alternative to help those people who abruptly lost their livelihood. Shaharanpur violence in August 2017 in which people of Dalit and Thakur castes clashed showed another dimension of Yogi Adityanath's regime. There were reports that the Lucknow government chose not to respond promptly and fairly to contain the violence because it had a bias towards Thakurs. Though as a Yogi, he has no caste, Yogi Adityanath was born to the Thakur caste.[16]

We need to look at the history of Hindutva movement in the region since the 1930s to grasp the reasons for the BJP's electoral resurgence in the elections of the 2014 and in 2017. This resurgence could be traced to a continuity of a political tradition seen prominently in four epochs of Uttar Pradesh's history. These four periods could roughly be described as follows:

- The first one was during the 1930s and the 1940s that created an impetus for the Pakistan movement. There was a counter-reaction by the RSS and other Hindu right organisations, though the political competition was visible between the secular politics of the Congress party led by Nehru and Muslim league led by Jinnah.[17]
- The second epoch was from the 1950s to 1970s, dominated by the political activities of the Bhartiya Jana Sangh (BJS), the first political party with a majoritarian agenda. Outside Delhi, Uttar Pradesh remained its main political playground. This was interrupted by the politics of *Emergency* (1975–1977), during which the BJS lost its identity to the new conglomerates of opposition parties called Janata Dal, which finally formed the government in New Delhi led by Moraraji Desai.[18]
- The third epoch began with the Ayodhya movement in the 1980s. A huge credit for the rise of the Hindu right would go to the

tactical part of the Ayodhya movement and its political implications, which led to dramatic electoral rise of the BJP in the 1989 and later.[19]
- After its dramatic rise in the late 1980s, the Hindu right was appearing to be heading for a decline until the Modi wave swept the Uttar Pradesh in 2014 and many other parts and sustained the momentum, as evident with the results of the 2017 elections. Underneath the so-called secular politics of the 1970s and 1980s – or the caste politics which Jaffrelot would describe as *Silent revolution*[20] – there was the politics of the Hindu Right simmering and gaining ground. Clearly, there was a social base of the Hindu right which already existed, which Modi–Shah leadership reactivated and created necessary conditions for a Modi wave to emerge and flow.

Implications for the Muslim politics

The issue of Muslim representation, based on the results of the 2014 Parliamentary election and the 2017 Assembly election, has become a matter of grave concern. In the 2014 election, not a single Member of Parliament (MP) from the Muslim community was elected from India's largest state, Uttar Pradesh, which elects eighty MPs to Lok Sabha. In the 2017 Assembly election, there were twenty-four Muslim MLAs, a significant decline in the Uttar Pradesh Assembly from its tally of sixty-eight in the 2012 UP Assembly. It fell down to 5.9 per cent from 17.2 per cent in the 2012 UP Assembly, almost equal to the 1993 Assembly results that took place after the Babri Masjid demolition on 6 December 1992. Also, the 17.2 per cent of the 2012 Assembly saw the highest percentage of the Muslim MLAs in independent India, and the lowest Muslim representation in the UP Assembly was in 1991 with a share of 4.1 per cent. More than half of the MLAs (fourteen of them) in the 2017 UP Assembly election were elected from the same constituency as before.[21]

In both the elections in 2014 and in 2017, the BJP decided not to field a single Muslim candidate in Uttar Pradesh. But the reason why the twenty-four Muslim MLAs are in UP Assembly today, unlike the Parliament, is because Muslim candidates fielded by non-BJP parties managed to win. That was not the case with Muslim candidates fielded by non-BJP parties in the 2014 Parliamentary election in Uttar Pradesh. It is crucial to flag off that the policy of not fielding Muslim candidates is not a new thinking in the BJP. Indeed, it is part of Hindutva ideology and often argued in the writings of its major thinkers.

It is also important to recall that in the three Assembly elections (in 2002, 2007, and 2012) that Modi won in Gujarat, the Modi-led BJP did not field a single Muslim candidate to run for Gujarat Assembly. What we saw in the BJP's ticket distribution policy in Uttar Pradesh is a repetition of what was practiced in Gujarat for many years under Modi. This deliberate exclusion of Muslims is aimed to deny them from becoming part of the political power structure and policy making processes.

In 2008 at the *India Today* conclave in New Delhi, when Modi as Gujarat Chief Minister was confronted by Digvijay Singh, the Congress party spokesman, at a panel discussion (moderated by Prabhu Chawla and also attended by Farooq Abdullah) regarding his decision not to field Muslim candidates, he argued that the only criterion for ticket distribution was the 'winnability' of a candidate and no such alleged discriminatory factor was in play. If winnability is such a stringent criterion for selection, then all of the supposedly winnable candidates of the BJP must win. Why do some the BJP candidates lose having passed the winnability criterion? Clearly, there are subjective factors and the winnability is not an entirely objective factor, which is why a predetermined bias could only be a natural cause. What has guided the ideological thinking is indeed the larger ideological understanding of the polity in which exclusion of particular communities are considered as the bottom line, thus no effort is made to be inclusive in the ticket distribution policy. We need to raise a few questions for the larger interest of Indian democracy such as the following: What could be the implications of the absence of Muslim political elites for a growing secular Indian polity? Can a secular polity be built in a multi-religious society without having anyone from a particular religious denomination? We can also raise further questions to make sense of this particular aspect of Hindutva ideology, and its challenge to secular thinking.

Should Muslims alone represent Muslims? Should their representation be proportional to their population in bodies like Assembly or Parliament? Why shouldn't it be more or less than their population? What secular or welfare purpose could be served if Muslims like Sayed Shahabuddin, a gangster from Siwan, Bihar, or Mukhtar Ansari of Uttar Pradesh, are elected? What do such representations do to the diversity or secular nature of the polity? In my view, while diversity could serve the secular character of a polity to some extent, it should not be the be all and end all game. What is important is that the polity should be sensitive enough to the diverse demands and minority interests of its society where minorities, religious or otherwise, do not feel discriminated. In the BJP case, the objective of denying Muslims tickets to run for office is clearly guided by prejudices, not aimed to enhance sensitivity towards minorities, and driven by the long-term goal to block the Muslim community from being part of decision-making processes. In part it has something to do with the interpretations of Indian history, where taking revenge for historical atrocities is central.[22]

Such a scenario of total exclusion of Muslims in a Hindu majority society could emerge in the Hindu India was perceived by Muslim leaders during the 1940s. That is why there was an attempt to have a separate constituency for religious minorities, particularly Muslims and Christians. It was debated in the Constituent Assembly. It was Sardar Patel who urged Muslim leadership at the time to give up the demand for a separate constituency in order to earn the goodwill of the Hindu community. And the Muslim leadership including Maulana Azad had to concede to Patel's argument. Today, we need it to ask where is the goodwill for Muslims now? At the end, the idea of separate Muslim constituencies was dropped, and the *goodwill* argument has also disappeared from our political conversations on Indian Muslims today. According to Raj Mohan Gandhi, biographer of Patel, Patel considered getting the separate constituencies for religious minorities in the Constituent Assembly dropped as one of his most satisfying accomplishment as a member of India's Constituent Assembly (Gandhi 1991). It is no surprise that Patel remains the Hindu right's the most favourite Congressman:[23] even for Narendra Modi who has a dream to build a Congress *mukta Bharat* (Congress-free India).

In any case, Muslims have been underrepresented in various sectors of the Indian economy according to the Sachar Report (2006). The idea not to let them take part in the decision-making body is indeed aimed to deny their political voice, a major objective of majoritarian Hindutva politics. In short, one of the major implications of the UP Assembly election is the reinforcement of this Hindutva reasoning, and the exclusion of Muslims from polity. If this politics continues to dominate, there is a distinct possibility that Muslim representation in various power sharing arrangements and bodies will be reduced and its political voice will be muzzled.

Over past several decades, even prior to 1947, there were allegations of Muslim appeasement by the Hindu right. Conservative or sectarian politics in both the major religious communities, Hindus and Muslims, have been part of the political tradition in Uttar Pradesh since the 1930s or even before. Conservative politicians from both the communities found place in the Congress party, whose commitment to

Table 16.1 Muslim MLAs in Uttar Pradesh

Constituency	Party in 2017 election	Name of the MLA	MLA since
Mau	Bahujan Samaj Party	Mukhtar Anshari	1996
Mubarakpur	Bahujan Samaj Party	Shah Alam Urf Guddu Jamali	2012
Gopalpur	Samajwadi Party	Nafees Ahmad	–
Nizamabad	Samajwadi Party	Alambadi	1996
Lal Ganj	Bahujan Samaj Party	Azad Ari Mardan	–
Isauli	Samajwadi Party	Abrar Ahmad	2012
Bhinga	Bahujan Samaj Party	Mohammad Aslam	–
Matera	Samajwadi Party	Yasar Shah	2012
Sambhal	Samajwadi Party	Iqbal Mehmood	1996
Kundarki	Samajwadi Party	Mohammad Rizwan	2012
Bilari	Samajwadi Party	Mohammed Faeem	2012
Amroha	Samajwadi Party	Mehboob Ali	2002
Rampur	Samajwadi Party	Mohammad Azam Khan	2002
Chamraua	Samajwadi Party	Naseer Ahmad Khan	–
Suar	Samajwadi Party	Mohammad Abdullah Azam Khan	–
Moradabad Rural	Samajwadi Party	Haji Ikram Qureshi	–
Thakurdwara	Samajwadi Party	Navab Jan Khan	2014
Najibabad	Samajwadi Party	Tasleem Ahmad	2012
Saharanpur	Congress	Masood Akhtar	–
Kairana	Samajwadi Party	Nahid Hasan	2014
Pratappur	Bahujan Samaj Party	Mohammed Mujtaba Siddiqui	–
Kanpur Cantt	Congress	Sohil Akhtar Ansari	–
Meerut	Samajwadi Party	Rafiq Ansari	–
Sishamau	Samajwadi Party	Hazi Irfan Solanki	2012

Source: Election Commission of India, New Delhi, India

the secularism was seen as questionable. Nehru was an exception, but everyone below and around Nehru, was not a Nehruvian. And Nehru was aware of it. It is this consciousness perhaps that forced Nehru not to press for the word 'secular' to be inserted into Indian Constitution during the Constituent Assembly debate.[24] Nehru was in a hurry for nation building and appeared satisfied with the fact that the set of fundamental rights already incorporated was good enough to take care of the secular character of the Indian Constitution. Historian Sabyasachi Bhattacharya has argued on this line in his Presidential Address of Indian History Congress in Malda, West Bengal in December 2016.[25]

On the other hand, after the creation of Pakistan, a vast number of Muslims migrated from Uttar Pradesh to Pakistan. The migration of well-educated, Urdu-speaking Muslims, a bulk of which found themselves being described as 'Mohajirs' is the key reason, some scholars argue, for Muslim backwardness even in India.[26] Urdu as a language also suffered for multiple reasons, including owing to the ambivalent attitude of various supposedly secular Lucknow governments.

The most significant political development, however, post-1947 for Muslim politics in north India was the failure of the attempt to rebuild the politics of the Muslim League that championed the separate homeland objective of Indian Muslims during colonial times under the leadership of Muhammed Ali Jinnah. A party with a similar name, Indian Union of Muslim League (IUML), found feet in south India and has been a key player in Muslim politics in Kerala, but not in any of the north Indian states, marking the end of identity politics the way it was practiced during the 1930s and 1940s. Muslim political behaviour, and voting behaviour have been secular in its orientation since the early days of Indian democracy.

However, a negligible, miniscule per cent of Muslim leadership has been trying to encourage Muslims to return to such religious identity–driven voting behaviour. The 2017 election results have once more proved that that was not going to be the case in Uttar Pradesh. In the 2017 Assembly election, the Hyderabad-based party, All India Majlis-e-Ittehadul Muslimeen (AIMIM) led by Asaddudin Owaisi, entered the fray and contested in thirty-eight seats, lost all, and secured only 0.24 per cent of valid votes in the entire Uttar Pradesh.[27] Out of the thirty-eight seats AIMIM fought for, twenty-two seats were won by the BJP, and the Samajwadi Party won in fifteen seats and Apna Dal won in one seat.[28] There were accusations that the decision by the AIMIM to enter the fray contributed to the division of Muslim votes and indirectly helped the BJP to win. Given that the AIMIM had fought only in 38 seats out of 403 seats, we need to look at the situations in rest of the 365 seats to take the accusations against AIMIM seriously. Apparently, the Indian Union of Muslim League (IUML) also entered the fray in Uttar Pradesh and fought in seven seats and lost all. From this data, it is obvious that there is no appeal for old-fashioned separatist

Muslim politics in Uttar Pradesh, where only a mainstream secular political party remains a choice for Muslims.

Yes, the conservative Muslim politics has survived through various institutions over the years. The politics of the All Indian Personal Law Board (AIPLB) and Deoband madarsa continue to champion old-fashioned conservative politics. The politics of the AIPLB became quite evident during the legal processes over the triple *talaq* issue in recent months, in which Supreme Court found the practice un-Islamic and gave the verdict for its abolition.[29] Doeband would, of course, claim to be the champion of Indian Muslims' national aspirations within the framework of Indian secular nationalism, a claim that was articulated in the farewell speech made by Mamood Madani in *Raya Sabha*. The Madani family, of course, remained the major link between Muslims and political parties, particularly the Congress party, for many decades in north India. In the post-Congress period since the early 1990s, the Madanis have changed their loyalties. Some of their family members have been part of various other non-Congress parties. For instance, Mahmood Madani served his term in Rajya Sabha (2006–2012) as a member of the Samajwadi party. The symbolic secularism that dominated the politics contributed to the creation of a small number of Muslims elites, particularly in Uttar Pradesh. A majority of them enjoyed the patronage of various Congress and non-Congress regimes in Lucknow and Delhi. Though there was evidence of progressivism in the art, culture, and other forms of creative writings, the politics remained largely under the grip of conservatives. Their commitment to Muslim welfare, particularly their economic well-being, remained limited as well, so the backwardness became a prominent debate.

A majority of Muslims voted for the Congress party, and their voting behaviour has been secular in the post-1947 era until Muslims in Uttar Pradesh began to look at other options, especially the Samajwadi Party (SP) and the Bahujan Samaj Party (BSP) during the 1990s and afterwards. However, there were two moments in Muslim politics when Muslim voters drifted away from the Congress party. The first one was during the anti-*Emergency* movement (1975–1977) during which, as part of the protest against Sanjay Gandhi's *nasbandhi*[30] and *Emergency* excesses, many Muslims voted against the Congress party. The 1984 Parliamentary election results could offer some evidence of Muslim forgiveness and reconciliation with the Congress party at the national level. But the Ayodhya movement in the 1980s and the Advani's *Rath Yatra* contributed to a massive churning in the Muslim community. There was evidence of Muslim alienation on the one hand from the Congress party again, and, on the other, appreciation for Mulayam Yadav's leadership for his secular commitment: he who almost saved Babri Masjid from being demolished in the first place. As there was a resurgence of the Hindu right, and a consolidation of the BJP with its fast expansion, Muslim politics again remained very secular. In the course of time, the SP and the BSP became its beneficiaries. The results of the 2007 UP Assembly election and the 2009 Parliamentary election give some hint of limited Muslim reconciliation with the Congress party, with some electoral benefits to the party.[31] Since the late 1980s when Ayodhya movement gathered momentum to the 2014 election, Muslims largely had broadened secular choices as three major political parties, SP, BSP, and the Congress, were seeking to woo them, which seemed to be lending advantage towards Muslims. This also contributed to checkmating the BJP electorally. During this period, the BJP's failure to consolidate was, however, less owing to the strength of Nehruvian secularism, but more owing to churning that took place in the Dalit and backward castes of Uttar Pradesh, for which Kanshi Ram particularly deserves especial appreciation.[32] Some would also like to give credit to Mandal politics. Sudha Pai has described it as 'deepening of democracy'.[33] For a while, it appeared that Hindutva has been caged forever in the cauldron of caste politics in Uttar Pradesh. India's secularism, particularly its commitment to religious minorities, would remain immune from any threat from the Hindutva politics, but the results of the 2014 and 2017 seem to have proved that wrong. In a hard-hitting op-ed in *The Hindu*, Zoya Hasan argued the essence of the dark influence of the Hindutva politics was shown after the 2017 results in the following words: 'Muslims have indeed been shown their place in this election'.[34]

Prior to the 2017 Assembly election, two events are very central to our understanding of Muslim attitudes and Muslim politics. The first is the Muzaffarnagar violence in 2013; and the second is the Dadri lynching in which Mohammad Akhlaq was lynched on 28 September 2015. Both contributed to the considerable alienation of Muslims from the BJP. In chapter seven of this volume, on Muslim voting behaviour, I have presented some evidence of Muslim voting for the BJP in Uttar Pradesh in 2014 election. But the political developments after 2014 should have destroyed any illusion Muslims have to see a changed face of the BJP. And, yet, why did not the consolidation against the BJP take place in 2017? The strategic voting behaviour for which Muslims are given credit so often by scholars was missing both in 2014 and 2017 (particularly in 2017). Some scholars have argued that it was a voting split that contributed to such a large-scale BJP victories. One could also argue that the lack of political mobilisation among the community members might have contributed, which in turn led to the disastrous trend of vote splitting in Muslim majority constituencies.

Muzaffarnagar violence took place when the Samajwadi party was ruling Lucknow after being elected in 2012.[35] The state topped the all India list as the highest number of communal incidents. Mohan Rao, who led a fact-finding team that visited Muzaffarnagar on 9 and 10 November 2013, noted that most of the eleven relief camps set up by the government (upon inspection) were in bad conditions.[36] The Senior Superintendent of Police (SSP) placed the death toll at fifty-two, out of which thirty-seven were Muslims and fifteen were Hindus. According to the UP government, 50,955 people were displaced, though non-official sources placed it to be more than 100,000. But the most significant aspect of this development is how it ruptured the relationship between the Samajwadi Party (SP) and the Muslims. The treatment of the victims of the Muzzafarnagar riots during the riot and after raised serious questions about the Samajwadi Party's secular commitment.

On the other hand, on 28 September 2015, there was the Dadri lynching in which Muhammad Akhalq was murdered in his home on the suspicion of beef eating, and his son also was brutally beaten and injured in front of his family. It triggered a debate on intolerance, and writers launched award wapsi as a matter of protest. The Akilesh Yadav government appeared rather ambivalent in its commitment to deal with the situation. Over all, these two incidents made it very clear to a majority of Muslims that the so-called secular parties are not adequately secular and their lives could be vulnerable under a Hindutva regime. Broadly, the failure of secular politics has created an opportunity for the Hindutva forces to present itself as an alternative.

Conclusion

No doubt, Muslim politics and the state of the Muslim community is going to witness a massive transformation under the influence of the Hindutva regime in Uttar Pradesh and elsewhere. While the socio-economic conditions of Muslims would deteriorate, the possibility of Muslim politics to descend to any sectarian politics is relatively less. Based on the signals coming from various Muslim leaders of different parties and also from civil society, Muslim politics will remain a part of mainstream secular politics.

There will be effort by sectarian leaders like Assaddudin Owasis to give it a sectarian direction and contribute to the evolving conditions of political polarisation; there is little evidence that such efforts would find any appreciation in electoral terms, though they may dominate discussions in partisan national media.

With the publication of the Sachar Report (2006), there were serious hopes that Muslim politics had moved from contentious identity politics to development politics. The resurgence of Hindutva politics has altered that scenario completely, and this has created a new context in which identity politics among Muslims remains the only game in town.

In the face of a hardline Hindutva regime in New Delhi and Lucknow, Muslim conservative politics would perhaps retreat or would appear less vocal and go underground as evident from its response to the Supreme Court's triple talaq verdict, a marked difference from how it reacted to the Shah Bano verdict in the 1980s. One of the limitations of India's populist secular politics was that it offered considerable patronage to Muslim conservative politics under the presumption that Muslim conservatives and clergy control Muslim voting behaviour. In the face of the current Hindutva offensive which may worsen in the days and months ahead, such a political trend would barely create the opportunity for emancipatory politics for Muslims leading to genuine secular democracy.

Notes

1 Omar Abdullah later clarified that by putting 'at this rate' in his twitter message he did hope there was some scope for change.
2 For an incisive analysis on the programmes like 'Love Jihad', ghar wapsi, see the Chapter 3 by Charu Gupta in this volume.
3 I am currently working on a more elaborate analysis of India's electoral politics as part of a new book project.
4 Why and how the BJP did so well and others lost in 2014 so miserably is a puzzle that many scholars have analysed in great detail. For a good analysis, see Sudha Pai and Avinash Kumar (2015), Chibber and Ostermann (2014), Louis Tillin (2015), Christopher Jaffrelot (2015), and several others.
5 For a good analysis of this part of the feud, see Sudha Pai, 'Who Is Samajwavi Party', *The Indian Express*, 28 September 2016; Also, see Gilles Verniers, 'Samajwadi Party, Family and Continuity', *The Indian Express*, 30 September 2016.
6 See 'Samajwadi Party and the Congress Announce Alliance for Uttar Pradesh', *The Hindu*, 22 January 2017.
7 See the interview by Mulayam Singh Yadav, *India Today*, 18 February 2017.
8 See the report, 'PM Modi Invokes Lord Krishna to Attack Akhilesh Yadav in Hardoi', *The Financial Express*, 16 February 2017.
9 See 'Communal Incidents Up 30% in 2013: UP Tops the List', *The Indian Express*, 5 February 2014.

10 See, 'BJP Gains After Every Riot, Says the Yale Study', *The Economic Times*, 5 December 2014.
11 For a good understanding of 2007 election, see Dipankar Gupta and Yogesh Kumar (2007); Vivek Kumar (2007).
12 See 'UP Assembly Polls: BSP Nominates 97 Candidates, Its Highest Ever', *The Indian Express*, 4 January 2017.
13 See 'What Is Yogi Adityanath's Hindu Yuva Vahini?' *The Indian Express*, 17 May 2017.
14 See 'Muslim Anxieties and India's Future', *The New York Times*, 27 May 2017.
15 See 'Long Before Yogi Adityanath: A Congress CM Banned Cow Slaughter in UP Against Nehru's Wishes', *India Today*, 26 March 2017.
16 See 'Shahranpur Dalit-Thakur Violence: 5 Things About Caste-Communal Couldron', *The Hindustan Times*, 21 July 2017.
17 Among others, John Zavos (2000) presents a very insightful analysis of this puzzle.
18 For this, Bruce Graham's book on Bhartiya Jana Sangh (BJS) remains the most scientific account on this subject, see Bruce Graham (2007).
19 There are several fascinating accounts on this aspect of Hindutva and its political face. For instance, see Thomas Blom Hansen (1999).
20 See Jaffrelot, Christopher. *India's Silent Revolution* (New Delhi: Permanent Black, 2003).
21 See 'Muslim Representation in Uttar Assembly Plummets With 2017 Election', *The Wire*, 14 March 2017 (accessed 24 September 2017).
22 For a nuanced understanding of this theme, see Mujibur Rehman, 'Reading the Past, Rewriting the Present', Seminar, October 2017.
23 For an incisive analysis of Patel's other roles that made him very dear to the Hindu Right, see A. G. Noorani (2014).
24 Nehru faced considerable resistance within the Congress when he was trying to push issues pertaining to minority rights, secularism, and socialism. In the early 1940s, some senior conservative leaders like Raj Gopalchari Patel threatened to resign to resist Nehru's programmes and were persuaded not to do so by Gandhi.
25 Speech by Sabyasachi Bhattacharya, Presidential Address, Indian History Congress, December 2016. (It was read out by Irfan Habib since Prof Bhattacharya was unwell on that day.)
26 There are several important works on partition and on the people on both sides. Some of the important works include these: Hasan (1994); Pandey (2002); Talbot (2009); Khan (2017).
27 For a very informative report on AIMIM, see 'The Seeker: Asaddudin Owaisis's Ambition to Unite India's Fractured Muslim Electorate', *The Caravan: A Journal of Politics and Culture*, September 2016.
28 AIMIM developed national ambition for which it chose to fight elections in various states where there are substantial Muslim votes. With the exception of Maharasthra, results for the party have been disappointing in states like UP, Bihar, Assam, etc. This shows the rejection of Muslim voters for a separatist ideology.
29 See an interview on triple talaq by Faizan Mustafa in www.aljazeera.com, 23 August 2017 (accessed 24 Septmber 2017); Tahir Mehmood, 'All Is Well That Ends Well', *The Indian Express*, 23 August 2017.

30 Vinod Mehta's book on Sanjay Gandhi presents very interesting portrait of the nasbandhi programme. See Mehta (2015).
31 For an interesting analysis on this, see Mirza A. Baig and Sudhir Kumar(2009).
32 For a detailed analysis, see Sudha Pai (2002), Jaffrelot (2003), and Kanchan Chandra (2007). Also see a fascinating biography of Kashi Ram by Badri Narayanan (2014).
33 Sudha Pai (2002).
34 See Zoya Hasan, 'Saffron Storm in Uttar Pradesh', *The Hindu*, 16 March 2017.
35 See Mujibur Rehman, 'The Consequences of Playing With Fire in Uttar Pradesh', 7 October 2016, www.The hinducentre.com (accessed 24 September 2017).
36 'Fact Finding Report: Independet Inequiry Into Muzaffarnagar Riots', *Economic and Political Weekly*, Vol. 49, No. 2 (11 January 2014).

Bibliography

Adeney, Katharine and Lawrence Saez. 2006. *Coalition Politics and Hindu Nationalism*. London: Routledge

Anderson, Walter and Shridhar Damle. 1987. *Brotherhood In Saffron: The Rashtriya Sevak Sangh and Hindu Revivalism*. New York: Westview Press.

Arendt Hanna. 2017. *The Origins of Totalitarianism*. London: Penguin

Baig, Asmer Mirza and Sudhir Kumar. 2009. 'Uttar Pradesh: Signs of Congress Reviva'l, *Economic and Political Weekly*, 44(39).

Banerjee, Mukulika. 2014. *Why India Votes? Exploring the Political South Asia*. London: Routledge

Basu, Amrita. 2015. *Violence Conjectures in Democratic India*. New York: Cambridge University Press.

Bilgrami, Akeel. 2011. *Democratic Culture: Historical and Philosophical Essays*. London: Routledge.

———. 2016. *Secularism, Identity, Enchantment*. New Delhi: Permanent Black.

Chandra, Kanchan. 2007. *Why Ethnic Parties Succeed? Patronage and Ethnic Head Counts in India*. Cambridge: Cambridge University Press.

———. 2016. *Democratic Dynasties: State, Party and Family in Contemporary Indian Politics*. New Delhi: Cambridge University Press. Chatterjee, Partha and Ira Katznelson. 2012. *Anxieties of Democracy: Reflections on Toquevillean Reflections on India and the United States*. New Delhi: Oxford University Press.

Chibber, P.K. and S.L. Ostermann. 2014. 'The BJP's Fragile Mandate: Modi and Vote Mobilizers in 2014 General Election'. *Studies in Indian Politics*, 2(2):137–151

De Souza Peter, D and E. Sridharan. 2007. *India's Political Parties*. New Delhi: Sage Publications.

Graham, Bruce. 2007. *Hindu Nationalism and Indian Politics: The Origins and Development of the Bhartiya Jana Sangh*. London. Cambridge: Cambridge University Press.

Guha, Ramachandra. 2014. The Past and the Future of the Congress Party. *The Hindustan Times*, August 3.

———. 2016. *Democrats and Dissenters*. New Delhi: Penguin.

———. 2017. *India After Gandhi*. London: Pan Macmillan.

Gupte, Pranay. 2011. *Mother India: A Political Biography of Indira Gandhi*. New Delhi: Penguin.

Jaffrelot Chrsiptophe. 1998. *The Hindu Nationalist Movement in India*. New York: Columbia University Press.

———. 2003. *India's Silent Revolution*. New Delhi: Permanent Black.

———. 2007. *Hindu Nationalism: A Reader*. New Jersey: Princeton University Press.

———. 2015. 'The Modi centric BJP 2014 Election Campaign: New Techniques and Old Tactics', *Contemporary South Asia*, 23(2): 151–166.

Jaffrelot, Christophe and Gilles Veniers. 2016. 'The Resistance of Regionalism: BJP's Limitations and the Resilience of State Parties', in Paul Wallace (ed), *India's 2014 Elections: Modi-Led BJP Sweep*, pp. 28–45. New Delhi: Sage Publications.

Jha, Prashant. 2017. *How BJP Wins*. New Delhi: Harper Collins.

Jha, Dhirendra K. 2017. *Shadow Armies: Fringe Organizations and Foot Soldiers of Hindutva*. New Delhi: Juggernaut.

Jha, D. N. 2009. *The Myth of Holy Cow*. New Delhi: Navayana.

Kaur, Ravinder. 2015. 'Good Times, Brought To You by Brand Modi', *Television and News Media*, 16(4): 323–330.

———. 2016. 'I am India Shining: The Investor- Citizen and the Indelible Icon of Good Times', *The Journal of Asian Studies*, 75(3):1–28, August.

Kiswhar, Madhu. 2014. *Modi, Muslims and Media: Voices from Modi's Gujarat*. New Delhi: Manushi.

Khan, Yasmeen. 2017. *The Great Partition: The Making of India and Pakistan*. New Haven: Yale University Press.

Khare, Harish. 2014. *How Modi Won It*. New Delhi: Hacchette India.

Kothari, Rajni. 1988. *State Against Democracy*. New Delhi: South Asia Books.

———. 1989. *Politics and People* (Vol 1). New Delhi: New Horizon Press.

———. 2012. *Politics in India*. New Delhi: Orient Blackswan.

Kumar, Vivek. 2007. 'Behind the BSP Victory', *Economic and Political Weekly*, 42(24): 78–85, 16 June.

Ghose, Sagarika. 2017. *Indira: India's Most Powerful Prime Minister*. New Delhi: Juggernaut.

Gupta, Dipankar and Yogesh Kumar. 2007. 'When the Caste Calculus Fails: Analysing the BSP Victory in UP', *Economic and Political Weekly*, 42(33): 33–42, 18 August.

Hansen Bloom Thomas. 1999. *The Saffron Wave: Democracy and Hindu Nationalism in Modern India*. New Jersey: Princeton University Press.

Hasan, Mushirul. 1994. *India's Partition: Process, Strategy, and Mobilization*. New Delhi: Oxford University Press.

Hasan, Zoya, Francine Frankel, Rajeev Bhargava, and Balveer Arora (eds.). 2002. *Transforming India: Social and Political Dynamics of Democracy.*
———. 2004. *Parties and Party Politics in India.* New Delhi: Oxford University Press.
———. 2009. *Politics of Inclusion: Caste, Minorities and Affirmative Action.* New Delhi: Oxford University Press.
———. 2012. *Congress After Indira: Policy, Power and Political Change (1984–2009).* New Delhi: Oxford University Press.
Malhotra, Inder. 2014. *Indira Gandhi: A Personal and Political Biography.* New Delhi: Hay House.
Marino, Andy. 2014. *Narendra Modi: A Political Biography.* New Delhi: Harper Collins.
Mehta, Vinod. 2015. *The Sanjay Story.* New Delhi: Harper Collins..
Mukhopadhaya, Nilanjan. 2013. *Narendra Modi: The Man, The Times.* New Delhi: Tranquebar Press.
Narayanan, Badri. 2014. *Kanshiram: Leader of Dalits.* New Delhi: Viking.
Noorani, A.G. 2014. *The Destruction of Hyderabad.* London: Hurst and Co.
Pai, Sudha. 2002. *Dalit Assertion and Unfinished Democratic Revolution: The Bahujan Samaj Party in Uttar Pradesh.* New Delhi: Sage Publications.
Pai, Sudha and Avinash Kumar. 2015. 'Understanding BJP's Victory in Uttar Pradesh.' In Wallace Paul (ed.) *2014 Elections: Modi- led BJP Sweep*, pp. 119–138. New Delhi: Sage Publications.
Pai, Sudha. 2016. 'Who Is Samajwadi Party?' *The Indian Express*, September 28.
Palshikar, Suhas; Sanjay Kumar and Sanjay Lodha(eds) 2017. *Electoral Politics in India: The Resurgence of Bhartiya Janata Party.* New Delhi: Routledge Publications.
Palshikar, Suhas, K C Suri, Yogendra Yadav (eds.). 2014. *Party Competition in Indian States: Electoral Politics in a Post-Congress Polity.* New Delhi: Oxford University Press.
Palshikar, Suhas, K C Suri, Yogendra Yadav (eds.). 2011. *Party Competition in Indian States: Electoral Politics in a Post-Congress Politics.* New Delhi: Oxford University Press.
Pandey, Gyanendra. 2002. *Remembering Partition: Violence, Nationalism and History In India.* Cambridge: Cambridge University Press.
Price, Lance. 2015. *Modi Effect: Narendra Modi's Campaign to Transform India.* London: Hodder and Stroughton.
Rehman, Mujibur. 2016. *Communalism in postcolonial India: Changing Contours.* London and New Delhi: Routledge.
———. 2018. *Rise of Saffron Power: Reflections on Indian Politics.* London and New Delhi: Routledge.
Rudolph, Sussane and Lyod Rudolph. 2010. 'An Intellectual History of the Study of Indian Politics' in Niraja Gopal Jayal and Prata Bhanu Mehta (eds), *Oxford Handbook on Indian Politics.* New Delhi: Oxford University Press.
Rupalia, Sanjay. 2015. *Divided We Govern: Coalition Politics in Modern India.* New Delhi: Oxford.

Sardesai, Rajdeep. 2014. *Election that Changed India 2014*. New Delhi: Viking.
Sharma Jyotirmaya. 2016. *Hindutva: Exploring the Idea of Hindu Nationalism*. New Delhi: Harper Collins
Shridharan, E (ed.). 2014. *Coalition Politics in India: Selected Issues at the Centre and States*. New Delhi: Academic Foundation.
Sen, Amartya. 2006. *Argumentative Indian: Writings on Indian History, Culture and Identity*. London: Penguin
———. 2007. *Identity and Violence: Illusions of Destiny*. London: Penguin.
Shastri, Sandeep, K.C. Suri and Yogendra Yadav (eds). 2009. *Electoral Politics In Indian States: Lok Sabha Elections in 2004 and Beyond*. New Delhi: Oxford University Press.
Sinha, Yaswant. 2007. *Confessions of a Swadeshi Reformer: My Years as a Finance Minister*. New Delhi: Penguin.
Talbot, Ian. 2009. *The Partition of India*. Cambridge: Cambridge University Press.
Taseer, Aatish. 2017. Anatomy of a Lynching. *The New York Times*, April 16.
Tachil, Tariq. 2014. *Elite Parties, Poor Voters: How Social Services Win Votes in India*. Cambridge: Cambridge University Press
Tawa Lama-Rewal, Stephanie. 2009. 'Studying Elections in India: Scientific and Political Debates', *South Asia Multi-Disciplinary Academic Journal (SAMAJ)*, (3): 1–15, online URL:http;//samaj.revue.org (accessed on 25 November 2017).
Tillin, Louis. 2015. 'Indian elections 2014: Explaining the Landslide', *Contemporary South Asia*, 23(2): 117–122.
Ullekh P N. 2016. *The Untold Vajpayee: Politician and Paradox*. New Delhi: Penguin Random House.
Vajpayi, Ananya. 2012. *Righteous Republic: Political Foundations of Modern India*. Cambridge: Harvard University Press.
Vaishnav, Milan. 2017. *Why Crime Pays*. Delhi: Harper.
———. 2017. 'Modi's Victory and the BJP's Future: Will Modi Remake the Party?', *Foreign Affairs*, 15, www.foreignaffairs (accessed on 25 November 2017).
Vinaik, Achin. 2017. *Hindutva Rising: Secular Claims, Communal Realities*. New Delhi: Tulika Books.
Wallace, Paul and Ramashray Roy (eds.). 2011. *India's 2009 Elections: Coalition Politics, Party Competition and Congress Continuity*. London: Sage Publications.
Wallace, Paul (ed.). 2015. *India's 2014 Elections: A Modi-Led BJP Sweep*. New Delhi: SAGE Publications
Wilkinson, Steve. 2004. *Votes and Violence: electoral Competition and Communal Riots in India*. New Delhi: Cambridge University Press.
———. 2010. 'Data and the Study of Indian Politics" in Niraja Gopal Jayal and Prata Bhanu Mehta (eds.), *Oxford Handbook on Indian Politics*. New Delhi: Oxford University Press.
Zavos, John. 2000. *Emergence of Hindu Nationalism in India*. New Delhi: Oxford University Press.

Index

Note: Page numbers in bold and italics indicate a table and figure on the corresponding page.

Aam Aadmi Party (AAP) 1, 155, 159, 181; anti-corruption movement 237–258; corruption, discourse of 242–244; at crossroads 251–256; current position of 225–226; electoral performance, in Punjab 215–230; middle classes 248–250; Modi wave, absence of 224–225; Naxalite movement in Punjab, suppression consequences 220–222; origins 238–239; people and political 244–248; in power 250–251; Punjab, specificity of 217–219; Rightwing technocracy 239–242; Sikh militant movement and 222–223; sources of support to 223–224
Aayog, Niti 135
Abdullah, Omar 5, 8, 173, 322, 368
Abe, Shinzo 66, 72
Achik National Volunteer Council (ANVC) 307
Achuthanandan, K. 58
Adi Granth 219
Advani, L.K. 7, 13, 30, 111, 140, 169, 172
African National Congress (ANC) 253
aggressive religious fundamentalisms 196
Ahmed, Bashiruddin 17, 18
Akali Dal 218, 223, 228

Akhil Bharatiya Vidyarthi Parishad (ABVP) 6
Aligarh Muslim Teachers Association (AMUTA) 180
All India Majlis-e-Ittehad-ul Muslimeen (AIMIM) 351, 356, 379
All Indian Personal Law Board (AIPLB) 380
All-Party Hill Leaders' Conference (APHLC) 301
All Regional Parties' Alliance (ARPA) 304
Almond, Gabriel 17
Ameeruddin, Maulana 93
Anand, Javed 144
Ananth, Krishna 16
Anderson, Walter 13, 175
Andhra Pradesh: sub-regional politics 51–54
Andhra Pradesh(undivided): election campaign 359–362; election issues 355–357; election manifestoes 357–359; election verdict 2014 350–355; Lok Sabha elections in 347–364; past elections, studying 347–350
Angad, Guru 219
Anna DMK (ADMK) 48, 49
Annadurai, C.N. 48
anti-corruption movement 237–258
anti-incumbency 11
'Anti Love-Jihad Front' 88

Antony, A.K. 162
aphorism 44
Apna Dal (AD) 112
Apna Punjab Party (APP) 226
Appadurai, Arjun 243
Arab Spring 237
Armed Forces Special Powers Act (AFSPA) 312, 320
Aryan supremacy 273
Arya Samaj 86
Asia Europe Meeting (ASEM) 69
Association of Southeast Asian Nations (ASEAN) 69, 74
Attenborough, Richard 178
Autonomous District Councils (ADC) 300, 301, 303
Ayodhya movement 3, 169, 173
Azad, Ghulam Nabi 15

'Babar's Santan' 169
Babri Masjid/Ram Janma Bhoomi 131, 140, 169, 381; demolition 121, 172–174, 375
Bahujan Samaj Party (BSP) 44, 111, 130, 182
Bajpai, Kanti 144
Bajpai, Laxmikant 90
Bajrang Dal 85, 91, 146, 201
Banerjee, Mamata 15, 16, 292
Banerjee, Mukulika 20
Barnett, Michael 62–64
Basit, Abdul 72
Basu, Amrita 3
Bavadam, Lyla 136
Bawa, Raghav 149
Berenschot, Ward 206
Bevan, James 175
Bhagwat, Mohan 13, 14
Bhagwati, Jagdish 135
Bharat: Darool Harab Darool Islam 91
Bharatiya Dharma Jana Sena 51
Bharatiya Jana Sangh (BJS) 2, 51
Bharatiya Janata Party (BJP) 1, 44–61, 64, 169; analysing, victory 121–126; attitudes 67–71; average victory margin of 125; election manifesto 67–71; ideological underpinnings 121–125; and Muslim voters in 2014 168–172; organisation and campaign, revamping 125–126; phase-wise total vote percentage 124; and RSS 197–199; victories 1, 3; victory in Uttar Pradesh 112–116; *see also* Modi, Narendra
Bhatt, Sanjiv 142
Bhave, Vinobha 373
BJP hatao and Desh Bajao 5
BJP's 2014 Election Campaign Committee (BNCC) 7
Bodos 147
Bofors scandal 194
botched campaign, Congress party 162–163
Brahmanical Hinduism 101
Brahmin castes 47
Brahminical social order 4
Brahmin-led Indian National Congress 47
Brahmin-Muslim-Dalit 118
Brahmins 116
Brass, Paul 206
Brazil-Russia-India-China-South Africa (BRICS) 69

Centre for the Study of Developing Societies (CSDS) 17
Ceylon Petroleum Corporation (CPC) 74
Chakraborty, Tapan 76
Chandra, Kanchan 15
Chandrababu Naidu, N. 53
Chandrashekhar Rao, K. (KCR) 53, 350
Chatterjee, Partha 243, 246, 247
Chatterjee, Somnath 29
Chauhan, Shiv Shankar 13
Chhottepur, Sucha Singh 225
Chibber, Pradeep 8
Chidambaram, P. 160
Christianity 105
Citizens and Politics: Mass Political Behaviour in India (Ahmed and Eldersveld) 18
civic activism 209
coalition jinx 3
Coalition Politics and Hindu Nationalism (Adeney and Saez) 20

coercion 94
collective mobilisation 63
communal antagonisms 203
communal polarisation 106, 154, 200, 203
communal violence 205, 206
communist movement 50
Communist Party of India (CPI) 16, 28, 44
Communist Party of India (Marxist) (CPIM) 44
Congress mukta Bharat 14
Congress nationalist movement 46
Congress party 2, 9, 10, 15, 30; botched campaign 162–163; collapse of 154–167; ideological drift 161–162; leadership crisis 160–161; Rightwing resurgence 163–165; turning point 159–160; UPA's record 156–158
Congress system 3
Contemporary South Asia 20
cooperative federalism 59
corruption, discourse 242–244
court packing 10
cultural nationalism 203

Data and the Study of Indian Politics (Wilkinson) 17
David *vs.* Goliath 307–310
de-dynastification 15
Defence Research and Development Organization (DRDO) 69
Delhi Assembly election 1, 12
democracy 191–212
Democratic Politics: State, Party and Family in Contemporary Indian Politics (Chandra) 15
Desai, Morarji 374
Dev, Guru Arjan 219
development paradigms antithesis 85
Devji, Faisal 246
Dharma Jagran Manch 85, 103
Dharm Jagran Samiti 100
Disturbed Areas Act 320
Divided We Govern: Coalition Politics in Modern India (Ruparelia) 20
'Do Parties Matter in Ethnic Violence: Evidence from India' 371

Dravida Munnetra Kazhagham (DMK) 45, 57
Dravidian identity politics 47
dynastic parties 15

Eaton, Richard 105
Economic and Political Weekly 149
economic expansion 157
Eldersveld, Samuel 18
elections of 2014 130–153; BJP and RSS 197–199; BJP win in 195–197; Congress loss in 193–195; epic saga 210–212; Gujarat model 203–205; marginalised and minorities 191–212; margins of modern India 263–276; minorities, implications for 199–203; possibilities, projecting 205–210; winners and losers 191–193
electoral democracy 2
Electoral Politics In Indian States: Lok Sabha Elections in 2004 and Beyond (Oxford 2009) 19
electoral transition, 2014 2
electoral waves 210
Elite Parties, Poor Voters: How Social Services Win Votes in India (Thachil) 19
Elwin, Verrier 300
Emergency 2, 27

Federation of Indian Chambers of Commerce and Industry (FICCI) 161
Fiction of Fact-Finding, The: Modi and Godhra (Mitta) 141
Figueira, Dorothy 273
First Past Post System (FPPS) 12
Foreign Direct Investments (FDI) 241, 305
foreign policy 64
'Foreign Relations – Nation First, Universal Brotherhood' 68
fraternity 149, 150
Frontline 136

G20 69
Gandhi 178
Gandhi, Gopal Krishna 149

Gandhi, Indira 27, 31, 53, 155
Gandhi, M.K. 273, 373
Gandhi, Rahul 11, 57, 118, 143, 155, 160–163, 180, 369
Gandhi, Sonia 5, 6, 53, 118, 155, 160, 163
Ganguly, Sumit 20
Garo Hills 301–303
Garo National Liberation Army (GNLA) 307
gau rakshaks 4
geopolitics 78
ghar wapsi 28, 84–110; anti-conversion and 100–104; Hindutva rhetoric, fissures in 105–107; nostalgia and 101
Goenka, Ramnath 27
Gogois 15
Golden Temple 217
Gramsci, Antonio 250
Gregor, James 272
Guardian, The 176
Gudavarthy, Ajay 246
Gujarat Assembly election, 2017 1
Gujarat genocide 291
Gujarati diaspora 175
Gujarat Investors Summit 175
Gujarat model 11, 111, 135, 138, 158, 173, 203–205
Gulbarg Society massacre 141
Gundu Rao, R. 55
Guruprasad, D.V. 98

Habib, Irfan 2
Hariss-White, Barbara 18
Haryana-Punjab conflict 216
Hasan, Zoya 24, 31
Hazare, Anna 226, 238, 239, 245
Hill State People's Democratic Party (HSPDP) 303
Himalaya Dhvani 99
Hind, Jamait Ulema 171
Hindi-speaking states 77
Hindu, The 147
Hindu fascism 274, 275
Hindu Mahasabha 86
Hindu majoritarianism 85
Hindu-Muslim riots 86
Hindu nationalist organisation 131
Hindu Rashtra 26–31

Hindustan Times 148
Hindu Swayamsevak Sangh (HSS) 14
Hindutva 168–187; 'Bahujanisation' of 274; double speech of 100–104; India's foreign policy and 62–79; politics, anxieties of 85; redefined 121–125; rhetoric, fissures in 105–107
Hindu violence 274
How BJP Wins (Jha) 21
Human Development paradigm 139
Hunger Index of Gujarat 138
hyper-nationalism 199

ideological drift, Congress party 161–162
Imam Khomeini Memorial Trust (IKMT) 332
inconvenient truths 168–187
India Against Corruption (IAC) movement 159, 238
'India Against Corruption' movement 243
India-Brazil-South Africa (IBSA) 69
Indian Council of Social Science Research (ICSSR) 17
Indian democracy, scholarship 2
Indian diaspora 14
Indian Express, The 70
Indian National Congress (INC) 28, 44–61, 130, 154; *see also* Congress party
Indian Peace Keeping Force (IPKF) 74
Indian political behaviour: inconvenient truths of 168–187
Indian Today Conclave 2008 176
Indian Union of Muslim League (IUML) 379
India's 2014 Elections: A Modi-led BJP Sweep 18
India's election studies, scholarship 16–21
India's foreign policy: Hindutva and 62–79
India's political landscape 2
India's population: religious composition 234; Sikhs share 235–236

India's soul, battle for 130–153
India Today 147
Indic civilisation 206
indigenous groups 147
Indo-US nuclear deal 160
Indus Waters Treaty 75
Integral humanism 2
Integrated Child Development Scheme (ICDS) 164
'Intellectual History Of the Study of Indian Politics, An' (Rudolph and Rudolph) 17
international economic policy 70
International Food Policy Research Institute (IFPRI) 138
inter-religious marriages 107
Islam 105
Islamic Relief Committee (IRC) 177
Islamist conspiracy 90
Islamiya School Kargil (ISK) 332

Jaffrelot, Christophe 15
Jafri, Ehsan 141
Jafri, Zakia 141
Jaintia Hills 301
Jaintia Hills District Autonomous Council (JHDAC) 303
Jai Parakash (JP) movement 29
Jammu and Kashmir (J&K): 2014 assembly election analysis 332–335; 2014 Parliamentary election in 322–323; analysis of verdict in 327–331, 338–342; assembly elections, key issues analysis 335; BJP's electoral strategy, reflections 335–338; communal polarisation and 317–345; election, overall verdict analysis 324–326; electoral politics in 317–345; historical background 319–342; Ladakh, electoral trends analysis 331–332; parliamentary elections, analysis of issues 323–324
Jammu-Poonch Parliamentary constituency 327
Janata Dal (JD) 5, 58, 172
Janata party and the Janata Dal 55
Janata Party/Janata Dal 52
Jayalalithaa, J. 57, 59

Jha, Dhirendhra K 28
Jha, Prashant 148
Johnson, Samuel 199
Joshi, Murli Manohar 7
Joshi, Suresh Bhayyaji 86
Journal Of Democracy 20

Kamaraj, Kumaraswami 47
Karlsson, Bengt 305
Karnataka: Southern 'national' exception 55–56
Karnataka Janata Paksha 28
Karunanidhi, M. 57
Kashmiri Pandits (KPs) 336
Kaur, Parneet 221
Kejriwal, Arvind 163, 181, 238, 242
Kerala: Congress Party in 50; left and communal accommodation, politics 49–51
Kerala Legislative Assembly 50
Kesavan, Mukul 148
Khaira, Sukhpal 216
Khalistan movement 217, 222
Khan, Bishmillah 181
Khan, Fawad 105, 106
Khandamal 202
khap panchayats 250
Kharge, Mallikarjun 161
Khasi Hills 301, 303, 305
Khasi Student Union (KSU) 301
Khattar, Manohar Lal 13
Khubsoorat 106
Khun Hyinniewtrep National Awakening Movement (KHNAM) 303
Khurshid, Salman 8
Kiswar, Madhu Purnima 178
Kodnani, Maya 142
Kothari, Rajni 3, 17, 59
Kumar, Nitish 5, 145, 172, 178
Kumar, Rajiv 20
Kumari, Mayawati 130, 372
Kurmis 116

Laclau, Ernesto 245, 254
Lahore University of Management Sciences (LUMS) 21
Lama-Rewal, Stephanie Tawa 18
land acquisition 194
language agitation 48

leadership crisis, Congress party 160–161
'Left Wing Extremism (LWE)' 16
Lindgren, Lars Olof 175
Lingayat–Vokkaliga political dominance 55
Lodha, R.M. 9
Lokpal and Lokayukta Act 194, 244
Lok Shakti Yatra 7
love-fraud-marriage-conversion-pain 92–93
love jihad 28, 84–110; bogey of 93; emotional bonding 91; hindus and 89–92; love-fraud-marriage-conversion-pain 92–93; propagating myths of 88; women and 90, 93
Love Jihad: Red Alert for Hindu Girls (Muttalik) 94
love-toting jihadist 94
loyal opposition 208
Lyngdoh, Paul 306

Macpherson Report 202
Madani, Mamood 380
Madani, Maulana Mahmood 171
Madhav, Ram 13
Mahagathbandhan 5
Mahatma Gandhi National Rural Employment Guarantee Act (MGNREGA) 156, 158
Majlis Ittehadul Muslimeen 54
Maken, Ajay 155
Malaviya, Madan Mohan 100
Malik, Muhammad Yasin 334
Manmohan Singh–led United Progressive Alliance (UPA) 6
Manoharpur tragedy 202
Manthan Shivir 13
Maoist Naxalite movement 217
March of Pride 140
market-led economic growth 138
Mazoomdar, Jay 146
Mazumdar, Siddharth 145
Meerut Bachao Manch 91
Meghalaya: competitive politics, conditions and dynamics 298–302; Lok Sabha elections, 2014 297–314; Shillong seat, BJP rise in Congress bastion 303–307; status quo 311–312; Tura seat 307–310
Meghalaya Congress Committee (MPCC) 302, 305
Meghalaya Pradesh Congress Committee (MPCC) 304
Mein Kampf 273
memoranda of understanding (MOUs) 137
Menon, Dilip 102
Menon, Nivedita 102, 107
militant piety 211
militarist triumphalism 134
Mirza, Saeed 144
Mishra, Satish 372
Mitta, Manoj 141
Modi, Muslims and Media: Voices from the Narendra Modi's Gujarat (Kiswar) 178
Modi, Narendra 2–3, 5, 15, 29, 57–59, 64–66, 111, 121, 133, 140, 141, 168–187, 192; anti-Muslim image and Muslim voters 172–182; early life of 6; in Gujarat 65–67; leadership style 134–135; maiden speech in Lok Sabha 3; Muzaffarnagar riots and 179–181; Varanasi and Muslim voters 181–182; wave 3, 6–12, 307
Modi factor 363
Modi-led BJP 2
Modi-Shah leadership 3, 30; electoral and political strategies of 3
Modi–Shah leadership 6, 370
Modi-Shah-led BJP 2
Mohalla concept 251
Mohan, Jagan 53
Mohan, Madan 347
Montagu-Chelmsford dyarchy reforms 47
Mouffe, Chantal 254
Mukherjee, Pranab 72
Mukherjee, Syama Prasad 4
Mukhopadhya, Nilanjan 12
Musaffarnagar riots 197
Muslim fundamentalism 90, 93
Muslim male 106
Muslim Nizam 52

Muslim population 103, 123
Muslim Rashtriaya Manch (MRM) 171
Muslim United Front (MUF) 320
Muslim veto 145
Muslim voters, 2014 168–187
Muttalik, Pramod 94
Muzaffarnagar riots 24, 123, 179–181, 382

Naicker, E.V. Ramaswamy 47
Nair, Janaki 107
Nanak, Guru 218, 219
Naroda Patiya 142
Narsimha Rao, P.V. 348
nascent foreign policy 71–78; multilateral and para-diplomacy dimension 76–77; regional and bilateral dimension 71–76
National Democratic Alliance (NDA) 2, 5, 30, 49, 54, 154, 191
national elections: in tribal state 297–314
national elections, 2014: margins of modern India 263–276
National Election Survey (NES) 17
National Food Security Act (NFSA) 158
Nationalist Congress Party (NCP) 44
National Rural Employment Guarantee Act (NREGA) 194, 247, 288
National Rural Health Mission (NRHM) 156
national *vs.* regional parties 45, 46
Naxalite movement 220–222
Nehru, Jawaharlal 164
Nehruvian Planning Commission 135
Nellis, Gareth 371
neo-con developmental model 204
neoliberal Gujarat model 197
neoliberal policies 164
new margdarshak mandal 7
New York Times 5
Nigam, Aditya 254
non-alignment 78
non-BJP parties, implications for 14–16
non-Brahmin Justice Party 47

North-East Regional Political Front (NERPF) 298
Nuclear Civil Liability Bill 160
Nussbaum, Martha 31
Nyaya Yatra 7

Obama, Barack 73, 75
O Brien, Derek 8
Ohm, Brita 31
One Belt One Road (OBOR) initiative 78
Ostermann, S.L. 8

Padnavis, Devendra 13
Pai, Sudha 370
Palshikar, Suhas 255
Panagariya, Arvind 135, 136
Pandey, Gyan 102
Parsoli Corporation 177
Party Competition in Indian States: Electoral Politics in a Post-Congress Polity (Oxford 2014) 20
Parvathi, Lakshmi 54
Patel, Aakar 7
Patel, Ahmed 12
Patel, Anandibehan 11
Patel, Hardik 9
Patkar, Medha 17
Patnaik, Biju 5
Patnaik, Prabhat 239, 252
Paulsen, Ole 175
People's Democratic Party (PDP) 321
People's Representation Act of 1951 200
pluri-religious civilisation 212
political identity 2
Political Liberalism (Rawls) 31
political violence 14
popularist welfarism 194
Potter, Stephen 44
poverty ratio 156
Power, Sharad 15
Prakasam, Tangutari 52
pre-election foreign policy statements 65–67
pre-framing concept 65–67
Press Trust of India 147
primordialism 103
Production of Hindu-Muslim Violence, The 206

Punjab: electoral performance, in 215–230; Naxalite movement in 220–222; specificity 217–219; vote share, elections 2014 232–233
Punjab's communist movement 220
Punjab's population, religious composition 234, 235
Punjab Students Union (PSU) 221
pyar andha dhandha 86

Quest for Modernity in Asia and Africa, The 210

Rajagopalachari, C. 47
Rajakdas, Baba 93
Rajasekhar Reddy, Y.S. (YSR) 53
Ramachandran, M.G. (MGR) 48
Ramachandran, Raju 142
Rama Rao, N.T. (NTR) 53, 348
Ramesh, Jairam 155
Ramjanmabhoomi campaign 104
Ramjanmabhoomi movement 88, 290
Ram Mandir movement 119
Rangarajan, Mahesh 10
Rashtriya Swayam Sevak Sangh (RSS) 2, 6, 46, 131, 192; role in 2014 election 12–14
Rawls, John 31
Reddy, Chenna 52
Reddy, Jagan Mohan 356
Reddy community 349
regionalisation 15
religious conversions 101
religious fanaticism 206
Resident Welfare Associations (RWAs) 250
Revolutionary Socialist Party 58
Richier, Francois 175
Right to Information (RTI) 194, 247
Rightwing economic policies 134
Rightwing resurgence, Congress party 163–165
Rightwing technocracy 239–242
riot, 2002 8
Roberts, Adam 5
Rosenzweig, Steven 371
RSS–BJP relationship 2
Rudolph, Lyod 17
Rudolph, Sussane 17

Sabka Vikas Sabka Sath, election slogan 10, 11
Sachar, Rajinder 26
Sachar Report (2006) 176, 178–180, 383
saffron neoliberalism 203
saffron system, making of 3–6
Samajwadi Party (SP) 28, 111, 172
Sampurnanda, Sarvsri 373
Sangari, Kumkum 103
Sangay, Lobsang 71
Sangh mukta Bharat 14
Sangh parivar 2
Sangma, Mukul 76
Sangma, P.A. 307, 308
sanjhi virashat bachhao 5
Sanskritisation 274
Sarabha, Kartar Singh 220
Sarkar, Tanika 93
Sarva Shiksha Abhiyan (SSA) 156
Savarkarite Hindu Rashtra 191
Sayeed, Mufti Mohammad 321
Schmitt, Carl 207
secular fever 174
secularism 132, 147, 171, 179
Seemandhra: issues and implications in 347–364; *see also* Andhra Pradesh(undivided)
self-fulfilling prophecy 209
Self-Respect Movement 47
Sen, Amartya 135, 139, 208, 211
Sepoy mutiny 168
sex ratio 138
Shadow Army, The (2017) 28
Shah, Amit 6–13, 77, 121, 123, 126, 145, 146, 176
Shah, Ghanshyam 201
Shanghai Cooperation Organization (SCO) 69
Sharanpur violence 4
Sharif, Nawaz 71
Sharma, Hemant 15
Shillong Lok Sabha constituency 304
Shiromani Akali Dal (SAD) 215
Shraddhanand, Swami 100, 103
Shri Amaranth Shrine Board (SASB) 321
Shridharan, Eswarn 20
Shri Guru Granth Sahib (SGGS) 219
shuddhi movement 100

Index

Siddaramaiah, K. 58
Sikh diaspora 223
Sikh militant movement 222–223
Sikhs 217–219
Silent revolution 375
Singh, Amarinder 221
Singh, Bhagat 220
Singh, Karan 317
Singh, Manmohan 156, 157, 160
Singh, Nirmal 336
Singh, Rajnath 66, 172
Singh, Ranjit 219
Singh, V.P. 5, 172
Singhal, Ashok 148
Sinha, Jaswant 13
social equity 139
social inequalities 204
social media 126
social reform movements 47
social winners 131
Som, Sangeet Singh 88, 146
Sood, Atul 137
South Asian Association for Regional Cooperation (SAARC) 69, 71, 76
South India: 2014 election in 56–60; BJP, Congress, and regional parties in 44–61
Special Economic Zones (SEZ) 283, 288
Special Investigation Team (SIT) 141
Special Marriage Act 91
Sree Narayan Dharma Paripalna Yogam (SNDP Yogam) 51
Sri Krishna Commission Report 202
state–citizen relationship 4
strategy of annihilation 30
Subramanium, Gopal 9, 10
Suhrud, Tridip 135
Sureshwala, Zafar 8
Swamy, Subramanian 49
Swaraj, Sushma 71, 73

Tamil Dravidian movement 46
Tamil Nadu: Dravidian bastion 47–49
Telangana: issues and implications in 347–364; sub-regional politics 51–54; *see also* Andhra Pradesh(undivided)
Telangana Praja Samiti (TPS) 52, 347
Telangana Rashtriya Samiti (TRS) 53
Television and New Media 20
Telugu Desam Party (TDP) 45, 52, 53, 348, 350
Telugu regional identity 51–54
Thachil, Tariq 19
Thackeray, Bal 7
Third Reich 207
Tourism, Infrastructure, Modernisation, and Empowerment (TIME) model 335
Trade Facilitation Agreement 76
trickle-down economic theory 208
Trinamul Congress (TMC) 16
Trivedi Centre of Political Data 18

Udhampur-Doda Parliamentary constituency 328
Ul Haq, Mahbub 139
United and Democratic Fronts (UDF) 51, 58
United Progressive Alliance (UPA): record 156–158
United Progressive Association (Two) (UPA-II) government 3, 6
Upadhyaya, Deen Dayal 2
Uttar Pradesh (UP): in 2017 assembly election 368–385; BJP, victory in 4, 112–116, 370–375; by-polls in 84; Dalits in 131; defeat of other parties in 116–121; electoral majority 4; Muslim MLAs in 378; Muslim politics, implications 375–382; saffron whirlwind 368–385

Vaishnav, Milan 19
Vajpayee, Atal Bihari 13, 29, 100, 111, 143, 175
Varanasi 181–182
Varshney, Ashutosh 20, 200, 206
Vasudeva Kutumbakam 68
Verma, Pavan 173
Vibrat Gujarat Summit 175
Vidhan Sabha elections 290
Vishwa Hindu Parishad (VHP) 49, 85, 148
Vivekananda, Swami 72

Votes and Violence: Electoral Competition and Communal Riots In India (Wilkinson) 19
vote share 2

Wadha, D.P. 201
Wallace, Paul 18
Waseem, Mohammed 21
Weaver, Michael 371
welfare state 132
West Bengal: big national parties in 279–293; BJP, game of 289–293; Congress, decline of 280–281; left, decline of 281–286; Trinamool Congress, consolidation of 286–289
When Crime Pays (Vaishnav) 19
Why India Votes? Exploring the Political In South Asia (Banerjee) 20

Wilkinson, Steven 17, 19
Women's Reservation Bill 160
World Trade Organization 76

Xi Jinping 72, 73, 75

Yadav, Akhilesh 28, 119
Yadav, Lalu 5, 7
Yadav, Mulayam Singh 119
Yadav, Sharad 5
Yadav, Yogendra 17, 181, 216, 238
Yedduyurappa, B.S. 28, 56
Young Indian Leaders Conclave 178

Zafar Sareshwala 177, 178
Zald, Mayer 63
Zelliot, Eleanor 18
Žižek, Slavoj 252